STUDENT SELF-ESTEEM

STUDENT SELF-ESTEEM

Integrating the Self

Edited by Gail McEachron-Hirsch

TECHNOMIC
PUBLISHING CO., INC.

LANCASTER · BASEL

Student Self-Esteem
a **TECHNOMIC**® publication

Published in the Western Hemisphere by
Technomic Publishing Company, Inc.
851 New Holland Avenue, Box 3535
Lancaster, Pennsylvania 17604 U.S.A.

Distributed in the Rest of the World by
Technomic Publishing AG
Missionsstrasse 44
CH-4055 Basel, Switzerland

Printed in the United States of America
10 9 8 7 6 5 4 3 2 1

Main entry under title:
    Student Self-Esteem: Integrating the Self

A Technomic Publishing Company book
Bibliography: p.
Includes index p. 431

Library of Congress Catalog Card No. 93-60638
ISBN No. 1-56676-031-3

To Karen Genevieve and Mark Alan

Contents

5. A Systems View of Family and School   91

STEVEN X. GALLAS – *Williamsburg/James City County School District*
GAIL B. HARDINGE – *Williamsburg/James City County School District*

6. The Assessment of Self-Esteem   113

SANDRA B. WARD – *The College of William and Mary*
THOMAS J. WARD – *The College of William and Mary*

7. The Developing Self in the Early School Years   143

KAORU YAMAMOTO – *University of Colorado at Denver*
GAIL McEACHRON-HIRSCH – *The College of William and Mary*

8. Adolescent Self-Esteem in the Family and School Environments   197

GAIL McEACHRON-HIRSCH — *The College of William and Mary*
THOMAS J. WARD — *The College of William and Mary*

9. Self-Esteem and Students with Special Needs   281

CHRISTINE WALTHER-THOMAS — *The College of William and Mary*

10. Developing Self-Concept in Gifted Individuals   311

JOYCE VANTASSEL-BASKA — *The College of William and Mary*

Foreword

FEW psychological variables affecting the lives of children are given as much emphasis by mental health professionals and the general public as self-esteem. Psychoanalyst Harry Stack Sullivan viewed the concept of self as the "bedrock of the human personality," and a deterioration in self-esteem has long been associated by both clinicians and researchers with a wide range of difficulties – from depression and delinquency to eating disorders and school failure. The message has not been lost on parents and teachers, who constantly search for ways to improve the motivation and well-being of their children by helping them enhance their self-concept. As one popular book on the subject tells its readers, self-esteem is no less than the "mainspring that slates every child for success or failure as a human being."

Careful observations of the child tend to reinforce the validity of such views – and thus the importance of this unusually rich volume. A host of findings demonstrates that, as early as in the second year of life, children begin to develop self-awareness – and with it a growing sensitivity to standards set by parents, as well as anxiety over their ability to live up to them. By age five, these early stirrings of self-evaluation are in full bloom, and with the child's entry into the demanding world of formal schooling, the forces affecting the nature and quality of self-esteem have grown both in number and complexity.

The process is complex, however, and one of the many strengths of this book is that it draws the reader's sustained attention to the mosaic of interacting forces – both psychodynamic and environmental – helping shape the child's self-perceptions from early childhood through adolescence. The reader is sure to come away from this volume with a renewed appreciation of the importance of the varied social and cultural contexts in which the child's self-concept evolves.

Special attention is directed to the salient role played by the educational environment. Such a focus is altogether warranted; nowhere are youngsters likely to feel as indelibly assessed and labeled as in the classroom. This book helps explain why it is often in the school context that children's perceptions of their capacities and competence take hold. In their journey through school, youngsters are likely to develop images of themselves that will serve them either well or poorly later, in the real world outside the classroom. Indeed, their emerging self-definition is likely to color not only their intellectual performance but their emotional and social adaptation as well.

The role of the teacher's personality is critical. Many parents and professionals can cite case histories of youngsters who were given up as "failures" — but who were later transformed into competent and achieving individuals by a charismatic teacher who was able to instill self-confidence and a sense of purpose. This book helps clarify the dynamic elements of such human dramas.

Because this book addresses various myths related to self-esteem, it is likely to help undo a number of the misconceptions that surround the topic. Despite the continuing emphasis given by mental health professionals to the development of self-esteem in children, the subject is still beset by simplistic notions and outright misconceptions. Efforts in public education related to child self-esteem — found in a continuing stream of books, magazines, pamphlets, lectures, and workshops — are often based not on solid research evidence, but rather on a particular idiosyncratic view, or on insights gained from limited clinical experience. Rarely acknowledged is the reality of individual differences in predisposition and temperament and in the varied sociocultural settings in which children grow and develop. Because the present book helps to clarify the role of such forces in the development of self-esteem, it will be of considerable benefit to those whose mission it is to communicate behavioral science findings to the general public.

Coverage offered in this volume is broad, with chapter emphases ranging from basic methodological issues of definition and assessment to applied areas such as the role of special education programs, the needs of particular groups such as gifted children and delinquents, and the lessons gleaned from resilient children. Also addressed is the generally overlooked role of national values — both cultural and political — in the shaping of self-esteem. Given its varied scope and important mission, the book will be a rich source of information and guidance for a broad range of readers—among them parents, educators, administrators, researchers, and other health care professionals.

Julius Segal, Ph.D.
Contributing Editor, *Parents*
Magazine, and formerly director of
scientific and public information
programs at the National Institute of
Mental Health

Preface

SELF-ESTEEM is a term that has been popularized to the extent that people attribute the source of nearly all events, with the exception of natural disasters, to self-esteem. For example, biographers suggest that major political leaders seek office as a result of supportive, loving family roots, the necessary ingredients for positive self-esteem. Others say political leaders such as Hitler sought political power to avenge the childhood forces that betrayed him. Social workers, psychologists, and educators say self-esteem is the reason that individuals do not want to improve their life or achieve at a level consistent with their potential. Despite the widespread use of the term, the concept of self-esteem continues to be shrouded in mystery and ambiguity. However nebulous the term in its current stages of development, self-esteem continues to inspire scholarship.

The authors in this book have broadened the scope of self-esteem research. They have taken traditional self-esteem research full circle to solidify linkages with cultural context, specifically, family and school environments. Conventional approaches to confronting self-esteem issues follow a typical scenario: an individual's "problem" is identified (e.g., juvenile delinquency, underachievement, teen parenthood, low self-confidence); the source of the problem is attributed to low self-esteem; efforts are devoted to building up the individual's positive self-perceptions so that he or she feels good about himself or herself; the individual with the "right" socially adjusted attitude is then sent on his or her way. This approach emphasizes that the source of personal well-being rests primarily upon the individual. Seldom does this approach include an examination of the social factors that may be supporting or impeding self-esteem. Often, the assumption is that the individual needs to learn how to conform to dominant social expectations.

One of the main purposes of the book is to challenge such lockstep notions of self-esteem. Individual states of mind and self-perceptions are key factors in shaping one's own identity, but they don't tell the entire story. An analysis of self must also include an examination of the social contexts that shape one's identity. The process is interactive and dynamic, changing from one context to another. The process is also embedded in cultural traditions and sources of power that pervade social institutions like families and schools. The current authors have not abandoned the groundwork that has been laid by previous self-esteem studies. Rather, they have built upon this foundation as a vantage point from which to raise questions about the role that family and school environments play in enhancing self-esteem. Viewing self-esteem as multidimensional and dynamic, the authors have addressed the interplay between individual and social factors that affect self-esteem.

By looking at individuals and social contexts, the authors have been able to identify patterns in individual personalities and patterns in families and schools that both inhibit and support self-esteem. In addition, the potential for families and schools to buffer each other during stressful periods or to go head-to-head with each other, thus creating stress, is also investigated as a means to capture their interactive relationships.

In order to make this relationship more explicit, several authors have been invited to place notions of self-esteem research in a broader political and philosophical context, thus examining the underlying assumptions in western culture. Their contributions, along with those authors who examine specific references to families and schools, raise important questions about how committed western culture is to families, schools, and individual well-being when so much emphasis is placed upon materialism, popular youth culture, power, and international superiority. Coming to terms with these seemingly inherent contradictions is reflected in the chapters that follow.

Acknowledgements

MANY people have contributed to the production of this book. I would especially like to acknowledge the support from elementary, junior high, and senior high school students and their families in Virginia, Ohio, Arizona, Egypt, Canada, Australia, Japan, and the Philippines who participated in the empirical studies featured in this book. Their willingness to make up missed class time to support the research efforts of others is commendable. In addition, school administrators, guidance counselors, and teachers at each of the respective schools contributed many hours of their time to ensure the collection of data. Our apologies and thanks for allowing further disruption to an already hectic and overburdened schedule.

The College of William and Mary has provided many resources over the course of this project. Dean John Nagle in the School of Education provided numerous resources for the longitudinal study and reception for participants, awarding additional graduate student support in the summer. With the assistance of five graduate students, Geoffrey Ludford, Barbara Smith, Lisa Bittner, Stephanie Snead, and Leigh Ann Foster, data processing procedures remained consistently on target. One chapter alone could be devoted to the procedures developed to obtain accurate descriptions of the wide range of everchanging family patterns. The graduate students' computer expertise and perseverance throughout the project is greatly appreciated. Michael Politano is responsible for setting up the computer programs, later run by Thomas Ward after Mike took a position at the Citadel. I would also like to thank Byrd Latham, Kathy Allen, Rosa Queman, Amy Whitcover-Sanford, Valise Shields, Sheila Brautigam, and Jill Eaton for their administrative and secretarial expertise.

Additional support from The College of William and Mary came from a summer research grant and a faculty seminar grant through the Women's Studies Program. Under the auspices of the Women's Studies

Program, Deborah Ventis and Virginia Kerns developed a faculty seminar entitled "Cultural Constructions of Race and Gender," attended by Joyce VanTassel-Baska and myself, as well as colleagues from other disciplines. The discussions and readings for this seminar were provocative and encouraged an ongoing examination of the underlying assumptions that shape identity. The opportunity to share viewpoints with colleagues from several disciplines was very stimulating, and yes, we could communicate after all, despite our varying academic orientations.

Kappa Delta Pi's Alpha Xi Chapter at The College of William and Mary sponsored a self-esteem colloquium, featuring Kaoru Yamamoto's current and longstanding research. The colloquium provided an opportunity for the authors to explore their research interests and plan for the development of this book.

One of the most rewarding aspects of this project was the collaboration with colleagues at The College of William and Mary, Virginia Commonwealth University, and The University of Colorado at Denver. The opportunity to pursue a personal area of study, begun in the 1970s, by revisiting it in more depth would not have been possible without the expertise added by colleagues from a variety of educational disciplines. Beginning with the Kappa Delta Pi colloquium and continuing with conversations in the Friends of the Library Room, the authors identified the salient aspects of self-esteem within a professional context where important issues often become clouded by educational jargonese.

In addition to the financial and collegial support of friends in the academic community, family and friends have also been devoted in more personal ways to self-esteem enhancement! Herb, Karen, and Mark give in so many ways, making home and family very special. Gratitude also belongs to my friends and tennis partners, Jane Bergquist and Betty Martin, whose team spirit has helped to keep many issues in focus.

Gail McEachron-Hirsch

CHAPTER 1

Self and Identity Formation

GAIL McEACHRON-HIRSCH – *The College of William and Mary*

HISTORIANS and anthropologists have provided us with rich analyses of collective identities through interpretations of ethnic, tribal, national, and gender relationships. At the same time sociologists have investigated the social basis of identity, while psychologists have been busy trying to untangle the knot of individual identity construction. Less is known about how these apparently discrete processes interact to formulate a person's identity.

Self-concept and self-esteem are terms that have evolved in this century to describe perceptions of one's identity. Self-concept is generally defined as the attributes one has whereas self-esteem is the judgment one makes about those attributes. Yet the very notion that ''self-esteem'' represents a judgment made about aspects of one's own identity is relative to culture. In some cultures, for example, identity is tied so closely to social categories that perceptions of individual significance within those social classifications would not be a part of the collective consciousness (Geertz, 1973).

Discussing dilemmas of identity in contemporary life, Gergen (1991) traces western views of self from the romantic, through the modern, to the post-modern periods. His analysis provides a useful framework for understanding how the term *self-esteem* has evolved in educational and popular discourse. For Gergen (1991, p. 27), the romantic period imbues identity with ''a vocabulary of passion, purpose, depth, and personal significance: a vocabulary that generates awe of heroes, of genius, and of inspired work.'' Romantics praised others who were willing to abandon the useful and functional for the sake of others; trusting moral values was the ultimate significance of the human venture. Gergen views Freud as a transitional figure between romantic and modern perspectives because he proposed that ''the major driving force behind human conduct was essentially beyond the reach of consciousness. Largely blocked from direct expression, it wended its tortuous path

1

to the surface through dreams, works of art, and distorted reasoning or neurotic action'' (p. 27). Where the ''romantics found the inner reaches potently self-evident, Freud was moved by modernist demands for objective evidence of the unconscious'' (p. 27).

With the rise of science and the emphasis upon objectivity and observation, subjects such as ''ethics, theology, and metaphysics virtually disappeared from university curricula'' during the modernist period (Gergen, 1991, p. 30). Gergen maintains that the present century succeeded in obliterating the ''romantic preoccupation with the deep interior'' and replaced it with the ''rational, well-ordered, and accessible self'' (p. 38). These seemingly polarized notions were met with mixed interpretations among American psychologists. Emerging theories captured the extremes of identity formations through observable emphases such as Skinner's behaviorism and through intrinsic emphases such as the quest for essence characterized by Rogers' humanism. Despite the increased following in humanistic psychology, terms such as intimate communion, intrinsic worth, creative inspiration, moral values, and passionate expression, so prominent in the romantic period, became overshadowed by scientific discourse such as objective, rational, orderly, quantifiable, achievement, improvement, and conquest (Gergen, 1991, pp. 27, 30).

A large portion of the modern language of self and identity formation stems from a psychological tradition based on empirical studies of individuals whose damaged selves were in the process of being restored to some imagined intact essence. According to Gergen (1991, p. 41) the emerging role of the therapist was ''to restore a full sense of self-acceptance to the individual.'' It was during the modern period, according to Gergen, that a deficit language of self flourished. At the same time, psychologists developed theories of cognition to coincide with the ''rational'' as opposed to the ''emotional'' aspects of one's identity formation, resulting in additional vocabulary that could be ascribed to the multidimensional aspects of self. As research into the multidimensional aspects of self became more refined, compartmentalization emerged and as a result the interrelationships among these characteristics remained obfuscated.

Bringing the cultural constructions of identity up to contemporary times, Gergen suggests that the post-modern period has saturated individuals with role expectations to the point that ''doubt is increasingly placed on the very assumption of a bounded identity with palpable attributes'' resulting in a ''general loss in our assumption of true and knowable selves'' (pp. 15 – 16). Citing Riesman's *Lonely Crowd* as the work that captured the modernist spirit and foresaw its demise, Gergen (1991) says that post-modern men and women are other-directed, conformists, constantly seeking approval from others, and submitting to the power of the group. The result is a constant state of inner conflict.

> For as new and disparate voices are added to one's being, committed identity becomes an increasingly arduous achievement. How difficult for the romantic to keep a firm grasp on the helm of an idealistic undertaking when a chorus of internal voices sings the praises of realism, skepticism, hedonism, and nihilism. And can the committed realist, who believes in the powers of rationality and observation, remain arrogant in the face of inner urges toward emotional indulgence, moral sentiment, spiritual sensitivity, or aesthetic fulfillment? Thus, as social saturation adds incrementally to the population of self, each impulse toward well-formed identity is cast into increasing doubt; each is found absurd, shallow, limited, or flawed by the onlooking audience of the interior (Gergen, 1991, p. 73).

Casting contemporary identity formation as more ambivalent than ever before is perhaps overstated by Gergen, but his depiction of the way vocabulary for the multidimensional aspects of self has multiplied in the first half of this century is particularly relevant to current research trends. Wylie (1961) traced the relationship between educational and psychological theories throughout the first half of the twentieth century, noting that educational discourse clearly followed developments in psychological theory.

Even though interest in self-theory and the dynamic of the self has continued to expand exponentially since the late 1950s, the results of empirical research do not seem to be readily available to parents, educators, and professionals who play important roles in influencing the identities of children and youth (Hansen and Maynard, 1973). Instead, the extensive literature base seems to be at odds with conventional wisdom and educational practice. As a result common misconceptions about self-esteem have emerged in American culture. A description of these commonly held myths is presented next, indicating that self-esteem is often confused with a host of social issues. One of the important contributions of this book is the authors' attempt to make more explicit the limitations of an educational tradition that has been overshadowed by psychological rhetoric that has not kept pace with the social, political, and spiritual realities of family and school environments.

Myth #1: Self-esteem can be isolated and measured in ways similar to testing intelligence. Neither self-esteem nor intelligence is an entity that can be isolated. Yet methods for measuring self-esteem are actually less well developed than are those for testing intelligence. Self-esteem scales developed by Rosenberg, Piers and Harris, and Coopersmith have had widespread use, but they continue to be criticized for lack of construct validity. In addition, instruments that measure self-esteem have not been carefully matched to appropriate developmental levels. Given temporary fluctuations in self-esteem due to significant life events or novel situations, as well as the multidimensional aspects of self-esteem, measures of self-esteem at a single point in time pose serious interpretation problems.

Myth #2: Women, minorities, and the poor have lower self-esteem than do men, non-minorities, and the more affluent. The seminal work of Rosenberg in the 1960s revealed differences in adolescent self-esteem based on gender. Since that time, however, self-esteem studies have been inconclusive in terms of demographic differences. Studies that had indicated racial differences in self-esteem were flawed because minority groups from one socioeconomic level were compared with non-minority groups from another level. Studies comparing gender, ethnicity, and class status have been criticized by researchers who point out that an emphasis upon global self-esteem does not take efficacy into consideration. That is, one may feel good about oneself, but societal expectations may be incongruous with personal expectations. For instance, Werner (1989) documented case studies in which native Hawaiians born into poverty defied typical societal expectations despite their ''at-risk'' status. In our own four-year study of adolescents in Virginia, Louis Messier and I found no significant differences in self-esteem among students of different gender, ethnicity, or socioeconomic status (with the exception of Black males who experienced *lower* self-esteem during their sophomore year and *higher* self-esteem during their junior year).

Myth #3: Children who grow up in intact families have higher self-esteem. Children who have experienced divorce and live in single-parent or reconstituted families are often portrayed as victims who inevitably have long-term psychological scars. Divorce, like other significant life events, requires periods of change and adjustment. Depending on the circumstances leading up to and following the divorce, and depending on the particular dispositions and attitudes of the children and their parents, adjustments to divorce may be smooth, rocky, or both. Research indicates that, in those families that experience high levels of conflict and low levels of cohesion either before or after the divorce, divorce has a more negative impact on the self-esteem of family members. This same combination of high conflict/low cohesion also affects, however, the self-esteem of members of intact families. Thus, family dynamics have a far more significant impact on self-esteem than do family structures. Evidence in our own research supports this conclusion. Overall, regardless of family structure, students whose families are more cohesive and have an active, recreational orientation experience higher self-esteem.

Myth #4: Smarter students have higher self-esteem. Studies indicate that students who perform better in school feel better about themselves. This is not the same, however, as saying that smarter students have higher self-esteem. Schools are clearly organized and inclined to reward students who perform well. Yet educational institutions are continuously faced with the challenge of motivating students who are performing below their potential. High ability students, students in special education programs, and students in regular classrooms experience threats to their self-esteem when their motivation to learn is thwarted by social expectations that are incongruous with self-perception and ability. Although such "diagnostic classifications can be useful in highlighting the need . . . for special services, . . . they are typically too broad and encompassing to describe the individual child in any meaningful way" (Segal and Yahraes, 1978, p. 214). In our noble effort to maintain an educational system that values students as individuals and attempts to provide all with equal human rights, we often blur the necessity to differentiate curricula and teaching strategies to meet diverse student needs. Differentiated treatment is not incongruous with the concept of equality; rather, it is the recognition of individual worth—a component of enhanced self-esteem.

Myth #5: Self-esteem is formed primarily in the first five years of life and remains stable throughout one's lifetime. The importance of nurturance during the early years of one's life has been well-documented by psychologists, physicians, and educators. Yet, regardless of the support and nurturance provided to children during their first phases of life, self-esteem remains malleable and is very much affected by subsequent life events. For example, children in the same family who have been abused by a parent at an early age may react quite differently. One may harbor feelings of resentment that will last a lifetime, thus affecting self-esteem. Another may work through his or her memories and past experiences in a way that reduces long-term debilitating effects upon self-esteem. Friends and members of the helping professions provide valuable services throughout these painful processes. More disconcerting, however, are the psychopaths who perpetuate abuse of others and who find no pause for self-reflection or reorganization.

Myth #6: People who have high self-esteem are valued members of society. Some people who feel good about themselves are also valued members of society. However, others may have an inflated image of themselves and may actually alienate others because of their arrogance. Self-esteem is often clouded by one's position of power and prestige, particularly when individuals who hold such positions manipulate others for their own ends. Under such circumstances, people in positions of leadership confuse their powerful role with notions that people like them. Elements of this myth also have implications for the power differentials perpetuated by dominant ideologies. For example, minorities and women who have traditionally held positions of lower status may demonstrate no differences in self-esteem when compared to their white male, or just male in comparison to female, counterparts. Yet the criteria by which they are "accepted" depends on one's social frame of reference. Social acceptance of minorities and women for some may be based on whether they fulfill subservient roles. In other words, as long as a social structure that reinforces one's position of political and social elevation can be kept in place, minorities and women are accepted because they are instrumental in achieving identities of superiority. Thus, isolating measures of self-esteem based on demographic characteristics is limited without an examination of political and economic power bases.

Myth #7: People who are well-liked by others have high self-esteem. Being liked by others is one way to build positive self-esteem. But social acceptance does not automatically bring about acceptance of self. This sentiment was humorously captured by Groucho Marx when he said, "Why would I want to join a club that would have me as a member?" Many individuals are wary of social interpretations of their actions or persona, and they deliberately choose to deny either positive or negative assessments, selecting instead from among a myriad of social cues and weaving their own assessment of self. The complexity of this relationship has been demonstrated throughout history, and in our lifetime Adolf Hitler and Jim Jones are gruesome examples. To large numbers of people, these two individuals, in distinct ways, were hailed as saviors to a host of political, economic, and spiritual needs. Yet one cannot help but conclude that anyone who was so driven to bring about mass murder in the case of Nazi Germany, and mass suicide in the cases of Guyana and Waco, Texas, surely was motivated by severely "damaged" feelings of self-worth. In fact, today, if someone expressed the desire to repeat the acts of these individuals, mental health professionals would rally to begin a process for "correcting" such personal aspirations.

But a paradox is illustrated by these two examples. What we know about cultures where human sacrifice was not only acceptable, but practiced in incomprehensible proportions, as in the case of the Aztecs, is that killing can be sanctioned by the masses of true believers who support the actions of their leaders. Killing, in other words, is not necessarily the result of damaged mental health or low self-esteem on the part of those who participate in it, but rather killing becomes legitimized and viewed as normal given a certain blend of cultural elements. Thus, low levels of self-esteem cannot be inferred from delinquency, acts of violence, and human destruction. Nor can it be said that support from a cadre of individuals results in higher levels of self-esteem for the designated leader.

Myth #8: More progress in self-esteem research can be made once humanistic psychology gains the recognition it deserves. Educators tend to relegate self-esteem as an area of study under the rubric of third force or humanistic psychology because it is defined in part by internal processes. The polarization between behaviorism and humanistic psychology only partially limits self-esteem research. More fundamental limitations are the blind spots created by western culture. For example, Descartes is credited with articulating a new vision of identity formation through his statement, "I think, therefore I am." The implications of this statement for western identity resulted in a further separation between individuals and their collective consciousness. While Descartes' philosophy has had a dramatic impact upon western thought, social deconstructionists would probably translate the importance of his statement to mean, "I am therefore what I think I am."

One of the tensions underlying western thought is the split between individual and collective consciousness. Self-esteem cannot be completely controlled by society, nor can it be entirely shaped by individual will. Yet the emphasis upon the importance of the process of identity formation for individuals, rather than for the good of some higher transcendent state of collective consciousness, is viewed by some scholars as the major impediment to well-being. Of all the myths, this one is the most difficult to understand because not only is it abstract, but it lies outside the typical realm of western educational scholarship.

Debunking these myths about self-esteem is an important step in understanding the role that educators can play in assisting students with issues related to their own self-esteem. When self-esteem is mythologized, broader social issues are obscured. In fact, one can argue that, if preoccupation with self-esteem is a national trend, as suggested by one English journalist (Sarler, 1992), that trend is actually a smokescreen to avoid dealing with social issues or value conflicts. To educators, parents, employers, or anyone who is quick to affix the label ''self-esteem'' in response to interpersonal conflicts, there may be risk of dismissing social factors by arguing that self-esteem issues are beyond their control. Consider, for instance, in the two following illustrations, Jerry and Susan.

It is not uncommon to hear professionals respond to a student's school problems by remarking, ''Jerry's self-esteem is low.'' When pressed further, the responses may include, ''His parents divorced, and he is now living with his mother who had to go back to work full-time.'' This statement sends several messages. First, the divorce has created problems that were not there before. Second, living with a single parent who is working full-time is not a desirable situation. And third, a desirable home environment is one in which there is one parent at home and one at work. These events and circumstances in Jerry's life may have much to do with his self-esteem, but they may also have nothing to do with it.

It is quite possible that, as a result of his parents' divorce, conflict levels in Jerry's home have been reduced dramatically. His attention to school work may be the best ever because Jerry and his mother now spend evenings together going over homework. What may, in fact, be troubling Jerry is that he was not selected for the advanced soccer team and that, as a result, he now feels dejected. Or it may be that Jerry's problems *are* the result of his not having enough time to spend with his mother on homework assignments. Too often, the typical reaction to students like Jerry is to blame their single parents for neglecting parental responsibilities, when a more substantive and useful response may be to restructure the workplace so that the fulfillment of school, family, and work responsibilities can be made more compatible.

As a second example, consider Susan, a pregnant teenager. Pregnant teenagers almost always cause others to raise the red flag of ''low self-esteem.'' The California Task Force on Self-Esteem, for instance, categorically identifies pregnant teenagers as being at risk for poor self-esteem! Perhaps, however, Susan is not really experiencing low self-esteem; rather, she may simply not ascribe to the middle-class value of upward mobility. Instead of working especially hard to maintain grades so that she can stay in school and someday go to college, she may prefer to have a child because, for her, that will be more meaningful. Most would argue that Susan is not enlightened about the consequences of her decision. Others might suggest that her values do not coincide with mainstream American culture. In fact, in a 1992 report of the American Association of University Women (AAUW), researchers suggest that early childbearing may be an adaptive response to social and economic deprivation.

Both of these illustrations reveal the complex web that educators and other professionals need to explore in order to get at the underlying pulse of individual self-esteem. Self-esteem and school performance are closely tied to broader social norms and values and to the very structures that influence family, school, and work environments. Studies of self-esteem provide important insights to the overall impact of these structures upon the individual, but their results should in no way be treated as logical outcomes. Rather, their results should represent individual testimonies in their own right, and they should be viewed as echoes of the strengths and tensions in the larger society.

Educational folklore hails the accomplishments of heroes and heroines who radically transform the lives of politically oppressed students. Movie roles played by Jon Voight in *Conrack,* Sidney Poitier in *To Sir with Love,* and Edward James Olmos in *Stand and Deliver,*[1] provide hope to those who tend to feel that it just takes commitment, enthusiasm, and the belief that all children can be motivated. The everyday lives of the majority of teachers are not typified by the experiences of these notable characters. In each of the well-known tales, the catalyst for overcoming poor school performance was unified by a greater notion of overcoming minority and/or socioeconomic oppression.

For most teachers, the self-esteem of students is expressed in a myriad of ways, and it rarely stems from a single or unified source. Given our diverse school population, the factors that affect self-esteem are not only multidimensional, but also diffuse within a particular classroom. In the same classroom, they may include academic performance; minority status; gender stereotypes; family discord; physical or sexual abuse; temporary feelings of loss and bereavement due to divorce, death, or a move to a new neighborhood; stigma based on labels such as *gifted, learning disabled,* or *blue group;* or teacher expectations that are either too high or too low—just to mention a few! Moreover, making these self-esteem factors explicit for each child is not only difficult, but sometimes undesirable, given the need to be sensitive to both individual privacy and a student's desire to belong to a particular group of peers.

Given the complexity of all the issues involved in self-esteem, over-simplified explanations and quick-fix solutions have little or no impact on individuals. Unless self-esteem research pursues the challenges posed by the multidimensional nature of self, it too will become another educational slogan that lacks documentation, is devoid of content, and has little or no impact on teaching and learning.

The title of this book, *Student Self-Esteem: Integrating the Self,* is based on the relatively modern western assumption that one plays an active role in creating one's identity. The notion that the self can be individually constructed has evolved within western scholarship as the field of psychology and psychoanalysis has turned its attention to the interplay between internal states and socialization. Eastern philosophers, on the other hand, have had a long tradition devoted to understanding one's inner life through reflection, yet the gains made in both eastern and western thought regarding the process by which one develops an identity continue along separate paths. A synthesis of the important contributions that eastern and western scholars have developed for understanding the self remains outside the purview of this book. Instead, an effort will be made to review American scholarly traditions regarding individual conceptions of self in educational and family environments. Representing a wide range of educational roles, each author brings a unique perspective to understanding the interplay between individual perceptions of self and the influence of the family and school. Most believe that education has the potential to be a positive medium through which individual identities can flourish. Yet, as the chapters reveal, no author is completely satisfied with the educational system and there is agreement that more can be done to address the needs of individuals.

Student Self-Esteem: Integrating the Self begins with a broad sociopolitical perspective, providing the cultural landscape from which contemporary family and school environments have emerged. Following this, the next group of authors looks more closely at the ways in which families and schools share common goals in preparing children and youth for adulthood. Together, the approaches reveal that preoc-cupation with the development of self-esteem in merely one domain will result in very narrow conceptualizations. Furthermore, the notion of shared goals becomes more complicated as many parents, teachers, and

students are faced with preparing for a future that seems more susceptible to change than it had been for previous generations.

Losito and Matthews take the challenging task of trying to link the
process of individual identity formation in the here and now to a more
inclusive unifying theme. For Losito, the alienation from personal
relationships and the world as a whole is precipitated by ontological
anxiety, a condition defined in existential philosophy. To the existentialist, self-esteem is enhanced by the ongoing affirmation of one's
significance. Thus, two of the fundamental existential questions crucial
to the formation of identity are "Who am I?" and "What is the purpose
of my existence?" The way individuals answer these questions and shape
their identity to reinforce a sense of purpose to their life is the crux for
understanding self-esteem. The assumption underlying these existential
parameters is that feeling a sense of purpose and significance to one's
being contributes positively to self-esteem, whereas feelings of alienation and worthlessness adversely affect self-esteem. According to May's
(1960, p. 3) existential analysis, individuals in Western culture are
particularly vulnerable to feelings of alienation because through our
emphasis on technical achievement over nature, "We repress the opposite, the 'awareness of being. . . .' "

In Chapter Two, Losito addresses the ontological anxiety manifested
by the existential quest of men and women today. Emphasizing the
important roles played by parents and professionals who work with
children and youth, Losito proposes alternative ways to model a more
meaningful sense of significance beyond "performing" for the sake of
reaping materialistic or externalized reinforcements. By using
hospitality as a metaphor, Losito presents a refreshing alternative to the
mechanistic, factory-model notion of education.

Matthews' approach, also expansive, is different. For him, Western
culture limits the enhancement of self because of its illusionary division
between the person and the environment, a division that even existentialist philosophy doesn't completely confront. In Chapter Three, he
begins with an analysis of the gains made in psychology and
psychotherapy toward a better understanding of individual identity. Then
Matthews argues that humanistic psychology met success in dealing with
Western culture's split within the mind and the split between the person
and the environment. Drawing upon Jungian psychology and the Eastern
concept of God as both transcendent and immanent, Matthews offers
both an explanation for our Western ideological limitations and suggestions for ways to reexamine our notions of self. Both Matthews and

Losito broaden the importance of identity formation as more than the enhancement of self-esteem as an end in itself. Instead, self-esteem is enhanced and imbued with significance in part by its being defined in relation to others and the rest of the world.

Many of the great political philosophers have advanced theories that allow for the simultaneous advancement of societal and individual progress. Indeed, the very rhetoric of politicians is based on the expectation that political leadership can better the lives of individual citizens. But history has demonstrated that certain kinds of political leaders are not only detrimental to the well-being of selected individuals and groups, but can undermine the well-being of society and become a threat to the rest of the world. Jung described the danger of individuals being manipulated by a set of symbols that enlist their commitment to abstract notions of the ''great society'' when in fact, it is the exploitation of the masses that results from corrupt political power. For Jung (1964, p. 45), ''The further we move away from the individual toward abstract ideas'' about humankind, the more consciousness will be influenced by prejudice and fantasy.

Without awareness of the political forces that can corrupt, there is great danger that the masses of people within society can be the victims of immoral acts or can be led to commit immoral acts. In fact, how one defines morality is the result of a complex process of political socialization. In Chapter Four, Hirsch will describe this process and contrast the effects of political corruption upon Europeans during the Holocaust. Examining altruistic behavior in extreme inhumane circumstances, Hirsch provides case illustrations to demonstrate the capacity of the self to combine self-consciousness with other-consciousness. By so doing, Hirsch's analysis spotlights the danger of being apolitical. That is, when individuals become self-absorbed or pursue individual self-aggrandizing activities without regard to the political realities that surround them, their political apathy may have self-defeating consequences. For Hirsch, notions of transcendence for collective consciousness run the risk of alienation from the here and now when self and identity are not linked to one's political culture. Political culture is much more complicated than the problem of whether one's homeland is governed by democracy or a military dictatorship. In fact, as Hirsch points out in Chapter Four, political behavior is closely entwined with family values.

The family is the primary source through which culture is transmitted from one generation to the next. In Chapter Five, Gallas and Hardinge discuss the ''family of origins'' and its significance for family systems theory. Looking at family dynamics and values as the most important source for enhancing or inhibiting self-esteem, Gallas and Hardinge discuss the positive roles that schools can play when educators attempt to understand the students' fit between family and school environments. Family systems theory provides educators with a basis for understanding the different behavioral patterns of students representing a wide range of cultural backgrounds and interactive styles. Awareness of these differences sensitizes educators to the need for a repertoire of responses that can accommodate lifestyle and cultural differences rather than expect all students to conform to narrowly defined expectations.

Just as social acceptance of a variety of cultural and interactive styles is necessary to enhance self-esteem, so too is it necessary to acknowledge the multidimensional nature of individual self-esteem. As Gergen noted earlier, the direction taken by psychology during the first half of this century has been primarily in delineating the multiple aspects of identity formation. As a result, the measurement of self-esteem has mushroomed as psychologists have attempted to define the gamut of possible dimensions and construct objective means to ascertain their presence or absence in individual identity formations. The proliferation of self-esteem and self-concept scales attest to this trend. However, as Ward and Ward demonstrate in Chapter Six, many of these scales have been formulated without sufficient attention to construct validity. Despite the limitations of the instruments themselves, educators and clinicians continue their use, making decisions about students based on limited and invalid information. Ward and Ward offer alternative approaches to making assessments of students whose self-esteem is at stake given problematic linkages between family and school environments. Because their model is designed to identify student strengths and weaknesses, practitioners can use it with students in a variety of classroom situations, not just with students whose needs require the attention of a school psychologist. By identifying strengths, self-esteem builds upon internal structures belonging to the individual rather than overemphasizing a series of strategies designed to correct deficit characteristics.

Few studies in education have attempted to clarify how student roles and norms in school settings coalesce with the individual's roles and expectations within the family. Typically, available case studies surface from the files of clinicians and child study teams that were created to solve problem situations. While these studies further our understanding of the lack of fit between family and school environments, we still know very little about the normal ways in which students negotiate school and family influences to develop self-awareness. In Chapter Seven, Yamamoto and McEachron-Hirsch focus upon the development of self during the elementary school years. Through two case illustrations, the roles of the school and family are portrayed in both a positive and negative light. In one case, the school plays a supportive role in buffering self-esteem during a transitional period of family difficulty. By contrast, the second case illustrates the damaging effects upon self-esteem when teacher expectations do not take individual capabilities into consideration.

Adolescents experience the same need to negotiate school and family influences. How the process of identity formation takes place amidst the many changing classrooms, teachers, peer groups, and work roles is not readily available to most researchers because of limited access to the many changing variables. Typically, studies of adolescent development may focus upon either emotional development, personality measures or academic achievement, but seldom focus upon the relationships among these dimensions. In a longitudinal study conducted by McEachron-Hirsch and Messier, adolescent self-esteem was investigated in relation to personality measures, as well as classroom and family environments. In Chapter Eight, McEachron-Hirsch and Ward report the results of this study spotlighting those factors in family and classroom environments that contribute in positive and negative ways to adolescent self-esteem. While Chapters Seven and Eight examine self-esteem and educational practice within general classrooms, Chapters Nine through Twelve present research conducted with special populations.

American public education has always prided itself in providing for the masses, though this ideal has not been consistently translated to all groups, particularly minorities, women, and those with disabilities. Nevertheless, greater access to an equal education has been more viable since *Brown v. Board of Education* in 1954, the passage of the Education of the Handicapped Act (Public Law 94-142) in 1975, and Title IX in 1972. In Chapter Nine, Walther-Thomas will examine the changing role of special educators as they respond to contemporary social issues and the impact on students with disabilities. Prior to the passage of this law, the self-esteem of many students must have been adversely affected since classroom teachers were not expected to differentiate the curriculum or learning environment to accommodate them. Yet, while singling out a student for special services can ameliorate individual learning problems, additional self-esteem issues emerge when social stigmas create unforeseen consequences. In some cases, going to ''special ed'' has signified deficiency, resulting in negative self-concepts because the emphasis upon deficiencies had not been balanced with the recognition of individual strengths. Walther-Thomas describes the collaborative efforts among special educators and classroom teachers as they develop strategies that provide students with the individual attention they need but in a setting that is conducive to both cognitive as well as social growth.

Placing the issues of special educators side-by-side with issues among educators of the gifted reveals that the singling out process may be more germane to the creation of stigmas than whether the basis for being singled out stems from deficient or proficient exceptionalities. Educators of the gifted and educators in regular classrooms have noted the pride as well as reluctance of some students who have been identified for gifted programs. These mixed reactions suggest that being recognized for individual strengths is perceived differently among students, and society in general, and may therefore, result in different effects upon self-esteem. In a society that assumes that the best and the brightest will rise to the top as if by some natural process, the threat of anti-intellectualism in the United States may be having unforeseen consequences. The self-esteem and realization of potential for many students who are endowed with greater than average capabilities as well as truly unique gifts, may be in greater jeopardy than previously understood. VanTassel-Baska presents an analysis of self-esteem studies of gifted populations in Chapter Ten. Noting discrepancies in ability and academic performance, VanTassel-Baska identifies pedagogical and philosophical weaknesses that are having adverse effects upon the self-esteem of gifted students. VanTassel-Baska's research demonstrates that when educators assume that those with above average abilities can rise above a host of social pressures, we have erroneously separated the intellect and other cognitive and physical abilities from the individual's emotional and social needs.

A good fit between individual student needs and the goals of educational institutions is the presumed magic formula for personal, educational, and societal progress. But when failure in school results in increased drop-out rates and juvenile delinquency the burden of responsibility is shared by all. Juvenile delinquency is a condition that sends a message of lives gone awry. When this happens, when failure to function within the laws of society becomes a way of life for misguided youth, low self-esteem is an assumed accompaniment. If juvenile delinquency signifies societal rejection, further rejection of self is sure to follow.

Blame is typically placed upon the family. Supposedly, family dynamics have created a situation whereby an individual family member has developed low self-esteem, thus creating a pattern of low school performance and failure, which leads to dropping out and juvenile delinquency. Occasionally, though less frequently, the schools are blamed because they have created the low rate of success in the first place, which has resulted in low self-esteem. Regardless of where the blame is placed, there are problems with this reasoning because the motivation to achieve is inextricably tied in with self-esteem, when they are really separate functions. Although probably related in some way, research to date has not made these relationships clear. In the meantime, while families blame the schools and schools blame the families, juvenile delinquency and drop-out rates have become a major societal problem. Few studies have attempted to examine the multidimensional aspects of self among juvenile delinquents. In Chapter Eleven, Messier and Ward will report the findings of a unique study, which assessed personality variables, self-esteem, family environment, ability, and depression among adolescent juvenile delinquents, some of whom are incarcerated. The chapter will describe the surprising, but previously unreported, prevalence of psychological depression, as well as the prevalence of intellectual giftedness among students in detention centers. Striking comparisons are made with the adolescents in the McEachron-Hirsch and Messier study, which is reported on in Chapter Eight.

Juvenile delinquency is an outcome that stems from many factors, but it does not imply a set of circumstances that are irreversible. Circumstances such as poverty, neglect, discrimination, wars, domestic violence, and damaged interpersonal relationships place children and youth in vulnerable situations that require strong will and fortitude in order for them to overcome psychological damage. Case histories reveal that certain children and youth are able to rise from their burdens, including some genetic predispositions, in ways that defy most odds. In Chapter Twelve, Yamamoto will provide an analysis of the factors that these individuals and their significant others mobilize for support. Contrasting coping styles of many children considered "at risk," Yamamoto reveals the more successful ways in which human beings respond to crisis situations. Awareness of these defenses and promotions of well-being not only provides further insights into the way individuals integrate an image of self, but reveals the importance of the help of significant others, not necessarily primary caregivers in the home. Illuminating the factors that help vulnerable children escape from adversity provides greater hope to those who may be in a position to make a difference (Werner, 1989).

Chapter Thirteen summarizes the important ways that schools and families can both promote and stifle developing selves. The intent of the book is not to end with a list of self-esteem enhancements that can be plugged into curriculum and parenting guides. To do so would be contributing to the smokescreen that detracts from dealing with broader social issues. Instead, the book attempts to make more explicit the interrelated factors that affect the process of integrating an image of self and to demonstrate that society cannot deny the school's role in influencing internal states such as self-esteem. Schools and society need to acknowledge the inseparability of the intellect from psychological dispositions and images of self. As Fromm points out, when the "I" has been split off into an intellect that, in turn, tries to control nature, the result is the transformation of the individual into a thing. The final chapter will discuss the strengths and limitations of the school's role in providing students with a healthy integration of psychological and intellectual growth. Sharing the responsibility with families and other social institutions is a necessary step in achieving these goals.

ENDNOTE

1 *Conrack* is a movie based on the book *The Water Is Wide* by Pat Conroy; the movie *Stand and Deliver* is based on the experiences of Jaime Escalante in East Los Angeles.

REFERENCES

The AAUW Report: How Schools Shortchange Girls, A Study of Major Findings on Girls and Education. 1992. Commissioned by the American Association of University Women (AAUW) Educational Foundation; Researched by The Wellesley College Center for Research on Women. A joint publication of the AAUW Educational Foundation and National Education Association.

Geertz, C. 1973. *The Interpretation of Cultures.* New York, NY: Basic Books, Inc.

Gergen, K. 1991. *The Saturated Self: Dilemmas of Identity in Contemporary Life.* New York, NY: Basic Books.

Hansen, J. C. and P. E. Maynard. 1973. *Youth: Self-Concept and Behavior.* Columbus, OH: Merrill.

Jung, C. 1964. *Man and His Symbols.* New York, NY: Dell Publishing Co.

May, R., ed. 1960. *Existential Psychology.* New York, NY: Random House.

Sarler, C. 1992. "Stiffen Your Lips, Yanks: No Self-Esteem, Please, We're British," *Newsweek* (February 17):52.

Segal, J. and H. Yahraes. 1978. *A Child's Journey.* New York, NY: McGraw-Hill Book Co.

Werner, E. E. 1989. "High-Risk Children in Young Adulthood: A Longitudinal Study from Birth to 32 Years," *American Journal of Orthopsychiatry,* 59:72–81.

Wylie, R. 1961. *The Self Concept: A Critical Survey of Pertinent Research Literature.* Lincoln, NB: University of Nebraska Press.

CHAPTER 2

Developing Self-Esteem through Meaningful Community Ritual and Narrative

WILLIAM F. LOSITO – *The College of William and Mary*

Both the starting and end points of my reflections pertain to an incident that occurred within the past few years. My son, Daniel, and I were alone on a Saturday afternoon at home watching a college tournament basketball game – I through the glazed eyes and foggy head of one suffering from early spring sinus allergies. Suddenly, Daniel spurted up, rummaged through the bookcase until he came upon his Cub Scout manual, and rushed outside. As he closed the sliding-glass door, he commented on the need to finish a number of activities for his Wolf Badge. For five minutes or so, he darted this way and that outside and I could hear the sporadic sound of a ball being thrown against the brick chimney. After that brief spurt of activity, he came in and thrust the scout manual in front of me for my signature, certifying the completion of one of the outdoor activities. Within another five minutes, the manual was back in my face with the request for a signature under a space where he had hastily scrawled five ways for ensuring household fire safety. I did so reluctantly, but a bit later, when yet another signature was solicited, I declared an autograph moratorium until we could talk further about the matter.

The incident prompted then, and with a clearer head later, reflections about the reinforcement system gone amok by Daniel's efforts to attain the Wolf Badge.[1] Zipping this way and then that, like the Sorcerer's Apprentice, he was a ludicrous caricature of the misuse of an important educational idea – positive reinforcement in this case – which can sabotage worthwhile achievement and its handmaiden, self-esteem. It is unlikely that Daniel will have an enduring appreciation for household safety measures because of his hasty scribbling. Likewise, any self-esteem developed through such spurious achievements is fragile at best. While my son's behavior was comical, the most worrisome aspect is that the episode is symptomatic of the greater cultural malady.

It is paradoxical that a culture that is preoccupied with promoting personal states of "feeling good" fails so miserably to engender a permanent sense of individual well-being in its populace. In fact, there seems to be a proportional relationship between our cultural investment in therapies of self and the amount of stress, anxiety, and violence in our society induced by low self-esteem. Any effort to develop a fruitful approach to building self-esteem needs to appraise critically the value/reward system inherent in the present cultural context and offer a foundational perspective for developing practical guidelines pertinent to particular social settings, such as the school and family. The reflections that follow will be directed toward identifying key considerations for developing an approach applicable both to the culture as a whole and particular social contexts.

CULTURAL CRITIQUE

There is a commonsense explanation for the failure of our culture to engender a durable sense of personal well-being in its members. It is no secret that our culture greatly prizes the acquisition of material goods, competitive achievements, speed, efficiency, productivity, power, beauty, and prestige. While there are personal and social benefits accrued from these prized activities, self-esteem, which is linked to normative success and achievement in all of these areas, is inherently inaccessible for large numbers of the population. And even for those who succeed in many of these areas, self-esteem is fragile; it is only as strong as the last compliment, performance on an academic test, or envy by others of the most recent purchase. Innumerable college students, whose family attics are full of smiley faces, ribbons, certificates, trophies, and even Cub Scout Wolf Badges, will give testimony to the feeling of utter despondency and worthlessness after receiving their first ''F'' on a test in calculus or physics. The emphasis on a wide array of competitive achievements is illustrated by the *Guinness Book of World Records,* which validates competitive attainments in everything from domino toppling to golf ball balancing. Such an emphasis only intensifies the anxiety to ratify a sense of personal worth and esteem through seeking greater individual achievement.

In addition to the commonsense explanation, there is a deeper framework for understanding the inadequacy of contemporary culture. The perspective developed by many twentieth century existential psychologists and philosophers, such as Rollo May (1983), is a useful and credible framework for the analysis.[2] Existentialism grounds its

rec(
exp(
an o
exist
time
indivi
ingly
whole,
to crea
never p
to exist(
life in a
transcen
to resist (
fulfillmei
life on de
individual

)eing in an analysis of the human
) existential analysis, humans share
;sibility of failing to live a meaningful
.tated by experiencing the passage of
;rceived as conferring significance on
intensifies, the individual feels increas-
relationships and the larger world as a
ife is then spent in the existential struggle
/ul existence. While the human condition
solution of ontological anxiety according
nificantly reduced through centering one's
realizes the deepest human potentialities in
sciplined centering of life requires courage
ion to patterns of behavior that frustrate the
nan potential. By habitually centering one's
of self-transcending, significant action, the
nse of "being in place" spatially and tem-

porally. An ontological sense of well-being and self-esteem emerges through "being in place."

But the individual does not always succeed in attaining ontological well-being. Because of the difficulty in disciplining intellect, will, and emotion to a centered way of life, the individual can easily repress and abdicate the responsibility of living out a committed course of action that enhances being. The abdication can take the form of allowing the shape of one's life to be dictated by attachments to lesser, self-centering values reinforced by the larger society. These attachments quickly develop into compulsive addictions, which control the life of the individual (May, 1988).[3] The compulsive addiction, instead of resulting in enhanced self-esteem, only exacerbates the sense of anxiety, guilt, and negative self-image. The individual feels intensely "dislocated" and out-of-place with respect to the centers of being.

The existential analysis of the human condition provides a framework for interpreting and critically assessing the failure of contemporary culture to provide a climate for enhancing individual and social self-esteem. Our culture has fostered addictive, self-centering attachments to power, symbols of prestige, and material goods. This pattern of attachments only facilitates an even greater psycho-cultural climate of ontological anxiety, guilt, and feelings of being dislocated. The problem needs, therefore, to be addressed at both the broader sociocultural level as well as in more personal social contexts, such as family and school.

The existentialist perspective provides a framework for understanding the problem at both the cultural and personal level. It also provides a general indication of resolution—the development of centered, self-transcending action. Since the problem has both a cultural as well as an individual dimension, it is important to examine other cultural models for concrete guidelines in the development of centered, self-transcending action. Anthropologists have frequently cited primitive societies for examining alternative cultural models.

PRIMITIVE RELIGIOUS CULTURES

In his seminal studies of primitive cultures, Mircea Eliade contends that it is a sense of the sacred that distinguishes them from contemporary cultures with their accompanying existential anxiety and guilt. Individuals in primitive societies tried "to live as much as possible in the sacred or in close proximity to consecrated objects" (Eliade, 1959, p. 12). To live in the sacred meant to conceive of one's being as present to the transcendent gods and participating in or imitating their actions. The impetus for sacralizing existence was, in Eliade's words, the deeply seated drive "to live in a pure and holy cosmos, as it was in the beginning, when it came fresh from the Creator's hands" (p. 65). The saturation of human existence with presence to transcendent reality conferred on primitive peoples an ontological sense of well-being and a cultural foundation for individual self-esteem.

Eliade contrasts the sense of sacred in primitive cultures with the "profane world"—a characteristic, invented dimension of modern societies (1959, p. 13). Contemporary cultures have maintained many of the sacred symbols, myths, and rituals of primitive cultures, but the drive to experience proximity to the gods has been transformed into a this-worldly self-centering of consciousness and action. For contemporary cultures, the valorization of being is derived from competitive, individualistic productivity and achievement.

Within Eliade's analysis, the "religious person" in primitive cultures—the person who achieved an existential sense of well-being—was the individual who consciously and fully tried to sacralize personal and social existence. The religious person created special spaces and times of divine presence so that all of human existence might be sacralized. With respect to space, the religious person desired to live at the "center of the world" in proximity to the gods (Eliade, 1959, p. 37). The religious person consecrated special places, such as temples and homes, where the epiphany of the gods could be experienced. Time was sacralized for the religious person by "reproducing the same paradigmatic acts and gestures of the gods," typically in the special sacred space, in a routinized pattern pervading the seasons of the year and one's life cycle. By viewing personal life as being present to the gods and a participation in their paradigmatic acts, an ontological sense of significance was conferred on personal action and being.

Myths and rituals were the critical factors for the religious person to understand and enact the sacralization of time and space. Sacred myths are the narratives that depict the primordial acts of the gods and their pertinence for human experience. The myths do not typically recount literally factual events; rather, they are meant to convey the essential truths about the hierophany of the gods in human experience. Rituals are the routinized patterns of actions for translating the meaning and events of the myths into contemporary time and space. Primitive religious peoples created myths and rituals to confer significance on almost every aspect of human existence – birth, marriage, entering adulthood, planting, harvesting, establishing human relationships, making war, and dying.

For primitive religious peoples, the paradigmatic myth was the creation myth, which recounted the original creation of the world by the gods. This myth has countless versions in different primitive cultures. The common theme is that the gods created the universe in primordial time and that the creation event is continually renewed in the present through ritual. The rituals included crossing the threshold of important dwellings, settling a new region, planting crops, sexual intercourse, and the like. Myth and ritual conferred significance for personal being which permeated all of individual and social existence. The sacralization of time and space through ritual empowered the individual to develop the deepest human potential for participating in the teleological design of the universe. For the primitive religious person, then, myth and ritual, which centered personal and social consciousness on the presence and acts of the gods, provided a foundation for a durable and fruitful sense of well-being.

Of what relevance is the experience of primitive religious cultures for contemporary societies and individuals? Contemporary societies have gradually lost their sense of the sacred as a means of centering personal and social existence in significant, transcendent human action. Western society, in particular, evolved into the modern secular era with an unbounded confidence in scientific reasoning and technological progress. Sacred myths and rituals were transformed into profane rags-to-riches sagas and the dehumanizing rites of industrialized, bureaucratic societies. According to Eliade, many religious symbols and observances remain in contemporary society, but they are weak traces of their vigorous roles in primitive cultures.

If Eliade is correct, a post-modern society needs to reclaim sacred myth and ritual as a means of self-transcendence and establishing an ontological sense of well-being. The cultural imperative to sacralize time and space emerges as a unique historical opportunity. In deconstructing all classical texts and their interpretations, our post-modern society has liberated us from the mandate to reclaim the specific sacred myths and rituals of primitive cultures. Many of the myths were fanciful and fostered unjustified pain and suffering for human, as well as other sentient, life. The opportunity is present to simultaneously reclaim and recreate a sacralized cultural foundation for individuals developing an ontological sense of well-being.

What Eliade rightfully points out is that individuals realize enduring self-esteem when personal action is perceived as participating in creative events of cosmic significance. Sacred myth and ritual enable the individual to transcend the particulars of fragmented, self-centered existence. Within a deconstructed, pluralistic society, there cannot be a hegemony of one ''sacred'' theology which undergirds reclaimed/created public myth and ritual. Rather, the new public ''sacred'' should refer to those transcendent themes of personal and social meaning that have stood the test of reasoned judgment for transforming action into cosmically significant events. The meaning of these new public ''sacred'' myths and rituals should be open-textured enough to encourage a pluralism of interpretations, applications, and subthemes.

Over the historical course of our civilization, there are several themes that have withstood the test of reasoned judgment for serving as a basis for reclaiming sacred myth and ritual. The creation and caring for being is the paradigmatic core idea for many of these themes. Primitive religious individuals, for example, interpreted their production of useful goods and helping of neighbors as participating in the creative/caring action of the gods. The paradigmatic ideas of creations provided the deeper structural meaning for myriads of myths and rituals in primitive cultures.

The rest of this chapter is devoted to identifying and giving an intro-

ductory explication of a mythical narrative exemplifying the paradigmatic theme of caring. The mythical narrative is the Greek classic,
The Odyssey, and the paradigmatic theme is that of hospitality. The
theme of hospitality is worthy of reclaiming and recreating in contemporary culture for developing a durable social and personal sense of
human well-being. After the concise explication, several suggestions for
incorporating the hospitality theme in educational contexts will be
pointed out.

THE HOSPITALITY TRADITION

Greek literature, as well as the Hebrew and Christian Scriptures, give
a preeminent place to the moral necessity and virtue of hospitality.
Homer's *Odyssey* (1963) lays out the paradigmatic narrative of life-as-
journey motif in our Western literature. Regularly throughout the epic,
the provision of hospitality is a key ingredient in supporting the heroes
and keeping them on course. The implication is that life's journey
requires the compassion and caring of others for a successful outcome.

In the early part of the story, Telemakhos, the son of Odysseus, sets
out with his compatriots in search of his father. They land on
Lakedaimon, the domain of Menelaos. King Menelaos himself had
participated in the siege of Troy and spent several treachery-filled years
returning to his homeland. Upon meeting Telemakhos, King Menelaos
emphatically exhorts his men:

> Could we have made it home again—and Zeus give us no more hard
> roving!—if other men had never fed us, given us lodging? These men to
> be our guests: unhitch their team! (Homer, Bk. 4, ll. 1—23).[4]

This passage clearly indicates important characteristics of the nature
and motive for hospitality. Each one of us is likely to be in need of food
and lodging at some time in life; we should feel compelled, then, to offer
it to others in need.

The most extended and profound treatment of hospitality centers
around the initial events of Odysseus' return to his homeland Akhaia.
When Odysseus first arrived after a twenty-year absence, he sought out
the shelter of the swineherd, Eumaios, who had remained faithful to him
for all those years. Because of Odysseus' aging and his disguise in poor
clothing, the swineherd did not recognize him. But spontaneously and
generously, Eumaios immediately offered hospitality, ''Come to the

cabin. You're a wanderer too. You must eat something, drink some wine, and tell me where you are from and the hard times you've seen'' (Homer, Bk. 14, ll. 1−22). After Odysseus thanks Eumaios profusely for the hospitality, the swineherd remonstrates him by indicating a fundamental reason for hospitality:

> Tush, friend, rudeness to a stranger is not decency. Poor though he may be, poorer than you. All wanderers and beggars come from Zeus. What we can give is slight but well-meant−all we dare. You know that is the way of slaves, who live in dread of masters−new ones like our own (Homer, Bk. 14, ll. 23−78).

So, ultimately, the reason for hospitality is that the strangers are sent by the gods; they are not simply accidental events in one's life. And the individual must respond accordingly.

Eumaios helped Odysseus eventually reunite with his wife, Penelope. Odysseus remained disguised, so that Penelope likewise did not recognize him. Nonetheless, she extended hospitality to the stranger and expressed eloquently another motive for extending compassion and caring:

> Men's lives are short. The hard man and his cruelties will be cursed behind his back, and mocked in death. But one whose heart and ways are kind−of him strangers will bear report to the wide world, and distant men will praise him (Homer, Bk. 19, ll. 263−332).

Here, Penelope points out that there is a reward for the individual who provides hospitality. Not only may the hospitality be returned, but the caring and compassionate person will be esteemed as virtuous by the community. Thus, we see that *The Odyssey* sets forth in narrative form guidelines concerning the nature, importance, and motives for the practice of hospitality in life's journey, both taken individually as well as for an entire culture.

The Odyssey is an excellent example of a classic narrative that portrays the myth and ritual of hospitality as a means for sacralizing human action in both space and time. The myth depicts action−the act of hospitality − which transforms individual action into a participation in the action of the god Zeus. It thus confers on the individual a sense of self-transcendent cosmic significance. Likewise, the myth spells out specific rituals − feeding, clothing, and nurturance−to the stranger. The ritual provides a repeatable coherence and sacralization of the individual's life which accounts for an ontological sense of well-being. It is the theme of caring as hospitality, which our post-modern society direly needs to hear. The reclamation/recreation of the hospitality theme has application at both the micro and macro levels in our culture.

EDUCATIONAL APPLICATIONS

It is important for the culture as a whole to reclaim traditional myths and rituals of hospitality as well as to recreate meaningful contemporary ones. But the transformation of a culture takes a long time. Individuals and smaller social settings, such as schools and families, can do something more immediately to effect a social climate conducive to fostering ontological well-being. It is in these more concrete social environments where we reinforce patterns of self-centering, individualistic achievements, which exacerbate the problem of ontological anxiety.

Through extreme forms of tracking and the emphasis on success on normative tests, particular school cultures inhibit the development of hospitality dispositions in students. Instead, the school cultures reinforce a sense of hostility and competition, at least insofar as the obtaining of grades are concerned. And in family settings, we frequently reinforce patterns of "getting ahead" behaviors and rigid insulation from "undesirable" classes of people. Certain paternalistic concerns for the well-being of the young are clearly justified, but we are talking here about those extreme forms of self-centering reinforcement, which keep dispositions of hospitality toward others from developing. The resolution is not to eliminate positive reinforcement and systems of rewards, but rather to redirect reinforcement toward actions embedded in myths and rituals, which have greater promise for enhancing ontological well-being.

The most profound impact on educational contexts from the above analysis is on the overall goals that we attribute to education in a democratic society. At present, there is not compelling consensus concerning the purpose of public education in American society. At its earliest beginnings, American education was conceived in Massachusetts to ensure Biblical and civil literacy. The contemporary debate about educational goals presents variations and extensions of those themes. E. D. Hirsch (1988, p. xi), for example, argues in a recent best-selling book that special emphasis should be placed today in American education on "cultural literacy" — "background knowledge necessary for functional literacy and effective national communication."

Former President George Bush, in his *America 2000* educational proposals, emphasizes the acquisition of competencies necessary for global economic development. Many of the educational goals included in the contemporary discussion, while worthy from a limited perspective, do not directly address the fundamental problem of individual/social existential anxiety, which was previously discussed.

As an implication of the analysis about the sacred dimension of primitive cultures, the overall goal of general education would be to help the student develop ontological well-being—a personal state characterized by the performance of self-transcending action understood to bear cosmic significance. Within the context of the hospitality theme, one component of general education would be to help students critically review and develop personally meaningful narratives/rituals of hospitality. Such an objective would not exclude positive reinforcement, but rather direct it toward action capable of sacralizing time and space.

The place to start for making concrete the educational goal of ontological well-being is with us individually as the adult educator, either as parent, professional teacher, scout master, coach, etc. We are the depositories of our culture. Since our culture is characterized by excessive ontological anxiety and an extravagant emphasis on esteem of self, then we are very likely to instantiate this culture and unintentionally transmit an addictive attachment to anxiety-producing achievements. Modeling the ability to sacralize action through appropriate myth and ritual is an effective instrument for helping the young to develop a durable and appropriate esteem of self.

Instead of merely serving as a passive receptor of the dominant culture, the adult educator should follow the Socratic prescription of leading the "examined life." Educators need to examine their personal level of ontological well-being honestly. As Arthur Jersild, in his classic study *When Teachers Face Themselves,* observed, "To have insight into the child's strivings and the problems he faces, the teacher must strive to face the same problems in his own life" (Jersild, 1955, p. 82). Educators, when facing themselves, should not be surprised or overly distressed at finding inadequately developed myths/narratives and rituals of caring-as-hospitality. The realization of our own failure to resolve ontological anxiety is a condition for personal growth.

The development of internalized hospitality myths and rituals are central goals of the life examination process for three reasons. First, as seen throughout the chapter, the sacralization of personal being through space and time is a condition of ontological well-being. Second, the modeling of sacred myth and ritual is an effective instructional method. And thirdly, the resulting relationship of hospitality between educator and student itself is enabling and supportive of the young in their striving for durable self-esteem.

Even though our contemporary society generally does not reinforce profound dispositions of hospitality, the individual can initiate his/her development through serious reflections on seminal mythic narratives within our tradition, such as *The Odyssey* or the "Good Samaritan" story found in Christian literature. In order for the individual to achieve ontological well-being, however, these reflections must eventuate into personally meaningful, committed patterns of action to hospitality myth and ritual. There is a common element in classical and primitive accounts of hospitality: the host treats the stranger as friend and does not require excessive accommodation to the manners of the host. Henri Nouwen, in *Reaching Out* (1975, p. 51), gives an eloquent account of this feature of the disposition to be hospitable:

> Hospitality, therefore, means primarily the creation of a free space where the stranger can enter and become a friend instead of an enemy. Hospitality is not to change people, but to offer them space where change can take place. . . . It is not an educated intimidation with good books, good stories and good works, but the liberation of fearful hearts so that words can find roots and bear ample fruit . . . free to sing their own songs, speak their own languages, dance their own dances; free also to leave and follow their own vocations. Hospitality is not a subtle invitation to adopt the life style of the host, but the gift of a chance for the guest to find his own.

The essential note here is that the host transcends concerns of self in order to help facilitate the development of another's well-being. The hospitality disposition is a form of caring. And all forms of caring, according to Milton Mayeroff (1971), embody the truth, "Through finding and helping to develop my appropriate others, I discover and create the meaning of my life" (p. 62). Paradoxically, then, the act of hospitality enhances the ontological well-being of the host.

For the educator, the personalization of the hospitality myth and ritual has many dispositional as well as practical pedagogical implications. At the more general level, the educator must develop dispositions of caring and accepting each of the children for whom the educator is responsible. The Jewish philosopher, Martin Buber (1965, p. 94), expressed most vividly the depiction of teachers who present themselves as educator-hosts and perceive their students as guest-strangers:

He enters the school-room for the first time, he sees them crouching at the desks, indiscriminately flung together, the misshapen and the well-proportioned . . . empty faces, and noble faces in indiscriminate confusion, like the presence of the created universe; the glance of the educator accepts and receives them all.

Because educators-as-hosts accept and receive all the students, they do not try to impose with coercion their own forms of mythic and ritualistic sacralization of action. Rather, they invite the young to critically and responsibly examine thematic myths and rituals, so that students can develop their "place" in the universe and ontological sense of well-being. Once again, the disposition of hospitality shares a central characteristic of caring, as enunciated by Mayeroff (1971, p. 7):

In helping the other grow I do not impose my own direction; rather, I allow the direction of the other's growth to guide what I do, to help determine how I am to respond and what is relevant to such response.

This does not mean that the educator does not insist upon any standards or objective goals for the educational process. There are objective standards of critical reasoning and valid community-shared values inherent in the educational process. But the educator tries to assume a posture of invitation rather than coercion; what is truly in the best interest of the student remains of paramount interest rather than the particular bias or convenience of the educator.

While there may not be specific, particular actions clearly required of the educator-as-host, there are a number of patterns of practice one would reasonably expect to be expressed by this kind of educator. First, one would expect the educator to have an interest in each student's well-being outside the school environment, insofar as possible. This might reasonably include the teacher's willingness to make home visits for better understanding and communication with parents and others responsible for the student's welfare.

Secondly, the hospitable educator should be personally and instructionally sensitive to cultural differences. Educators necessarily bring with them to the teaching situation their own backgrounds of culture, gender, religion, and so on. Educators who truly embody the caring-as-hospitality disposition recognize that ontological well-being will almost certainly be different for each student, as well as for the teacher. Practically speaking, this may mean that the teacher needs to accommodate and not discriminate on the basis of dialect or natural language of the student, religious beliefs and celebrations, and patterns of forming personal relationships.

The key here is that the teacher-as-host goes beyond passive acceptance of multicultural differences and tries to respond positively to and enhance the student's ontological well-being within that student's cultural context. As Virginia Shabatay (1991, p. 136) has thoughtfully expressed this idea, "The stranger by her presence, asks something of us: she asks that her heritage or her condition be respected." A most challenging aspect of responding with hospitality to multicultural differences lies in the area of curriculum content selection. The educator needs to be courageous enough to step outside of his/her particular tradition, texts, and ideas into the heritage of the student and then critically review their own mythic narratives and rituals among others. Only in this way can the student develop a personally meaningful sacralization of being, which is not radically disconnected from personal tradition.

Likewise, the educator-as-host would attempt to minimize instructional methods and social arrangements, which would exacerbate ontological anxiety through an overemphasis on individualistic, competitive achievements. To this end, we would expect such an educator to experiment with nonabusive forms of grading and evaluation. Also, the educator could introduce more cooperative forms of learning, such as have been proposed by Robert E. Slavin (1990). Several practices for differentiating instruction—such as categorization, ability grouping, and tracking—are susceptible to misuse in ways that militate against the development of personal ontological well-being. While these practices are frequently controlled as systemic policies and are therefore beyond the direct authority of the individual school educator, the teacher can develop creative ways for minimizing any negative effects of these practices within the classroom.

As we have seen, the individual educator can have significant impact on the student's development of ontological well-being. Nonetheless, the efforts of the individual educator are greatly enhanced if the school as a whole embodies the qualities of ontological well-being. The same is true with respect to the efforts of parents being greatly enhanced by local civic communities, which exhibit and reinforce the goals pursued by the individual families. For the school community, as for the individual educator, the most important initial step is a reexamination of goals. Otherwise, the school community can reinforce addictive, anxiety-producing behaviors, which do not alleviate the problem of ontological anxiety. The school community must articulate and commit itself to sacralize being and action through the adoption of cosmically significant myth and ritual.

The inclusion of the hospitality theme should be central to this overall effort of sacralization through myth and ritual. Therefore, the school should develop a conception of itself as a hospitable community with the purpose of helping students develop these same dispositions. The school-as-host metaphor can be expressed and incorporated in the music, mottoes, and sagas generated by the school community. Certainly, there are other legitimate educational objectives of schooling—preparing civic leaders and competent workers, for example—but these other conceptions can be integrated into the overall school ethos as a community that both embodies ontological well-being and strives to develop/reinforce this quality in its students.

The commitment to embody the hospitality theme entails ritualistic action by the school community. While it is inappropriate to spell out *a priori* what the action should be in specific cases, one can depict the kinds of action that would reasonably be expressed in a hospitable school community. The common element of these ritualistic patterns of action would be the effort to respond effectively to the needs of individuals-as-strangers (and here the "strangers" would include, in addition to the students, all the members of the school community). As we have already seen, the perplexing term *need* is to be interpreted as referring to the fundamental human striving for "ontological well-being." As a consequence of the effort to meet individual needs, one might reasonably expect, for example, that the hospitable school would be *particularly* sensitive to multicultural differences in students. It is differences in cultural backgrounds that profoundly make us strangers to one another; the specific mythic narratives and rituals inherent in each culture attempt to resolve the problem of ontological anxiety for its members in a different manner. More concretely, this multicultural sensitivity should inform school policy and practice in all areas of the school life, particularly significant areas such as family and social values, language acquisition, and the learning styles of the various students. Whether it be general policies, such as discipline and grading procedures, or particular interactions with one another, the hospitable community is sensitive to legitimate differences. Sensitivity to the stranger should extend beyond heritage to any "condition" that individualizes the person. Rightly, then, the hospitable community would be sensitive to any important differentiating characteristic, such as gender, religion, mental and physical characteristics, etc. The entire ecosystem of the community would be nondiscriminatory and help each individual develop a sense of "in place" and ontological well-being.

If the school community were to embrace the goal of promoting ontological well-being—and caring-as-hospitality as one of its central ingredients—there would be no entailment of a radically new inclusion or exclusion of subjects conventionally taught in public schools. But that does not mean that there would not be major structural changes in the selection of curricular content, instructional methods, and the organization of learning activities. The most important attribute of such a curriculum would be the thematic question that would give coherence for teaching/learning at every level: How should humans conduct themselves so as to live a meaningful life and achieve a state of ontological well-being? The conventional curriculum, whether acknowledged or not, tends to emphasize the development of the human as a civic and economic animal. Certainly, these are aspects of the human condition and education ought to take into account these dimensions in a significant way. But the civic and economic, as well as the aesthetic and the other dimensions of human life, can and should be subsumed under the broader and more fundamental quest for ontological well-being. This does not mean that each and every learning activity needs to explicitly relate to the ideal of ontological well-being, but it ought to be contributory to the ideal in some general sense, and the ideal should drive and give fundamental coherence to all of the curriculum components.

A curriculum that took this goal seriously would use history as the backdrop and resource for structuring the curriculum. It is through critically assessing the way various historical cultures have attempted to answer the central question through myth and ritual that the students can develop a response appropriate for themselves personally and the contemporary community. The view of critically assessing a culture assumed here goes well beyond the superficial acquaintance with political events, military battles, names of important persons, and other information that contributes to "cultural literacy." What is indicated here is the kind of critical assessment that probes more deeply the ethos that informed conduct in a given period and cultural framework. That probing would reasonably extend to the social intellectual history of what drove the common person in a given culture and not just the intellectual and aristocratic elites.

Given our continuing focus on the theme of caring-as-hospitality, the examination of how various cultures mythically and ritually depicted relationships with strangers in all contextual forms would be a valuable strand in the curriculum. Needless to say, all past and present cultures could not be equally treated, and some not at all. The effort here would be to understand and critically assess a representative sample of primitive and contemporary world cultures. While certain cultural models would be selected because of their apparent quality for fostering ontological well-being through significant myth and ritual, the educator should not assume a posture of indoctrination or emphatic advocacy for any one cultural system. However, it would be reasonable for the educator to propose standards and logical procedures for critical assessment of a cultural ethos. The ultimate objective, after all, is for the student to develop personally meaningful myths and rituals, which facilitate ontological well-being for the individual and serve as a basis for the individual participating in the development of community well-being.

In returning full-circle to the anecdote presented at the outset, I think I would have done well to probe with Daniel the meaning of his activities rather than the rewards. This probing would rightly include reflection on persona and traditional narratives, as well as ritualistic patterns of action, which would instantiate the significance of the action. Education for ontological well-being may include positive reinforcement, reward systems, concern for achievement and competence, and individual competition. It is a matter of emphasis and proportion. The ultimate goal, however, is the development of individuals who feel that their very being is saturated with significance through a participation in cosmically significant action—the meaning of which is expressed in appropriate myth and ritual.

ENDNOTES

1 My criticism is not directed toward the merit badge system used in the Scouts or reward systems in general. Rather, I am concerned about the overdependence on indicators of competitive achievement for the confirmation of personal worth rather than the performance of significant action.

2 For the most part, I am trying to follow the existential line of analysis explicated by May. There are, of course, numerous other existential psychologists whose interpretive perspectives would differ.

3 May describes how addictive behaviors, resulting from excessive concern for the self, result in the loss of personal life control and the frustration of ontological well-being.

4 For *The Odyssey*, the general book and line citations are given for the convenience of the reader using a different edition.

REFERENCES

Buber, M. 1965. *Between Man and Man.* New York, NY: Macmillan Company.

Eliade, M. 1959. *The Sacred and the Profane.* New York, NY: Harcourt, Brace & World, Inc.

Hirsch, E. D., Jr. 1988. *Cultural Literacy: What Every American Should Know.* New York, NY: Random House.

Homer. 1963. *The Odyssey.* (R. Fitzgerald, Trans.) Garden City, NY: Doubleday & Company, Inc.

Jersild, A. T. 1955. *When Teachers Face Themselves.* New York, NY: Teachers College Press.

May, G. G. 1988. *Addiction and Grace.* San Francisco, CA: Harper & Row.

May, R. 1983. *The Discovery of Being.* New York, NY: W. W. Norton & Company.

Mayeroff, M. 1971. *On Caring.* New York, NY: Harper & Row.

Nouwen, H. J. M. 1975. *Reaching Out: The Three Movements of the Spiritual Life.* Garden City, NY: Doubleday.

Shabatay, V. 1991. "The Stranger's Call," in *Stories Lives Tell: Narrative and Dialogue in Education,* Carol Witherell and Nel Noddings, eds. New York, NY: Teachers College Press.

Slavin, R. E. 1990. "Ability Grouping, Cooperative Learning and the Gifted," *J. for the Education of the Gifted,* 14(1):3−8.

CHAPTER 3

Beyond Self-Esteem

CHARLES MATTHEWS – *The College of William and Mary*

THE intent of this chapter is to explicate the differences between humanistic and transpersonal psychology's treatment of the concept of self-esteem. The concept of self-esteem will be traced from William James to Abraham Maslow to Ken Wilber. The works of C. H. Cooley, G. H. Mead, Erik Erikson, Karen Horney, H. S. Sullivan, and Carl Jung will be visited along the way. Maslow is pivotal in this journey since he was a founder of both the "Third Force" in psychology, humanistic psychology, and the "Fourth Force," transpersonal psychology. As a chief architect of humanistic psychology, he was instrumental in laying the foundation for the prominence of the concept of self-esteem; as a founder of transpersonal psychology, he helped to sow the seeds for its potential deemphasis, or more accurately, its relativization, as evidenced in the work of transpersonal theorist Ken Wilber.

ORIGINS OF THE CONCEPT OF SELF-ESTEEM

According to Wells and Marwell (1976), William James (1890, 1892) "is generally identified as the earliest 'self' psychologist, and his writings are still standard reference for developmental discussions of self-esteem" (p. 14). James differentiated the person, or total self, into the "self as knower and the self as that which is known" (p. 15). By conceptualizing the self as both the agent of experience and the object of experience, James included both elements necessary for a self-reflexive act, thus making self-consciousness possible. James postulated that "to the extent that people experience successes, they experience heightened self-esteem, although this was not described as some kind of stable self-evaluation, but rather as a barometer which 'rises and falls from one day to another' " (p. 15).

Baldwin (1987) states that "despite the efforts of William James, John Dewey, and others to examine the self on an empirical basis, the concept of a self, complete with philosophical, social and religious connotations, was largely ignored by an emerging psychology seeking to establish itself as a scientific discipline'' (p. 30). The driving force behind this quest was behaviorism, which disavowed the possibility of ever scientifically studying such an imprecise concept as a self.

"John B. Watson (1916, 1925) was the leader of this movement. He rejected the then dominant conception of psychology as a unique type of science, aimed at discovering the structure of consciousness by introspection. Psychology, he proposed, should study *behavior,* using the same types of objective techniques as other natural sciences'' (Hall and Lindzey, 1970, p. 418). Two schools of behaviorism emerged, the stimulus-response school of Clark Hull (1952) and Kenneth W. Spence (1956) and the operant reinforcement school of B. F. Skinner (1938, 1968, 1969, 1971). Skinner was careful to explain in *Beyond Freedom and Dignity* (1971) that the notion of a self was a dangerous illusion. We are nothing other than the sum total of our contingencies of reinforcement, that is, puppets of whatever we have been conditioned to find reinforcing.

Behaviorism has been called America's contribution to psychology and its impact on American education is hard to overestimate. Virtually every teacher trained in the last twenty-five years has been taught the importance of reinforcing desired behavior of students and ignoring or punishing undesirable behavior. Trying to understand why the undesirable behavior was manifested in the first place or how the school context may bring about undesirable behavior were not typical concerns of behaviorist pedagogy.

However, while behaviorism, called the "Second Force" in psychology, was developing in the United States, the "First Force," psychoanalysis was developing in Europe. "Otto Kernberg (1976) points out that 'psychoanalytic theory has always included the concept of the self, that is, the individual's integrated conception of himself, as an experiencing, thinking, valuing and acting (or interacting) entity. . . In fact, Freud's starting point in describing the 'I' ('das Ich,' so fatefully translated as 'the ego' in English) was that of the conscious person whose entire intrapsychic life was powerfully influenced by dynamic, unconscious forces'' (Baldwin, 1987, pp. 35 – 36).

It was only when neo-Freudians emphasized this self (ego) and its social roots and deemphasized the libidinal unconscious forces, that a comprehensive view of self emerged in psychoanalysis (Erikson, 1950, 1959; Fairbairn, 1954; Horney, 1939,1950; Kernberg, 1976; Klein,

1952; Kohut, 1971, 1977; Mahler, Pine, and Bergman, 1975; Sullivan, 1953; Winnicott, 1971).

Therefore, Wells and Marwell (1976) cite a contemporary of Freud's as the next major self theorist, a sociologist, C. H. Cooley. He is known for his theory of *"the looking glass self,"* which postulates that "an individual's conception of him- or herself is determined by perception of other peoples' reactions to him or her" (Wells and Marwell, p. 16). George Herbert Mead added to the work of James and Cooley by conceptualizing how people utilize symbols to create a "generalized other," as well as a "generalized self." According to Mead's symbolic interaction theory, "People's innate impulse to realize themselves over or against other persons was not just a drive for self-enhancement, but for *superiority.* For a sociological theorist like Mead [as well as for Cooley], enhancement must be relative to other people and clearly presumes not only self-evaluation but a social comparison process" (Wells and Marwell, 1976, p. 18).

Getting back to the neo-Freudians, three of those mentioned previously must be singled out for their contributions to development of the concept of self and self-esteem: Erikson, Horney, and Sullivan. Erikson's (1950, 1959) work transposed Freud's psychosexual stages of development into psychosocial stages of development. In doing so, Freud's libidinal drives were deemphasized, and the social experiences of the person were made prominent. Thus, the human being struggles through Erikson's eight stages of development by fighting age-appropriate battles of ego development. The stages and their conflicts are oral sensory (basic trust vs. mistrust); muscular-anal (autonomy vs. shame and doubt); locomotor-genital (initiative vs. guilt); latency (industry vs. inferiority); puberty and adolescence (identity vs. role confusion); young adulthood (intimacy vs. isolation); adulthood (generativity vs. stagnation); maturity (ego integrity vs. despair). The legacy of each battle is a ratio of both qualities, e.g., basic trust/mistrust. To the extent that ratio is weighted toward the positive quality (basic trust), the energy of the person is freed up to be invested in the next battle, e.g., autonomy vs. shame and doubt.

Erikson posited that each culture has an intrinsic folk wisdom about what children need to be successful as adults; consequently, their child-rearing practices were consciously and unconsciously designed to produce that type of adult. For instance, toilet training has been so important to North Americans and Europeans because the industrialized societies their children must grow up to fit into require that bodily functions not get in the way of 8:00 A.M. to 5:00 P.M. jobs. In contrast, an Indian tribe studied by Erikson in South America doesn't even bother to toilet train its toddlers. Things are simplified because they don't wear clothes and they don't have toilets; thus, it becomes only a matter of them following the older children out into the bushes. This approach is congruent with their adult lives as hunter-gatherers. Thus Erikson explicates the same theme as Cooley and Mead in emphasizing the importance of society and significant others in the child's battle to construct a self; self-esteem then becomes a barometer of how he/she is doing in the eyes of significant others, as well as in taking on age-appropriate challenges.

When significant adults support developmentally appropriate growth of children, they have a relatively smooth transition from one stage to the next and the healthy self-esteem of the child is a natural consequence. However, when adult expectations are out of line with the developmental plan, the self-esteem of the child suffers. Karen Horney (1939, 1950) developed the implications of a child's betrayal of self in order to please these neurotic parents; in order to please the parents, and thus feel secure, the child either has to take on the developmental challenges too soon, too late, or not at all. She saw that the only way children could do this was to develop a false self, thus pleasing the parents, but at great cost to their real selves.

She formulated a theory that the vicissitudes of preserving one's integrity in the face of ʌ ʌcial pressures are severe enough for many children so that they may develop one of three strategies: moving away from people, moving toward people, or moving against people. All three strategies are the result of a combination of the child's constitutional endowments and the parenting he/she receives. Those who choose the defense of moving away from people do not feel safe with others. Those who choose the defense of moving toward people do not feel safe with others either, but hope that if they do enough for them, they will be safe. This stance has recently been popularized as "co-dependency" in the self-help literature. And those who choose the defense of moving against people, likewise, do not feel safe, but have adopted the strategy of "the best defense is a good offense" or 'hit them before they hit you.' The main theme of Horney's work can be seen as formulating theories that delineate children's attempts to compensate for lack of true self-esteem.

Sullivan (1953) posited that there are two primary driving forces of interpersonal human behavior: (1) the need for satisfaction and (2) the need for security. Both of these needs develop in infancy and childhood. The need for satisfaction originates in the interactions between caregivers and infant, which relieve biological derived tensions; out of these early interactions evolve the need for tenderness and intimacy. Sullivan defined the need for security as the need to avoid disapproval from real or fancied others. Thus, the goal in interpersonal situations is to achieve satisfaction while maintaining or enhancing security.

This is the task of what Sullivan calls the "self dynamism," which develops gradually since birth. The self dynamism is essentially an image of self constructed originally in the parataxic mode of experiencing. The parataxic mode is characterized by "an appreciation of relationships among experiences – not logical, causal relationship, but relationships of coincidence and concomitance, of similarity and difference. This is said to be the primordial form of knowing, and it makes its appearance within the first year of life" (Carson, 1968, p. 29).

Thus, the foundations of self-image are laid in pre-verbal awareness: without language, the child cannot obtain feedback on his or her parataxic "reasoning." However, during this phase of development, the child comes to feel itself as a "me." The attributes of this "me" consist, "most importantly, of *reflected appraisals* from the environment" (Carson, 1968, p. 30). Children, in fact, construct separate images or personifications of themselves for each of the appraising states of their environments.

Sullivan posited that parental attitudes, thus, can cause a child to develop originally as three selves: a "good me," a "bad me," and a "not me." The *not me* has behavior that was so upsetting to the parent that the child had to banish it from awareness. *Good me* and *bad me* are direct precursors of self-esteem; indeed, Sullivan has identified the phenomenological introjects which correlate with the more or less normal parental injunctions of socialization. On the other hand, his *not me* category has been heuristic in the development of the field of child psychopathology, which charts the lack of normal development of ego and self-esteem.

Erikson, Horney, and Sullivan were neo-Freudians who did much to develop the concept of self-esteem in both normal and abnormal development. Maslow, on the other hand, as we shall see in the next section, was more interested in studying what can only be termed supernormal development.

ABRAHAM MASLOW

Maslow thought that perhaps Freud's personality theory had been skewed by his research population—his clients, who by definition were not on good terms with their lives. He asked, "What would a theory of personality look like if it were derived from studying those we think of as the very best human beings?" He dedicated his life to correcting psychoanalysis' bias toward pathology by studying the lives of the exemplary (e.g., Eleanor Roosevelt, Albert Einstein, Abraham Lincoln) and formulating his theory of personality accordingly.

Maslow concluded that human beings have a hierarchy of needs. In order of their appearance developmentally, they are physiological needs, safety needs, the need to be loved and belong to a group, the need to have self-esteem, the need to self-actualize, and the need for self-transcendence. Maslow can also be added to the list of theorists who emphasize the social comparison process in the building of self-esteem. He was careful to distinguish the need for self-esteem from the need for self-actualization. In meeting self-esteem needs, Wells and Marwell (1976, p. 22) state,

> A person is not trying to actualize her inborn potential, but to establish superiority over others. As a result of this, Maslow's notion of self-esteem was identified with the notion of "dominance-feeling"—a kind of sureness, pride, sense of mastery, or feeling of superiority when dealing with other people and objects (Maslow, 1937, 1942, 1954).

Maslow's (1954, 1961) emphasis on the needs for love and to belong to a group, self-esteem, and self-actualization undoubtedly spurred him to help found the "Third Force" in psychology—humanistic psychology, which would concentrate on these needs in its literature. The concept of self-esteem blossomed in the fertile ground of the humanistic psychology of the 1960s. This provocative new Third Force was eager to challenge its elders, psychoanalysis, and behaviorism. At that time behaviorism believed that research with pigeons and rats would shed light on human behavior. Freud did not hold the candle of being a human being very high either. He had said that the purpose of psychoanalysis was to lighten the suffering of the neurotic up to the ordinary misery of normal people.

But humanism found it easier to do battle rhetorically with psychoanalysis and behaviorism than with human nature. Although this emphasis on discovering ways to encourage human potential led to many important ways of nurturing the psyche, it also had its down side. The down side involved the differences between the concepts of self-esteem and self-actualization. Maslow was careful to point out that self-esteem comes from a sense of superiority and, thus, is at least implicitly at the expense of others, whereas self-actualization is a fulfilling of one's own potentials, irrespective of others.

The phenomenon of the Human Potential Movement in the 1960s, which was the crucible for highlighting the differences between self-esteem and self-actualization was the encounter group. Theorists as different as Carl Rogers (1951, 1961, 1970, 1980) and Fritz Perls (1951, 1969a, 1969b) championed this new forum for developing the authentic human. The goal was self-actualization, but the method of necessity concentrated on unmet needs on the lower levels of Maslow's hierarchy. The need to love and be loved and to be part of a group was a foundational criterion for many of the groups—especially those embracing Rogers' approach. The problem came when group members' needs for self-esteem clashed with each other. One person's need to feel dominant in some way over another person collided with that person's need to feel dominant over him or her. Lieberman, Yalom, and Miles (1973) published the definitive study of encounter groups, in which they demonstrated that, although one-third of the participants had significant positive changes, another third had significant negative changes. Experience with encounter groups and research such as this led a small group of leaders of the humanist movement to reexamine the distinctions between self-esteem and self-actualization. They realized that the key to making the leap from win-lose self-esteem contests to win-win self-actualization lay in Maslow's last level of development.

In 1968 Maslow stated, "I consider Humanistic, Third Force Psychology, to be transitional, a preparation for a still 'higher' Fourth Psychology, transpersonal, transhuman, centered in the cosmos rather than in human needs and interest, going beyond humanness, identity, self-actualization and the like" (Walsh and Vaughn, 1980, pp. 19–20). He added this level because so many of the exemplary people he studied had seemed to move beyond an emphasis on self-actualization to an emphasis on self-transcendence that he split them into two groups: the doers and the transcenders. The doers were practical people who concentrated on improving the world, whereas the transcenders were more mystically oriented. It has been suggested that this is an artificial distinction: that the doers simply were not as vocal about their mystical inspirations as were the transcenders. For instance, Piechowski and Tyska (1982) and Matthews (1990) argue that a careful study of the life of Eleanor Roosevelt, labeled by Maslow a doer, indicates that she was also a transcender, at least by Western standards.

Such quibbling aside, the point is that Maslow (1971) proposed that beyond the need for self-actualization lay the need for self-transcendence. He also realized that humanistic psychology was ill-equipped to research this dimension because its focus was the personal, not the transpersonal. As a result, shortly before his death, he helped found the Association for Transpersonal Psychology.

TRANSPERSONAL PSYCHOLOGY

Walsh and Vaughn (1980) define transpersonal psychology as follows: Transpersonal psychology is concerned with expanding the field of psychological inquiry to include the study of optimal psychological health and well-being. It recognizes the potential for experiencing a broad range of states of consciousness, in some of which identity may extend beyond the usual limits of the ego and personality. Maslow's hierarchical view of human development was the seminal theoretical work in transpersonal psychology. Thus, rather than seeking to displace the previous three psychological models (psychoanalysis, behaviorism, and humanism), transpersonal theorists created a meta-model, which gives each of them its due but also goes beyond into the uncharted spiritual or transpersonal realm. This transpersonal meta-model is the most ambitious and comprehensive yet produced by Western psychology, yet, in many ways it echoes views of the psyche, which are over 5,000 years old in the East, as we shall soon see.

Although Maslow died before he was able to contribute to the exploration of this new transpersonal dimension, he at least pointed the way. One theorist who took him seriously was Ken Wilber, who subsequently developed a spectrum of consciousness that included the realm of transpersonal experience. Wilber is the first Western theorist to develop a comprehensive model, which also includes Eastern models of reality.

Wilber's research into Maslow's last and highest level of need – the need for self-transcendence – led him to two very different sources – the world of mystics and the world of quantum physics. He discovered to his great surprise that the description of ultimate reality from these two disparate sources were virtually interchangeable. The West had channelled many of its best minds into physics and the East had channelled many of its best minds into mysticism. The former concentrated on charting the external physical world with increasing precision and the latter, the internal phenomenological world. And by going in opposite directions they had come up with the same description of ultimate reality.

This description from the perspective of physics was developed in the first quarter of this century when physicists turned their attention to quantum, or subatomic, physics. Until then, classical physics had viewed the cosmos as a collection of discrete objects in space. They naturally hypothesized that subatomic particles would be but a miniature solar system. To their great shock, they found that these particles did not even exist as they had expected. Measured one way, they seemed to be particles; measured another, they seemed to be waves. At best they could only come up with statistical formulae to estimate where they were and how they behaved. Heisenberg's uncertainty principle and Einstein's relativity theory were instrumental in this paradigm shift (Capra, 1976; Wilber, 1979; Zukav, 1984).

> As Henry Stapp put it, "An elementary particle is not an independently existing unanalyzable entity. It is, in essence, a set of relationships that reach outward to other things." These "'atomic things,'" the ultimate building blocks of all reality, couldn't be located because, in short, they had no boundaries (Wilber, 1979, p. 37).

Thus, Wilber notes the metaphor for ultimate reality offered by Alfred North Whitehead — "the seamless coat of the universe." Reality was not represented by discrete objects moving through empty space, but a gigantic system of interrelated energy patterns. This interrelatedness of everything is fundamental to the mystic's vision of the universe.

Wilber's research on Maslow's need for self-transcendence of necessity became an attempt to describe the experiences of those who had gone beyond the usual levels of ego development into this "seamless coat of the universe." He agrees with Maslow that, after a threshold amount of self-actualizing behavior, human beings are pulled toward the transpersonal level — they then feel a need to transcend their individual identities and experience this unitive vision — realizing their "place" in this gigantic interrelated energy pattern. Thus, Wilber concludes that:

> There are not just one but many *levels of identity* available to an individual. . . . As regards these different levels, it's almost as if that familiar yet ultimately mysterious phenomenon we call consciousness were a spectrum, a rainbow-like affair composed of numerous bands or levels of self-identity (Wilber, 1979, pp. 8–9).

For Wilbur, this need for transcendence exists because, after a certain amount of actualizing our potential from the paradigm of experiencing ourselves as separate from the rest of the universe, we exhaust that viewpoint, just as a toddler, after actualizing certain potentials by seeing him- or herself from the perspective of narcissism (being the center of the universe), outgrows that false and limiting viewpoint. Alan Watts (1961) speaks of the illusion of the skin-encapsulated ego—that our skin is the boundary between us and the world. Yet without the rest of the world (or only a part of it called oxygen, or other parts called sunlight, food, and water), we would not exist. The mystics and the physicists see beyond this illusion of the skin-encapsulated ego, while at the same time knowing that on the level of material reality, they must still open a door in order to pass through it. In other words, the laws that pertain to the level of individual consciousness do not necessarily pertain to the level of transpersonal or collective consciousness. A growing number of scientists, as well as mystics, proclaim this principle (Capra, 1975, 1982; Ferguson, 1980; Huxley, 1945; Prigogene, 1984; Small, 1982, 1991; von Bertalanffy, 1968).

According to Wilber the first boundary drawn in the evolution of homo sapiens was this illusionary one between self and environment. The second boundary was the equally illusionary distinction we make between our bodies and our psyches. The third boundary is the false one between those parts of our psyches we are proud of or at least neutral toward and those parts we are ashamed of (Wilber, 1981). In fact, Wilber would probably argue that the impetus in psychology to examine the multidimensional aspects of self-concept and self-esteem is based to a great extent upon the illusion of a compartmentalized self.

Anthropologists have documented how this first boundary—between the person and the environment—is not yet fully formed among traditional peoples, such as the aborigines or the American Indians before the arrival of the Europeans (Eliade, 1964; Harner, 1982; Levy-Bruhl, 1985; Levi-Strauss, 1963, 1966, 1979). Fortunately the work of the anthropologists is not merely deductive from archeological remains; small pockets of so-called primitive peoples have been discovered and studied. Their image of self-in-the-world is very different from ours. They commune with the spirits of the animals and plants in a way that indicates that they are still very much in connection with the natural world. They are also good examples of humankind before the second split developed—between mind and body. Wilber would say that their knowledge and behavior indicates that, because they have not split the body off from the mind, they have access to the deeper reality of the bodymind, which he calls the centaur.

Wilber (1979, p. 117) describes this reality in the following:

Your willful ego can consciously deal with perhaps two or three things at one time. Yet your total organism, without any help from the ego, is at this moment coordinating literally millions of processes at once, from the intricacies of digestion to the complexities of neurotransmission to the coordination of conceptual information. This requires wisdom infinitely greater than the superficial tricks of which the ego is so proud. The more we are capable of resting in the centaur, the more we are capable of founding our lives on, and giving our lives over to, this wider store of natural wisdom and freedom.

In developing his notion of the centaur, Wilber draws upon the works of disciples of Wilheim Reich, a student of Freud's who broke with him to develop his own theory of how people embody their defenses. His seminal work was *Character Analysis,* published in 1949. Alexander Lowen (1976), John Pierrokos (1987), Stanley Keleman (1985), and Ken Dychwald (1977) are all neo-Reichians who have developed their schools of bodywork to compete with talk therapy. They claim to be able to find the specific muscular blocks that embody the defenses erected by the ego against the traumas of childhood. By working with the muscles and energy of the body, in addition to listening to the client's phenomenological description of his/her pain, they take psychotherapy to the level of the centaur.

As a group, they would join Wilber in claiming that happiness is not to be found in a reservoir of self-esteem, but in the energy of the body, which is available to everyone. Wilber quotes William Blake: "Energy is eternal delight, and is from the body" (Wilber, 1979, p. 118). Rather than enjoying this natural flow of energy, we modern peoples, thinking ourselves far superior to the "primitives," feel that self-fulfillment is determined from outside of us—it must be garnered in the reflected glow of another's admiration or envy, or come in the form of images on a screen in our dens. To the centaurs, on the other hand, the original meaning of happiness is simply an appreciation of what happens (Johnson, 1987), and what happens most consistently is the energy streaming of the body, as well as the prosaic happenings of life—experiencing the many faces of nature, the companionship of relatives and friends, eating, sleeping.

As Wilber (1979, p. 119) puts it,

To find egoic meaning in life is to *do* something in life, and up to a point that is appropriate. But beyond the ego is beyond that type of meaning—to a meaning that is less of doing and more of being. As e.e. cummings put it, "If you can be, be. If not, cheer up and go on about other peoples' business, doing and undoing unto others 'til you drop."

Thus, in summary we see that Wilber is positing that from the broadest perspective—the transpersonal—there are no human beings as we know them and even as we think of ourselves. He would say that the "self" in "self-esteem" is an illusion. It is an illusion because it is the result of the three illusory boundaries we draw—between ourselves and the rest of the world; between our minds and our bodies; and between the acceptable and unacceptable parts of our minds.

Viewed from the transpersonal perspective our feeling of selfhood is nothing more than a "more or less accurate mental *self-image,* along with the intellectual and emotional processes associated with that self-image" (Wilber, 1979, p. 7). Wilber states that all of our suffering and problems stem from our attachment to this self-image, that is, our belief that this is who we really are. Thus, self-esteem, which seems so promising a concept from a lower perspective, becomes a stumbling block at a higher one. In summary, if by self-esteem we mean our evaluation of our self-image or ego, then Wilber would declare that, by seeking satisfaction and happiness in such esteem, we will be less successful than "primitive peoples" who merge with the essence of what is. However, he also says that the answer is not to try to return to the primitive ways; we have developed egos for an evolutionary purpose, just as we will be called to transcend them for an evolutionary purpose.

SELF AS PERSONAL AND TRANSPERSONAL

Before we explore the conundrum of primitive connection versus contemporary alienation, reconnection and transcendence, however, we must look more closely at how we have become fragmented creatures driven by fictional images of ourselves. To explain the split between acceptable and unacceptable parts of our minds, Wilber borrows from Putney and Putney (1966). According to the Putneys, all children are born into this world needing the love of their parents for survival. Early on, most children learn that they feel sure of their parents' love only when they please them; that is, they feel in grave danger of losing that love when their parents are upset and angry at them. The exception is the fortunate child whose parents effectively communicate *unconditional* love for the child while disciplining his/her behavior. However, the outcome for many children in Western culture, however, is that they learn, with increasing sophistication, to present their "best sides" to their parents. Their parents, in turn, unwittingly reinforce this central lesson: they coach their children to "put their best foot forward" when meeting others. Thus, they teach them that the world will not accept them in their totality — that in order to gain acceptance from others, they must only show the facets of themselves that are most likely to be acceptable.

As a result, the foundation of children's self-esteem is based on whether others find them acceptable. But the strategy they are taught for gaining the approval of others *precludes* that approval from translating into true self-esteem, unless they have been loved unconditionally. For when children, or adults for that matter, make new friends by presenting primarily their best sides, they then feel: "But if they knew the *real* me they would not like me." The Putneys label the behavior of trying to gain self-esteem from the approval of others as misdirection, which they define as a behavior designed to meet a need, but which does not meet that need. A simple example they give is drinking saltwater in an attempt to quench one's thirst. Attempting to gain self-esteem through working for the approval of others they see as equally faulty. They then quote philosopher Eric Hoffer who says, "We can never get enough of that which we don't need." And what we need is *self* approval, not the conditional approval of others.

It should be apparent that the Putneys' theory is quite consistent with the previously described work of James (1890, 1892), Cooley (1902), Mead (1934, 1956), Horney (1939, 1950) and Sullivan (1953). In other words, Wilber is on firm theoretical ground when he claims that our image of self is greatly conditioned by what we think others think of us. He posits that we are so willing to buy such a contracted self-image, not only because our parents pushed it, but also because we are afraid of death.

> Thus man comes to nurse the secret desire that his self should be permanent, static, unchanging, imperturbable, everlasting. But this is just what symbols, concepts, and ideas are like. They are static, unmoving, unchanging and fixed. The word "tree," for example, remains the same word even though every real tree changes, grows, transforms, and dies. Seeking this static immortality, man therefore begins to center his identity around an *idea* of himself — and this is the mental abstraction called the "ego." Man will not live with his body, for that is corruptible, and thus he lives only as his ego, a picture of himself, and a picture that leaves out any true reference to death (Wilber, 1979, pp. 80–81).

The split within the mind and the split between the mind and the body were addressed by humanistic psychology, which developed not only the body therapies, but also therapies to deal with the split within the mind (Rogers, 1951, 1961, 1970, 1980; Perls, 1951, 1969a, 1969b) to compete with the psychoanalytic approaches. However, humanistic psychology was not equipped to deal with the split between the person and the environment.

The split between the person and the environment is harder to describe than the other two splits because Western civilization rests on this illusionary division. According to Heacox (1990), this illusion was not firmly in place until the Renaissance. Before this time, the average European had more in common with his/her Native American and aboriginal brothers and sisters: they did not have clearly differentiated concepts of self. They apparently had more of a group type of identity; they were members of the serf or noble class, and they were members of a certain family or clan, but they did not think of themselves as autonomous from these groups in a way that we take for granted today.

The French essayist Montaigne was one of the first modern men (Heacox, 1990). By keeping a diary to disseminate, it was clear that he thought of himself as an individual whose views might matter to others. His contemporaries in the art world, Michelangelo and Leonardo da Vinci, likewise kept diaries, which were made public. Of course, this paradigm shift in consciousness among the intelligentsia was the spearhead of a cultural movement that has, only after the fact, become known as the Renaissance. For the purposes of this chapter we can view the Renaissance as the beginning of humanistic psychology as an academic discipline—that is, the study of humankind for its own sake—apart from any reference to the spiritual or transpersonal. When Montaigne, Michelangelo, Leonardo da Vinci, and their colleagues began a process that eventually extracted men and women from the religious context of the Middle Ages to look at them apart and anew, humanism was born.

The chief architect of this new humanism was Descartes. He split mind and matter, declaring, "I think, therefore I am." Thus, in one fell swoop, the split between human beings and the environment and the split between the mind and the body were accomplished. It was not until Freud (several hundred years later) that the arrogance of this position was challenged in the intellectual community. Freud's discovery of the unconscious brought the brilliant simplicity of "I think" into serious question. In fact, as has been noted, Freud did not put much stock in the individual's capacity to utilize the ego to control either the instinctual demands of the id or the harsh dictates of the superego. At best, one could perhaps keep them both at bay enough to be normally miserable.

As has been noted, Wilhelm Reich broke off from Freud to try to heal the split between mind and body. Another of Freud's disciples, Carl Jung, also broke with Freud, but his mission was to make inroads into healing the split between the person and the environment. He felt that Freud was essentially correct as far as he went in his charting of the unconscious. He, too, found in his investigations with his patients a personal unconscious filled with the rejected traits and characteristics which society found unacceptable; he called this area of the psyche the shadow. But he discovered much more in the unconscious than toxic waste. Jung would agree with Wilber's description of the wisdom of the integrated bodymind, but he went even further.

Jung postulated that, far from being skin-encapsulated egos, we are all connected by the collective unconscious. That is, beyond the personal unconscious or shadow lies the collective unconscious, which at its deepest level is shared by all human beings. He argued that, just as the process of evolution selected the opposable thumb for its beneficial effect on survival, it selected an organization of the psyche, which is beneficial to our survival also. In other words, we are not born with a mind that is a blank slate, a *tabula rasa* waiting to be filled in by experience. Rather, we are born with a psyche that has been prewired for human experience. For starters, a baby comes into this world looking for a caregiver to bond with. Recent research supports Jung's position. Whereas previously it was thought that the first six months of an infant's life was a "blooming, buzzing confusion," now it has been documented that "innate abilities enable the child to distinguish its own caregivers from strangers soon after birth" (Campbell, 1989, p. 26). Furthermore, according to Campbell, infants reared in hospital nurseries show a preference for their mother's voice; thus, it apparently isn't just a question of rein-forcement as the behaviorists postulate.

This prewiring of the psyche Jung posited was the work of the archetypes; we are born with an archetype of every common human experience in our psyches. It is our phylogenetic inheritance: the wres-tling of humanity with these situations for aeons has resulted in our having this reservoir of wisdom to draw upon in our individual lives. However, for this wisdom to be tapped, the ego must be receptive to its appearance in non-ego dominant activities—dreams, meditations, con-templation of symbols, intuition, and imagination. Jung thought that the ego was meant to be the servant of the Self. The Self is the preeminent archetype that organizes the entire psyche, that is, all of the other archetypes. It contains all of one's potential. Its overarching aim is for

each individual to strive toward wholeness, to actualize his/her potentials. It does this by directing the ego to those resources in the psyche,
which it overlooks in its daily grappling with outer reality. The character
represented by us in our dreams is our ego. All the other characters are
parts of the psyche our ego needs to interact with and learn from. By
dialoguing with these neglected parts, the ego is serving the ends of the
Self, rather than its own ends.

It is as if the ego is a chauffeur who has forgotten he is a chauffeur — he
thinks he is driving his own car and can go anywhere he likes. Rather,
his purpose is to drive where the Self directs. When human beings act
as skin-encapsulated egos, they think they are driving their own cars.
The Self is there to orient them to their place in the cosmos (to direct
them to where they fit in the big picture) and, ultimately, to direct them
toward unity consciousness. The Self is both personal and transpersonal;
it is the blueprint for what we have the potential for becoming on this
earth in relation to the cosmos. The Eastern notion of *dharma* is helpful
here. The closest translation into English is ''destiny,'' but not destiny
in the existential sense of the post-hoc piecing together of the apparently
random events in a person's life. Rather it is a teleological concept — we
are put here with a unique purpose — and aligning with that purpose is
the only source of true esteem. For such esteem is Self-esteem, not
self-esteem. It is the felt contentment of inner certainty that one is doing
the right thing, regardless of how others view one's actions. As we have
seen, self-esteem is, by definition (James, Cooley, Mead, Maslow, and
Putney and Putney), dependent on what others think of us. Indeed, it
could be no other way because the ego is a product of the interaction
between our nature and our nurture and thus always at the mercy of what
others think.

Wilber cites Jungian psychology as applying to the transpersonal
bands of experience, which serve as a bridge for the individual to heal
the split between him/herself and the environment, or self (ego) and Self.
Jung (1953, 1976) was greatly influenced by the Eastern concept of God
as both transcendent (Atman) and immanent (atman). He saw the persistence of the God archetype in all civilizations throughout history. Just
as the infant needs a caregiver, the adult needs a God, and the Self is the
conduit to that ultimate reality. He believed that if any given civilization,
such as ours, had lost its connection with God as a result of the loss of
power in the symbols of institutional religions, then the individual could
reconnect through his own dreams and intuitions.

The messages of Jung and Wilber go against the modern grain. As chronicled earlier, the Renaissance western civilization has identified increasingly with the ego. Ours is the age of the imperialism of the ego. It is clear that the environment has suffered drastically in this age. It is also clear that the enthronement of the ego has not brought about human happiness. The catalogue of modern ills that have led to the call for programs to raise the self-esteem of children attests to that.

However, how we approach the raising of self-esteem is crucial. If we teach children how to better please others, the Putneys (1966) say it will not result in true self-esteem; Horney (1939, 1950) and Sullivan (1953) say it can actually hurt their development. If we teach them how to better please their own egos, surely the world will not be a better place: many of the problems of both the classroom and the world can be traced to people who have no empathy and care for others (Lasch, 1979; Rieff, 1968). According to transpersonal psychology, here represented by Wilber and Jung, we feel true self-esteem only when we are aligned with the Self, which aligns us with the All.

Perhaps going back to Maslow's hierarchy of needs can shed some light on this problem. He thought that needs develop sequentially. As one is satisfied to a certain extent, another one becomes dominant. Therefore, children need to learn how to feel safe and secure first. This is difficult if they live below the poverty level in a crime-infested neighborhood or if they are abused by their parents, no matter what neighborhood they live in. To the extent that they are able to feel safe and secure, they will feel the need to belong to a group and to have self-esteem in the sense that they are good at something. If successful at meeting those needs, they then will feel the need to actualize their potentials. And, ultimately, after some success with this, they will feel the need to transcend their limited identity for unity consciousness. The successful traversing of this hierarchy of needs is considered in the East to be an endeavor lasting many lifetimes. From our perspective of ego imperialism, we claim we can raise children's self-esteem in the classroom in such a way that it will solve many of society's ills. Perhaps we would have a better chance if we knew first of all what we mean by "self." The most recent developments in psychology have brought us back to the impossibility of defining self in a vacuum. The worth of transpersonal psychology should be judged on how it helps us fill in that vacuum. Such a task will not be easy, for the very data of transpersonal experience—intuition, dreams, mystical visions, altered states of consciousness—are those human experiences the reigning philosophies—materialism and logical positivism—have been most eager to condemn.

Ironically, such contempt is based on physics as the source and paradigm of modern knowledge; the extrapolation is that only if psychology can become as rigorous as physics will it produce anything worthwhile. The irony rests in the fact that this rigor is the rigor of a physics that is fifty years old and at least one paradigm out of date. The new physics, as noted above, has been unable to hold itself aloof from these mystical realms (Capra, 1976; Zukov, 1984). This paradigm shift in the physical view of reality has prompted thinkers to examine the implications for various disciplines, as well as society in general (Capra, 1982; Ferguson, 1980; Wilber, 1983; Zukav, 1990). Inspired by the new physics, Prigogene (1984) has created the new chemistry and von Bertalanffy (1968), the new biology. The transpersonal theorists are creating the new psychology (Assagioli, 1971; Jung, 1953 – 1976; Maslow, 1971; Small, 1982, 1991; Tart, 1975; Wilber, 1977, 1979, 1980, 1983). And self-esteem will never be the same.

REFERENCES

Assagioli, R. 1971. *Psychosynthesis*. New York, NY: The Viking Press.

Baldwin, D. 1987. ''Some Philosophical and Psychological Contributions to the Use of Self in Therapy,'' in *The Use of Self in Therapy*, M. Baldwin and V. Satir, eds., New York, NY: The Haworth Press, pp. 27 – 44.

Campbell, A. 1989. *The Opposite Sex*. Topsfield, MA: Salem House.

Capra, F. 1976. *The Tao of Physics*. Boulder, CO: Shambhala.

Capra, F. 1982. *The Turning Point: Science, Society, and the Rising Culture*. New York, NY: Simon & Schuster.

Carson, R. 1968. *Interaction Concepts of Personality*. Chicago, IL: Aldin Publishing Company.

Cooley, C. 1902. *Human Nature and the Social Order*. New York, NY: Charles Scribner's & Sons.

Dychtwald, K. 1977. *Bodymind*. New York, NY: Pantheon Books.

Eliade, M. 1964. *Shamanism*. New York, NY: Pantheon.

Erikson, E. 1950. *Childhood and Society*. New York, NY: Norton.

Erikson, E. 1959. *Identity and the Life Cycle*. New York, NY: International University Press.

Fairbairn, W. 1954. *An Object Relations Theory of the Personality*. New York, NY: Basic Books.

Ferguson, M. 1980. *The Aquarian Conspiracy*. Los Angeles, CA: Tarcher.

Hall, C. and G. Lindzey. 1970. *Theories of Personality*. New York, NY: John Wiley & Sons, Inc.

Harner, M. 1982. *The Way of the Shaman*. New York, NY: Bantam Books.

Heacox, T. 1990. ''The Birth of the Self,'' Honors Lecture, College of William & Mary, Williamsburg, VA.

Horney, K. 1939. *New Ways in Psychoanalysis*. New York, NY: Norton.

Horney, K. 1950. *Neurosis and Human Growth.* New York, NY: Norton.

Hull, C. 1952. *A Behavior System.* New Haven, CT: Yale University Press.

Huxley, A. 1945. *The Perennial Philosophy.* New York, NY: Harper & Sons.

James, W. 1890. *Principles of Psychology, Volume I.* New York, NY: Henry Holt.

James, W. 1892. *Psychology: The Briefer Course.* New York, NY: Henry Holt.

Johnson, R. 1987. *Ecstasy: Understanding the Psychology of Joy.* San Francisco, CA: Harper & Row.

Jung, C. 1953–1976. *The Collected Works of C. G. Jung.* Princeton, NJ: Princeton University Press.

Keleman, S. 1985. *Emotional Anatomy.* Berkeley, CA: Center Press.

Kernberg, O. 1976. *Object Relations Theory and Clinical Psychoanalysis.* New York, NY: Jason Aronson.

Klein, M. 1952. "Some Theoretical Conclusions Regarding the Emotional Life of the Infant," in *Envy and Gratitude and Other Works, 1946–1963,* M. Klein, ed., (1975), New York, NY: Delacorte Press, pp. 61–93.

Kohut, H. 1971. *The Analysis of the Self.* New York, NY: International Universities Press.

Kohut, H. 1977. *The Restoration of the Self.* New York, NY: International Universities Press.

Lasch, C. 1979. *The Culture of Narcissism.* New York, NY: Norton.

Levi-Strauss, C. 1963. *Structural Anthropology.* New York, NY: Basic Books.

Levi-Strauss, C. 1966. *The Savage Mind.* London: Weidenfeld.

Levi-Strauss, C. 1979. *Myth and Meaning.* New York, NY: Schocken.

Levy-Bruhl, L. 1985. *How Natives Think.* Princeton, NJ: Princeton University Press.

Lieberman, M., I. Yalom, and M. Miles. 1973. *Encounter Groups: First Facts.* New York, NY: Basic Books.

Lowen, A. 1976. *Bioenergetics.* New York, NY: Penguin.

Mahler, M., F. Pine, and A. Bergman. 1975. *The Psychological Birth of the Human Infant.* New York, NY: Basic Books.

Maslow, A. 1937. "Dominance Feeling, Behavior, and Status," *Psychological Review,* 44:404–429.

Maslow, A. 1942. "Self-Esteem (Dominance-Feeling) and Sexuality in Women," *J. of Social Psychology,* 16:259–294.

Maslow, A. 1954. *Motivation and Personality.* New York, NY: Harper.

Maslow, A. 1961. *Toward a Psychology of Being.* New York, NY: Van Nostrand Reinhold.

Maslow, A. 1971. *The Farther Reaches of Human Nature.* New York, NY: Viking.

Matthews, C. 1990. "Reaction to the 'Inner Growth and Transformation in the Life of Eleanor Roosevelt,' " in *Proceedings from a Symposium on the Developmental Potential of the Gifted,* Williamsburg, VA: School of Education, College of William and Mary.

Mead, G. 1934. *Mind, Self, and Society.* Chicago, IL: Chicago University Press.

Mead, G. 1956. *The Social Psychology of George Herbert Mead.* Chicago, IL: University of Chicago Press.

Perls, F., R. Hefferline, and P. Goodman. 1951. *Gestalt Therapy Integrated: Excitement and Growth in the Human Personality.* New York, NY: Dell.

Perls, F. 1969a. *Gestalt Therapy Verbatim.* Moab, UT: Real People Press.

Perls, F. 1969b. *In and Out of the Garbage Pail.* Moab, UT: Real People Press.

Piechowski, M. and C. Tyska. 1982. "Self-Actualization Profile of Eleanor Roosevelt, a Presumed Nontranscender," *Genetic Psychology Monographs,* 105:95–153.

Pierrakos, J. 1987. *Core Energetics.* Mendocino, CA: LifeRhythum.

Prigogene, I. and I. Stengers. 1984. *Order Out of Chaos: Man's New Dialogue with Nature.* New York, NY: Bantam Books.

Putney, S. and G. Putney. 1966. *The Adjusted American.* New York, NY: Harper.

Reich, W. 1949. *Character Analysis.* New York, NY: Farrar, Straus.

Rieff, P. 1968. *The Triumph of the Therapeutic.* New York, NY: Harper Torchbooks.

Rogers, C. 1951. *Client-Centered Therapy.* Boston, MA: Houghton Mifflin.

Rogers, C. 1961. *On Becoming a Person.* Boston, MA: Houghton Mifflin.

Rogers, C. 1970. *Carl Rogers on Encounter Groups.* New York, NY: Harper & Row.

Rogers, C. 1980. *A Way of Being.* Boston, MA: Houghton Mifflin.

Skinner, B. 1938. *The Behavior of Organisms.* New York: Appleton-Century-Crofts.

Skinner, B. 1968. *The Technology of Teaching.* New York: Appleton-Century-Crofts.

Skinner, B. 1969. *Contingencies of Reinforcement: A Theoretical Analysis.* New York: Appleton-Century-Crofts.

Skinner, B. 1971. *Beyond Freedom and Dignity.* New York, NY: Knopf.

Small, J. 1982. *Transformers: The Therapists of the Future.* Marina Del Rey, CA: DeVorss & Co.

Small, J. 1991. *Awakening in Time.* New York, NY: Bantam Books.

Spence, K. 1956. *Behavior Theory and Conditioning.* New Haven, CT: Yale University Press.

Sullivan, H. 1953. *The Interpersonal Theory of Psychiatry.* New York, NY: Norton.

Tart, C., ed. 1975. *Transpersonal Psychologies.* New York, NY: Harper & Row.

von Bertalanffy, L. 1968. *General Systems Theory.* New York, NY: Braziller.

Walsh, R. and F. Vaughn. 1980. *Beyond Ego: Transpersonal Dimensions in Psychology.* Los Angeles, CA: Tarcher.

Watson, J. 1916. "The Place of the Conditioned Reflex in Psychology," *Psychological Review,* 23:89–116.

Watson, J. 1925. *Behaviorism.* New York, NY: Norton.

Watts, A. 1961. *Psychotherapy East and West.* New York, NY: Random House.

Wells, E. and G. Marwell. 1976. *Self-Esteem: Its Conceptualization and Measurement.* Beverly Hills, CA: Sage Publications.

Wilber, K. 1977. *The Spectrum of Consciousness.* Wheaton, IL: Quest.

Wilber, K. 1979. *No Boundary.* Los Angeles, CA: Center Publications.

Wilber, K. 1980. *The Atman Project.* Wheaton, IL: Quest.

Wilber, K. 1981. *Up from Eden: A Transpersonal View of Human Evolution.* Boulder, CO: Shambhala.

Winnicott, D. 1971. *Playing and Reality.* London: Tavistock Publications.

Zukav, G. 1984. *The Dancing Wu-li Masters: An Overview of the New Physics.* New York, NY: Bantam Books.

Zukav, G. 1990. *Seat of the Soul.* New York: Fireside/Simon & Schuster.

CHAPTER 4

Political Reality and Identity: Developing Self in the Context of Politics

HERBERT HIRSCH — *Virginia Commonwealth University*

INTRODUCTION

SELF-ESTEEM does not develop in a vacuum. While this simple notion seems obvious, scholars interested in the development of identity often neglect important contextual environments within which the self not only develops, but which have important effects on that development throughout the life cycle. Attempts to measure and analyze self-esteem have, as one observer notes, "often run aground in a conceptual fog" (Adam, 1978, p. 68) because they ignore the context of politics. What does it mean to talk about self-esteem or to compare levels of self-esteem between different ethnic, racial, or class groups, if the analyst does not specify the conditions? All social phenomenon are, after all, embedded in social and political structures, and any research that hopes to be remotely isomorphic with reality must consider these an integral part of the conceptual framework. In fact, identity is manifestly political since it reflects and is influenced by the social, economic, and political circumstances within which a particular individual or group of individuals finds him- or herself.

Identity becomes a sociopolitical creation when it is related to power and to the dominant or subordinate position in which an individual or group is placed (Adam, 1978, p. 10). For example, access to or denial of opportunities in a society are generally related to the characteristics that have been declared by that society to be valued, to be positive or negative. It might be the value placed on the color of a person's skin, religion, or gender. These subjective judgments are transformed into objective categories as they are used by those occupying positions in society that allow them to bestow or withhold the rewards of the system. In short, seemingly objective criteria are actually the result of highly subjective political evaluations that have developed within a society over time. Once these criteria are established, groups will engage in political battle to maintain or change them. Hence, they also become political means and ends and are tied to the maintenance of the status quo or to change. The battles over these definitions may become heated and occasionally violent, and they, in turn, have an impact on the identity that is developing within that context. In other words, self-esteem cannot be divorced from a serious consideration of politics, and research on self-esteem is more complete if it is analyzed within the context of politics. This chapter will examine the process of identity formation as it operates within boundaries formed by the political environment. To accomplish this it is first necessary to define that environment.

THE POLITICAL ENVIRONMENT OF IDENTITY FORMATION

> To pass from civilization to extremity means to be shorn of the elaborate system of relationships—to job, class, tradition and family, to groups and institutions of every kind—which for us provides perhaps ninety percent of what we think we are (Des Pres, 1976, p. 214).

Even though Des Pres was referring to the experience of concentration camp survivors, in a very real sense his comments are applicable to the development of self in the modern world. He identifies the foundations of identity as well as the agents that transmit, through the process of socialization, the cues that will be vital to the formation of individual identity. This process will be elaborated upon in detail, but before discussing the process of political socialization it is necessary to engage in what has historically been a foolhardy attempt to define precisely the "political" context.

Political thinkers have grappled with this problem for thousands of years. From Aristotle to Marx they have struggled to define "politics," and there is a multiplicity of definitions. I want to adopt a rather unorthodox definition, which may not be any definition at all, but will clarify for me, and hopefully for the reader, what is involved. Most contemporary definitions involve the concept of "power," which itself is very difficult to define. Other definitions use terms such as *influence,* and attempt to distinguish between influence and power. These efforts at definitional clarity ultimately, in modern political science, give way to attempts to frame the concepts in mathematical symbols and, thus, to make them "scientific." While scientific definitions are useful for empirically based studies, especially if they are grounded in theory and based on historical understanding, very often the method becomes an end in itself and results in trivialization in the name of science. Method replaces content, and human emotions and feelings may be reduced to techniques of measurement. Since I believe that the human being must be the primary focus of inquiry (Hirsch, 1989), the definition I wish to use is that of a humanist.

Terrence Des Pres approached politics by writing about poetry. He once defined politics as:

> acts and decisions that are not our own but which nonetheless determine how we live; events and situations brought about by brute force or manipulations of power. . . . Politics, then, as the condition we find ourselves in when, without consent, we become the means to others ends — politics as endured by the victims, as seen by the witnesses, as beheld by the poet (Des Pres, 1981, p. 73).

This view of the political means that identity formation takes place in an environment in which politics is, as Des Pres (1981, p. 74) notes "insistent," "penetrating," and "widespread." Even if the individual does not personally experience incidents such as terrorism or violence or political chaos and uncertainty, he/she cannot escape "knowing" such facts and the mere "knowing" "changes the way you feel about being in the world" (1981, p. 74). Politics now intrudes on all aspects of life and there are no more bystanders. The personal has been transformed into the political and the disintegration of the boundary between them has left the modern individual face to face with the power of the modern state.

The reality formed by this erosion of boundaries means that the human person is no longer isolated and that his or her identity is formed within a crucible of political turmoil and unpredictability. The realities of contemporary political life intrude upon the formation of identity and these political realities may be destructive or constructive — may destroy or preserve life. If we adopt Des Pres' definition and focus on the acts of power addressed toward generally powerless people, then the realities are often not pretty.

Reflect for a moment on some of the more somber realities. Within the United States individuals face poverty; homelessness; environmental destruction and disintegration; increasing gaps between rich and poor; unemployment; recession; drugs; violence; disintegrating cities and a disintegrating infrastructure; and increases in the incidents of racism, sexism, and anti-Semitism. Internationally individuals are confronted with and exposed to war, nationalism and ethnic hostility rising and giving birth to violence, the widening gap between rich and poor nations, increasing inter-ethnic conflict, starvation and famine, the destruction of the rain forest, and genocide against indigenous populations. The list is almost beyond comprehension and almost immediately depressing. These negative realities are, of course, balanced by counter-trends, which are also part of the political context. This context, naturally, varies over time. For example, in the late 1960s and early 1970s the context of identity development included political movements to broaden the base and exercise of political power. These movements were devoted to empowering previously powerless people and, undoubtedly, had an effect upon the development of identity. At present there are, in the international context, certain hopeful and positive happenings such as Glasnost, Perestroika and the restructuring of the former Soviet Union, the apparent decline of totalitarian regimes, peace talks in Southeast Asia and the Middle East, and the hopefully not episodic and momentary quest for self-rule and democracy, to name but a few.

These political episodes become an integral part of our daily diet of overwhelming information. The desire to maintain some sense of psychological balance between the apparent tranquility of a person's everyday life and the apparent chaos and violence of the political context is constantly challenged. Daily newspapers and Cable News Network (CNN) inundate the mind with information—most of it concerning death, tragedy, or war. Knowing such facts not only changes the way people feel about being in the world, but must influence the type of person one becomes. Politics, thus, intrudes into the process of identity formation. Forming identity within such a political context must affect one's sense of self. If this is the case, it is important to explain how identity is being formed in the political cauldron of contemporary civilization.

POLITICAL SOCIALIZATION[1]

People learn to perceive political reality and assimilate their political ideas and opinions from a process called political socialization. This process is the same as the psychological processes of learning, but the content of what is transmitted and learned differs markedly from culture to culture, from state to state. For example, there is extensive research documenting the impact of culture on political socialization. Perhaps the clearest demonstration of cultural differences may be found in the Lambert and Klineberg study (1967), in which children from several nations were asked, "What are you?" The cultural differences are interesting and demonstrate how one's sense of self is influenced by culture.

Many, but not all, of the students interviewed by Lambert and Klineberg described themselves by referring to gender. This was true for American, English, and Canadian students, who also referred to their role as students (Lambert and Klineberg, 1967, p. 91). Describing oneself in terms of gender was also characteristic of the Brazilian, French, and German six and ten year olds and for the fourteen-year-old Bantu children, who also described themselves by referring to racial background. Israeli fourteen year olds, however, referred to themselves primarily as "children" and generally emphasized the fact that they are persons and students. As Israeli children got older, they referred more often to their national and religious backgrounds (Lambert and Klineberg, 1967, p. 94).

Turkish children rarely described themselves as boys or girls, referring, instead, to themselves as children, persons, or students. Lebanese children did use gender, but also used religion as reference points. Finally, they discovered that Japanese six year olds described themselves as persons and ten and fourteen year olds typically referred to themselves as "Japanese boys or girls" (Lambert and Klineberg, 1967, p. 94). These data clearly indicate that culture influences conceptions of self and that the use of national, racial, gender, or religious categories places these descriptions within a political context. Cultural differences in the content of what is socialized are not limited to inter-country comparisons. In the United States, for example, a child born and raised in an Appalachian (Hirsch, 1971), African-American (Abramson, 1977), or Hispanic (Hirsch and Gutierrez, 1977), community does not view the police, or political authority in general, in the same way as a child born into a white, middle-class context. These variations mean that the process is more complex than normally thought and emphasizes the importance of the context in determining the boundaries of the process.

In addition, there is the complicating factor that, along with individual self-concept, people have a collective self. This means that self-esteem must be analyzed as it operates at the societal and the individual level. In short, a person may manifest low individual self-esteem which might result in high societal self-esteem or some other of the various possible combinations (see Table 4.1). This means that both high and low self-esteem may lead to visions of superiority or inferiority and could conceivably provide a justification for hostility toward other groups. Or as Staub puts it, ''Both an inflated and a weak self-esteem can enhance threat'' (Staub, 1989, p. 55). For example, ''Low self-esteem may even intensify the need to compensate by seeing one's group in a positive light. Individuals who vary in self-esteem may share a belief in the superiority of their culture, nation, society, or way of life'' (Staub, 1989, p. 54). The relationships are much more complex than generally thought, and high self-esteem does not necessarily lead to a concern for others. In fact, in some cases high self-esteem may mask self-doubt and may also ''be associated with limited concern for others'' (Staub, 1989, p. 55). This collective or societal self-image ''includes shared evaluations of their group, myths that transmit the self-concept and ideal self, goals that a people set for themselves, and shared beliefs (e.g., about other groups). It may also include or mask uncertainties, insecurities, and anxieties'' (Staub, 1989, pp. 104 – 105). In other words, when a member of a group is dependent on the group for supporting his or her feeling of self-esteem and confidence, he or she will be more likely to follow what the group decides (Janis, 1982, pp. 257 – 258).

When identity is wrapped tightly in the actions of the group or community any perceived threats to the group or community become more real and potentially more devastating, thus, more likely to motivate a behavioral response (Sigel, 1989, p. 381). This is the ironic fact about identity. The more atomized and disconnected the person, the easier time they have coping with community crises and the less connected they may feel to the community. At the same time, the more disconnected they are, the more likely they will be unconcerned about members of their own

Table 4.1. Individual and societal self.

Individual	Societal	
	Low	High
Low		
High		

community. The great puzzle is: How does one maintain both a feeling of belonging and connection without becoming a person willing to follow the leaders or the group in the pursuit of negative action such as violence?

Questions about obedience are especially important when group identification and self-esteem are related to the nation state and are coupled with militarism or a streak of authoritarianism, which emphasizes unquestioning obedience to authority (Hirsch, 1985). Belonging to groups and in the modern era to nations

> . . . is of profound significance for human beings. It fulfills deep needs and provides satisfactions inherent in connections. It provides a feeling of security. It is essential in defining the self: as a member of a family, a profession, a religious group, voluntary associations, a nation. Individual identity is defined and the self gains value and significance through identification with groups and the connection to others that membership provides (Staub, 1989, p. 252).

In short, individual and collective identity are influenced by the cultural and political context within which the formation of those identities take shape. This context often involves questions of power, which are tied closely to the dominant or subordinate positions to which groups within a society are assigned, as well as to dominant or subordinate positions to which groups or nations are assigned within the international political community. As stated earlier, this might very well be related to any number of factors, including skin color, religion, or gender.

How individuals, groups, or even nations are described and perceived influences the way they are treated, which, in turn, influences their perceptions of their own identity. Very often, skin color, religion, or gender are used as the basis of myths, which may function to dehumanize those stigmatized as possessing the less desirable characteristics. Examples may be found in every historical epoch. Perhaps the most obvious is the Nazi appeal to what is referred to as ''The Aryan Myth'' to justify and rationalize the ''Final Solution.''

Myths such as the Aryan Myth simplify a complex political reality. As Edelman (1971) points out, the basic themes often revolve around a threatening outgroup conspiracy against the ingroup from which the benevolent political leaders will save the people. Victory, according to the leaders, may be achieved if the group works hard, sacrifices, and, most importantly, obeys its leaders (Edelman, 1971, p. 77). These types of myths, which often form the basis of a policy of genocide, perform at least four functions. First, they define the outgroup. Second, they call for certain actions on the part of the in-group, which are justified by the myth. Third, they require unquestioning obedience to the leaders who will function, if they are obeyed, as the saviors of the people. Fourth, they disguise reality and justify the acts of destruction. It is not difficult to imagine the impact this might have on the formation of identity. This is all part of what is called the "terminology of contempt" (Hirsch and Smith, 1991), and its applicability is not restricted to Jews or even to religious, racial, or ethnic groups.

The terminology of contempt depersonalizes and dehumanizes the subject of the negative stereotypes, and the use of such language cannot help but have profound effects on the formation of a person's identity. Assigning such negative attributes shapes not only the identity of the individuals or groups to whom the negative characteristics are assigned, but also profoundly influences the manner in which these groups are viewed by those in the dominant group, as well as the way the dominant group perceives themselves. Obviously, if people in the subordinate group are "savages" or "vermin," to deal harshly with or even kill them becomes a viable and justifiable option. Vermin, after all, carry disease, and savages may be a threat to the dominant group's existence. In addition, the dominant group is clearly superior and stronger. Hence, the self-esteem of the dominant group may be elevated, or at least defended, by repressing or killing the subordinate group. Self is, in this fashion, related to the political context, which is transmitted to succeeding generations via the process of political socialization. The content of what is transmitted is carried by language. In fact, as well as theory, self-esteem is connected to both mass and elite political behavior in extreme circumstances involving dominance and subordination, as well as in more nearly "normal" circumstances of routine political activity.

IDENTITY AND POLITICAL BEHAVIOR

The connection between identity and political behavior has been explored at both the mass and elite levels. That is, studies have examined both followers and leaders, as scholars wrestled with the puzzle of how self-esteem relates to political behavior at both levels. These attempts to understand the relationship between self-esteem and political behavior usually derive their hypotheses and borrow their concepts from psychological and psychoanalytic theory. The works of Freud, Erikson (1958, 1969, 1975, 1980), Maslow, and Fromm (1973) are among the most important sources of theory which have been applied to the study of politics (Lasswell, 1930, 1936, 1948).

The problem with most of the attempts to adapt these thinkers to interpreting the relationship between identity and politics is that most of the derivative theory remains abstract and mired in jargon. For example, Renshon (1989, p. 223) summarizes Erikson's core notion of identity by noting that identity

> is a by-product of the ego's synthetic functions, namely its capacity to integrate an individual's selves (both actual and aspired-to) within the context of available (or potentially available) roles.

But what does this mean and how is it related to politics? The human self remains a mystery, shrouded now in social science jargon instead of "pagan" or "civilized" mythology. What is most evident when one cuts through the abstractions is that the idea of self-esteem or identity appears to be central to almost all theories of political behavior.

Political scientists have hypothesized that self-esteem is related to a number of forms of political behavior (Knutson, 1972, p. 47). For example, a recent textbook in political psychology compares individuals with high and low self-esteem and concludes:

> A person with high self-esteem is more confident than the person with low self-esteem about her ability to cope with the problems of life. Compared to individuals with high self-esteem, those with low self-esteem are much more likely to exhibit feelings of political impotence, a lack of a sense of political efficacy, and possibly, have a sense of helplessness (Barrier-Barry and Rosenwein, 1985, pp. 64–65; also Stone and Schaffner, 1988, p. 120).

Other studies (Sniderman, 1975) found that high self-esteem is related to a commitment to democratic values while low self-esteem is related to the possibility that a person will be influenced by extreme political views. These, in turn, are hypothesized as contributing to a higher probability that a person with high self-esteem will be more likely to engage in political action and be "successful" in politics. But the relationship between self-esteem and politics has been found to be more complex.

Barber points out that both

> those who have such *high* self-esteem that they can manage relatively easily the threats and strains and anxieties involved . . . , and those who

have such low self-esteem that they are ready to do this extraordinary thing to raise it (Barber, 1965, pp. 223–224)

may motivate political candidates. One way to illuminate the confusing relationship between self-esteem and political behavior is to examine such behavior within specific, well-defined, yet very different contexts. Accordingly, the remainder of this chapter will examine the relationship between self-esteem and political leadership and then look at the effect of extreme political contexts on self-esteem.

IDENTITY AND POLITICAL LEADERSHIP

Studies of the relationship between self-esteem and leadership are ambiguous. Some find that persons with high self-esteem are more likely to be leaders than followers, while others find that this is not the case. In his seminal book on leadership Burns summarizes the results as follows:

> . . . Across the whole range of studies, correlations between self-esteem and leadership objectively measured often were not high, with the implication that other significant factors were involved, and that leaders and followers were not all that different (Burns, 1978, p. 100).

This, of course, makes sense. After all, the studies of leaders are undertaken after the fact—that is, after they had already become leaders. There are few longitudinal studies following a selected population to determine whether those with high self-esteem are more likely to become leaders than those with low self-esteem. In addition, we cannot determine whether the attainment of leadership positions has affected the level of self-esteem because there are no pre- and post-test studies. There are, moreover, few comparisons with the general population as attention is focused on leaders. Consequently, most of our generalizations about self-esteem and political behavior focus on how people who become leaders perform in that role.

For example, self-esteem has been found to be related to presidential behavior. Barber (1985) concluded that presidents with high self-esteem had a greater capacity to learn from experience and context and were more "successful" in office. Studies have also tried to establish a relationship between self-esteem and leadership with a particular interest in whether high self-esteem causes people to seek to become political leaders or to go into politics. The results of these studies have, for the most part, been ambiguous.

Studies of leaders have also utilized several different approaches. One early perspective focused on social background. This was closely related to the approach that examined individual life histories (Lasswell, 1930, 1948). These early studies "examined aspects of the leader's past, especially childhood, for clues to understanding later political behavior" (Renshon, 1989, p. 213). Much of this work was guided by psychoanalytic theory, which involved, as Renshon points out, "two related assumptions. The first was that unconscious and therefore unresolved conflicts originating in childhood would persist into adulthood and be instrumental in shaping political behavior" (Renshon, 1989, p. 213).

The second assumption, also based on the psychoanalytic model, predicted that "unresolved childhood conflicts not only influence the leaders' adult political behavior, but do so repeatedly" (Renshon, 1989, p. 214). A primary example of a work based on these assumptions is the Georges' study of Woodrow Wilson (George and George, 1964). They argued that Wilson's inner dispositions combined with external circumstances to create unfortunate political results. These types of studies draw from sources such as interviews with acquaintances and autobiography. Based on this type of material, analysts attach characteristics to leaders and argue that these attributed characteristics are at least one of the causes of the leader's behavior. I call this psychoanalysis by long distance and it is of questionable validity.

In addition, this approach generally argues that there is a "potent need for esteem, prestige, for reputation, for admiration," that produces the ambition of political leaders (Burns, 1978, pp. 113–114). Burns even argues that this is evident in the effect that damaged self-esteem has upon the political leader. As an example, he cites "Woodrow Wilson's insecurity over his father's love for him" (Burns, 1978, pp. 113–114). For additional support he also includes the examples of "Thaddeus Stevens' sensitivity over his origins, his absentee father, his physical deformation" and the "discrimination practiced against both Disraeli and Gandhi in their early years" and "Bismarck's ambivalent feelings toward his mother and his hypochondria" (Burns, 1978, pp. 113–114). But does every person who is insecure about his or her father's love or who is sensitive over his or her origins or who lives with a deformity or who experienced discrimination act in a fashion similar to Wilson, Stevens, Disraeli, or Gandhi? Is it not more likely that additional, complicating factors are involved?

Later studies added new categories to try to help understand political ambition. Renshon (1989), for example, focuses on the concept of "character," which he believes stands at the center of a leader's personality system. Character is not, however, a new concept. Fromm (1973, p. 255), in his modification of Freud, proposed the concept of character as a central construct in his theory (Hirsch, 1990). Without really paying attention to Fromm, in fact without citing him at all, political scientists nonetheless proceeded to adopt the idea and incorporate it into their study of political leadership.

For example, Barber (1965, 1985) in his celebrated studies of *The Presidential Character* argues that character is persistent throughout the life cycle. He studied different presidents and developed a typology of character, which could be used to predict their behavior. One of the problems, of course, is that the character is reconstructed from sources such as autobiography and memoirs, and the predicted behavior already occurred. It comes dangerously close to being tautological. In the long run, therefore, we are still puzzled by the riddle of self as it relates to political behavior and political leadership. One of the persistent questions involves whether self-esteem is involved in the production of positive or negative, constructive or destructive leaders and how it is influenced by, or influences, behavior in dramatic or extreme circumstances.

IDENTITY AND "NEGATIVE" LEADERSHIP

Generalizations concerning these questions are very similar to those made about the effect of self-esteem on leaders. Once again, based on psychoanalytic concepts, there has arisen an entire industry devoted to explaining, in individual terms, why, for example, people such as Hitler became mass murderers (Fest, 1970; Bullock, 1992). A major problem with psychoanalytically derived explanations of violent leaders is that they focus on destructive behavior as a manifestation of individual pathology or as caused by some significant event from the leader's childhood. This is too easy and ignores the possibility that, given the "right" set of conditions, any human person might be motivated to become a victim or a killer (Hirsch, 1985). Conceptions of self figure prominently in attempts to isolate the causal factors.

Staub (1989) for example, argues that low self-esteem is related to violent crime, and that

A poor or shaky self-image, easily threatened, and a tendency to see the world, other people, or institutions as hostile may cause a constant need for self-defense and elevation of the self. People with such characteristics may be especially sensitive to life problems. A low level of well-being and much frustration and pain – a negative hedonic balance – heighten the desire to enhance the self. Diminishing others raises at least one's relative well-being (Staub, 1989, p. 70).

But in the modern era the self is diminished by the constant assault of politics as the intimate connections within which the self is formed and exposed to the chaos and disorder of the contemporary political world. Within this context, as stated earlier, attachments to the smaller units such as the family may be in the process of being replaced by connections to the nation. As the smaller units have lost their importance or been transformed, the individual's sense of allegiance and belonging has been shifted to the nation. This type of identification has, as Staub (1989, p. 253) notes, "destructive potential if the members stop questioning" the "beliefs, values, ideals, policies, and actions" of the state. Self-concept is related to views of "the other," of outsiders: "If groups do not have valid ways of defining themselves on the basis of their past history, tradition, values and customs, they will have to define their identity by contrast to outside groups" (Staub, 1989, p. 253). Groups and nations set themselves up as "good" by setting others up as "bad." This is related to self-esteem, according to Staub (1989) in the sense that

> The more a group has succeeded in encoding most aspects of its experience into its self-concept, and the more this self-concept is realistic and moderately positive, the less likely that it will give rise to nationalism as an important goal. There will be less need to protect and enhance the nation by "purifying" it or by enlarging its territory or power (pp. 253–254).

These, according to Staub and others, were some of the elements that combined in the Third Reich. It was, as Staub notes (1989, p. 108), "the elevated German self-concept" that became dangerous when combined with these other elements.

In a similar fashion the Khmer Rouge demonstrated a comparable sense of superiority along with "underlying feelings of inferiority and vulnerability" (Staub, 1989, p. 199). The sense of having a mission to create and implement the "true" people's communism based on a model of the glory of the rural worker, along with the sense that the entire world was against them, led the Khmer Rouge, in the years 1975 to 1978, to kill over one million of their own people (Becker, 1986). But self-esteem is only one of a rather complicated set of contributing conditions.

Clearly, there may have been an elevated sense of self among the Germans, but without the historical conditions of postwar instability and the historical development of anti-Semitism along with cultural hierarchy, the elevated sense of self would not have been translated into the deadly mix that led to the extermination of the European Jews. Similarly, the past history of the Khmer people provided a glorification of militarism and a romanticization of a warrior tradition that combined with the feelings of inferiority and vulnerability on the one hand and superiority on the other to lead to the violence. This combination is not unknown in contemporary history, as self-esteem may be seen as related to violence when the combination of factors turns it in that direction. Elevated or low self-esteem in and of itself is not sufficient to cause mass murder. Self-esteem becomes of particular importance in the formula when one realizes that it not only influences the behavior of leaders who are involved in programming and manipulating the murderous mix of conditions, but it is also an important element motivating the followers who are, in many cases, only too willing to carry out the destructive acts. In addition, self-esteem is influenced by the context created by the destructive situation. We must, therefore, now ask what happens to the individual self when it experiences the trauma of war or repressive incarceration in a concentration camp.

This is important because it illustrates the dialectical nature of self. Identity is one of the motivating factors stimulating people to harm others while at the same time an adaptive self is formed within the context of that very same negative behavior.

IDENTITY AND VIOLENCE: WAR AND CONCENTRATION CAMPS

Identity is not always formed under conditions of apparent autonomy. Very often, and this is especially true for minorities — both racial, sexual, and ideological — identity is formed under conditions involving violence. What is most important here is the "limitation of life possibilities" (Adam, 1978), which are not equally experienced by all people. Participation, either as a willing or coerced perpetrator, or as a victim, appears to function as a kind of primitive socializing event in a person's life. Studies have shown that trauma has quite profound impacts on the individual's sense of who they are — especially on their identification with various types of authority and their predilection for participating in political violence. As Laufer (1989) notes:

The literature on the survivors of war indicates that exposure to the trauma of war leaves lasting scars on individuals and potentially serves as a turning point in life trajectories. What we know about the experience of war indicates that the resources, beliefs, and experiences individuals bring to it are wholly inadequate to cope with the actual experience. Warfare in the imagination cannot compare with warfare in situ; and the latter, especially modern warfare, is without romance, glamour, or melodrama, it is terrifying beyond imagination, horrifying beyond what is known in civil society and, for those trapped in its grip, inescapable. The experience of warfare is so overwhelming that individuals rapidly find it necessary to develop a new repertoire of adaptive coping mechanisms for functioning in the warfare environment, i.e., the situation imposes a new subjective reality on the neophyte (p. 418).

The effect of modern warfare is so overwhelming that even the military estimates that most individuals cannot endure sustained exposure to conflict for "more than thirty to fifty days" (Laufer, 1989, p. 419, citing Marlowe, 1983).

The parallels to incarceration in any total institution are obvious. The inmates in the Nazi concentration camps faced a similarly overwhelming experience for which nothing in any of their previous backgrounds could prepare them. As Des Pres (1976) summarizes,

In the camps prisoners lost their possessions, their social identity, the whole cultural matrix which had previously sustained them. They lost, in other words, the delicate web of symbolic identifications available to men and women in normal times. In Nazi camps they lost even their names and their hair. They were reduced to immediate physical existence . . . (p. 214).

The experience of both war and the concentration camps reduced those exposed to "primal acts and to an awareness circumscribed by primitive needs. They are naked to the roots, radically compressed to their essence as creatures of flesh" (Des Pres, 1976, p. 223). Even time is destroyed as the usual habits and "rhythms of change and motion," of seasons, work, cultural rituals are lost. The person in war or in the camps has no idea how long the ordeal will last and the situation often appears to be endless. As Des Pres (1976) notes, "The death of time destroys the sense of growth and purpose, and thereby undermines faith in the possibility that any good can come from merely staying alive" (p. 12). In extremity there are, then, two basic problems of existence, which have a serious impact on identity: first, "how not to despair" and, second, "how to keep moral sense and dignity intact" (Des Pres, 1976, p. 16). These are crucial to the maintenance of a semblance of what one might call a civilized self as opposed to the development of a war or concentration camp self. Undoubtedly, the person experiencing either of these extreme situations will have to adapt and that is, in fact, what happens. What is important, however, is whether they are able to reassert their civilized self at the conclusion of the extreme events.

Laufer (1989, pp. 419–420) identifies nine factors that might influence the results of exposure to extremity. All involve the experience of one or another form of stress. These include (1) direct experience of combat; (2) loss of buddies; (3) proportion of unit which suffers casualties; (4) witnessing abusive violence or atrocities; (5) direct participation in abusive violence or atrocities; (6) age of exposure to war stress; (7) a particularly dangerous assignment such as graves' registration, tunnel rats, demolition, etc.; (8) knowledge of personally killing enemy soldiers; and (9) length of time in war situation. In order to survive such horrible experiences, the human person must develop mechanisms to adapt. Lifton (1986; Lifton and Markusen, 1990) points out that both perpetrators and victims developed a new version of the self through a process he calls "doubling." In the concentration camp, he points out, the perpetrators developed an "Auschwitz self" which allowed them to go about their jobs of destruction. Likewise, the prisoners of the camps developed a self that aided their survival. This occurs through what Lifton calls doubling or numbing, which involves adaptation to an environment that is highly unusual, while at the same time being able to invoke their prior self when, for example, the perpetrators made periodic visits to their wives and children (Lifton and Markusen, 1990, p. 13).

Doubling involves the "division of the self into two functioning wholes, so that a part-self acts as an entire self" (Lifton and Markusen, 1990, p. 106). These selves acquired a logic and purpose that seemed appropriate to the environment even though the environment was extreme. The self is, therefore, able to adapt to almost unbelievable conditions and to, consequently, engage in and justify acts of great cruelty or great courage. The Nazi doctors at Auschwitz were able to justify their actions by investing their work with such great significance that any feelings of guilt were diffused. This, as Lifton (1986, p. 458) notes, is "part of a universal proclivity toward constructing good motives while participating in evil behavior." Lifton identifies several elements involved in the doctors' construction of their Auschwitz selves. These include force of routine, the justification that they were the ultimate biological soldiers doing important medical work, blaming the victim, and the overall notion of performing, which seems, according to Lifton, to be characteristic of the male ego (Lifton, 1986, p. 458).

By extension, one suspects that similar justifications occur in persons asked to serve in warfare and, in particular, if they are ordered to engage in actions that, in normal civilian circumstances, might be morally suspect. Hence, when a civilian person is exposed to the military and to "basic training," their civilian self is being erased as the doubling process occurs. Obviously, it is not desirable to erase completely the civilian self since it is necessary at some stage to reintegrate the citizen-soldier back into society. This problem is put off for a longer stretch of time in the case of the professional soldier. Consequently, as Lifton notes, professionals are particularly susceptible to doubling. He includes physicians, psychologists, physicists, biologists, clergy, generals, statesmen, writers, and artists and points out that they have a "special capacity for doubling. In them, a prior, humane self can be joined by a 'professional self' willing to ally itself with a destructive project, with harming or even killing others" (Lifton, 1986, p. 464).

Of course, Lifton assumes that two selves exist, that, in essence, the human person is basically moral or good and that the "bad" or evil self is created through the process of doubling. Assuming that he is correct, an assumption necessary to maintain one's hope for the species, this means that to some degree we are doubling every day. Our work self and our home self may be quite different from each other. Doubling is role-playing and we learn to discriminate, to play different roles according to the conditions or the circumstances within which we find ourselves. To a very large extent, how we play these different roles, how, in short, we double and what type of acts we are willing to pursue when ordered or given the opportunity to do so, depends upon the type of internalized self that exists at the moment of choice. Doubling, in fact, is similar to Staub's notion of the individual and collective self. The collective self, the societal self, may be that doubled self, the self developed to allow the person to adapt to extreme circumstances. In this case, the doubled, or the societal or institutional, self a person develops may very well be dependent upon the prior individual self. In other words, our self-image or self-esteem is one determining factor in how we react to extreme situations.

In a similar fashion extreme experiences become a filter through which subsequent events may be given meaning (Laufer, 1989, p. 445). Experiencing the trauma of war, for example, is related to delayed stress reactions.[2] Any exposure to extreme events, such as war or incarceration in a concentration camp, would likely have a similar impact on the self. In fact, the self that emerges from extremity will "play the central role in defining the identity available to the individual" (Laufer, 1989, p. 445). The construction of a self-system, "congruent with civil society or with the non-military non-concentration camp environment will occur through the process of 'serialization' " (Laufer, 1989, p. 445). The extreme discontinuities between the military or concentration camp self and the civil self, Laufer believes (1989, p. 445), "constantly creates a special vulnerability to identity diffusion or disintegration through the demands of developmental transitions of adulthood and subsequent stressful life events which either recall the original trauma and/or challenge" the individual to resolve the self conflicts. Just such a conflict faced the Nazi doctors who conducted experiments at Auschwitz.

At the conclusion of World War II, the doctors had to find some way to establish a postwar self. They had to find a way to cast off their "Auschwitz or Nazi self and to see themselves (and of course represent themselves to the world) as essentially decent and moderate postwar German burgher-physicians of a conservative stamp" (Lifton, 1986, p. 457). This presented problems because it was difficult for them to face forthrightly their Auschwitz or Nazi self. They sometimes found themselves without moral clarity about who they were at the moment — what was their "contemporary self?" As a result of these difficulties, as with soldiers who have experienced combat, they were not all successful at reintegrating themselves to civilian society. Some committed suicide after the German defeat, some were tried and executed, some served prison sentences, a few escaped, and "a considerable number returned to medical practice and continued until retirement or natural death" (Lifton, 1986, pp. 456–457). In short, the relationship between extremity and self is complicated. Clearly, common sense dictates that we believe that exposure to such horrible events must significantly affect self-esteem. What those effects are is not clearly spelled out. We can say with some assurance, however, that, while the individual is experiencing the events, the self is adjusting. Whether we call it doubling, numbing, the development of an institutional or societal self, or some other term, it raises important questions about the relationship between self-esteem and political behavior. If an individual is able to adapt him- or herself to virtually any situation, is it possible to create a self-image, an identity that refuses to participate in atrocity? That is, do human beings develop "good" and "bad" selves depending upon the conditions of their socialization? The remainder of this chapter will summarize the possibilities by first discussing the relationship between identity and altruism and then discussing an alternative view of the development of self in a political context.

IDENTITY AND ALTRUISM

While most of the research has focused on war and the perpetrators of violence, some scholars have tried to figure out why, in the midst of violence and evil, some people are willing to help others even though the commission of these acts could result in the loss of their life. Generally, these types of acts are referred to as "altruistic behavior." Examining altruism in the face of malevolence provides a needed counterbalance to the focus on violence and evil. After all, if identity is related to the commission of "evil," it must also be related to the commission of "good."

Philip Hallie quotes the American poet John Peale Bishop as noting that the tragic thing about war is that it destroys the "tragedy of death" (Hallie, 1979, p. 274). The very prevalence of war and violence causes people to lose their "awareness of the pricelessness of life" because they become accustomed to killing. This, he argues, "destroyed the foundations of a life-and-death ethic. War substituted military heroism for dignity" (Hallie, 1979, p. 274).

It seems quite likely that this demise of an ethic of life and death has spilled over into modern life in general. The prevalence of state-sanctioned mass murder and the technology of death have created a commonness of violence that continues to erode our awareness of the pricelessness of life along with our capacity for outrage at injustice and cruelty that appear in the modern period to be the "normal" state of human existence. People are numbed and no longer react with horror and disgust at the massive destruction of life. If this is the case, then the people who resist death, those who actively refuse to participate in the killing and take action to oppose it, deserve the status of modern heroes and heroines, and we need not only to celebrate their acts, but to attempt to understand the development of their motivations to the same extent that we examine those of the killers.

Scholars have conducted rather extensive research on different aspects of what is often referred to as altruistic or helping behavior. For the most part, scholars who have studied altruism anchor the idea of helping others with heavy weights of academic jargon. Instead of looking for good or evil in events that take place in people's lives, they begin with definitions and proceed to examine trivial and mundane forms of behavior exhibited, usually in artificially created situations. Altruism is sometimes defined as exhibiting a certain kind of behavior, such as intervening in a crisis to which one is a bystander (Latane and Darley, 1970), mailing unmailed letters (Forbes, TeVault and Gromoll, 1971), dimming one's headlights for an approaching car (Ehlert, Ehlert, and Merren, 1973), writing letters on behalf of others (Haynes, 1972), helping someone pick up groceries they dropped (Schneider and Mokus, 1974), and giving money to a stranger in a supermarket (Bickman and Kamzan, 1973).

Most of the studies of bystander intervention have been conducted by psychologists who have come up with a number of hypotheses to explain why people refuse to intervene. These include: the victims are to blame for their suffering and hence, "deserve," their fate (Lerner, 1970); others will or can help so they do not have to—the diffusion of responsibility (Latane and Darley, 1970); the longer an emergency continues without help being offered, the less likely it will be forthcoming (Piliavin, Rodin, and Piliavin, 1969). Other hypothetical determinants of altruistic behavior include an optimistic, as opposed to a fatalistic, vision of the future (Sorokin, 1950) and an internal locus of control (Midlarsky, 1986).

While these studies resulted in some hypotheses about why individuals might or might not help others, actions undertaken in a laboratory or in a supermarket are significantly different from those taken in the midst of a situation such as the Nazi destruction of the Jews, because as Tec notes, "The price to be paid is insignificant when compared with the risks of one's own life" (Tec, 1986, p. 151). While consideration of other remains important as a mechanism to establish the habit and idea of helping, a more poignant examination of altruism would focus on helping in a situation where to do so endangers the life of the rescuer. Examining helping behavior in a life and death situation such as the Holocaust[3] raises what is perhaps the most important question:

> Why did some people during that era resist Nazism by rescuing and in other ways helping Jews often at great risk to themselves and their families while the majority of the population remained passive bystanders or, worse, active participants in genocide? (Baron, 1986, p. 307).

As Baron (1986, p. 239) notes, most of the attempts to explain why people helped the Jews operate at a macroscopic level "reveal little about either the type of individuals who engaged in Jewish relief or the reasons which motivated them to do so." Generally, there have been two broad approaches to studying why people helped Jews. The first deals with "the historical conditions that fostered collective rescue operations at the national and local levels. The second has analyzed the psychological traits and sociological profiles of individuals who rescued Jews as revealed in intensive interviews with them" (Baron, 1986, p. 238). Neither considers the role of identity or self directly, but the discussions will allow us to draw some tentative conclusions about the role of self in rescue.

The first approach, the general, historical approach, considers examples such as the Danish rescue of the Jews and concludes that the Danes helped the Jews because of some combination of the following:

> . . . Denmark's long heritage of democracy and religious toleration, the high degree of social integration and acceptance achieved by native Jews, the lenient nature of the German occupation until 1943, the timing of the Nazi attempt to deport the Jews which coincided with the imposition of martial law on the increasingly unruly Danes who resented growing German economic exploitation, and finally the proximity of neutral Sweden which publicly offered to receive the escaping Jews (Baron, 1986, p. 238; Jegstrup, 1986).

In short, the Danes viewed the Jews as humans who were entitled to all the rights of citizens and they set about to rescue the Jews. Left out of these general historical observations are any ideas concerning why individual people were willing to help—what the motivating factors were. Studies of those who helped Jews during the Holocaust have been able to identify a number of different factors and derive several explanations.

Baron (1986, p. 240) cites a German study in which letters and other evidence were gathered from seventy Germans who helped Jews. A group portrait based on age, gender, marital status, geographical distribution, religious affiliation, vocation, political outlook, and involvement in other forms of resistance against Nazism revealed that many of the rescuers were born before 1910 and had achieved adulthood prior to the Nazis assuming power. They were, thus, not as susceptible to the influences of Nazi propaganda manifested in the socialization process, but they were still a distinct minority. This was, in fact, the major finding of this study, and it clearly reveals the inability of this type of study to uncover more in-depth reasons people were willing to risk their lives to help Jews.

Another study (Gordon, 1984) examined data from 452 Gestapo files on individual opponents of racial persecution in the government district of Dusseldorf. These files included "203 cases of individuals who aided Jews," 42 on "critics of racial persecution," 30 on "individuals suspected of aiding Jews," 137 on "Germans who had sexual relations with Jews," 40 on "persons who were suspected of having sexual relations with Jews," and 255 on "Jews arrested for these reasons" (p. 211). Gordon found that German males over fifty years of age were the most active in helping Jews and hypothesized that this happened because the political socialization of older men occurred when anti-Semitic movements were not as strong and because older men had access to the financial resources and contacts that helped them to hide Jews. Gordon also indulges in several speculative hypotheses which are of doubtful validity (Gordon, 1984, pp. 210–245). The basic criticism remains that Gordon's analysis does not allow one to achieve any insight into individual reasons for helping Jews, and it certainly says absolutely nothing about the role of self. In order to approximate some under-standing of individual motivation, it is necessary to turn to in-depth, interview studies of individuals who rescued Jews.

Nechama Tec (1986) interviewed Polish rescuers and attempted to ascertain what influenced them to help Jews. She looked at social class, political beliefs, degree of anti-Semitism, extent of religious commit-ment, the prospects of monetary reward, and friendship with Jews. She found that, while each of these may have offered a partial explanation, none was a "wholly reliable predictor of precisely who would attempt the protection of Jews" (Tec, 1986, p. 150). As a result she proceeded to look for "core characteristics" and identified six from which she derives three hypotheses.

The six characteristics are:

(1) Individuality or separateness (p. 188)—Tec defines these as "the inability of the rescuer to blend with the environment." This closely resembles an earlier finding of London (1970) that rescuers were socially marginal to their societies, but Tec points out that mar-ginality has a negative connotation and she prefers to describe the characteristic as "individuality" or "separateness" (p. 154).

(2) Independence or self-reliance—Individuals are motivated to "pur-sue personal goals regardless of how these goals are viewed by others" (p. 154).

(3) Commitment to stand up for the helpless and needy (p. 188)—

Usually, the commitment started before the war and included a variety of activities (p. 154).

(4) Attitude toward rescue as a duty—The rescuers do not see themselves as doing anything unusual or heroic (p. 154).

(5) Rescue efforts were not premeditated and were spontaneously undertaken (pp. 154, 188)—Rescuers were often not able to explain how they began to rescue Jews.

(6) Universalistic perception of the needy (pp. 154, 188)—People in need were viewed as human beings who needed help. They were not perceived according to ethnic, racial, or other categorization.

Tec (p. 190) then derives three hypotheses to explain what she calls selfless rescue of the Jews. First, individuals who are freed from the constraints and control of their community are more likely to resist the pressures for conformity and act independently. Second, these independent acting individuals may be motivated by moral imperatives expressed as a strong desire to help the needy. This is often, as we shall see shortly in the case study of two rescuers, learned through early socialization from parents. Third, helping behavior becomes a habit. "The longer people act in accordance with such strong moral imperatives, the more likely are these actions and values to become traditional patterns. The more firmly established such actions become, the easier they are to follow and the greater the likelihood that they will be taken for granted as natural reactions and as a duty" (Tec, 1986, p. 191).

Rescuers appear, therefore, to be independent thinkers, freed from obedience and conformity, willing to follow their moral conscience to "do the right thing" even in the face of threats to their own lives. While self-esteem is never mentioned as a characteristic, it is logical to believe that individuals possessing the above characteristics would have a very strong sense of self. This likelihood becomes very clear when we turn our attention to two individuals who devoted their lives to rescuing Jews during the Holocaust.

Pastor Andre Trocme (Hallie, 1979) and the people of the Village of Le Chambon sheltered and saved hundreds of Jewish children. Herman "Fritz" Graebe, a German engineer (Huneke, 1985), also used his courage and ingenuity to save Jews during the period of Nazi domination. Their stories are not only inspiring, but bring us closer to an understanding of the relationship between self-image and altruism.[4]

In most of the literature on altruism and rescue, self or self-esteem was connected to positive behavior in only one case. While it was clearly present in others, it was explicitly discussed only in the case of Le Chambon. Sauvage (1986, p. 256) conjectured that helping Jews in the face of the horrible penalties meted out by the Nazis required a "very secure, very anchored sense of self—a spontaneous access to the core of their being—that resulted in a natural and irresistible proclivity to see the truth and act upon it. . . ." Rescuers of Jews come from many different backgrounds, but appear to have had in common a "caring human concern for the suffering of others and the ability to endure personal risk in order to alleviate the suffering" (Henry, 1986, p. 318). How this was developed is the important question.

As Sauvage notes, it is important to recognize that "to care about other people is also to care about yourself" (Sauvage, 1986, p. 259). If one cares about oneself, this may be indicative of a strong sense of self-esteem. Surely, one cannot undertake dangerous acts, such as the rescue of Jews from the Nazis, without a strong inner core of identity. If this is the case, if self-esteem is a characteristic of those who helped Jews, then how did it develop?

Huneke (1985) and Grossman (1984) suggest that parental and role models were responsible for inculcating an ethic of tolerance, justice, and equality. Grossman in fact, argues that "the type of parenting they received endowed them with an acute sense of personal responsibility, a great deal of empathy toward others, and the independence and confidence to act upon their feelings and values despite the legal or social consequences" (Baron, 1986, p. 242). The recollections of the rescuers were that they learned these traits from communicative and non-authoritarian fathers and affectionate mothers who established a warm and trusting relationship with their children. As might be expected, children who had "experienced security, acceptance, and love could readily empathize with another human being in trouble . . ." (Baron, 1986, p. 243). It is, consequently, not so much "what a child is taught, but how it is treated which determines the kind of human being he or she will be, and the way he or she will relate to others" (Baron, 1986, p. 243).

The in-depth interviews with specific rescuers reinforced this idea. The study of the German engineer, Fritz Graebe, led to the identification of a number of factors related to rescuing. Among these, the most important is probably the influence of a moral parental role model (Huneke, 1986, p. 323). Graebe is said to have learned his moral values of compassion from his mother, Louise, who "taught him to be an independent thinker and to care for the less fortunate and for those who were the victims of society. She showed him how to be hospitable and instilled in him a profound sense of justice that enabled him to resist ill-willed, inhumane authorities'' (Huneke, 1985, p. xviii). As Graebe noted, he grew up ''in a world of distinct right and wrong, but that sense of righteousness was always tempered by an equally strong sense of charity, a willingness to understand and appreciate the position of the other person'' (Huneke, 1985, p. 6).

A second characteristic was social marginality or independence. This is similar to the ideas of London and Tec. This marginality is in terms of social class, political affiliation and viewpoint, economic status, religious beliefs and practices, educational status, geographic location, family style, and personal characteristics. Graebe was taught to be an independent thinker and he had the confidence not to conform, to be marginal. At one point he noted

> I marched to my own tune. I was not taught to be political. Therefore, I did not oppose or support National Socialism on ideological grounds. I became opposed to it when I personally witnessed its injustice and inhumanity (Huneke, 1986, p. 324).

Graebe did what he thought was right and did not seek the approval of authority figures.

A third ''value strongly emphasized in the Graebe household was the virtue of hard work and diligence'' (Huneke, 1985, p. 7). When he was young Graebe overcame a problem with stuttering. He also worked hard to become a licensed engineer who used his position to help rescue Jews.

From this examination of Graebe and other rescuers of Jews during the Holocaust, Huneke (1985, 1986) identifies ''seven traits of the caring person – the rescuer'' (Huneke, 1986, p. 325).

(1) Empathic imagination – This is the ''ability to place oneself in the actual situation or role of another person and to imagine the long-term consequences of the situation or the role on that person'' (p. 325).

(2) The ability of an individual to dramatically present himself or herself and seize control of a critical situation – Graebe had trained as an actor and was ready to seize control of situations and play different roles as needed to further his efforts at rescue. On several occasions he was confronted by the SS or Gestapo and accused of various illegal acts. Instead of accepting their authority, Graebe

used his dramatic talents to confuse the investigators by claiming that he was on a secret mission for high German authorities. His audacious bluffs succeeded on at least three separate occasions.

(3) Previewing for a purposeful life—"In order to be altruistic, a person must be both proactive and prosocial. *Proactive* (its opposite reactive) and *prosocial* (its opposite is anti-social) behavior is characterized by (1) careful planning to act in a cooperative and responsible way; (2) anticipating opportunities for having a positive and beneficial impact in the lives and circumstances of others; and (3) actively promoting the well-being of self and others" (p. 326).

(4) Significant personal experiences with suffering and death prior to the war—Graebe, for example, remembers watching the returning veterans of World War I. He recalls, in particular, "one bandaged young man . . . , much of whose face had been blown away by a bullet . . . [and] recalls thinking that this man and others like him were going through such unnecessary and wasteful suffering" (Huneke, 1986, p. 327). These experiences sensitized him to death and tragedy and heightened his empathic identification.

These appear to be the primary characteristics of rescuers. Huneke added three additional points:

(5) The ability to confront and manage one's prejudices

(6) The development of a community of compassion and support

(7) The ability to offer hospitality

Standing out from all of these studies, one gets the very clear impression that those courageous individuals who risked their lives to attempt to save or help Jews during the Holocaust must have had, as was noted of Fritz Graebe, a deep "faith in his own abilities" along with a "capacity for difficult, sustained work . . ." (Huneke, 1985, p. 8). This deep faith in one's own abilities is another way of talking about high self-esteem or a positive self-image. Whatever term is used, the act of rescue must have come from a deep inner core of self, and to sustain it in the face of the German atrocities must have necessitated calling up all of the strength of character a person possessed. It seems logical to believe that a strong and positive sense of self must have been part of that inner support mechanism. In addition, it also seems readily apparent that it is very difficult to understand both the rescuers and the murderers. We cannot assume that they experienced different contexts for their socialization since both were subjected to the same political, cultural, and social forces. In short, while we can identify characteristics of both, we can come to no definitive outline of their character or motivations. Perhaps the best we can do is to attempt to outline some final thoughts on the adaptive self.

THE ADAPTIVE SELF: DEVELOPING SELF-ESTEEM

Whatever lies at the heart of the human person remains an enigma, and how the self relates to politics remains at the heart of that enigma. In-depth case studies of individuals have, however, provided some directions to follow in trying to untangle the complex knot of motivations. At least there is now information on some of the background characteristics of victims, killers, bystanders and rescuers. In addition, the realization that most previous theoretical models were inadequate led scholars to develop alternative perspectives.

The most generally accepted perspective is that people are socialized or learn an image of themselves, which is reinforced and transmitted by the culture and political context in which they live and to which they must adapt. If the self is adaptive, malleable, think of the consequences of the previous discussion. It means, literally, that individuals are able to adapt themselves to war, to concentration camps, to politics of all forms, and this implies that within every human person there exists the capacity for both great good or great evil—perhaps within the same person at the same time. Where, then, does one find one's "true self," if one can survive as an inmate or doctor at Auschwitz? Conceivably, in our pursuit of identity, we have asked the wrong questions.

An individual self is not necessarily evil or genocidal. Yet, under certain conditions, virtually any self is capable of becoming all of these. Just as there are many different types of people, there may be different selves—even within the same person. A self is not a single fixed entity, but a representation or symbolization of the way a person perceives him- or herself; the way one thinks others see him- or herself; one's identifications with groups, nations, and other institutions; and the survival and adaptive mechanisms one has developed. Noting this complexity, some social scientists have realized that many of the earlier attempts to include self-esteem as a variable explaining political behavior have foundered on the shoals of oversimplification. The general perspective on self conveyed by most of the social science models is constricted. As McCollough (1991) notes,

[If] we add the social science disciplines together, especially those of psychology and economics, we find them converging on a model of human nature as self interested and acquisitive, an atomistic individual abstracted from history and from all that makes a person identifiable, known, and respected and cared for as a person. The economic individual motivated solely by rational calculation of narrow self interest is an "encumbered self," without friendship, loves, loyalties, values, obligations, and commitments. The result is a concept of self that influences our actions and our public policy (pp. 102 – 103).

In fact, this perspective is not compatible with the way people live their lives when they are most fulfilling. The realization of the problem with this view of self led to attempts to develop a more dynamic and realistic perspective more in line with the above discussion. It is now more common in the literature to find a recognition that, while experiences in childhood might affect adult perceptions or behaviors, development does not stop in childhood – recognition, in short, that development of self is a life-long process that includes change and the importance of adult life experiences. The most important question for our purpose is to ascertain how self-esteem interacts with, influences, or is influenced by the political context through the explication of the lived out roles. Particularly important is the notion of choice. In fact, the focus on choice reinstates the individual as a responsible actor and puts the human person and the human self back into the calculations of political behavior. As Des Pres (1976) put it:

People still free must decide how much their "freedom" is worth: how many lies they will live by, how far they will acquiesce while their neighbors are destroyed. The choice is always there (p. 18).

While one cannot argue that the person victimized by a strong oppressor necessarily has choice, it is the case that, as the murderers made choices, the victims also had, more limited to be sure, choices. They did not choose to become victims, but having been placed in that role, they had then to choose how to behave. The essential "distinction is between those who live at any price, and those who suffer whatever they must in order to live humanly" (Des Pres, 1976, p. 19). The killers did not have to become killers and even the victims could, until choice was taken from them when finally herded to the gas chambers, decide how they would attempt to structure their survival. In short, there is a direct and reciprocal relationship between the self and the environment. The previous self determines the types of choices one makes, while the context influences the self that will be. It is in the choices that one makes that the individual identity surfaces. This is where the importance of educating people to be aware of and critically evaluate the contextual importance of the many choices they will face throughout their lives becomes a determining factor in the developing self. While most of the choices one must make appear on the surface to be insignificant, they are, in reality, part of a larger pattern. If a person consistently ignores inhumanity, however small, for example racist or sexist jokes, and this becomes a life-long pattern of not recognizing or ignoring oppression and injustice, it is likely that the same person will be unable to recognize inhumanity when it confronts him and that he will, consequently, lose his sense of outrage at acts of oppression and injustice. It is in these seemingly small areas of everyday life that people find protection and relief from the reach of the intrusive state and from the seemingly sad realities of political life. It is also the place where they may develop attachments, a sense of identity, and the support to make moral choices. These seemingly insignificant choices assume ever greater importance in a person's life as they develop the habit of making or not making moral choices. Although these attachments to the small islands of love and affection may create a supportive structure, they do not exist in a vacuum.

They are part of the larger context, and educators must focus attention on the everyday realities and forthrightly confront injustice and in-humanity so that their students develop the capacity to make the choices between destruction and preservation of life. A person who is so edu-cated also develops a positive self-image as he or she realizes the potential of empowerment—they are not powerless, they do have choices, and if multiplied by every individual the making of these choices can influence local, national, and perhaps international politics. As Camus noted, if we all choose to be neither victims nor executioners, those who wish to make us either will have a difficult time sating their appetites for destruction.

ENDNOTES

1 Since 1959 when Herbert Hyman published his pioneering study of political socializa-tion, political scientists have tried to understand how the process operates and what eventually results when the child becomes an adult. From the derivative systems theory studies of Easton and Dennis, through the ''benevolent leader'' studies of Greenstein, and even down to the extensions of these studies, the focus has been on the maintenance of stability and perceptions of political authority. Even after years of critical interpretations, the focus on stability and a tendency to dismiss cultural

variations remain a major thrust of the literature. See Hyman, 1959; Easton and Dennis, 1969; Greenstein, 1965, 1975. For dissenting interpretations, see Jaros, Hirsch, and Fleron, 1968; Hirsch, 1971; Hirsch and Gutierrez, 1977; Hirsch, 1988.

2 While precise connections are difficult to substantiate, there is evidence of "psychopathology associated with the trauma of war. . . ." These include problems with careers and marriages, delayed stress reactions, and others. Laufer does note that, "Although the vast majority of Vietnam veterans continue to function without institutionalization, the evidence indicates that war stress irreparably alters the intrapsychic life trajectories by creating series of identity crises whose resolution requires the integration of serial crystallized selves that often can only be partially integrated. The early adult development crisis around the integration of the serial self creates confusion in social relations, career development, and parenting which, because they often come close together, negatively affect interlocking life trajectories" (Laufer, 1989, p. 435).

3 As with self-esteem, altruism is also influenced by context. There are, for example, important differences between the penalties faced by rescuers of Jews during the Holocaust as opposed to rescuers of Armenians during the Armenian Genocide (1915–1918). As Hovannisian (1992, p. 180) notes, "Unlike the circumstances during the Holocaust, therefore, at certain places and at certain times there was little or no risk in having persons born as Armenians in a household. This point underscores a significant difference between the Young Turk perpetrators of the Armenian Genocide and the Nazi perpetrators of the Holocaust. The Young Turks were extreme nationalists, but they were not racists in the Nazi sense. They wanted to create a Turkic empire and to eliminate all obstacles to the realization of that goal. The Turks had absorbed subject peoples for centuries and the continued absorption of powerless and defenseless Armenian survivors did not jeopardize the fulfillment of their objectives. On the contrary, in some areas Armenian orphans were gathered into Turkish orphanages to be "Turkified." Hence, while many Muslims who took in Armenian women and children must be regarded as performing humanitarian deeds, on the whole they had little to fear in case of exposure." This was in stark contrast to the situation of rescuers of Jews. Any person who helped Jews was either sent to a camp, killed, sometimes by themselves, sometimes along with their entire family, or, in some cases, the entire village was destroyed. While rescuing in both contexts was clearly a humanitarian act, rescuing Jews during the Holocaust was, if one may talk about degrees of altruism, more altruistic than the other.

4 While these are two of the best known stories, they are not the only rescuers of Jews during the Holocaust. Rank and file people of both sexes sometimes risked their lives to help individuals or in some cases families. For some of these stories, see Tec, 1986. It is also important to keep in mind the overwhelming fact that most people did not help.

REFERENCES

Abramson, P. 1977. *The Political Socialization of Black Americans*. New York, NY: The Free Press.

Adam, B. D. 1978. *The Survival of Domination*. New York, NY: Elsevier.

Barber, J. D. 1965. *The Lawmakers*. New Haven, CT: Yale University Press.

Barber, J. D. 1972 and 1985. *The Presidential Character: Predicting Performance in the White House*. Englewood Cliffs, NJ: Prentice-Hall.

Baron, L. 1986. "The Holocaust and Human Decency: A Review of Research on the Rescue of Jews in Nazi Occupied Europe," in *Altruism and Prosocial Behavior*, a special issue of *The Humboldt Journal of Social Relations*, Elizabeth Midlarsky and Lawrence Baron, eds., 13(1 and 2):237–251.

Barrier-Barry, C. and R. Rosenwein. 1985. *Psychological Perspectives on Politics*. Englewood Cliffs, NJ: Prentice-Hall.

Becker, E. 1986. *When the War Was Over*. New York, NY: Simon and Schuster.

Bickman, L. and M. Kamzan. 1973. "The Effect of Race and Need on Helping Behavior," *The J. of Social Psychology*, 89:73–773.

Bullock, A. 1992. *Hitler and Stalin: Parallel Lives*. New York, NY: Knopf.

Burns, J. M. 1978. *Leadership*. New York, NY: Harper & Row.

Des Pres, T. 1976. *The Survivor: An Anatomy of Life in the Death Camps*. New York, NY: Pocket Books.

Des Pres, T. 1981. "Emblem of Diversity," *Harpers* (March):73–77.

Easton, D and J. Dennis. 1969. *Children in the Political System*. New York, NY: McGraw-Hill.

Edelman, M. 1971. *Politics as Symbolic Action*. New York, NY: Academic Press.

Ehlert, J., N. Ehlert, and M. Merren. 1973. "The Influence of Ideological Affiliation on Helping Behavior," *The J. of Social Psychology*, 89:315–316.

Erikson, E. 1958. *Young Man Luther*. New York, NY: Norton.

Erikson, E. 1969. *Ghandi's Truth*. New York, NY: Norton.

Erikson, E. 1975. *Life History and the Historical Moment*. New York, NY: Norton.

Erikson, E. 1980. *Identity and the Life Cycle*. New York, NY: Norton.

Fest, J. C. 1970. *The Face of the Third Reich*. New York, NY: Pantheon Books.

Forbes, G., R. K. TeVault, and H. F. Gromoll. 1971. "Willingness to Help Strangers as a Function of Liberal Conservative or Catholic Church Membership: A Field Study with the Lost Letter Technique," *Psychological Reports*, 28:947–949.

Fromm, E. 1973. *The Anatomy of Human Destructiveness*. New York: Fawcett.

George, A. L. and J. L. George. 1964. *Woodrow Wilson and Colonel House: A Personality Study*. New York, NY: Dover.

Gordon, S. 1984. *Hitler, Germans and the Jewish Question*. Princeton, NJ: Princeton University Press.

Greenstein, F. I. 1965. *Children and Politics*. New Haven, CT: Yale University Press.

Greenstein, F. I. 1975. "The Benevolent Leader Revisited: Children's Images of Political Leaders in Three Democracies," *The American Political Science Review*, 69:1371–1398.

Grossman, F. G. 1984. "A Psychological Study of Gentiles Who Saved the Lives of Jews during the Holocaust," in *Toward the Understanding and Prevention of Genocide*, Israel Charny, ed., Boulder, CO: Westview Press, pp. 202–216.

Hallie, P. P. 1979. *Lest Innocent Blood Be Shed*. New York, NY: Harper and Row.

Haynes, M. B. 1972. "The Effect of Performing One Altruistic Act on the Likelihood of Performing Another," *J. of Social Psychology*, 88:65–73.

Henry, F. 1986. "Heroes and Helpers in Nazi Germany: Who Aided Jews?" in *Altruism and Prosocial Behavior*, a special issue of *The Humboldt Journal of Social Relations*, Elizabeth Midlarsky and Lawrence Baron, eds., 13(1 and 2):306–319.

Hirsch, H. 1971. *Poverty and Politicization: Political Socialization in an American Sub-Culture.* New York, NY: The Free Press.

Hirsch, H. 1985. "Why People Kill: Conditions for Participation in Mass Murder," *International Journal of Group Tensions*, 15(1−4):41−57.

Hirsch, H. 1988. "Nazi Education: A Case of Political Socialization," *The Educational Forum*, 53(1):63−76.

Hirsch, H. 1989. "Trivializing Human Experience: Social Studies Methods and Genocide Scholarship," *Armenian Review*, 42(4):71−81.

Hirsch, H. 1990. "'To Love or to Hate?' Erich Fromm's Reflections on Human Destructiveness," paper presented at the *20th Anniversary Scholar's Conference on the Holocaust, March 4−6, 1990, Nashville, TN.*

Hirsch, H. and A. Gutierrez. 1977. *Learning to Be Militant: Ethnic Identity and the Development of Political militancy in a Chicano Community.* San Francisco, CA: R & E Research Associates.

Hirsch, H. and R. Smith. 1991. "The Language of Extermination in Genocide," in *Genocide: A Critical Bibliographic Review, Vol. 2,* Israel Charny, ed., London: Mansell Publishing, pp. 386−403.

Hovannisian, R. G. 1992. "Intervention and Shades of Altruism during the Armenian Genocide," in *The Armenian Genocide: History, Politics, Ethics,* Richard G. Hovannisian, ed., New York, NY: St. Martin's, pp. 173−207.

Huneke, D. K. 1985. *The Moses of Rovno.* New York, NY: Dodd, Mead & Company.

Huneke, D. K. 1986. "The Lessons of Herman Graebe's Life: The Origins of a Moral Person," in *Altruism and Prosocial Behavior,* a special issue of *The Humboldt Journal of Social Relations,* Elizabeth Midlarsky and Lawrence Baron, eds., 13(1 and 2):320−332.

Hyman, H. H. 1959. *Political Socialization; A Study in the Psychology of Political Behavior.* Glencoe, IL: The Free Press.

Janis, I. L. 1982. *Groupthink.* New York, NY: Houghton Mifflin.

Jaros, D., H. Hirsch, and F. J. Fleron, Jr. 1968. "The Malevolent Leader: Political Socialization in an American Sub-Culture," *The American Political Science Review,* 62:564−575.

Jegstrup, E. 1986. "Spontaneous Action: The Rescue of the Danish Jews from Hannah Arendt's Perspective," in *Altruism and Prosocial Behavior,* a special issue of *The Humboldt Journal of Social Relations,* Elizabeth Midlarsky and Lawrence Baron, eds., 13(1 and 2):260−284.

Knutson, J. 1972. *The Human Basis of the Polity.* Chicago, IL: Aldine.

Lambert, W. E. and O. Klineberg. 1967. *Children's Views of Foreign Peoples.* New York, NY: Appleton-Century-Crofts.

Lasswell, H. D. 1930. *Psychopathology and Politics.* Chicago, IL: University of Chicago Press.

Lasswell, H. D. 1936. *Politics: Who Gets What, When, How.* New York, NY: McGraw-Hill.

Lasswell, H. D. 1948. *Power and Personality.* New York, NY: Norton.

Latane, B. and J. M. Darley. 1970. "Social Determinants of Bystander Intervention in Emergencies," in *Altruism and Helping Behavior,* J. Macaulay and L. Berkowitz, eds., New York, NY: Academic Press.

Latane, B. and J. M. Darley. 1970. *The Unresponsive Bystander: Why Doesn't He Help?* New York, NY: Appleton-Century-Crofts.

Laufer, R. S. 1989. "The Aftermath of War: Adult Socialization and Political Development," in *Political Learning in Adulthood,* Roberta Sigel, ed., Chicago, IL: The University of Chicago Press, pp. 415–457.

Lerner, A. W. 1970. "The Desire for Justice and Reactions to Victims," in *Altruism and Helping Behavior,* J. Macaulay and L. Berkowitz, eds., New York, NY: Academic Press, pp. 205–229.

Lifton, R. J. 1986. *The Nazi Doctors.* New York, NY: Basic Books.

Lifton, R. J. and E. Markusen. 1990. *The Genocidal Mentality.* New York, NY: Basic Books.

London, P. 1970. "The Rescuers: Motivational Hypotheses about Christians Who Saved Jews from the Nazis," in *Altruism and Helping Behavior,* J. Macaulay and L. Berkowitz, eds., New York, NY: Academic Press.

McCollough, T. E. 1991. *The Moral Imagination and Public Life.* Chatham, NJ: Chatham House.

Midlarsky, E. and L. Baron, eds. 1986. *Altruism and Prosocial Behavior,* a special issue of *The Humboldt Journal of Social Relations,* Elizabeth Midlarsky and Lawrence Baron, eds., 13(1 and 2), pp. 1–408.

Midlarsky, M. 1986. "Helping during the Holocaust: The Role of Political, Theological, and Socioeconomic Identifications," in *Altruism and Prosocial Behavior,* a special issue of *The Humboldt Journal of Social Relations,* Elizabeth Midlarsky and Lawrence Baron, eds., 13(1 and 2):285–305.

Piliavin, I. M., J. Rodin, and J. A. Piliavin. 1969. "Good Samaritanism: An Underground Phenomenon?" *Journal of Personality and Social Psychology,* 13(4): 289–299.

Renshon, S. 1989. "Psychological Perspectives on Theories of Adult Development and the Political Socialization of Leaders," in *Political Learning in Adulthood,* Roberta Sigel, ed., Chicago, IL: University of Chicago Press.

Sauvage, P. 1986. "Ten Things I Would Like to Know about Righteous Conduct in Le Chambon and Elsewhere during the Holocaust," in *Altruism and Prosocial Behavior,* a special issue of *The Humboldt Journal of Social Relations,* Elizabeth Midlarsky and Lawrence Baron, eds., 13(1 and 2):252–259.

Schneider, F. W. and Z. Mokus. 1974. "Failure to Find a Rural Urban Difference in Incidence of Altruistic Behavior," *Psychological Reports,* 35:294.

Sigel, R. S. 1989. *Political Learning in Adulthood.* Chicago, IL: The University of Chicago Press.

Sniderman, P. 1975. *Personality and Democratic Politics.* Berkeley, CA: University of California Press.

Sorokin, P. A. 1950. *Altruistic Love: A Study of American "Good Neighbors" and Christian Saints.* Boston, MA: Beacon Press.

Staub, E. 1989. *The Roots of Evil.* New York, NY: Cambridge University Press.

Stone, W. and P. E. Schaffner. 1988. *The Psychology of Politics.* New York, NY: Springer-Verlag.

Tec, N. 1986. *When Light Pierced the Darkness: Christian Rescue of Jews in Nazi-Occupied Poland.* New York, NY: Oxford University Press.

CHAPTER 5

A Systems View of Family and School

STEVEN X. GALLAS – *Williamsburg/James City County School District*
GAIL B. HARDINGE – *Williamsburg/James City County School District*

FAMILIES and schools are the two most important social systems in the life of a child from approximately five years of age to adolescence. Typically, children spend at least seven to eight hours a day in school, not to mention additional time spent on school buses, and after-school activities. Although both family and school systems have a major impact on a youngster, there is no doubt that the family's influence on a child is more personal and pervasive than that of the school system (Hansen and Okun, 1983). However, because of the necessity and reality of two-income families, working single parents, and unavailability of local extended family networks, an increasing number of children may be spending considerably more time with adults within the school milieu than with their primary caregiver in the home. While the school is a major context for children, little attention has been given to the interactive effects of these two major social systems.

Fine and Holt (1983) point out that the essential systems in a child's life, home, and school, often overlap and what occurs in one setting will affect the child's behavior in the other. According to Aponte (1974, p. 307), "A child having trouble in school is not having trouble alone." While the notion that schools or families in isolation cannot solve the problems of youth may seem obvious, a careful examination of this vital working relationship has only recently received the attention it deserves. Educators often romanticize about the social, political, and parental support awarded schools during the nineteenth century, where education was valued as the means for social mobility. As political and economic trends in the last half of the twentieth century seem to be in a constant state of flux, educators and parents occasionally seem at odds with one another when educational goals are daily staples of political debate.

Members of the school community may respond to this conflict by casting blame on the child, e.g., "Tommy is socially maladjusted," or casting blame on the family, e.g., "The family's values, language, and

communication are not what we want to encourage in our school."
Parents, on the other hand, may have their own reasons for criticizing
the schools. Statements such as, "I can't believe your teacher assigned
that project," and "It's your teacher's responsibility to teach you that,
not mine!" only serve to undermine a positive working relationship and
make the child feel caught in a world of competing systems. Such
responses do not create positive learning environments, nor do they
foster the positive concept of self, family, and school, and the importance
of cooperative relationships among all three.

Utilizing systems theory within the context of child-family-school
may be an important link in addressing the current concerns regarding
the self-esteem of youngsters in our schools. By utilizing a systemic
approach within the schools, those responsible for teaching children
have an alternative way, a different "lens" through which to see and act
upon problems. As both family and school members recognize that the
problem is shared, there is less emphasis on blaming the child, which
can result in the reduction of conflict (Tucker and Dyson, 1989). By
removing blame, parents and teachers are given the opportunity to feel
less defensive and the child feels less at fault. The kindness and efficacy
of systems theory is in not finding fault, but altering communication
patterns in a way that creates a renewed harmony. The focus of this
chapter will be to familiarize the reader with a systems theory orientation
and the interactive dance of systems with systems, as well as the potential
effect it can have on learning and self-esteem. The structure of schools
and families will be addressed along with roles and responsibilities
school personnel may have in the system.

OVERVIEW OF SYSTEMS THEORY

A family system and a school system are both organizational structures. Each is composed of a set of interdependent parts (Okun and
Rappaport, 1980). A behavior that affects one part of a system has a
ripple effect upon other parts of that system and those within the system.
Families and schools can be seen as two subsystems within a larger
macrosystem, which share a common member, the child. The school,
as an institution, has roles and functions that overlap with the family.
While it is imperative that these roles and functions remain separate and
distinct, the awareness of systems theory proves to be beneficial when
attempting to understand and optimally affect the interaction between
home and school (Fine and Holt, 1983).

Historically, when school personnel viewed a child's learning or behavior problems, they focused primarily upon the individual child utilizing psychoeducational and projective assessment in addition to behavioral observations to understand intrapsychic factors influencing the child's behavior. The prevailing assumption from a Newtonian linear perspective was that the primary locus of health or pathology rested within the child. Reasons for behavior envisioned psychodynamic aspects of unresolved oedipal conflicts or behavioral aspects regarding primarily environmental factors of contingency awareness (positive or negative reinforcement and punishment). The way the interventions based on these assumptions were carried out varied, but the orientation of school staff was towards viewing the child apart from his or her family.

In contrast to the linear model, utilizing a triadic model of school, student, and family implies a circular process of causality (Minuchin, 1974; Haley, 1976; Selvini-Palazzoli et al., 1978). Each member of a family and school system influences the other and is in turn influenced by others within the system. The movement of a mobile illustrates systemic dynamics. As one section or individual part of the mobile is set in motion, it affects another, and sometimes all parts of the mobile. Change occurs for the entire unit regardless of what component is initially touched. In linear thinking, one usually has an impact at one point resulting in a chain reaction, whereas, with the mobile in mind, at any point in a circular system, change can be effected. Much like the mobile, school and family systems involve relationships that are interconnected, and a change in one part of the system affects other parts (Minuchin and Fishman, 1981). Changing from linear to more circular reasoning greatly increases the opportunity to accept responsibility for change.

Regardless of the system in question, there are rules that influence behavior, communication patterns, and information exchange, both overt and covert. From a systems perspective, a child's problematic behavior reflects the problems and stressors within and between the school and family system. Problem school behavior usually has its correlates within the home, typically helping to define the nature of family relationships (Green and Fine, 1980). From a systemic viewpoint, the child's problem does not reside solely within the intrapsychic mechanisms of the child, nor exclusively in the realm of the environment; it is born out of the interaction of the child with the systems of which he is a part.

Using a systems approach to solve problems within schools contributes to a youngster's healthy concept of self. On one level, taking the position that the problem is one of systems incongruence, rather than the fault of one member, suggests that a child's reactions may, to a large degree, be a reflection of some systemic or intersystemic imbalance. If school personnel have the knowledge of alternative strategies for understanding these family and school dynamics, less time will be spent blaming and more time attempting to alter the imbalance. The key to an improved concept of self lies not only in addressing issues of self, but of the environments in which the child lives. The child internalizes life experiences and integrates them in his or her own way, creating the essence of an individual. The phenomenological construct, self-concept, is typically communicated through functional, observable characteristics. One can evaluate these variables from a behavioral, psychoanalytic, or social perspective. However, regardless of orientation, it is difficult to ignore the impact of systems, the first of which is the family.

FAMILY SYSTEM

The family develops patterns of interacting over time. These patterns make up the family structure, which governs the functioning of family members, delineating their range of behavior and facilitating their interactions (Minuchin and Fishman, 1981). Within the family there are four major subsystems: the marital (husband and wife), parental (parent and child), sibling (child and child), and extra familial (extended family, friends, teacher, professional). The marital subsystem sets boundaries that allow the couple to take charge without intrusion from children, in-laws, and others. This subsystem also acts as a model for interaction for the children in the system. In the marital subsystem, the child learns how intimacy, conflict resolution, and support under stress is acted out.

The parental subsystem involves the childrearing and socializing functions within the family. Here the child learns what to expect from people who have greater authority, power, and strength. According to Minuchin and Fishman (1981, p. 17), the child learns which communication patterns will be effective, the family's style of dealing with conflict and negotiations, and whether to think of authority as "internal or arbitrary." In addition, Minuchin and Fishman maintain that, within the family context, the child's sense of adequacy, an important aspect of self-esteem, is shaped by the recognition of elders who may signal age appropriate behavior.

The sibling subsystem is the child's initial foray into the world of peer interaction. He or she develops patterns and styles of conflict resolution, negotiations, and the way to make friends. How they utilize those patterns and styles when interacting with the world outside the family is important in understanding the inner workings of the family. Siblings develop subsystems among themselves based on age and roles and, to a large degree, the family's expectations. These roles and expectations may cause conflict when brought into the world of the classroom.

For instance, a child who, within the family system, is in charge of younger siblings may run into problems when he tries to assert this power and authority with same-age classroom peers. Likewise, a child whose family allows and promotes aggression as a means of establishing power and position within the sibling subsystem may run into serious problems in the classroom if he uses these same techniques.

The extrafamilial subsystem can have advantageous or deleterious effects on the nuclear family. Outside influences can be a powerful source of support and nurturance to the family. However, they may also be a threat to the family's daily functioning if alliances formed between members of the family and those outside the family serve to undermine the power and authority of the spousal or parental subsystem. The family's utilization of outside influences as supports to shore up an already well-functioning family, or as a means to disguise dysfunction, is determined in part by their world views or "frames."

Family frames are the cognitive underpinnings supporting the family's transactional patterns. Frames guide how the family construes reality. They may also serve to limit or distort the system's ability to move towards more effective patterns of interaction. According to Green and Fine (1980), each family has a homeostatic ideal that maintains the family's balance. Regardless of how destructive some behaviors appear, they often serve the purpose of protecting the family from a perceived greater harm. Frames provide the rationale for the "how and why" this ideal is maintained.

For instance, problematic behavior in a child may serve as a system-maintaining device if the child's behavior helps in some way to support the spousal subsystem. The parents reinforce the behavior, drawing attention to the child and away from conflict within the spousal subsys-tem. It may seem much safer to focus on the child's behavior than on the problems between the parents, which may lead to the dissolution of the family.

There are different types of frames such as labels (he's bad, sick, crazy, disrespectful), causality (because of how his parents raised him), and family/school roles (clown, bully, scholar, troublemaker). From a school perspective, these frames may guide how school personnel view the child. How one views the problem and, thus, the intervention approach, is greatly influenced by the frames one uses. Frames also help support and define the hierarchy in a system.

In most organizations, a hierarchy exists. With regard to family structure, hierarchy is generally determined by generation. Historically, grandparents held the greatest status and power. Presently, in Western civilizations by and large, parents are accorded the most power and status, with grandparents relinquished to an auxiliary role at best and children the least amount. In systems thinking, it is essential that the hierarchical arrangement in a family be firm, with boundaries among the subsystems clearly defined. When an individual shows symptomatic behaviors, the organization has a hierarchical arrangement that is confused (Haley, 1976).

SYSTEMIC TRIANGLES

It is not uncommon for a child's family system style to clash with the classroom system style (Hansen and Okun, 1984). Children bear the brunt of any incongruence between the value system of the family and that of the school. There are various ways members within and between systems align themselves with each other that can be functional but also potentially destructive. Some of these patterns of interacting are known as triangles, coalitions, and alliances. Bowen (1976) refers to the triangle as a three-person system, which is the smallest stable relationship system. Triangulation occurs when a third person or situation is brought into a dyadic relationship (Green and Fine, 1980). A child can be a third point in a triangle involved in the family or schools dysfunctional system (Minard, 1976).

Coalitions develop when two or more people join in action and behavior against a third person. Coalitions often develop when generational boundaries are violated. Alliances are seen when two people share a common interest that does not belong to the third member of a system. Some common transactional patterns that illustrate boundary violations between school and family are as follows:

(1) *Father/Mother/Child*—Here conflicts between parents are played out by pulling the child into the interactional dance. A parent may violate generational boundaries and form a coalition with the child against the other parent. For instance, a mother and son may enter into a coalition against father, undermining father's authority. The child may also act as the scapegoat by developing symptomatic behaviors that shift the focus away from the marital discord onto himself, resulting in parents uniting to work together to help the child. While the child's behavior places him or her in a vulnerable position, it is less threatening than the fear of parental separation or divorce.

(2) *Parent/School/Child*—Conflicts that arise between parent and school involving a child invariably leave the child caught in a loyalty conflict between the two authorities. Sometimes the child's problematic behavior serves to activate the adults in both systems to resolve a particular problem. The child is often left to be the communication link between both systems.

(3) *Mother/Father/Teacher*—This usually occurs when parents are in disagreement over rules and expectations and the teacher is pulled in as the authority to side with one of the parents. This position is ripe for the teacher to respond inadvertently to the child in a manner that replicates the dysfunctional pattern within the family. For example, if the child is accustomed to aligning with the mother against father, the mother/father/teacher triangle serves to replicate a continued split in power between parents.

(4) *Teacher/Child/School*—Here the triangle involves two school personnel putting the child in the middle. Staff may have differences in opinion regarding what actions best serve the child. There is also the possibility that staff may have conflicts not related to the child, but use the child to serve some other purpose. Foster (1984) likens this to the loyalty conflicts that children experience when two parents compete for the child's affections.

In all of the previous illustrations, boundaries were violated, and members of unequal power and status form relationships against others. The boundary permeability between and among members, subsystems, and the total system determines the rigidity or flexibility of interactions not only within the family system, but also the school system. It determines what information is let into the system and how that information is handled within the system.

Boundary violations can be particularly destructive between school and family and may, when the school is trying to intervene with a child's problem behavior, inadvertently perpetuate or exacerbate the problem they were working to rectify. The beginning of a child's academic career brings an entirely new set of interactions both within the family and with the outside world that parents and child must reconcile. Parents are affected by their child's first days of school. There will be tensions related to "letting go" of the child, concerns regarding what the world will hold, and finally, coming to terms with one's own changing position as it relates to the family. There are various new roles, such as who is responsible for helping with schoolwork, getting the child ready for school in the morning, going to school meetings and after-school activities, etc. In addition, the child now brings home information about classmates' families, including rules and expectations that may seem better to the child than his or her own and that may challenge the frames by which his or her family lives.

Difficulties emerge when parents cannot resolve issues regarding responsibility or sharing the inherent duties in daily living. Often there is a "too soft" or "too hard" position taken by one parent with disagreement or abandonment by the other in determining and carrying out rules and functions. The parent may be unable to set the limits needed to demonstrate the necessary authority. In some cases, the parent may lack the patience to allow the child to explore his or her own parameters of self.

Carter and McGoldrich (1989) describe these various pressures on the family as vertical and horizontal stressors. Vertical stressors involve the family's pattern of relating, family myths, secrets, and legacies passed down through the generations. These are the notions, beliefs, frames, and life experiences both parents bring to the family.

Horizontal stressors encompass the social, economic, and daily life occurrences, along with the traumas of untimely death, chronic illness, or loss of employment—what Carter and McGoldrich (1989, p. 2) aptly describe as the "slings and arrows of outrageous fortune." While the stressors are felt throughout the life of the family, they can be especially disruptive to healthy family functioning at the various transition points along the life cycle of the family.

Even though both vertical and horizontal stressors within the family carry over to the school environment, there are at least three developmental milestones within the family life cycle that hold particular importance for school personnel: entrance into school, adolescence, and leaving school. These milestones follow, more or less, a developmental sequence over time. Because a system itself has basic needs to survive and maintain itself, it must remain fluid and be able to adapt. The way children have learned adaptability and cohesiveness in the home is also crucial for adjustment during these transitional periods.

Cohesion and adaptability are terms describing how family members interact and change over time. *Cohesion* involves the concepts of enmeshment and disengagement. Minuchin (1974) describes enmeshed families as having weak boundaries between subsystems. Enmeshed families can be categorized as overly involved and/or overly protective. Such families have difficulty allowing for a sense of individuality. Conversely, disengaged families often have rigid subsystem boundaries (Minuchin, 1974) and typically demonstrate under involvement. Well-functioning families strike a healthy balance between enmeshment and disengagement. Boundaries between subsystems remain clearly defined. While members are emotionally connected, there is encouragement in the expression of self and autonomy.

Adaptability refers to the family's ability to change over time and to overcome stressful situations. If problems occur, issues regarding system boundaries, stress, and equilibrium are typically overlooked as members of both families and schools seek out the ''cause'' of the problem. School personnel or parents may look for fault. However, instead of casting blame, progress can be made by acknowledging the lack of fit between various factors. Upon this recognition, competent patterns of functioning inherent in both systems can be called upon to work out a cooperative solution. For counselors, consultants, and teachers, it is helpful not only to be aware of the stage of development of the child's family, but also to be sensitive to where each member of the child's triad is in relation to his or her own family's development. Compatibility and understanding among systems creates a healthy network for enhancing the self-esteem of family and school members.

SCHOOL SYSTEMS

Schools are similar in administrative and personnel structure; however, in practice, there are considerable differences in how they function. Members of the school ''family'' comprise, perhaps, the most vast range of personalities, complete with interdisciplinary education, experience, goals and objectives. School's formal goals, informal norms, staff relationships, and procedures can have a differential impact on the behavior of students and teachers (Schmuck, 1974).

Like families and all other systems, schools are hierarchically organized. Viewing school personnel from a family system's perspective, principals act as the parent member of each school. They yield the most power and typically set the tone for developing norms regarding the flexibility of boundaries. There are many administrative styles. Some principals may be at the center of all educational, curricular, and disciplinary concerns. Information and advice might be sought from staff members and the principal may be highly visible in the daily working of the school. As a result of such accessibility, communication boundaries may be more permeable. Relationships that have the potential of becoming more fluid and relaxed allow more flexibility between systems, as well as between personal boundaries. Flexibility in boundaries is viewed, from a systemic standpoint, as healthier (Tucker and Dyson, 1989). Other principals may take a more distant or singular stand, leaving much of the pragmatic, day-to-day activities to the educational staff. Distant principals may not be as accessible to staff, students, or families. In this instance, a more rigid boundary may be set up between the school "family" head and staff. Principals vary, too, in how broadly or narrowly they interpret school system guidelines and rules as applicable to their own school (Foster, p. 130).

The status of other members in the school community is often determined by alignments with the principal or whomever exercises power within the school. By definition, the principal should hold the power. If this is not the case, there is likely to be a hierarchical problem resulting in boundary violations throughout the school. Any conflict regarding boundary violations or misalignments will be felt, at some point, by the entire system. Teachers are part of the larger school ecosystem, but they also represent the leadership role within individual classrooms.

The primary subsystem within the school is the teacher within the classroom. Interactions within the subsystem are related to a variety of variables, including personal and interpersonal characteristics, size of class, and amount of assistance available to the teacher. A teacher with a classroom of twenty-five students may have a different way of interacting with his or her students than a classroom teacher with an aide or two teachers "teaming" together in an expanded classroom setting.

If a teacher has difficulties developing and maintaining his or her power with the class, the effects will be felt by students who inappropriately take on too much control. The teacher's development of a professional self-concept is essential in assisting students in developing a healthy concept of self and what it means to be a student.

In addition to the classroom subsystem, there are a host of educational support staff and itinerant personnel that are often actively involved when a student demonstrates academic or behavioral concerns. The itinerant people—school psychologists, social workers, special education specialists—join with in-school counselors, teachers, and administrative staff to form another subsystem known as the Child Study Team. The different roles and types of power these individuals yield within this subsystem can be confusing and transitory depending on the focus of the intervention. For instance, a school psychologist or special education teacher may have considerable influence in a special education eligibility meeting, but have little or no influence on the daily workings of the school.

Another important member of the school community is the guidance counselor, who may be perceived as closely aligned with the student or with the teacher and/or principal. There are, again, strong implications regarding how this alignment will be felt by students as well as by other school personnel or family. The guidance counselor who may be more closely aligned with the student may be at risk of triangulation, contributing to the development of unproductive coalitions. Both counselors and teachers are much like family members who, over time, may develop a sense of possessiveness toward "their" students. This can be more a factor with counselors who follow students through a number of years of schooling, in comparison to the teacher who typically has a child in his or her classroom for one academic year. The effect of this sense of close ownership (and possibly rigid boundaries) can be seen in staff members who do not adapt well to support service intervention. If a teacher or counselor reacts strongly to assistance from a social worker, psychologist, or learning specialist, perhaps the answer lies in assessing the situation from a systemic perspective. While there are often personal and interpersonal factors to consider, thinking in a systemic manner may provide answers not otherwise considered.

Underlying any evaluation of how school personnel function is the belief that a healthy system will prove to be a productive environment in which the child can develop. Robert Chin (1976) has recognized the connection between various systems and the importance of relational issues in the helping professions. Even the "helper" can be part of the problem. He states that helpers are prone to "not see that their own systems as change agents have boundaries, tensions, stresses, equilibria, and feedback mechanisms which may be just as much part of the problem . . ." (p. 204). The helper's relationship with the student, the school, and the family affects the outcome and should be considered when analyzing the process of change.

Within the school environment, there are a variety of opportunities for a child to receive individual attention through counseling. Whether this opportunity becomes reality depends upon a complex array of variables, all of which can be viewed from a systemic "lens." As mentioned previously, school community factors, such as principal, teacher, and counselor characteristics, all play an important part in how the youngster is perceived. Intersystem variables have a strong impact on the services provided to children. How individuals work together within the system contributes to how services are delivered to the students. The way helpers view problems determines how and what type of interventions will be utilized. Typically, norms within schools are as varied as the families who attend them.

Providers of counseling services include counselors, social workers, and school psychologists. Counselors are building-level staff and often are the first to respond to initial problems. Whether referrals are made to the school psychologist depends upon the counselor's boundary definition and competence in the area of concern, as well as his or her flexibility in assessing the appropriateness of the referral. Additional factors might include the role of the psychologist, some of whom, due to time constraints or lack of counseling experience, may not choose to provide extensive counseling services. While psychologists were first employed within schools to provide mandated psychological testing, it has become a well-established practice to utilize their training in other areas. There has been an increase in school psychology training programs, recognizing the needed emphasis on primary prevention strategies such as consultation and counseling.

Counseling services have received a much needed increase in attention; however, assessment of a child's academic progress has remained in the forefront. Throughout a child's years in school, he or she undergoes countless evaluations. In addition to day-to-day assessment through homework and class work, there are exams and national standardized tests that are required. There are also times when staff find it necessary to complete individual assessment of a youngster's cognitive and emotional status. It is helpful to remember, when considering the makeup of an individual, that behaviors and experiences arise out of a social, intersystemic context. The current trend in psychological testing is to provide an ecological component that assists in validating a youngster's social and emotional functioning. It has long been the practice and is a requirement for schools to include an adaptive, social component when assessing the skills of mentally handicapped students. In addition, the increase in numbers of students diagnosed with attention deficit disorders has contributed to an increase in behavioral rating scales, often completed by both school and family. Likewise, with evaluations of children occurring at age two or younger, there has been an increase in realizing the importance of the family component. All attempts at evaluating a child through the eyes of both school and family contribute to the improved understanding of self-esteem and how and why a child functions as he or she does.

There are now concerns emerging within the schools regarding training of staff to address multicultural issues. It is important to consider the cultural variations and the potential barriers that may exist within the school setting and between school and home. Cummins (1986) suggests that attempts to decrease the minority student's rate of failure within schools has been largely due to the fact that programs have been ineffective in altering the relationships between educators and minority students and between schools and minority communities. He goes on to say that the existing pathology is not within the student, but within the "societal power relations" between dominant and dominated people.

From a system's perspective, the school does present a potentially different world to many minority students. The obvious ethnic, racial, and cultural factors give way to the more subtle differences which may influence children and youth. According to Pedersen (1988), culture, much like a network of traits, is located within a person. School staff need to identify a student's "cultural disposition" in order to communicate appropriately and accurately (Pedersen, 1988). Breakdown in communication often results between members of the same culture, but often becomes exacerbated between individuals of different racial or ethnic backgrounds (Sue, 1981). Awareness of one's own culturally learned assumptions is the first step to increasing multicultural knowledge. Multicultural awareness and knowledge increases an individual's intentional decision making by accounting for the many ways that culture influences different perceptions of the same situation (Pedersen, 1988). Staff members need to be aware of their own values and be flexible in adapting to cultural differences.

Given the importance of not only an individual staff member's role, but that of the family, child, and additional school staff, one begins to understand the breadth of study involved in understanding how all participants influence the development of the child. The following case illustrations were chosen to highlight typical student-family-school interactions. Following each description of a case are interpretations utilizing a systems approach to effect change.

CASE ILLUSTRATION 1

This first illustration is an example of how dysfunction in the family boundary can cause behaviors that may be mistaken for learning and behavioral difficulties.

Jason, a ten-year-old fourth grader, was referred for a special education evaluation because of suspected learning problems and disruptive behavior in the classroom. According to his classroom teacher, Jason was "frequently cutting up" when he wasn't daydreaming. Jason performed within the gifted range cognitively on standardized tests but was barely passing his courses. He was described as disorganized and forgetful, and his teacher was concerned about the presence of Attention Deficit Hyperactive Disorder (ADHD), in addition to a learning disability.

In spite of Jason's classroom behavior, his teacher was very nurturing towards Jason and often looked after him in his dealings with other school staff. It was clear she genuinely liked him. Jason's mother was viewed by the classroom teacher as "excitable" and somewhat intrusive, in that she frequently (sometimes three times a week) dropped in on the classroom to deliver something Jason forgot at home. She frequently tried to engage the teacher in a mini-conference regarding Jason's difficulties, which served to take the teacher away from the rest of her class. After Jason nearly failed the first marking period, a parent/teacher conference was requested, and the guidance counselor was asked to attend as a consultant.

As Jason's family entered the room, the consultant was able to get a visual picture of some of the family dynamics and could then begin to generate a hypothesis. Jason's father entered the room first and sat approximately four feet away from the rest of the family. Jason followed with his mother's arm on his shoulder and Jason's five-year-old sister skipping happily behind. Jason's parents seemed personable, articulate, and concerned about Jason's school difficulties.

After the social amenities were completed and the parents thanked for attending, the guidance counselor asked the classroom teacher to describe her concerns. The parents were then asked how they viewed the problems. Jason's father, Mr. D., spoke first, indicating that his employment took him away from home for days at a time and that, while the frequency was much less than it used to be, he was still gone a few weeks each month. Jason's mother reported the difficulties of "running a household on her own." She described a special closeness to Jason and felt like, in the first five years of Jason's life, it was just the two of them.

Mr. D. then explained he was confused about Jason's behavior in school in that he didn't experience similar problems with him and felt that his wife and, perhaps, the classroom teacher might be "too soft" with Jason. Mrs. D. felt her husband was "too hard," laughingly stating Jason is "still my baby." Mrs. D. was also well-read in the areas of learning disabilities (LD) and ADHD and shared the teacher's concerns.

Throughout the interview, Mr. D. often spoke for his wife and Jason when a question was directed at either of them and seemed disinterested when his wife did speak. When Jason's parents were asked to question Jason regarding how he viewed what was going on, Jason said that, while he loved his mother and really liked his teacher, they both "kinda nagged him all the time." Both women agreed that it felt like they were "after him all the time."

At this point, the guidance counselor asked the parents if Jason and his sister would leave the room while the adults decided what to do next. The counselor then asked if some other ideas could be tried before a formal evaluation for LD-ADHD was initiated and asked the parents if they had any ideas about how to change Jason's behavior.

Mr. D. volunteered to keep in contact with the teacher and asked for progress reports. Mrs. D. was complimented by the guidance counselor for the hard work she'd done with Jason, but it was suggested that she not rescue Jason's forgetfulness and that the teacher need not stay "on top of him." Since Mr. D. volunteered to take a more central and active role in Jason's school performance, the teacher and Mrs. D. were asked by the counselor if they would be willing to help Mr. D. in developing reasonable positive and negative consequences, which Mr. D. would enforce. Mr. D. was asked if he would be willing to hear and incorporate their suggestions.

After agreement was reached among the parents and teacher, Jason was called back into the room and the parents explained the plan. It was further volunteered by the counselor that he meet with the parents over the next few weeks and that the counselor would also meet with the classroom teacher.

This illustration demonstrates a family system where an alliance was formed between mother and son. The original hypothesis assumed the mother was overly involved (enmeshed) with her son and the father was distant. Through the course of consultation with the family, the father was asked to take a more active role, thus allowing the mother a less active one. Likewise, it was seen that the teacher inadvertently replicated some of the same patterns of interaction that Mrs. D. displayed.

Another hypothesis generated from the first case study is based on the assumption that, when a child presents a problem, it is because his or her parents do not agree on some issue. By creating a problem, the parents are pushed to focus on the child rather than their own conflicts. Madanes (1981) suggests that, when a child demonstrates a problem, it can aid the parents in an indirect way. The child's authority is exaggerated in relation to the parents and a hierarchy problem surfaces. Helping the parents to resolve the problem by getting their agreement on a solution puts them back in charge, thereby reestablishing the hierarchy.

It was speculated that a problem between the parents was the lack of emotional intimacy. With the father being away, it was easy for this to form. Once formed, it was easy to perpetuate, and the child was caught in the middle. Over time, the consultant made a recommendation to the family to address these issues. In addition, the mother's frame of Jason being the baby was reframed by the counselor as follows, "By allowing him to be the baby," he doesn't have to take you or himself seriously. Through individual consultation with the classroom teacher, the same message was conveyed to move away from the label of "impaired" (LD-ADHD).

Over the course of the year, Mrs. D. was encouraged to get involved in other activities at school that did not directly involve her with her son's classroom or academic performance. As the relationship between Mr. and Mrs. D. reestablished itself, Mrs. D. did not find it necessary to interact with the school as frequently and developed other enjoyable interests. Jason passed the school year with honors.

CASE ILLUSTRATION 2

Situations arise within the school setting where coalitions and alliances work against the best interests of the child.

Mary, an eleven-year-old child, was first referred to the school's child study team by her classroom teacher and the guidance counselor because of poor motivation and behavioral problems. The counselor presented the case to the team, indicating she was representing the first-year classroom teacher (who was in attendance). Given the teacher's presence, it was unusual that she did nct speak for herself. This is suggestive of a hierarchical problem among staff members, with possible overinvolvement on the part of the counselor resulting in taking too much ownership of Mary's problem. This was particularly evident, given that the primary concern was the youngster's academic performance.

Reportedly, Mary seldom completed her work in class and never returned homework assignments. She was described as a sullen youngster who argued with teachers and peers. She often sat in class with her head on her desktop, making no attempts to follow class directions.

The teacher and counselor had met with Mary's mother on one previous occasion; however, the counselor was reluctant to contact her again because, according to Mary, her mother hit and starved her whenever a bad report came home from school. Instead of continued contact with Mary's mother, Mrs. H., the counselor met with Mary daily. The child study team recommended a second meeting and requested that the school psychologist attend.

On the day of the appointment, only Mary's mother arrived, explaining that her husband was unable to leave work. It was immediately evident that Mrs. H. was angry. She folded her arms, clenched her jaw, and sat in silence, waiting for one of the school personnel to speak. The school psychologist thanked her for attending and expressed hope that now that Mrs. H. was here, a solution could be found. Mrs. H. was then asked how she viewed Mary's difficulties.

Mrs. H. described her husband as having a problem with alcohol. Reportedly, he was generally unavailable and distant when it came to family concerns. An older daughter had dropped out of school, and Mrs. H. expressed concern that Mary was "headed down the same road." She indicated she didn't want Mary to quit school, but feared her daughter was lazy and disrespectful, and the school staff unable to effect change.

The school psychologist reframed Mary's laziness and anger as being sad about her father and worried for her mother. When the school psychologist asked the consequences if Mary refused to do her work, Mrs. H. responded that she placed restrictions on Mary and took away privileges. She stated her husband was sometimes abusive when drunk, and she did not want her children further exposed to violence; therefore, she tended to handle problems herself.

The counselor offered information regarding Mary's account of "beatings and starvation" when uncomplimentary reports were sent home regarding her school performance. Mrs. H. explained that the "beating" was a spanking for Mary being disrespectful, and the "starving" on another occasion was being sent to her room without dinner because of disobeying her mother.

Mrs. H. was also concerned that Mary's daily visits to the school counselor were taking her out of the classroom more than was necessary. While the counselor was reluctant to relinquish seeing Mary, all agreed to a two-week trial period of Mary staying in the classroom. The reluctance on the part of the counselor was indicative of the degree to which the counselor was inducted into a dysfunctional coalition with Mary. Imposing distance between the child and the counselor equalized and realigned the relationship between parent, guidance counselor, and teacher.

The school psychologist asked Mrs. H. and the counselor if they would be willing to work together in developing alternatives to corporal punishment that both the school personnel and Mrs. H. could use consistently. Since Mrs. H. wanted to be kept informed regarding Mary's school performance, the teacher agreed to contact Mrs. H. on a weekly basis or at any time Mrs. H. felt something was amiss.

Mrs. H. and the teacher developed a behavioral plan with Mary's input, and it was understood that Mrs. H. and the classroom teacher could adjust and/or modify the plan as needed. Mary was presented the contract and asked to sign. This united presentation was used to demonstrate agreement among all parties.

A follow-up meeting was planned for four weeks later. Mary still struggled with classroom work, but she stayed with the tasks at hand and stories about starvation and abuse did not resurface. At a subsequent meeting with Mrs. H., the school psychologist recommended that she and Mary seek assistance in dealing with Mr. H's alcoholism and the impact it had on the family.

In the preceding scenario, a coalition had formed between the guidance counselor and the child against the mother. The classroom teacher appeared virtually powerless and was often excluded. Although the counselor had Mary's "best interests" at heart, her overinvolvement was intrusive to both the mother and the teacher. It helped maintain a wedge between mother and daughter and suggested to Mary that she needed protection against her mother. The effect increased the stress between the mother-daughter subsystem. Furthermore, the counselor's actions implied that she perceived incompetence on the part of mother, teacher, and child. This is antithetic to systems thinking, which is based on the belief that families and teachers are capable of finding effective solutions together. By her lack of communication with Mrs. H., the counselor inadvertently undermined the mother's power and authority for maintaining family loyalty and cohesiveness.

Consequently, when the counselor was able to hear Mrs. H.'s concern for her daughter, she was able to give up her central position with Mary. By having the plan developed by the adults present with Mary's input, it placed the mother back in control of her daughter and the teacher back in the role of expert in her field. Encouraging direct communication between the teacher and Mrs. H. forced Mary to take responsibility for her own learning and decreased the possibility of miscommunication between the systems when relayed through the child.

While nothing was done directly with the family, acknowledging mother as the expert regarding her daughter and the teacher as expert in the classroom, the hierarchy for these collaborative efforts was established. This allowed the daughter to remove herself from the middle and free the tension of divided loyalties between mother and counselor.

As the previous case studies demonstrate, any initial meeting between parents and school personnel regarding a child's problem behavior or learning difficulties should be arranged to establish interaction patterns within and among family and school systems. The self-esteem issues affecting school performance can then be seen as requiring shared ownership among several parties, rather than the result of one child's psychological dispositions.

The following questions have been helpful in generating effective strategies to reach cooperative solutions, rather than inadvertently contributing to the maintenance of the problem.

(1) What are the boundary and hierarchical definitions of the family? Are they too permeable or too rigid? Do they let information and people into the system or are they closed?
(2) What coalitions, alliances, or triangles have occurred?
(3) How differentiated is the family? Is it enmeshed or disengaged?
(4) What are the family's or school personnel's world views? How do they frame the problem?

(5) What purpose does the behavior have in maintaining the family? What function does it serve and who gains or loses if it is changed?

(6) What strengths or competencies in the family or school personnel can be utilized?

CONCLUSIONS

Once family and school communication networks are understood more clearly, utilization of a systems approach enables school personnel and members of the helping profession to move beyond an encapsulated view of the child within the school. Using an intersystem model shows recognition of the impact of environment upon the youngster. Tucker and Dyson (1989) suggest that bringing family and school together in developing a solution unburdens the child and reinforces the importance of the two systems.

When there is a heightened sense of conflict or lack of cohesiveness, the sense of one's self and one's fit with the world is disrupted. The result can be a threat to one's concept of self. In *A Humanistic Psychology of Education—Making the School Everybody's House,* Schmuck (1974) proposes that a major challenge for schools is to confront the student's conflicts, which are viewed as normal reactions to anxiety and problems in life, in a constructive and creative manner.

Whereas school personnel are at risk of feeling helpless in effecting change due to what they perceive as familial dysfunction in a child's life, parents may feel that educational and social issues are at the root of their child's adjustment problems. Tucker and Dyson (1989) suggest that families often view schools as "one undifferentiated mass that represents authority." School personnel would do well to remember that parents arrive at their child's school with memories of their own school experiences. From a systemic perspective parents enter school doors with their own family becoming part of a different, larger system. Once the child is at school, the interaction between systems creates a shift in the world of the child, parent, and school members. This shift can often be painful for all involved, and occasionally results in dysfunctional behavior on the part of one or more members.

Within the school environment, staff members who have a constructive plan for viewing and working with issues feel a greater sense of empowerment. They realize that there are alternative ways of addressing problems. In addition, because members of the system know that sole ownership of problems is not realistic, their feelings of isolation and hopelessness decrease, thus creating a more cohesive and supportive workplace. Students certainly benefit from a climate of camaraderie in their school environment.

Using a systemic approach is one way of recognizing the importance of all the pieces of a youngster's life and creatively addressing the issues of youth. While there has been no published research providing information on how utilizing a system's approach within the schools contributes to a healthy sense of self, the practical application of respecting and responding to all components of a child's life certainly reflects a more humanistic approach to education. A systemic approach assumes that each family is competent to effect change and resolve problems. The marriage of family and school reflects how systems merge to effect change within the child. If the goal of school is to contribute to the healthy development of a youngster's capabilities and values, then the major family and school resources, as well as the mediating factors (e.g., quality of interaction between the resources), should be viewed as essential in that development.

REFERENCES

Aponte, H. 1974. "The Family-School Interview: An Eco-Structural Approach," *Family Process,* 15:303 – 311.

Bowen, M. 1976. *Family Therapy in Clinical Practice.* New York, NY: Jason Aronson.

Carter, B. and M. McGoldrich, eds. 1989. *The Changing Family Life Cycle.* Needham, MA: Allyn & Bacon.

Chin, R. 1976. "The Utility of System Models and Developmental Models for Practitioners," in *The Planning of Change: Readings in the Applied Behavioral Sciences,* W. G. Bennis, K. D. Benne, and Robert Chin, eds., New York, NY: Holt, Rinehart & Winston, pp. 201 – 214.

Cummins, J. 1986. "Empowering Minority Students; A Framework for Intervention," *Harvard Educational Review,* 56(1):18 – 36.

Fine, M. and P. Holt. 1983. "Intervening with School Problems: A Family Systems Perspective," *Psychology in the Schools* (January):20.

Foster, M. A. 1984. "Schools," In *Practicing Family Therapy in Diverse Settings,* M. Berger and Associates, San Francisco, CA: Jossey-Bass, pp. 110 – 141.

Green, K. and M. Fine. 1980. "Family Therapy: A Case for Training for School Pathologists," *Psychology in the Schools,* 17:241 – 248.

Haley, J. 1976. *Problem-Solving Therapy: New Strategies for Effective Family Therapy.* San Francisco, CA: Jossey-Bass.

Hansen, J. C. and B. Okun. 1983. *Family Therapy with School Related Problems.* Rockville, MS: Aspen Publications.

Madanes, C. 1981. *Strategic Family Therapy.* San Francisco, CA: Jossey-Bass.

Minard, S. 1976. "Family Systems Model in Organizational Consultation: Vignettes of Consultation to a Day-Care Center," *Family Process,* 15:313—320.

Minuchin, S. 1974. *Families and Family Therapy.* Cambridge, MA: Harvard University Press.

Minuchin, S. and C. Fishman. 1981. *Family Therapy Techniques.* Cambridge, MA: Harvard University Press.

Okun, B. and L. Rappaport. 1980. *Working with Families: An Introduction to Family Therapy.* North Scituate, MA: Duxbury Press.

Pedersen, P. 1988. *A Handbook for Developing Multicultural Awareness.* Alexandria, VA: American Association for Counseling and Development.

Schmuck, R. A. and A. Patricia. 1974. *A Humanistic Psychology of Education—Making the School Everybody's House.* Palo Alto, CA: National Press.

Selvini-Palazzoli, M., G. Cecchin, G. Prata, and L. Boscolo. 1978. *Paradox and Counter Paradox.* New York, NY: Jason Aronson.

Sue, D. W. 1981. *Counseling the Culturally Different: Theory and Practice.* New York, NY: John Wiley and Sons, Inc.

Tucker, B. Z. and E. Dyson. 1989. "The Family and the School: Utilizing Human Resources to Promote Learning," *Family Process,* 15:125—414.

CHAPTER 6

The Assessment of Self-Esteem

SANDRA B. WARD — *The College of William and Mary*
THOMAS J. WARD — *The College of William and Mary*

THE assessment of children's and adolescents' well-being typically includes an evaluation of social and emotional adjustment, with a heavy emphasis placed on self-concept and self-esteem. However, the literature in this area does not offer consistent or universally accepted definitions of terms (Byrne, 1983). Definitions vary without consensus and remain vague, which seriously limits the generalizability of research findings and the validity with which we can measure these constructs (Alsaker and Olweus, 1986; Benner et al., 1983). Reliable and valid assessment is critical because it is the process through which we obtain information about individuals in order to specify strengths and weaknesses and develop treatment plans. Thus, the interpretation of scores from measures and subsequent recommendations can have long-lasting effects upon students' self-esteem. This chapter describes a variety of techniques used to measure self-esteem, delineating advantages and disadvantages. Drawing upon the strengths of the various approaches, a multifaceted model of evaluation will be presented.

Hamachek's (1988) distinctions between self and self-concept will be used as a basis for understanding the assessment terminology used in this chapter. For Hamachek, the self refers to one's sense of personal being. Self-concept is the cognitive awareness of the self or the way people imagine how they appear to others. Self-esteem refers to the extent to which one values oneself, or the judgment one makes about one's self-concept (Beane and Lipka, 1986). In addition, Damon and Hart's (1982) analysis of self-esteem as having positive and negative affective orientations is a useful extension of these definitions.

A review of literature on self-concept and self-esteem supports the premise that the feelings children and adolescents hold about themselves are related to a number of constructs. Positive self-esteem was related to greater expectations for success and higher school achievement (Damon and Hart, 1982; Gilberts, 1983; Johnson et al., 1983). Gilberts

(1983) reported self-concept to be positively related to physical health and overall psychological adjustment. Self-esteem was also found to influence social relationships (Damon and Hart, 1982).

Given the relationship between self-esteem and intellectual, social, and psychological functioning, it is critical for healthcare professionals, teachers, and parents to understand the important role they play in the development of positive self-esteem in children and adolescents. In order to understand this role, however, it is necessary first to understand what is being measured and whether or not what is purported to be measured is being assessed with reliable and valid instruments. A careful scrutiny of the assessment process will provide a greater understanding of the utility of the measures and meaningfulness of the results. Careful assessment should produce a description of the individual's functioning, including feelings and behaviors, which can be used to develop treatment plans that promote positive mental health and social adjustment. Without such scrutiny the children and youth we are supposed to be helping may be adversely affected by programs based on misdiagnosed needs.

DEVELOPMENTAL ISSUES IN THE ASSESSMENT OF SELF-ESTEEM

Psychosocial theorists have contributed to our understanding of how the conception of self changes with development. Between three and eight months of age, infants can recognize themselves via contingency cues. For example, babies will respond to the sound of a parent's voice. It is not until fifteen to twenty-four months of age that they are able to distinguish themselves from others and become aware of their capabilities and physical characteristics (Damon and Hart, 1982). In early childhood individuals distinguish the self on the basis of physical appearance and activities. Around eight years of age, children begin to see the self as separate from body parts and realize the influence of subjective thoughts and feelings on behavior. The young adolescent demonstrates an increase in self-awareness and reflection, but it is not until later adolescence that a more abstract underlying dimension of the self is conceived to influence behavior. At this level one believes that unconscious mental experiences can influence actions, and no one can comprehend one's experience as fully as oneself (Damon and Hart, 1982).

This developmental sequence has serious ramifications for measures of self-esteem. It is essential to incorporate the changing conception of the self and self-understanding into such measures. For example, items for younger children should center around physical features, situations, and activities. Introspection on thoughts and feelings can be expected in later childhood and early adolescence. Not until later adolescence will items successfully tap the more abstract evaluations of the self.

Unfortunately, many instruments commonly used to assess self-esteem do not reflect the developmental changes of self-understanding, and little attention is given to this issue in the interpretation of results. Too frequently, the same items are used for age ranges from early childhood to later adolescence. Even when different scales are used for different age levels, there is considerable overlap of item content. Additionally, the age groupings are too broad. For example, clustering ages eight to fifteen on one scale ignores the differences between later childhood and early adolescence. Many scales require advanced verbal skills to complete the task and expect students to read an item and keep it in memory while deciding the degree to which it is descriptive. Younger children and those with lower ability have not yet reached the level of cognitive development that enables them to successfully process information in this manner (Byrne, 1983). The extent to which we can describe self-esteem through self-reporting measures by younger children requires closer examination.

Alsaker and Olweus (1986) attempted to extend the Rosenberg's Self-Esteem Scale downward to early adolescence. They eliminated four items that were deemed more suitable for adolescents and adults than for children and added two items to assess general lack of satisfaction with oneself. Their research established preliminary reliability and validity data for the measure. More studies of this nature are needed to ensure that instruments measure appropriate constructs at different age levels. However, the use of different instruments with individuals of various age levels raises the issue of whether the instruments are measuring the same construct. It is possible that the factor structure of the various measures will not remain stable. If this proves to be the case, then such differences must be considered when interpreting results, so that readers are not misled by general descriptions of children's and adolescents' self-esteem.

CURRENT PRACTICES IN THE ASSESSMENT OF SELF-ESTEEM

Types of Measures and Their Use

Self-esteem is assessed through a variety of techniques, including projective measures, rating scales, and behavior checklists. Although the instruments exhibit a great deal of diversity, some common components have been identified and include physical, social, personal, family, school, peer, and behavioral aspects of the individual. Typically, these elements are measured by statements reflecting self-worth, personal competence, and aspirations (Gilberts, 1983).

Projective techniques allow individuals to assign their own thoughts and feelings to neutral stimuli. In other words, individuals reveal aspects of their personalities in their responses. Drawings are a popular projective technique to assess self-esteem. Such measures include the Draw-a-Person Test, the House-Tree-Person Test, and the Draw-a-Family Test. The drawings are analyzed according to a number of criteria, including line quality, size and placement of figures, overall organization and symmetry, amount of detail, distortions, and behavioral observations. The incomplete sentence technique is another common projective measure in which examinees are requested to complete unfinished sentences. Their responses are expected to reveal underlying thoughts and feelings about themselves and significant others. Despite their widespread use, interpretation of projective measures involves considerable intuition and clinical impressions. Reliability and validity data for these techniques are usually insufficient and too low for making diagnostic decisions about children and adolescents, and many lack adequate standardization norms (Salvia and Ysseldyke, 1991).

Self-report measures of self-esteem require individuals to evaluate themselves and complete items regarding their personal thoughts and feelings. The measures follow a similar format whereby examinees respond to declarative statements by indicating the degree to which the content is descriptive of themselves. Coopersmith's Self-Esteem Inventories (1981) are commonly used and consist of a School Form (ages eight to fifteen) and Adult Form (ages sixteen and over). Examples of items from the School Form include "I have a low opinion of myself," and "I'm proud of my schoolwork," to which the examinee responds "Like me" or "Unlike me." The Piers-Harris Children's Self-Concept Scale (1984) is a self-report measure developed for grades four through twelve. Children circle "Yes" or "No" to items such as "My looks bother me," and "I am a good person" (Piers and Harris, 1969). The Self-Esteem Scale by Rosenberg (1965) was designed specifically to assess self-esteem in adolescents. This ten-item instrument requires students to rate items such as, "I feel that I have a number of good qualities," and "I certainly feel useless at times," on a four-point Likert scale from Strongly Agree to Strongly Disagree. Generally, the reliability of popular self-report measures of self-esteem is suitable for screening purposes only, which means that diagnostic decisions should not be made on the basis of this data alone. Additionally, the reliability of individual items is considerably lower, which warrants caution against overinterpretation of separate items. Systematic validation of these measures is needed in order to establish predictive and construct validity (Beitchman and Corradini, 1988; Byrne, 1983; Gilberts, 1983; Mc-Loughlin and Lewis, 1990).

Behavior checklists are also available to assess various aspects of self-esteem. These are typically completed by someone familiar with the child such as parents and/or teachers who rate the extent to which the child exhibits certain behaviors believed to be related to self-esteem. The Behavioral Academic Self-Esteem Scale (BASE) (Coopersmith and Gilberts, 1981) is part of the Coopersmith Self-Esteem Inventories and is completed by an observer to provide behavioral indicators of academic self-esteem in children from kindergarten through eighth grade. Items were developed to tap student initiative, social attraction, and self-confidence. There is some evidence for reliable use of the BASE (Johnson et al., 1983).

The teacher rating scale of The Self-Perception Profile for Children (Harter, 1985) requires the teacher to rate the child's actual behavior and adequacy in five domains: scholastic competence, social acceptance, athletic competence, physical appearance, and behavioral conduct. The scale consists of fifteen items such as, "This child usually acts appropriately, or this child would be better if s/he acted differently," and "This child has a lot of friends, or this child doesn't have many friends." The teacher decides what kind of child the student is like, then rates whether the statement is somewhat true or very true of the student. Specific information on the psychometric properties of this rating scale, including reliability, validity, and standardization, are not provided. Consequently, the meaningfulness of results cannot be determined. Nevertheless, the overall advantage of behavior checklists is that they offer the opportunity for input from different sources regarding individuals' self-esteem and, because of their specificity, may reduce the likeliness of ambiguity due to rater subjectivity.

The use of these measures of self-esteem is as important as the instruments themselves. Assessment is the process of collecting data for the purpose of making decisions about individuals (Salvia and Ysseldyke, 1991) and should therefore reflect sensitivity to the complexity of psychological constructs. Testing is a part of assessment but constitutes only one source of information. Administration of a battery of instruments using multiple techniques is generally recommended to fully assess an individual's needs and enhance the reliability of the evaluation (Sattler, 1988). It is important that the battery include different sources of information and reflect behaviors across a number of settings.

Unfortunately, current practice in the assessment of self-esteem relies heavily on administration of a single self-report measure and/or projective techniques with limited technical adequacy. There is minimal consideration of situation specific behaviors or the influence of the environment on self-esteem. Little use is made of behavioral observations despite findings that observational estimates of self-esteem are frequently better predictors of behavior than self-reports (Gilberts, 1983).

The reliance on single measures seriously limits the reliability and validity of diagnostic decisions. Test results may simply indicate positive or negative global self-esteem and offer few suggestions for treatment. Consequently, recommendations for remediation in a variety of contexts remain vague. In addition, there is often no follow-through with the prescribed course of action, nor is there an evaluation procedure to accompany the intervention plan.

Furthermore, limited data exists on the equivalence across instruments, so it is unknown whether they are actually measuring the same constructs (Benner et al., 1983). In other words, results from one instrument may not mean the same thing as results from another instrument, despite similarity in titles and content. An individual's evaluation of self-esteem may vary as a function of the instrument. Therefore, it is important to reference the instrument used when describing an individual's measured self-esteem and to interpret results cautiously. Another factor that may introduce variability to the results of self-esteem measures is subjectivity and bias of the rater.

Disparity between Self-Perceptions and Others' Perceptions

The majority of scales designed to measure self-esteem include primarily self-report or third-party ratings. Given parents' closeness and familiarity with their children, they are logical evaluators of behavior and are frequently asked to complete rating scales of self-esteem. Parents represent valuable sources of information about the child's relationships with family members, peer relationships, and behaviors at home. Children also spend considerable time in school, which makes the teacher(s) another important source of information about academic performance, peer relations, and classroom behaviors.

When studying behaviors across settings, it is often useful to obtain information from a variety of people. However, potential sources of bias must also be examined in the interpretation of results. Research findings have indicated that teachers tend to view children they feel close to more positively. Emotional bias becomes apparent when teacher ratings of self-esteem merely reflect the teachers' own perceptions of the student. For example, Itskowitz, Navon, and Strauss (1988) found a gap between teachers' ratings of self-esteem and the children's self-reports. The inaccuracy of the teachers' ratings was directly related to perceived closeness with the children. In another study parents and teachers rated students' self-esteem higher than the students rated themselves (Ensink and Carroll, 1989). Beitchman and Corradini (1988) reported nonsystematic overestimation and underestimation of children's self-esteem by parents. Parents' variability in evaluating their children's self-esteem could not be explained by any one factor, nor were their evaluations biased in a single direction.

A question often asked regarding the limitations of third-party reports of self-esteem is whether parents and teachers can accurately infer self-esteem from behavior. If one believes that no one understands one's experience as completely as oneself, then the best source of information is the individual. Therefore, it is equally important to tap the child's and adolescent's point of view in order to understand his/her genuine feelings. For regardless of what others may say, the individual's perceptions of self can be tenaciously protected as stated in Chapter Seven. Great disparity between self-reports and third-party ratings, however, can be indicative of a number of factors. There could be third-party bias or an unrealistic self-image on the part of the individual in question. It is also possible that there are genuine differences of opinion regarding what constitutes appropriate or inappropriate behavior. In school settings, for example, what is perceived as inappropriate behavior by the classroom teacher may be perceived as healthy and appropriate by the parent, or vice versa. In either case, these inconsistencies suggest a need for further analysis.

Another common problem inherent in self-report measures is social desirability effects. This refers to answering questions the way one thinks they should be answered to be socially acceptable. Brody et al. (1990) found that reports of self-esteem were influenced by prior completion of questionnaires. This suggests that reporting negative memories, focusing attention on the self, and mental fatigue may adversely affect the reliability and validity of self-report instruments. In some cases the mere act of having to take a battery of tests may adversely affect students' self-esteem.

Given the findings that self-ratings differ from teacher and parent ratings the question remains, "Which reflects the individual's true self-esteem?" This question is not easily answered, but the importance of utilizing multiple measures with a variety of sources is highlighted. Even if the individual is deemed the best source of information about inner feelings, children and adolescents may be unwilling to reveal such aspects of themselves. Their responses may be influenced by social desirability effects or the lack of abstract thinking skills required of the task. Information obtained from parents and teachers can supplement children's reports and assist in arriving at accurate diagnoses. Therefore, the interpretation of results must not place undue emphasis on one source over another.

Multidimensional Assessment of Self-Esteem

As mentioned previously, a central problem in the measurement of self-esteem is the lack of validity among the various instruments. This is likely related to the issue of vague and inconsistent definitions of the construct or the dimension of self-esteem, which the instrument purports to measure. Further complicating the matter is acceptance of the multi-dimensional nature of self-concept but differing opinions on the extent to which the different dimensions can be measured separately (Byrne, 1983).

Harter (1985) attempted to specify the different dimensions of general self-esteem and reduce social desirability effects evident on many self-report scales. The Self-Perception Profile for Children (Harter, 1985) was developed for children in grades three through six. As noted previously, the measure consists of five domains: scholastic competence, athletic competence, social acceptance, physical appearance, and behavioral conduct, as well as a global self-worth scale. Students are asked to choose which sort of child typifies their own behavior. Examples of items include "Some kids find it hard to make friends, but other kids find it's pretty easy to make friends," and "Some kids like the kind of person they are, but other kids often wish they were someone else." Children are asked to decide which kind of kid is most like them, and then determine whether the statement is sort of true or really true of themselves.

The manual reports reliability coefficients of the separate scales to be in the range acceptable for screening purposes. Validity data support the scale structure in grades five and six; however, results for younger children must be interpreted with caution since a different factor structure emerges (Harter, 1985). It appears that the test does not measure the same dimensions at the younger age levels.

The School Form of the Coopersmith Self-Esteem Inventories (1981) consists of five subscales: general self, social self—peers, home-parents, school-academics, and a lie scale. The lie scale is included to determine the truthfulness of the individual's responses. A total score is obtained from the sum of all subscales except the lie scale. Consequently, this measure provides information about general self-esteem as well as specific attributes. The reliability of the individual subscales is relatively low compared to that of the total score, which was adequate for screening purposes only. Therefore, interpretation of the scores from the subscales must be made with caution.

Although the Piers-Harris Children's Self-Concept Scale (1984) was designed to be a unidimensional measure, the manual refers to six cluster scales, which can be scored from the responses, in addition to a total score. The clusters include behavior, intellectual and school status, physical appearance and attributes, anxiety, popularity, and happiness and satisfaction. These clusters represent an attempt by the authors to distinguish the different dimensions of self-esteem, but the technical data do not support the validity of these clusters as separate factors. Therefore, it is recommended to focus on the total score when interpreting results.

Roid and Fitts (1988) developed the Tennessee Self-Concept Scale to assess the following areas of self-concept: identity, satisfaction, behavior, physical, moral-ethical, personal, family, and social. The total test and subscale scores have adequate reliability for clinical uses. The largest barrier to the use of the Tennessee Self-Concept Scale is that it was designed for use with those age twelve and older, which severely limits its application to the entire range of school-age populations.

The Self-Esteem Index (Brown and Alexander, 1990) is an eighty-item instrument designed for use with children ages eight to nineteen. The Self-Esteem Index (SEI) breaks self-esteem into the following subscales: familial acceptance, academic competence, peer popularity, and personal security. The SEI has total and subscale reliabilities adequate for clinical and research uses. The SEI is also one of a few tests in this area that has been standardized on a national sample. Although the SEI is technically stronger than most of the other tests discussed, it does not provide for interpretation beyond norm-referencing scores.

The Multidimensional Self Concept Scale (Bracken, 1992) is a 150-item instrument designed for use with ages nine to nineteen. The MSCS measures self-concept in the following domains: social, competence, affect, academic, family, and physical. The total and subscale reliabilities are adequate for clinical and diagnostic purposes. In addition to providing standard scores based on a national sample, the MSCS also provides information on test interpretation. Although the MSCS is a promising new measure, more research is necessary on its validity and practical application as a diagnostic tool.

A primary advantage of scales that specify the separate dimensions of self-esteem is the ability to investigate different attributes of self-esteem across different situations. It is possible to discern whether an individual evaluates themselves more positively with regard to academic competence, athletic competence, or peer acceptance. It may be that an individual with an overall low rating of self-esteem may actually feel academically competent but socially unaccepted. The global measures of self-esteem are unidimensional and do not consider the situation specificity of self-esteem. Unfortunately, the psychometric properties of many scales that purport to assess the different dimensions of self-esteem are not adequate to justify use of the instrument.

The Utility of Measures of Self-Esteem

As indicated in the previous sections, the multiple definitions and perspectives used by those investigating self-esteem have led to the availability of numerous scales for the assessment of self-esteem. A question that is likely to arise is which of these scales is best for measuring self-esteem. Unfortunately, there is no easy answer to this question since the scales in question are not parallel.

One way of determining the best self-esteem measure is to ask the question of intended use. It is apparent from the descriptions of measures provided by the authors who developed them that the scales have different purposes and thus different uses. Some scales concentrate on a general measurement of self-esteem, while others concentrate on self-esteem as related primarily to school. Some claim to examine happiness and satisfaction while others focus on acceptance and security.

Although all the scales are identified as measures of self-esteem, the particular foci of the scales vary greatly.

Scale developers' descriptions may provide a good indication of the intent of the instruments but do not provide evidence of the instruments' utilities and functions. This presents a major problem with relying on the descriptions and titles of instruments alone. Although a scale developer may make claims for the composition and use of a particular scale, the best evidence is the actual functioning of the scale. The functioning or utility of an instrument is most closely related to the concept of validity. The validity of an instrument is established by comparing the scores it yields with scores from other instruments that measure related and unrelated traits. It is hoped that scores on the new instrument correlate highly with related measures and not with those that are unrelated.

Another problem with selecting a measure of self-esteem is that different scales produce different relationships. For example, the Children's Self-Concept Scale (CSCS) (Piers and Harris, 1969) has been shown to correlate with measures of intelligence while the Self-Observational Scale (SOS) (Stenner and Katzenmeyer, 1979) and Culture-Free Self-Esteem Inventories (CFSEI, Battle, 1981) do not. Since traits that correlate with the instrument help to define what is being measured, while traits that do not correlate help to define what is not being measured, the CSCS is apparently measuring something different from the SOS and CFSEI. To complicate matters, all three of the scales correlate with achievement, thus leading one to see a pattern between self-esteem and achievement without any clearer understanding of self-esteem.

Added to these complications is the inconsistency among self-reports and third-party observations of self-esteem. As mentioned previously, parent and teacher ratings of a child's self-esteem have not been found to agree with the child's own rating. Studies have found that parents underestimate and overestimate the self-esteem of their children (Beitchman and Corradini, 1988) and that teachers are influenced by their closeness to the child (Ensink and Carroll, 1989). With such known conflicting results it is hard to determine which method to use. Information from several sources is better than relying on one measure, but if multiple measures don't converge, at least in a general sense, they are problematic. Although several studies have been done to validate the results of third-party measures by relating them to results from self-reports, none have compared the relative utility of such measures. To determine the best scale for an intended purpose, it is necessary to systematically study which measures of self-esteem are the best predictors of particular outcomes related to self-esteem. Improvements in the area of self-esteem measurement need to focus on the use of multiple data sources and comparisons among various measures.

FUTURE DIRECTIONS IN THE ASSESSMENT OF SELF-ESTEEM

Given the information presented in the previous sections, the valid assessment of self-esteem may seem to be a hopeless endeavor. Although existing measures and their use are problematic, it is possible to integrate them into a more comprehensive and multifaceted model of evaluation known as behavioral assessment. The focus of behavioral assessment is the identification of positive and negative behaviors and the environmental variables that maintain those behaviors. This is contrasted with traditional assessment practices that place considerable emphasis on enduring personality traits that explain behavior. A general assumption of traditional assessment is that behavior during testing and one-time observation is representative of the individual's behavioral repertoire. Consequently, environmental influences are not considered and collected data are most applicable to classification decisions only (Shapiro, 1987).

The behavioral assessment model is much broader in scope and includes the identification of individual strengths and weaknesses, so intervention strategies can be developed. Thus, assessment is directly linked with intervention. The belief that human behavior is multifaceted is an underlying assumption of behavioral assessment. In other words, the environment in which the behavior occurred, contingencies for performance, and the individual's thoughts and feelings all exert influence on behavior to some degree. Therefore, assessment must be multifaceted to address more than a single dimension of behavior and account for situation specificity (Shapiro, 1987). Proponents of behavioral assessment advocate a multiple assessment approach in order to obtain data from different sources and across settings and to consider the cognitive and affective influences on behavior (Ollendick and Hersen, 1984).

The techniques of behavioral assessment fall on a continuum from direct to indirect. The more direct approaches involve recording behavioral data during its occurrence. Examples include direct observation, self-monitoring, and role-plays. Indirect methods include interviews, questionnaires, and rating scales in which the collection of behavioral data is removed from the time and place of occurrence (Bellak and Hersen, 1988). The following sections expand on the application of a behavioral assessment model to the evaluation of self-esteem.

The Model

Figure 6.1 represents one way to conceptualize a behavioral assessment model for self-esteem. At Level I indirect measures are used to obtain information from multiple sources about the individual's

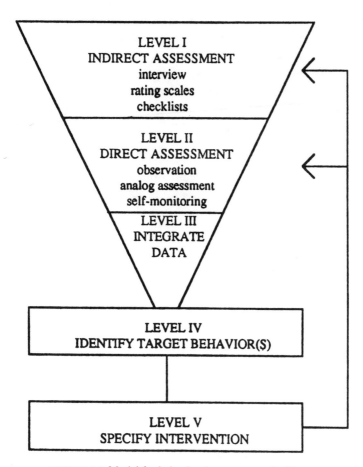

FIGURE 6.1 Model for behavioral assessment of self-esteem.

strengths and weaknesses, behavioral manifestations, and environmental conditions, which are maintaining the behaviors. This level represents an information-gathering stage. Data are used primarily to generate hypotheses regarding the target behavior(s) and to guide further assessment. Level II represents more direct methods of assessment. Specific behaviors identified at Level I and the conditions of their occurrence within the environment are more thoroughly evaluated. At Level III all of the data are integrated, and support for hypotheses generated at Level I is determined. Level IV represents the outcome, that is the identification of positive and negative behavior(s), including strengths and weaknesses, and the contexts in which they are more likely to occur. Once the intended outcome is developed, it is possible to proceed to Level V where intervention strategies are outlined. In this model assessment is ongoing and continues after intervention is initiated. If positive effects on behavior are not evident, then further assessment is needed to verify or re-identify the target behavior and modify interventions accordingly.

Behavioral assessment represents a more comprehensive approach than traditional assessment of self-esteem, which typically includes measures at Level I only. Consequently, the results of traditional approaches indicate only the degree of self-esteem and offer no direction for intervention. Behavioral assessment takes this a step further by specifying and investigating the behavioral, cognitive, and emotional manifestations of self-esteem and the influence of situational variables. Therefore, the more general concept of self-esteem is translated into specific behaviors that can then be the focus of treatment to enhance psychological adjustment.

Level I: Indirect Assessment

Level I includes, primarily, checklists, questionnaires, rating scales, and interviews. As mentioned in a previous section, behavior checklists and rating scales are commonly used in the traditional assessment paradigm to classify high or low self-esteem. Within a behavioral assessment model, however, they are administered as a screening device to identify potential areas requiring further investigation. These instruments allow for multiple sources of information, so parents', teachers', and children's perceptions of the problem can be compared. Their disadvantages are related to social desirability effects and inaccurate recall of past behavior (McMahon, 1984). Data obtained from these measures should be used in conjunction with interview data to provide direction for further assessment. Therefore, they are used as a means to an end rather than a final product.

Interviews are one of the most commonly employed indirect methods of assessment, however, the reliability, validity, and comprehensiveness of obtained information is largely a function of the competence and skill of the interviewer. Therefore, training in interview techniques is strongly recommended. It is important to interview parents, teachers, and significant others, as well as the target child. Children rarely refer themselves to healthcare professionals, so their perceptions of the problem may differ dramatically from those of parents and teachers (Gross, 1984). These disparities are useful in identifying the informants' beliefs, values, and attitudes towards the behavior.

Interviews with children represent a challenge. Often children's self-reports are biased due to the misunderstanding of questions or inaccurate recollection of past events. It is important to consider the developmental stages of children's cognitive and emotional growth, and adjust the interview format accordingly. For example, open-ended questions are not recommended for young children because they are unable to provide the extensive information required of such broad-based questions. Instead, the interviewer could request the child to select a response from different options. It is also necessary to consider the age level of the child in wording questions. Direct questions tend to increase anxiety. The use of scenarios such as, "I once knew a girl who was sad because she didn't have any friends. Do you ever feel like that?" will often encourage a child to talk about her own feelings. Play materials such as dolls, games, blocks, and clay can also serve as prompts for children's self-expression (Witt et al., 1988).

Projective measures are useful to facilitate discussion with children as well. In the assessment of self-esteem, projectives are typically interpreted within a psychodynamic framework to assist in the diagnosis and classification of disturbance. The integration of these methods into a behavioral assessment model requires an alternative conceptualization. Minimal emphasis is placed on the interpretation of unconscious motivations. Projectives are used instead to help children reveal thoughts and feelings. Drawing techniques can be administered in conjunction with further inquiry about feelings, beliefs, and behaviors. For example, a boy who is asked to draw a picture of himself on the Draw-a-Man test draws a child crying. Questions such as, "Why is he crying? How is he feeling? What happened?" are used to probe the issue further. Sentence completion techniques also serve as a springboard for more in-depth interviewing. Therefore, the active content of the responses to projectives is more important than their latent meaning. Projective measures that require a high degree of inference like the Thematic Apperception Test and the Rorschach Inkblot Technique are less useful in behavioral assessment because their interpretation requires symbolic analysis (Prout and Ferber, 1988).

The following areas should be included in the content of the interview: demographic information, academic performance, classroom behavior, peer relations, interests, and relations with family. The interview should reveal the child's present concerns, including thoughts, emotions, and behaviors. The antecedent conditions and consequences of behavior need to be investigated to identify environmental variables maintaining behavior. Information regarding interpersonal relationships and social variables influencing behavior will also be useful to the evaluation of self-esteem (Bellak and Hersen, 1988). It is important to remember that children possess strengths as well as weaknesses; therefore, the interview should focus not only on problem areas but should reveal positive aspects of the child, which can promote change. An excerpt from a child behavioral interview between a school psychologist (SP) and a third-grade child, Jimmy, referred for difficulties completing schoolwork follows. Some interesting issues emerge regarding self-esteem.

SP: Do you know why you're here today, Jimmy?

J: I guess it's because I'm not doing so well in school.

SP: When you say not doing too well, what do you mean?

J: Well, I never get my work done all the way.

SP: So, you're not doing well in school because you don't complete the assignments. Are they too hard for you?

J: No, not really. I just can't seem to finish them. . . . I lose my place.

SP: You lose your place like you're not paying attention.

J: Kind of. I start thinking about other things.

SP: Like daydreaming.

J: Yeah.

SP: What types of things do you think about?

J: Well, school work is real hard for me, and I know I'm in the lowest math and reading groups. I'm afraid the kids will make fun of me.

SP: You're afraid other kids will think you're dumb.

J: Yeah . . . I don't like schoolwork.

SP: Do you feel like this all the time or just at certain times during the day?

J: Sometimes in reading class, but mostly in math.

SP: So, you believe that math is your worst subject.

J: Yeah, but I don't read very well either.

SP: What do you do well in Jimmy?

J: I'm good in gym class, and I really like recess.

SP: You're proud of your sports activities.

J: I'm always the first picked for teams. The other kids know I'm the best.

SP: You're the best.

J: Yeah, I'm pretty good.

SP: Do you have certain friends that you like to play with?

J: There's a bunch of us who play together at recess.

SP: How about outside school? Do you have friends to play with then?

J: Some of the same kids come over to my house and there's a couple friends who live in the neighborhood.

SP: Do you have a best friend?

J: I guess I have two, Scott and John.

SP: What types of things do you like to do with friends?

J: We ride bikes, play Nintendo, watch TV.

SP: You seem happy with your friends.

J: Yeah, we have a good time.

It appears that Jimmy's negative feelings about himself center around academic performance, especially his math ability. These negative feelings are prompted by his thoughts regarding his performance; however, his interpersonal skills and athletic ability represent areas of strength for him. The accuracy of his perceptions, the situational variables affecting his behavior, and the consistency of his behavior across settings are still unknown. Additional information needs to be obtained about Jimmy's academic ability and classroom behaviors, the classroom environment, behaviors at home, and the home environment before the problem can be identified and effective intervention initiated.

Interviews with teachers and parents also focus on identifying strengths and weaknesses and situational variables. It is important that the interviewer elicit specific descriptions of the behavior in observable terms. It is not enough for the parent or teacher to state, "I think he has low self-esteem." People have different conceptions of what constitutes self-esteem. Therefore, it is necessary to ask follow-up questions such as, ''What do you mean by low self-esteem?'' or ''What does the child do to indicate low self-esteem?'' The answers will reveal specific behavioral manifestations of the problem. In addition to a description of behavior, information about the duration, frequency, intensity, and conditions of occurrence must be collected. It is also possible to detect irrational beliefs and unrealistic expectations of teachers and parents. In these instances, the problem may not be with the child but in the belief system of the parents or teachers (Gresham and Davis, 1988). After the interview, it is often necessary to collect data on the occurrence of the specific behaviors through observation in the environment. Parents and teachers can participate in this effort, which will be discussed more thoroughly in the following section.

The interview is a useful technique because of its flexibility. The interviewer can control the type of questions, probe relevant areas further, obtain extensive information about the behaviors and the situational variables, and investigate differences in informants' perceptions of the problem. Although the interview is a good starting point, it alone is not enough to fully comprehend the problem behavior. Additional measures are needed to understand the behavior within the context of the entire case.

Level II: Direct Assessment

Up to this stage of the assessment process, data have been collected via indirect methods to generate hypotheses about the problem behavior and the influence of situational variables and to provide direction for further assessment. At Level II the potential problem areas suggested by the findings from Level I are more systematically and objectively evaluated through direct methods of assessment including observation, analog assessment, and self-monitoring.

Direct observation is a method of recording overt motor and/or verbal behavior of an individual without subjective evaluation (Barton and Ascione, 1984). It is a useful approach with children and adolescents because it does not require advanced cognitive processes or verbal responses. A variety of techniques exists for direct observation. Narrative recording provides a running record of the behavior including antecedent conditions and consequences. The behavioral description is frequently used in conjunction with interview data to identify and operationalize specific behaviors to be observed through more systematic methods such as event and interval recording. For example, poor interpersonal relations can be translated to observable behaviors such as "failure to maintain eye contact when speaking with another child" or "does not initiate conversation."

Event recording focuses on the frequency of occurrence of behavior within a specified interval. Duration recording notes how long each occurrence of the behavior lasted or the time from the beginning to the end of the behavior. Interval recording focuses on whether the behavior occurred or not during a specified interval (Sattler, 1988). The choice of which technique to use will depend on the nature of the behavior to be observed. The length of the observation varies but is usually at least thirty minutes. It is also recommended that more than one observation be conducted since the child's behavior on a single day may not be representative of his/her typical behavior. Observations in different settings also highlight situational factors influencing behavior. The result is an objective description of the behavioral manifestations of the problem in the natural environment including data on frequency, intensity, and/or duration.

It is possible to train individuals in self-monitoring procedures in which they record data on themselves. Self-monitoring requires minimal investment of time and has a wide range of applications. It has been employed successfully by children, but it is often necessary to include visual prompts and more objective recording measures such as checklists to increase accuracy of reporting. Children can be provided with a checklist to mark the behaviors that occur during a specific time period. This is analogous to narrative recording. In many cases specific occurrences of the behavior(s) are recorded by simply keeping a frequency count on paper or using a mechanical counter. An alternative is to provide the child with a signal at the end of specified intervals at which time s/he assesses whether the behavior occurred during the interval. Self-monitoring is particularly useful for the recording of covert actions like thoughts and feelings, which are not apparent to an outside observer (Gardner and Cole, 1988). A common side effect of this method is reactivity or a positive change in behavior as a result of attending to it (Shapiro, 1987). Effective application of these methods will require prior training.

In some cases behaviors do not lend themselves to direct observation because they occur only in specific situations or occur at low frequencies. An example would be compliance with requests, which can be observed only when the child is asked to do something. Analog assessment involves observation in a contrived setting that represents the conditions in which the behavior normally occurs (Shapiro and Kratchowill, 1988). For example, a child who evidenced low self-esteem on rating scales with regard to social acceptance is asked to role-play a situation on the playground and to respond as if it were actually occurring. The observer would note posture, eye contact, verbalizations, and gestures. The child may also be questioned about how s/he feels and what s/he is thinking. Although considered a direct method, analog assessment is less direct than naturalistic observation because the child may not completely transfer natural behaviors to the contrived setting.

Another target of observation that is frequently overlooked in the assessment of self-esteem is the environment. Information collected through interviews often suggests aspects of the environment that require further investigation. The focus is not on the child but on the interaction between the child and the environment (Shapiro, 1987). This often provides insight into the context in which the problem behavior occurs. In some cases it becomes apparent that the problem does not rest solely with the child. For example, a child with low self-esteem, as measured on rating scales, is observed to labor over academic assignments, rarely finishing them on time. Careful analysis of the classroom environment reveals strict discipline on the part of the teacher who expects perfection on class worksheets. Mistakes are viewed as carelessness and result in disproportionate reductions in grades and loss of privileges. Consequently, some children who feel they can never achieve such standards assume they are not good enough, which results in low self-esteem. The primary problem here is with the teacher's expectations for success. In some instances the home environment may be adversely affecting self-esteem. For example, a child who scored low on self-esteem rating scales has been placed in foster care because of parental neglect. In addition to serious emotional concerns, aspects of the environment that impact on the child's self-esteem and psychological adjustment must be addressed.

Thus far, the model of behavioral assessment has operated as a funnel. At the first level general information about the possible problem and behavioral manifestations has been obtained through screening devices. Areas of concern have been selected for more systematic evaluation. Direct assessment required the translation of problems into observable behaviors to identify specific behavioral strengths and weaknesses, and situational variables that can be addressed through intervention strategies. At the third level all the data is integrated to arrive at treatment recommendations.

Level III: Integrate Data

The integration of data actually occurs at each level of the model. Information obtained at Level I from screening devices is used to generate hypotheses, which guide the collection of further data at the same level or through more direct techniques at Level II. The results of direct measures at Level II may support the hypotheses or suggest alternative domains, which need to be assessed to fully understand the problem. Consequently, at each level the conceptualization of the problem becomes more specific and detailed. The following case study represents an example of this progression.

> Sara is an eight-year-old girl who was referred to the school psychologist by her teacher who suspects low self-esteem. In an interview, her teacher described Sara as isolated. Sara appears sad and disinterested much of the time and seldom plays with other children. At first the teacher believed Sara to be shy, but it now seems more than just timidness. She behaves awkwardly around other children and often does not respond to their initiatives to make friends. The teacher's ratings on the Harter Self-Perception Profile indicate low self-esteem with regard to social acceptance and physical appearance. Sara's strengths lie in the academic realm where she performs above average. Sara's parents also rated their daughter's behavior on the Child Behavior Checklist. Although their ratings were below average, they were not as significant as those of the teacher. Sara's parents do not perceive the same problem behaviors at home. They reported satisfactory family relations. When asked about her peer relationships, her parents admitted that she is an only child, and there are few children her age in the neighborhood. In an interview, Sara reported feelings of loneliness and a desire to have more friends. She doesn't understand why other children do not like her. Her self-ratings on the Harter Self-Perception Profile were consistent with those of her teacher. Based on this information, Sara's difficulties seem to center around interpersonal relationships with peers.
>
> A direct observation of Sara during free time in class, which

provided more opportunities for peer interactions, was scheduled. She was observed to remove herself physically from group activities. She did not make eye contact and refused others' initiatives to participate. When she did respond to classmates, the content and context of her expressions were inappropriate. Interestingly, she freely initiated conversation with her teacher. An analog assessment was conducted to further investigate Sara's interpersonal difficulties. In role-plays Sara frequently did not know what to say to initiate conversation with peers or respond to their inquiries, but could freely express herself to the school psychologist and admitted her insecurity in interacting with children her age.

Sara's referral problem was low self-esteem; however, the assessment data indicate the specific nature of these negative feelings, which center around peer relationships. This negative self-image needs to be addressed, but equally important is her need for social skills education, which will hopefully enable her to interact successfully with peers and enhance her feelings of self-worth.

During the integration stage comparisons are made across sources of data to detect different perceptions of the problem. In Sara's case it is likely that her parents did not perceive her interpersonal difficulties as serious because there was little opportunity for peer interaction in the home environment, and Sara's interpersonal skills with adults are adequate. Comparisons across settings are equally important because of the multidimensional nature of self-esteem. Sara's negative feelings centered around peer relationships, but her perceptions of academic competence were satisfactory. Therefore, the problem may not be evident under all conditions. In the final analysis at Level III, it is important not to overlook inconsistencies in the data, because they often indicate situational variables influencing behavior.

Level IV: Identify Target Behaviors

Level IV represents a direct product of data integration. Target behaviors include positive and negative behaviors that will be the focus of intervention. Their identification requires a specific observable description of the behaviors. Equally important, however, are the environmental conditions in which the behaviors occur.

Referring to the previous case of Sara, it appears that poor interpersonal relationships with peers is central to her difficulties. However, "poor interpersonal relationships with peers" is a general description, which can include a broad range of behaviors. Therefore, any intervention based on that description alone is unlikely to address the child's specific needs. However, data from the behavioral observation and analog assessment reveal specific behavior difficulties including not maintaining eye contact, avoidance, and inappropriate verbalizations. It is also apparent that these problem behaviors are only manifested in the context of social relationships with peers. Sara exhibits socially appropriate behaviors with adults, which represents a strength. This information is more useful because an intervention can now be developed to address those specific target behaviors in a particular context.

Level V: Specify Intervention

Treatment within a behavioral assessment model is typically multi-faceted to address the multidimensional nature of the target behaviors identified at Level IV. Consequently, a single approach will not resolve all the difficulties. Interventions are directed at the individual, as well as the environmental variables, which impact on behavior. It is optimal to capitalize on the individual's strengths when trying to enhance functioning. This will not only facilitate change and increase the likelihood of success but will also make the process a more positive experience than that in which only the child's deficits are considered.

To illustrate the process at Level V the case of Sara will be used again. Sara's behaviors differed with the environmental context. Interactions with peers were more problematic than those with adults in which she exhibited appropriate behaviors. Further analysis may reveal increased tension and anxiety in peer situations. If this were the case, it may be beneficial to use relaxation techniques with Sara. However, it is unlikely that these alone will be sufficient to change behavior because Sara still needs to learn critical social skills with peers such as maintaining eye contact, initiating conversation, and appropriate topics of conversation. These can be modeled for her in role-plays and applied through guided practice. It is important to include a variety of situations that Sara may encounter when teaching these skills in order to foster generalization.

After Sara has successfully demonstrated these skills in role-play, it is possible to combine the relaxation training with imagery. This requires Sara to imagine interacting with peers using learned skills under relaxed physical conditions. This often helps reduce anxiety. Situations should be structured within the classroom and at home, which allow Sara to apply her learned skills successfully with peers. Successful application should be followed by positive reinforcement to maintain motivation. As her skills improve, Sara may also benefit from participation in a group counseling situation, which will enable her to interact with peers, as well as provide her with positive role models.

Until this point intervention has only focused on the child. As mentioned previously, interventions are also directed to the environmental context. If Sara's teacher is willing, the physical structure of the classroom can be changed. For example, arrange desks in a formation that will promote interaction. The teacher could also use cooperative learning groups for a unit or lesson each day, which also provides more opportunity for interaction. Given Sara's academic competence, peer tutoring may be beneficial. Sara could be assigned as tutor to a classmate who needs academic assistance but exhibits appropriate social skills. This would benefit both parties and likely be rewarding for Sara by showing her that she has something to contribute to her peers. The teacher should also reinforce Sara's appropriate interpersonal behaviors.

Sara's parents can participate in the intervention. An important contribution from parents is merely their support of their child's efforts. Additionally, they can structure group activities for Sara at home. This may be accomplished by designating one afternoon a week for Sara to invite friends over to play. Sara may also benefit from extracurricular activities involving peers such as Girl Scouts, 4-H, sports, etc. Parents can assume a vital role in encouraging such activities and supporting participation.

The interventions outlined above are specific to Sara's case and are by no means inclusive. The strategies developed at Level V of this model will be specific to the individual's target behaviors. Interventions must be selected in consideration of the specific characteristics of the individual, the environmental context, and the willingness of significant others to support them, if they are to be successful.

CONCLUSION

Traditional assessment of self-esteem has relied predominantly on behavior checklists, rating scales, and projective measures. The technical adequacy of these techniques for making important diagnostic decisions is questionable. Too often there is reliance on a single instrument to assess self-esteem with minimal consideration of the developmental level of the child, the multiple dimensions of self-esteem, or the influence of the environment. The results of this type of assessment only indicate the degree of self-esteem with little understanding of what is represented by the measure and, therefore, few suggestions for intervention.

There is a great need to change this approach if we intend to better serve children and enhance their psychological adjustment. It is apparent from the literature that self-esteem is a difficult concept to isolate and, therefore, difficult to understand as a single entity. A better approach would be to accommodate its multidimensional nature by incorporating the various aspects into an assessment model. Behavioral assessment accomplishes that.

The behavioral assessment model presented in this chapter is much broader in scope than traditional assessment practices. The focus of assessment becomes the behavioral manifestations of self-esteem and the environmental variables that maintain behavior, in addition to underlying personality traits. The outcome of assessment is a more comprehensive and specific description of the individual's strengths and weaknesses, including cognitive and affective components and the situational variables influencing behavior.

The flexibility of this model allows for application at various ages. Children's concept of self changes with development. Therefore, any assessment approach must consider that child's developmental stage to measure self-esteem accurately. Behavioral assessment does not rely solely on standardized instruments, which tend to obscure developmental differences, but emphasizes the need for individualized measures through direct assessment. The outcome is a specific description of the child's behavioral strengths and weaknesses, which can then be considered developmentally appropriate.

Additionally, this model can be applied in a variety of situations due to the importance of environmental variables that maintain behavior. Consequently, behavioral assessment can be effective in addressing milder cases of low self-esteem due to inappropriate peer relationships, as well as more severe cases resulting from child neglect. There is always the consideration of the child's behaviors within the environmental context, and that context is also targeted for intervention.

The results of behavioral assessment indicate the child's difficulties as well as competencies and the environmental variables that impact on behavior. This information is used to design intervention strategies. Thus, assessment is directly linked with intervention. These interventions may include one or more of the following: modifying behavior, changing negative thought processes, teaching coping mechanisms, altering the environment, and counseling for emotional difficulties in family or classroom environments. Therefore, the treatment is multi-faceted to deal with the multiple dimensions of self-esteem and capitalize on the individual's strengths.

Most importantly, the comprehensive assessment of the model goes beyond merely labeling a child. Assessment is directly related to inter-vention, which is designed to meet the needs of the individual. The specific recommendations for the child are based on the information obtained from parents, teachers, counselors, psychologists, and social workers through indirect and direct assessment. Collectively, all parties are more informed of the child's specific strengths and weaknesses in behavioral terms. They can then adjust expectations and implement interventions accordingly. This approach accounts for the multidimen-sional nature of self-esteem and the situation specificity of behavior. Another valuable aspect of the more extensive approach is that it promotes consultation among parents and teachers, which is often neces-sary to effectively address the needs of students.

DIRECTIONS FOR FUTURE RESEARCH

The multidimensional assessment of self-esteem requires more re-search on both the instruments and models used. The majority of instruments that currently exist are lacking in the reliability and validity necessary to make individual decisions. Their use is limited to examina-tion of self-esteem as a unidimensional construct and provide only for a labeling of the degree of general self-esteem. There is a need for the development of instruments that offer more than a global evaluation of self-esteem. Instruments and methods are needed that can guide efforts to remediate or enhance self-esteem. If individual strengths and weak-nesses are examined, there is a greater likelihood that remediation and enhancement can take place simultaneously, rather than focusing merely on deficits. Such instruments and methods would address the multi-dimensional nature of self-esteem and provide for reliable and valid measurements within the domains assessed. These instruments and methods should also account for the developmental aspects of self-es-teem by adapting items to match the developmental level of the respon-dent.

An important area of inquiry is the validity of self-esteem measures. Investigations into the relationships of self-esteem measures with other important outcome measures, such as school success and psychological adjustment, should be undertaken so that we can better interpret the results of self-esteem measures. Such studies would also allow for better selection of self-esteem instruments since they would provide information as to which measures are most closely related to the outcome of interest.

Investigations should also attempt to examine the role that parents, teachers, peers, and the environment play in the development of self-esteem. There is a need to examine self-esteem in the dynamics of the real world rather than relying on a self-report. The strengths and weaknesses that individuals display are certainly dependent on the environment around them. A complete examination of self-esteem requires an examination of the environmental factors that are operating to encourage or undermine the development of positive self-esteem.

The model presented in this chapter attempts to go beyond a global and unidimensional assessment of self-esteem. The behavioral assessment approach should help to identify strengths and weaknesses, as well as suggest a plan for the remediation or enhancement of self-esteem. The model is complex and needs to be investigated. Study of the indirect assessment devices that provide the necessary information at the first step of the model was discussed previously.

Direct methods of assessment are implemented at the second stage of the model. The training of individuals to observe or self-monitor behaviors related to self-esteem is a critical issue. Will it be possible to train individuals in a timely and efficient manner and will these individuals be successful in real settings? If the issues surrounding the collection of data are overcome, there remains the issue of integrating the information and moving to an intervention plan. Training individuals to interpret data from multiple sources is a formidable task. Ensuring that they are consistent and accurate is critical to the correct implementation of the model.

Research will be necessary on the specific interventions. Although much is known about self-esteem in general, not much is known about the particular interventions that may help produce better self-esteem. Most importantly, it will be necessary to assess whether the implemented model improves the self-esteem of those individuals identified as needing help. Since self-esteem is the individual's interpretation of personal value and, therefore, tied to self-reports, interventions will have to balance these interpretations. If the components of the model can be implemented and individuals trained to interpret the information for each component, then behavioral assessment of self-esteem has the potential to provide assessment of self-esteem and plans for remediation and enhancement.

REFERENCES

Alsaker, F. and D. Olweus. 1986. "Assessment of Global Negative Self-Evaluations and Perceived Stability of Self in Norwegian Pre-Adolescents and Adolescents," *J. of Early Adolescence*, 6(3):269–278.

Barton, E. J. and F. R. Ascione. 1984. "Direct Observation," in *Child Behavioral Assessment*, T. H. Ollendick and M. Hersen, eds., New York, NY: Pergamon Press.

Battle, J. 1981. *Culture-Free Self Esteem Inventories for Children and Adults.* Seattle, WA: Special Child Publications.

Beane, J. A. and R. P. Lipka. 1986. *Self-Concept, Self-Esteem and the Curriculum.* New York, NY: Teachers College Press.

Beitchman, J. H. and A. Corradini. 1988. "Self-Report Measures for Use with Children: A Review and Comment," *J. of Clinical Psychology*, 44(4):477–490.

Bellak, A. S. and M. Hersen. 1988. *Behavioral Assessment.* New York, NY: Pergamon Press.

Benner, E. H., D. H. Frey, and R. Gilberts. 1983. "A Construct Validation of Academic Self-Esteem for Intermediate Grade-Level Children," *Measurement and Evaluation in Guidance*, 16:127–134.

Bracken, B. A. 1992. *Multidimensional Self Concept Scale.* Austin, TX: PRO-ED.

Brody, G. H., Z. Stoneman, M. Millar, and J. K. McCoy. 1990. "Assessing Individual Differences: Effects of Responding to Prior Questionnaires on the Substantive and Psychometric Properties of Self-Esteem and Depression Assessments," *J. of Personality Assessment*, 54(1 and 2):401–411.

Brown, L. and J. Alexander. 1990. *Self-Esteem Index.* Austin, TX: PRO-ED.

Byrne, B. M. 1983. "Investigating Measures of Self-Concept," *Measurement and Evaluation in Guidance*, 16:115–126.

Coopersmith, S. 1981. *Coopersmith Self-Esteem Inventories.* Palo Alto, CA: Consulting Psychologists Press.

Coopersmith, S. and R. Gilberts. 1981. *Behavioral Academic Self-Esteem, A Rating Scale.* Palo Alto, CA: Consulting Psychologists Press.

Damon, W. and D. Hart. 1982. "The Development of Self-Understanding from Infancy through Adolescence," *Child Development*, 53:841–864.

Ensink, T. and J. L. Carroll. 1989. "Comparisons of Parents', Teachers', and Students' Perceptions of Self-Concept in Children from One and Two Parent Families," *Psychological Reports*, 65:201–202.

Gardner, W. I. and C. L. Cole. 1988. "Self-Monitoring Procedures," in *Behavioral Assessment in Schools: Conceptual Foundations and Practical Applications*, E. S. Shapiro and T. R. Kratchowill, eds., New York, NY: The Guilford Press.

Gilberts, R. 1983. "The Evaluation of Self-Esteem," *Family and Community Health* (August):29–49.

Gresham, F. M. and C. J. Davis. 1988. "Behavioral Interviews with Teachers and

Parents," in *Behavioral Assessment in Schools: Conceptual Foundations and Practical Applications,* E. S. Shapiro and T. R. Kratchowill, eds., New York, NY: The Guilford Press.

Gross, A. 1984. "Behavioral Interviewing," in *Child Behavioral Assessment,* T. H. Ollendick and M. Hersen, eds., New York, NY: Pergamon Press.

Hamachek, D. E. 1988. "Evaluating Self-Concept and Ego Development within Erikson's Psychosocial Framework: A Formulation," *J. of Counseling and Development,* 66:354–360.

Harter, S. 1985. *Manual for the Self-Perception Profile for Children.* Denver, CO: University of Denver Press.

Itskowitz, R., R. Navon, and H. Strauss. 1988. "Teachers' Accuracy in Evaluating Students' Self-Image: Effect of Perceived Closeness," *J. of Educational Psychology,* 80(3):337–341.

Johnson, B., D. L. Redfield, R. L. Miller, and R. E. Simpson. 1983. "The Coopersmith Self-Esteem Inventory: A Construct Validation Study," *Educational and Psychological Measurement,* 43(3):907–913.

McLoughlin, J. A. and R. B. Lewis. 1990. *Assessing Special Students: Third Edition.* Columbus, OH: Merrill Publishing Co.

McMahon, R. 1984. "Behavioral Checklists and Rating Scales," in *Child Behavioral Assessment,* T. H. Ollendick and M. Hersen, eds., New York, NY: Pergamon Press.

Ollendick, T. H. and M. Hersen, eds. 1984. *Child Behavioral Assessment.* New York, NY: Pergamon Press.

Piers, E. V. and D. B. Harris. 1969. *The Way I Feel about Myself; The Piers-Harris Children's Self-Concept Scale.* Los Angeles, CA: Western Psychological Services.

Piers, E. V. and D. B. Harris. 1984. *The Piers-Harris Children's Self-Concept Scale: Revised Manual.* Los Angeles, CA: Western Psychological Services.

Prout, H. T. and S. M. Ferber. 1988. "Analogue Assessment: Traditional Personality Assessment Measures in Behavioral Assessment," in *Behavioral Assessment in Schools: Conceptual Foundations and Practical Applications,* E. S. Shapiro and T. R. Kratchowill, eds., New York, NY: The Guilford Press.

Roid, G. H. and W. H. Fitts. 1988. *Tennessee Self-Concept Scale: Revised Manual.* Los Angeles, CA: Western Psychological Services.

Rosenberg, M. 1965. *Society and the Adolescent Self-Image.* Princeton, NJ: Princeton University Press.

Salvia, J. and J. E. Ysseldyke. 1991. *Assessment.* Boston, MA: Houghton Mifflin Co.

Sattler, J. M. 1988. *Assessment of Children.* San Diego, CA: Jerome M. Sattler, Publisher.

Shapiro, E. S. 1987. *Behavioral Assessment in School Psychology.* Hillsdale, NJ: Lawrence Erlbaum Associates.

Shapiro, E. S. and T. R. Kratchowill, eds. 1988. *Behavioral Assessment in Schools: Conceptual Foundations and Practical Applications.* New York: The Guilford Press.

Stenner, A. J. and W. G. Katzenmeyer. 1979. *Self-Observational Scales: Technical Manual and User's Guide.* Durham, NC: NTS Research Group.

Witt, J. C., T. A. Cavell, R. W. Heffer, M. P. Carey, and B. K. Martens. 1988. "Child Self-Report: Interviewing Techniques and Rating Scales," in *Behavioral Assessment in Schools: Conceptual Foundations and Practical Applications,* E. S. Shapiro and T. R. Kratchowill, eds., New York, NY: The Guilford Press.

CHAPTER 7

The Developing Self in the Early School Years

KAORU YAMAMOTO – *University of Colorado at Denver*
GAIL McEACHRON-HIRSCH – *The College of William and Mary*

YOUNG as they might be, all children have certain ideas about who they are and what they are like. The global concept of self has been developed over the years, first on the basis of perceived appraisals by others, and later also on the added basis of one's own assessment. Sociologist Charles Cooley coined a very descriptive phrase, "the looking-glass self," to characterize the process involved. Indeed without adequate interpersonal relations, we will be hard pressed to develop, maintain, and change our self-concept, because we need someone else first to hold up a mirror so that we may see the reflected image in it (Yamamoto, 1972). In other words, our concept of self is largely based upon the social network surrounding us.

The influence of the immediate family on the formation of self-concept is a powerful one because the home is indeed the cradle for a child's perceptions of his or her identity. If parents, siblings, and significant others constantly belittle the child by playing up weaknesses and shortcomings, he or she is bound to depict a picture of self as an inferior or worthless human being. The basis for such external assessments may be transient, or it may be more longstanding. For example, if a healthy child cannot control bodily functions as skillfully as others of the same or similar age, he or she might be momentarily subjected to parental disfavor, disappointment, and disapproval. Meanwhile, the same sort of ridicule and rejection tends to be directed to the so-called mentally retarded.

Interpersonal appraisal is indeed *social* in nature and not dependent upon any absolute standard of behavior. Given two brothers in the same family, parental treatment typically varies between them. It does not matter that both boys may be academically successful; if one is always at the top of his class, while the other is not, the comparison is often critical in inducing differences in parents' responses to them. Snide remarks, constant reminders, or telltale rewards (given or withheld) are

143

some of the forms these may take. Moreover, what counts is the *child's* perceptions of how others perceive or treat him or her, and not the accuracy of such perceptions. If, let us say, a girl believes that her parents, teachers, siblings, or peers regard her as ugly, dumb, or bad, it makes little difference whether they do or do not, in fact, see her as such.

SELF-CONCEPT, RIGHT OR WRONG

There is an unfortunate, but strong, tendency for us to remain true to our self-concept, even when it has no valid basis. In other words, we act so as to preserve our sense of identity, our image of self, at almost any cost. Once painted, we are very hesitant to add touches to our portrait, much less to repaint it. Because we would rather believe in the picture (self-concept), or the way we imagine how we appear to others, than take a close look at who we may actually be (the self), we often deceive ourselves in thought, feelings, and action.

Some extreme cases would help make the point. A clinical psychologist told the story of three people in a single state hospital, each believing that he was Jesus Christ, reincarnated (Rokeach, 1964). When the three confronted each other, they were very much threatened by this reciprocal challenge to their sense of current identity and tried hard to maintain their beliefs (clinically, ''delusions'') by denial, recrimination, rationalization, and other means of defense. None was willing to accept the possibility of his not being Christ, and all strove for apparent consistency, continuity, and sameness rather than for a painful reexamination of his personhood. The picture (self-concept) was kept intact at a high price.

The consciousness of who one is comes into focus quite early, and it is inseparable from the consciousness of others. Goodman (1964) reported that, by the age of two or two and a half, children begin to show an awareness of differences in such physical features as the color of skin pigmentation. By four or five, a distinct acceptance-rejection orientation to these differences seems to be formed and, by the time a child becomes seven or eight, full-fledged attitudes are in evidence and these reach their ethnocentric peak at early adolescence. The classic studies conducted by Clark (1965, pp. 64 – 65) illustrate this phenomenon:

> When Negro children as young as three years old are shown white- and Negro-appearing dolls or asked to color pictures of children to look like themselves, many of them tend to reject the dark-skinned dolls as ''dirty''

and "bad" or to color the picture a bizarre shade like purple. But the fantasy is not complete, for when asked to identify which doll is like themselves, some Negro children, particularly in the North, will refuse, burst into tears, and run away. By the age of seven most Negro children have accepted the reality that they are, after all, dark skinned. But the stigma remains; they have been forced to recognize themselves as inferior. Few if any Negroes ever fully lose that sense of shame and self-hatred.

Additional, vivid testimonies have come from such literary observers as W. E. B. DuBois *(The Souls of Black Folk)*, Richard Wright *(Native Son)*, James Baldwin *(Notes of a Native Son)*, Ralph Ellison *(Invisible Man)*, Claude Brown *(Manchild in the Promised Land)*, and Maya Angelou *(I Know Why the Caged Bird Sings)*, not to speak of many others of "different" or "handicapped" backgrounds. A dawning awareness, at least among those who work with children, of the unfathomable damage wrought on the young mind is encouraging, even though the challenge remains enormous indeed.

If the image of inferiority and worthlessness in such children is inaccurate, so is that of gratuitous superiority and bloated confidence in many majority or "mainstream" children and adults. It has been noted that those who are prejudiced against one group of people, say, African-Americans, tend to be also prejudiced against others, like Jews and Asians (e.g., Adorno, Frenkel-Brunswik, Levinson, and Sanford, 1950). The generalized attitudes about *them* (the out-group) and *us* (the in-group) perpetuate various social stereotypes and distort perceptions of the self as well as of others. In other words, the sword cuts both ways.

One (but only one) of the many postulated ways in which unfriendly orientations are revealed against the weak and downtrodden is the well-known frustration-aggression-displacement sequence. A person may be frustrated for various reasons in the quest of such goals as self-esteem, social status, economic security, and occupational achievement. The typical coping process in the face of frustration is a range of efforts to surmount the obstacle and solve the perceived problems. Beyond one's limit of tolerance, however, these attempts become erratic and self-defeating. Some would blame themselves to carry the feelings of guilt and get deeply depressed. Many regress to earlier patterns of behavior such as denial, repression, overdependence, and withdrawal.

Others turn against their brethren and displace their hostility upon hapless victims (Allport, 1958). A recent, flagrant example was the brutal killing of an engineer of Chinese heritage by two unemployed automobile workers in Detroit. During their trial, these disgruntled murderers, who had beaten the young victim to death with baseball bats, blurted out that they had believed him to be a Japanese! A clear reasoning and a fine "defense," to say the least! This process of rationalization is quite common in such acts of aggression. One's own faults and guilt are ascribed to the scapegoat (clinically, "projection") so as to justify blaming the latter. It is much easier to find shortcomings in, for example, those "dirty, lazy, and drunk" Indians than to face up to the very same characteristics in ourselves and admit to our prejudicial feelings. Even to label a child "problem" assuages many a parent's remorse and self-hatred for having a handicapped, retarded, disturbed, or errant offspring and helps teachers to divert their feelings of frustration and powerlessness.

HELPING OR HINDERING

Displacement of one's aggression is the very last thing a teacher or parent should find in their own interactions with children. Nevertheless, the incidence of open ridicule, sarcasm, and other forms of hostility and cruelty seems pretty high in the allegedly *helping, caring,* or *nurturing* relationship. This is indeed unfortunate, particularly since for many children the family and school represent the last hope and haven for finding the precious sense of competence and self-respect.

The potential effects of one variety of the scapegoating orientation are summed up in the so-called "self-fulfilling prophecy" (a phrase coined by sociologist, Robert K. Merton), or "the countless subtle ways in which expectancy of certain behavior in others evokes that very behavior" (Allport, 1958, p. 156). Put in another way, "One's reputation, whether false or true, cannot be hammered, hammered, hammered, into one's head without doing something to one's character" (Allport, 1958, pp. 138–139).

This phenomenon has typically been observed in its destructive form. If, for example, a child is constantly told that he is no good, he tends to develop, indeed, into a no-good individual because of his perception of self as such. This is one of the real dangers in, e.g., the multi-track system of teaching, if and when it becomes inflexible and serves only to pigeonhole pupils into the smart, so-so, and dumb groups. The pervasive and often blind faith in a single, rough index called IQ has certainly done much harm in touching off such a vicious circle (Yamamoto, 1975).

"Children who are treated as if they are uneducable almost invariably become uneducable" (Clark, 1965, p. 128).

While not, hopefully, meaning to do so, adults can hurt children through their words, uttered unawares, or their subtle acts. This is especially true during the period when youngsters are striving to gain independence from their parents and, hence, rejecting them as a valid source of information and guidance. In the words of Wigginton (1986, p. 235),

> During that critical age . . . the only adult feedback they get about themselves may be from us [teachers]. Scarier still, they may *trust* it. What happens if we confirm, even unconsciously, the dark fears some have that they'll never amount to anything? What happens when one tells us of hopes to go to college, and we laugh? What happens when one says he wants to be a photographer for *National Geographic* and we tell him that's impossible? What happens when we get angry and state, "This is the worst class I've ever had" [?]

He then reminds us of a keystone rule for the teacher (as well as for any adult): "The one sin that is unforgivable is to diminish a student's sense of dignity and worth" (p. 235).

However, there is no reason why the same mechanism of self-fulfilling prophecy should not be used in affecting children in a constructive manner. As a matter of fact, when we speak of the teacher's faith in and respect for pupils as the basic requirements in teaching, a part of the story is precisely these dynamics. Through changes in teachers' expectations of themselves and of their pupils, some dramatic improvements in academic performance have been effected even in difficult or "impossible" schools (see, e.g., Cadwalader, 1989; Clark, 1965; Collins and Tamarkin, 1982; Freedman, 1990).

An additional testimony comes from Rosenberg and Simmons (1972) who, at the end of their massive study on the self-esteem among 1,900 black and white children randomly selected from the third through twelfth grades in twenty-six schools in the city of Baltimore, came to the following conclusion of importance (p. 144):

> In sum, given the environments in which most of these black children currently live, many of the factors which might be expected to reduce their self-esteem — the low prestige of their race, the rejection of the black physical model, poverty, the broken family structure, and, to a lesser extent, poor school performance — do not turn out to have the anticipated consequences. . . . What does have an unequivocal impact on their self-esteem in these environments is *what they believe their significant*

others think of them. The great proportion of the child's daily interpersonal interactions occur with parents, friends, and teachers. If these significant others hold favorable opinions of him, respect him, and like him, then a firm foundation for healthy self-esteem may be established.

THE GIFT OF THE TEACHER

"In all memorable educational achievements enthusiasm [on the part of the teacher] has borne distinguished part. There are not wanting instances of them in which it was the capital source of power—in which but for its inspiration and contagion overwhelming failure must have ensued" (Spring, 1946, p. 82). Many a teacher has successfully guided her charges to the appreciation of love of life, not by words or activities alone, but by the totality of her or his life (e.g., Ashton-Warner, 1963; J. Gordon, 1970; Marshall, 1963; Pratt, 1990). Knowingly or unknowingly, teachers serve as models for pupils, thus exerting a powerful influence upon multitudes. Lucky are those who have met a teacher offering himself or herself as a mature and compassionate fellow traveller in life. That is why it is critical for the teacher to know, accept, and share herself or himself better. That is the first challenge. Closely behind comes the challenge for the teacher to know his or her children better, both as individuals and as a group.

"Life comes from life and the teacher is the living agent in the school" (Moustakas, 1966, p. 7). The teacher must thus be alive, sharing himself or herself with children and striving for maturity. As aptly put by Baruch (1964, p. 24), "A reservoir without water cannot take water to those who are thirsty. Neither can a starved person feed another out of full bounty." If one feels deeply hurt and insecure, he or she is likely to hurt others in various ways, be these through open hostility, power struggle, sarcasm, smothering, or overdependence. When one does not love oneself properly, the person is ill-equipped to love others in an authentic manner. If teachers do not accept themselves, there is little likelihood for their trusting others. If teachers have faith in themselves, on the other hand, they can let others know them as they are. Bonds of genuine human relationship can scarcely be built upon misrepresentation of the self, either to oneself (self-deception) or to others (faking and alienation).

In Buber's expression (1965, p. 205), "*I* and *Thou* exist only in our world, because man exists, and the *I*, moreover, exists only through the relation to the *Thou.*" In this sense, knowing one's self is dependent upon letting oneself be known without pretense or duplicity. Since the essence of education has to be an authentic human encounter, the place where that encounter ought to begin is, as usual, our relationship with ourselves.

Of course, self-disclosure is not the same thing as exhibitionism (which, ironically, is a mask in itself). There are wide individual differences in the tendency for disclosure and, besides, there are wide variations in relation to culture (nationality, ethnicity, religious orientations, etc.), age, sex, occupation, and other social factors. What is important here is simply the fact that openness to oneself and others is a necessary, if not sufficient, condition for anyone's being and becoming a mature human and an authentic teacher (Jourard, 1968; Moustakas, 1966; Rogers, 1983). When such a teacher, awakened to the richness of life, discloses oneself to youngsters, the latter has a chance to catch a glimpse of what is possible and potential, to broaden their perspectives, to deepen their faith in themselves and others, and to carve out their world with imagination and compassion. Henry Adams (1961, p. 300) captured the essence of the teacher's role in the following statement: "A parent gives life, but as a parent, gives no more. A murderer takes life, but his deed stops there. A teacher affects eternity; he can never tell where his influence stops."

KNOWING CHILDREN

As a way to shift our focus from *I* to *Thou*, we now examine some of the numerous ways to see and understand children. No single approach or information source suffices, and merely occasional attempts will not allow the teacher to know her children well. The efforts must be continuous. Anecdotal records, autobiographies, tests, questionnaires, structured observations, and other avenues must be utilized with discretion. Comments coming from other teachers, counselors, parents, and children themselves are also invaluable. (Useful, more detailed references include Almy and Genishi, 1979; Beagle and Brandt, 1973; Boehm and Weinberg, 1977; Brandt, 1972; Cohen et al., 1983; I. Gordon, 1966; Irwin and Bushnell, 1980; Medinnus, 1976; Millard and Rothney, 1957; Rowen, 1973; Strang, 1959; Torgerson, 1947; and Wright, 1967.)

Within the classroom or out on the playground, a teacher can glean many indicative signs of a child's world. For example, does the child spontaneously tell stories? If, yes, what kind and to whom? What types of books does the child like to read? With whom does the child speak and play? Does the child laugh often? Cry? Sing? Have temper tantrums? Is the child willing to make something with others? To follow the rules of a game? Is the child generally relaxed? Interested in living things? Pick on younger children? These and many other questions are relevant in assessing what is going on in a child's life and how the youngster sees himself or herself.

Self-Portraits of Children

One of the readily available, yet very revealing, means for knowing children happens to be their simple drawings, particularly drawings of themselves. Beyond a sheet of paper and pencils or crayons, no special materials or preparations are necessary. No elaborate instructions are in order, other than merely inviting them to draw a picture of themselves (or simply of a person). Most preliminary questions require nothing but a noncommittal response, "Just as you please," and no rigid time limit needs to be set.

> Underlying the drawing technique is the wide and basic assumption that personality develops not in a vacuum, but through the movement, feeling, and thinking of a specific body. . . . In general terms, the drawing of the person represents the expression of self, or the body, in the environment. What is expressed may be characterized as *body image,* a term that has been described variously by different authors. Briefly put, the body image may be regarded as the *complex reflections of self-regard—the self-image* (Machover, 1951, p. 348).

Many pages have been written on the expressive meanings of human drawings, and it takes some serious study to learn all the interpretive details (see, e.g., DiLeo, 1973; Hammer, 1980; Koppitz, 1984; Machover, 1980). A teacher is not a clinician and, therefore, should not be expected to develop the same level of skill as that shown by psychologists or psychiatrists specializing in such tasks. Nevertheless, alertness to some of the characteristic features and, hence, to any exceptional indications in such drawings will go a long way in the teacher's efforts to be of help to children.

Look at some sample pictures (Figures 7.1−7.14) rendered by primary-elementary age children. As you note, in some instances, two self-portraits are shown for the same child, the first done in October of one year and the second in February of the following year.

FIGURE 7.1 Kindergartner [A].

151

FIGURE 7.2 Kindergartner [B].

FIGURE 7.3 Kindergartner [C].

153

FIGURE 7.4 First grader [D].

FIGURE 7.5 Fourth-grade boy [E] (fall).

FIGURE 7.6 Fourth-grade boy [E] (spring).

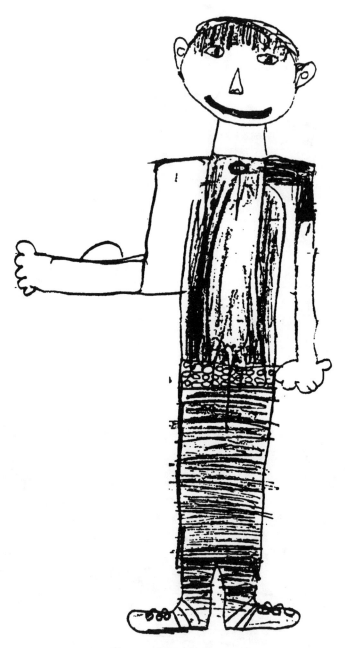

FIGURE 7.7 Fourth-grade boy [F] (fall).

FIGURE 7.8 Fourth-grade boy [F] (spring).

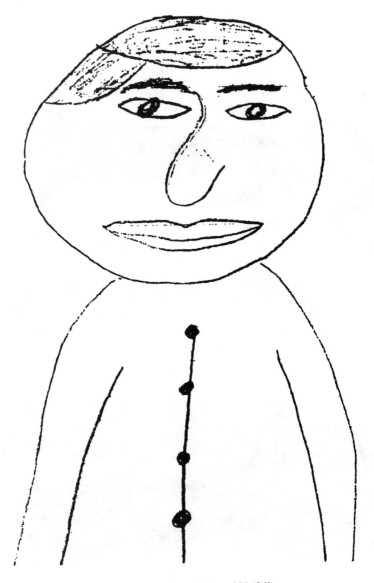

FIGURE 7.9 Fourth-grade boy [G] (fall).

FIGURE 7.10 Fourth-grade boy [G] (spring).

159

FIGURE 7.11 Fourth-grade girl [H] (fall).

FIGURE 7.12 Fourth-grade girl [H] (spring).

FIGURE 7.13 Fourth-grade girl [I] (fall).

FIGURE 7.14 Fourth-grade girl [I] (spring).

163

It is obvious that considerable differences exist between younger and older children in their drawings. Although it is always dangerous to pigeonhole a child on the mere basis of his or her chronological age, most observers agree that there is a recognizable developmental trend. The following overall pattern has been summarized from descriptions by two scholars (Burt, 1963, pp. 17–19; Machover, 1960, pp. 238–257):

At age two to three, children move gradually from the enjoyment of scribbling movement itself to some appreciation of the results. Imitation of adult movement and efforts to reproduce part of objects may be noticeable. At four and five, distinct lines based upon single movements of the pencil begin to replace gross oscillations in scribbles. Figures tend to be large, showing only the principal parts of the body. With little attention to shape or proportion, the figures may be readily mistaken for animals of one sort or another. At this stage, sex difference (i.e., pictures drawn by boys vs. those by girls) are still small.

At about six or seven, girls start surpassing boys by drawing pictures more mature in body concept, more realistic, and more differentiated. Greater expressive fluency and flexibility, as well as orderliness and attention to clothing and other details, are revealed by girls. From seven or eight to nine or ten, drawings become realistic for both sexes, even though girls continue to show better controlled pictures of themselves. At ten or eleven, attempts at visual representation are initiated, and two- and three-dimensional drawings appear. These include silhouettes, three-quarter views, background landscapes, and perspective.

From about eleven to fourteen, drawings tend to show loss of spontaneous quality to degenerate into an empty, geometric, and oversimplified version. At this point, sex differences cease to be consistent and pronounced. Many children stop at this prepubertal repression stage. Some, however, go on to the artistic revival stage of early adolescence in which definite esthetic elements become discernible. Drawings are now made to tell a story, and some abstract use of line, form, color, and design may be seen. Utilization of the principles of composition, arrangement, balance, and the like helps to enhance the communicative effects of concepts and affect.

Because of the imperfect stabilization in self-image, as well as graphic skills, variations in drawings over time are greater in younger children than in older ones. By the same token, those with an uncertain sense of self are more inclined to give vacillating portraits from one drawing to another than self-confident individuals. When the teacher notices some sudden and radical changes in a child's picture of himself or herself, it is usually worthwhile to look into the possible reasons. In general, figure drawings readily lead children to another expressive medium of storytelling about the characters. The teacher will also find it easy to sit down with individual children to have a conversation to learn more about their inside-out view of themselves. Simple answers to such questions as, What is he doing? Is she happy? What does he worry about? and What are the nicest things about her? reveal much about the child.

Altogether, drawings vary in terms of both structure and contents. Among the structural features are

- size of the figure
- location of the figure on paper
- sex identification of the figure
- stance of the figure
- pressure of line
- degree of completion and detailing
- perspective, and joining
- proportions and symmetry
- coloring and shading
- erasures and reinforcement of line
- background

Among the contentual features would be

- individual parts of the body
- facial expression
- postural tone (vigorous, collapsed, inconsistent, etc.)
- clothing and other accessories

To start out, a child may be reluctant to draw himself or herself (or a person), or may draw merely a portion of the body and omit the rest. The figure may be *very* small (usually a sign of feelings of insignificance) and located in the bottom corner (often chosen by a timid, self-conscious child). A child may draw a figure inconsistent with one's own age, color, or body type. The portrait may show disproportionate size or details of a single body part or joints (frequently signifying somatic preoccupation), or it may show frequent erasures or vigorously reinforced lines in a particular area of the body (reflective of emotional conflicts, uncertainty, etc.). The child may randomly shade (potentially a sign of anxiety), depict internal organs (generally evidence of somatic delusions), or draw a transparent figure (poor or disturbed judgment). These and many other leads, *when combined with additional information and placed in a proper perspective,* aid the teacher to make reasonable inference into the child's inner world. The integration and contextualization of information is critical, since teachers can ill afford to fall in the popular trap of typing and stigmatizing people on the basis of flimsy, incomplete evidence.

In addition to possible interpretations of affective nature, figure drawings are open to readings to yield a rough indicator of children's maturity in the cognitive realm of development. Thus, in the well-known Goodenough-Harris system of human figure drawings, a picture of a man, a picture of a woman, and a picture of self are scored to give credit to many aspects identified in a detailed scheme involving seventy-three dimensions for the "man" drawing and seventy-one for the "woman" drawing (Harris, 1963). Some examples of these are given below ("man" and "woman" scales mixed):

Head present	Knee joint shown
Neck present	Feet I: any indication
Neck, two dimensions	Feet II: proportion
Eye present	Feet III: heel
Eye detail: brow or lashes	Feet IV: perspective
Eye detail: pupil	Feet V: detail
Eye detail: proportion	Motor coordination: lines
Eye detail: glance	Motor coordination: junctures
Bridge of nose	Superior motor coordination
Hair I	Clothing indicated
Hair II	Sleeve I
Hair III	Sleeve II
Hair IV	Neckline I
Fingers present	Neckline II: collar
Correct number of fingers	Waist I
shown	Waist II
Details of fingers correct	No transparencies in the
Opposition of thumb shown	figure
Hand present	Sketching technique
Legs present	"Modeling" technique

A given drawing is accorded one point when showing each of these items, and the raw score is derived by summing all points. In the 1963 – 1965 Health Examination Survey conducted by the U.S. Public Health Service, a national sample of roughly 7,100 children was studied on numerous health and developmental factors. This sample was chosen to be representative of the approximately 24 million non-institutionalized U.S. children of ages six through eleven with respect to age, sex, color, region, and characteristics of their place of residence. Raw score means on the Goodenough-Harris drawing test in this group ranged from about sixteen in six-year-olds to close to forty in eleven-year-olds. When drawing a man, both sexes scored at about the same level. With a ''woman'' drawing, however, girls surpassed boys, as well as their own ''man'' drawings, by three to four points at every age (Harris et al., 1970).

For better comparability, these raw scores are usually converted to standard scores by referring to tables provided in the test manual (Harris, 1963). This is done separately for ''man'' and ''woman'' figures, and the two standard scores are then averaged to obtain a single estimate of intellectual maturity. The manual allows such conversion for children aged three through fifteen for drawings of a man and aged six through fifteen for drawings of a woman. The standard score expresses a child's relative standing on the test in relation to groups of his own age and sex. For each sex-age group, the mean standard score is 100, and the standard deviation is fifteen. What this means is that, in the general population of children of a given age and sex, about 68 percent would be expected to score between 85 and 115, about 95 percent between 70 and 130, and about 99 percent between 55 and 145. This standard score system is also used in the Wechsler Intelligence Scale for Children (WISC), with which the Goodenough-Harris Test has been found to show a reasonable degree of correspondence. Unfortunately, the scoring scheme for the self-drawing itself has remained merely tentative in the Goodenough-Harris system and, as a result, there have been dissenting views on the interpretations (Kellogg, 1969).

Picture of the Whole Child

All told, then, seemingly innocuous figure drawings can be both an enjoyable medium of self-expression for children and a useful means for enhancing teacher knowledge of these same children. As emphasized before, however, the teacher should always be wary of basing judgment on information from any single source, particularly if obtained at a single time point in a single social setting (e.g., only on the playground, in the classroom, in the home, etc.). Integration of accounts from various sources over time and across contexts is indispensable to a compassionate understanding of the child as a whole being. Also keep in mind that, while commercial and standardized tests, largely of academic achievement and cognitive functions, are useful in many ways, they are restricted in scope and, typically, a poor monitor of the child's daily struggle for growth. In fact, teacher-made means of assessment are often preferable to these for the immediate needs of teachers and children. There are numerous informal channels through which to reach the child (see Bourisseau, 1972).

One device that has often been found helpful is "Incomplete Sentences." Here, children are to finish each of ten to fifty incomplete sentences to their own liking. Many of the sentences have to do with personal wishes, fears, and other feelings, and the first association ("the first thing that comes to your mind") is sought. Simple as it is, the task is surprisingly revealing, particularly when repeated at certain intervals. Some actual responses to sample questions, given by several fourth graders, are shown below (as they were):

I often wish I could . . .
                                                  fly.
                                                  make myself small.
                                                  scream my head off.
                                                  buy a gun.
                                                  be a dog.
                                                  be grown up already.

The worst thing a person can
    do is . . .
                                                    liy (lie).
                                                  steel something.
                                                  is kill themself's.
                                                  start a fire.
                                                  spank me.
                                                  die.

Most people don't know
    that I . . .
                                                    am an Indian.
                                                  can make a cake.
                                                  fiell (feel).
                                                  hate my brother.

	like them.
	erased the sentence itself and added, "It's personal."
I wish my father would . . .	be home more than he's gone.
	visit me.
	come home.
	play.
	come from the sky.
	stop yelling at me so much.
I do not like people who . . .	get mad when I make a mistake.
	be mean.
	welly (yell) at me.
	call names.
	smoke and drink.
	act big.
I am happy when . . .	my dad koms house.
	I give someone a gift.
	I get my work done.
	I'm proud of myself.
	I spi on people.
	nowon is hurt.
I love . . .	the holy Jesus and god.
	horses and my mom and dad.
	John Doe (a classmate).
	my family (sometimes).
	everybody who loves me.

It can easily be seen that the children are typically very candid unless, of course, they are defensive or intentionally silly in answering. Repeated administrations at intervals help in detecting these diversionary patterns of response, as well as the matters of lasting concern to children. Various themes are apparent even in such fragmentary samples as above—for example, achievement, competence, dejection, frustration, and morality.

Although we cannot discuss them here, other means for increased teacher understanding include storytelling, creative drama, puppetry, finger painting, and so on and so forth. These serve, in common with drawings and associations, the dual purposes of being a good medium for creative self-expression in children, and of being a window to their mind. Their frequent and imaginative applications would be of use to both the teacher and children (see Chukovsky, 1963; McCaslin, 1986; Oaklander, 1978; Sutton-Smith, 1981; Torrance and Myers, 1972; Wagner, 1976; Way, 1990).

Classroom as a World

It has been emphasized that, to know any child, the teacher must observe him or her in varied social settings over time. Certainly, one of the most accessible of these settings for the teacher is the classroom, the dynamics of which deserve close attention and careful study. There, the sociometry is another very useful, yet simple, procedure to use. By asking children to name a few of their classmates with whom they would like to work, play, or do something else, it is possible to identify those who are most often selected (called the *stars*), as well as those who are seldom or never selected (the *isolates*). For example, a two-choice question, "Who are your best friends?" in a group of eighteen children may give such results as shown in Table 7.1 and Figure 7.15. The first is a nomination matrix (who chose whom), and the second is a sociogram constructed from the matrix.

On the sociogram, the fact that everyone gives two names is seen by the arrows emanating from each name. In this group, Julie with eight nominations is the obvious star, while Tom, Gerry, and Jean with none are the isolates. Julie, Bunny, and Mary, also Bill, Don, and Chuck, form cliques of three with reciprocal choices (shown by double-headed arrows) among them. The first clique, however, is a leading crowd with additional unilateral nominations from other children (single-headed arrows). The second clique of three boys is apparently closed to anyone else. Obviously, Julie and, to a lesser extent, Bunny were enjoying good peer relationships in the classroom. Jean, Tom, Gerry, Cindy, Linda, Pat, and Dick were followers in a marginal position. Frank and Mary also occupied a position of fair popularity, and the rest fell in between them and the least popular ones.

It must be kept in mind that this technique yields a rough ranking among children *on that particular question at the specific time*. It has been known that nominations vary according to the questions asked, and the same children are not necessarily chosen on different criteria, e.g., friendship, homework, sports, and class council. In other words, social leadership does not always go with academic, athletic, or political

Table 7.1. Nominating matrix.

The Nominating	The Nominated																		Total Nominations Received
	Bill	Bobby	Bunny	Chuck	Cindy	Dick	Don	Frank	Gerry	Henry	Jean	Joe	Johnny	Julie	Linda	Mary	Pat	Tom	
Bill				1			1												
Bobby												1	1						
Bunny														1		1			
Chuck	1						1												
Cindy								1						1					
Dick				1						1				1		1			
Don	1													1					
Frank		1												1					
Gerry													1				1		
Henry								1											
Jean			1																
Joe						1								1					
Johnny								1				1							
Julie			1													1			
Linda			1		1														
Mary			1											1					
Pat														1	1				
Tom		1								1									
Total Nominations Received	2	2	4	2	1	1	2	3	0	2	0	2	2	8	1	3	1	0	

171

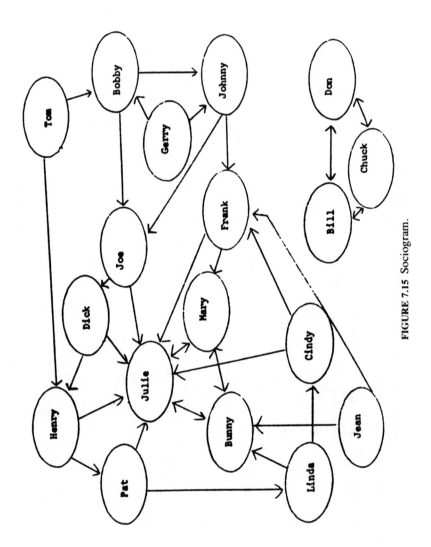

FIGURE 7.15 Sociogram.

leadership, and children do differentiate among these. The teacher can enroll pupil participation in his or her efforts to reach some of the class members. By identifying typical roles that different children seem to play in a group situation and by arranging carefully for a suitable subgroup composition, the teacher may let the peers affect each other toward a desired and desirable goal. For example, a child associating himself with a "star" tends to gain his confidence and social acceptance, and a cohesive, task-oriented group can carry its members to higher motivation for learning. Needless to say, changes over time are to be expected even on the same nomination criterion, and the nature of such variations would reveal something of the child's position in the social cosmos of the classroom.

TWO YOUNG LIVES

Now, let us meet two children with the pseudonyms of Tommy (kindergartner) and Susan (a fourth grader). Their stories have been selected to show a contrast in a home and school influence on children's self-concept.

Tommy

For many children the encounter with a nursery school or kindergarten teacher is the first introduction to established routines outside the family environment. When the family has been supportive of the child's development at home, the expectation is that a similar environment will be provided in the classroom. Unfortunately, not all children receive such a welcome reception when their personalities, abilities, or social characteristics are negatively judged by a teacher. Tommy's kindergarten experience illustrates the harmful effects that treatment by an insensitive teacher can have on a child.

Tommy was born into a white upper-middle-class family as the third child, first boy. His two older sisters were five and seven at the time of his birth. Tommy's father, Mr. W., has an MBA degree and is an investment advisor. The mother has worked as a teacher of learning disabled students.

At three months of age, Tommy had a viral infection requiring a week of hospitalization and four days of oxygen therapy. As a small child he had urethral surgery, and at four years of age he had hernia surgery. He has had ruptured eardrums twice and two febrile seizures at the ages of five years, nine months, and five years, ten months. According to his mother, Tommy continues to have very brief staring episodes during which he cannot be distracted.

Tommy entered nursery school at the age of four. Mrs. W. noted occasional discipline problems due to "squirmy" behavior and short attention spans. However, his performance appeared to be well within the appropriate developmental ranges because his teacher recommended that Tommy proceed to kindergarten. In fact, based on a Gesell Reading Readiness test administered when Tommy was four years, eleven months, he was above average on questions pertaining to perceptual motor skills, while below average in emotional maturity.

Figure 7.16 shows Tommy's self-portrait that was completed as a part of the reading readiness test when he was four years, eleven months. The portrait is age appropriate and does not reveal suggestions of social or developmental difficulties. However, Tommy's parents became concerned about his school performance and self-esteem during his kindergarten year when he persistently complained about school, saying he didn't want to go. At this point, several factors alerted the parents that the situation should be carefully watched. First, his father and uncle had a history of learning difficulties during the early years. According to Mr. W., as a youngster he responded to rebukes from teachers by defending himself in an assertive fashion. On one such occasion when a young Mr. W. "backtalked" a teacher, she slapped him.

Second, because Mrs. W. was a teacher of the learning disabled, she was especially "tuned in" to reports of Tommy's progress. Most important in parental judgments, however, were the changes seen in Tommy from the onset of kindergarten. He was becoming an unhappy child.

Tommy's teacher informed Mrs. W. about difficulties he had been having with certain activities. During a class party in December which Mrs. W. was attending, the teacher asked Tommy to perform a particular task. It required following several directions given at the onset. When he could not handle it because he did not remember the sequence, the teacher said to Mrs. W., "See, he's dumb." Three boys, including Tommy, in a class of about seventeen could not perform these and other designated tasks. As a result, they were separated from the larger group and each other and given separate seats in the back of the room. When Mrs. W. arrived the day this took place, Tommy was rocking in his chair while the other two boys were standing on top of their chairs. The teacher's comments through clenched teeth to Mrs. W. were, "See what I mean?"

FIGURE 7.16 Tommy, in September of kindergarten year.

The incidents greatly alarmed Mr. and Mrs. W. They therefore asked that the school conduct tests to assess Tommy's learning problems. They also asked that the boy be moved to another class because they felt that there was a "mismatch" between the teacher and him. Tommy's artwork in Figures 7.17 through 7.21, depicting pictures of what he wanted for Christmas, also alerted the parents that there seemed to be regression in his cognitive and emotional growth. Because the parents recognized that he had certain learning difficulties requiring attention, they felt that the teacher's unrealistic expectations were exacerbating his learning problems and consequently adversely affecting his willingness to learn and his overall self-esteem. Nevertheless, the administration claimed that they never honor such requests. The school also advised the parents to have Tommy tested at a children's hospital for attention deficit disorder (more commonly known as hyperactivity). Mr. and Mrs. W. followed the suggestion as they were eager to get the appropriate help for the child.

After inquiring about the boy's history and the family's concerns, the hospital recommended a battery of tests. Since Tommy had taken the Wechsler Preschool and Primary Scale of Intelligence (WPPSI) at the age of four years, nine months, the hospital felt that a repeated measure would provide comparison data. In addition, the child development clinic recommended electroencephalogram (EEG) to rule out the possibility of the "petit mal" seizures, a hearing test to examine potential central auditory processing problems, and a test to rule out lead exposure (because Tommy had a history of exposure to an old farm house). It has been known that lead poisoning could lead to short attention spans.

The results of the EEG and the lead poisoning test were negative (i.e., nothing abnormal). The central auditory processing screening indicated developmental delays—seven months below chronological age. On the *WPPSI—Revised,* the children's hospital reported a Full Scale Score of 89 with a Performance Score of 90 and Verbal Score of 90. When Tommy had taken the same test at the age of four years, nine months, his scores were higher—a Full Scale Score of 111 without significant scatter. Meanwhile, his school achievement had been adequate except for the low achievement in mathematics.

Based on these findings, the hospital staff stated, "We are very concerned about the drop in his intellectual scores. . . . He is not seen by us as a child with primary Attention Deficit Hyperactivity Disorder, but a child who is somewhat anxious secondary to his current school experience" (quoted from the hospital report by permission of parents).

FIGURE 7.17 Tommy's art, December of kindergarten year.

FIGURE 7.18 Tommy's art, December of kindergarten year.

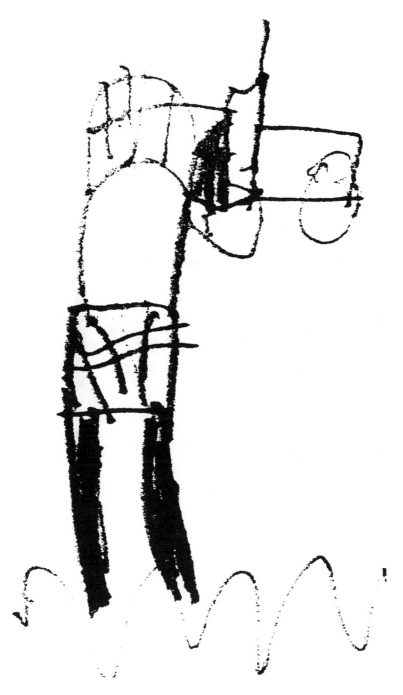

FIGURE 7.19 Tommy's art, December of kindergarten year.

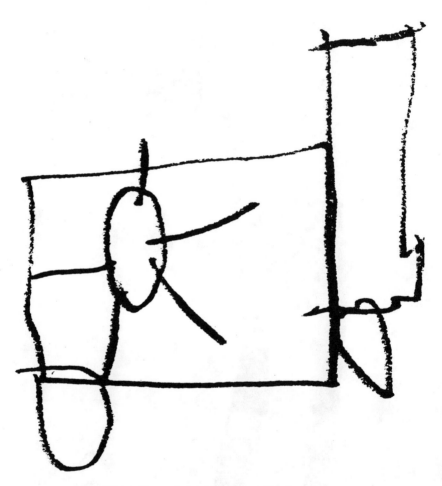

FIGURE 7.20 Tommy's art, December of kindergarten year.

FIGURE 7.21 Tommy's art, December of kindergarten year.

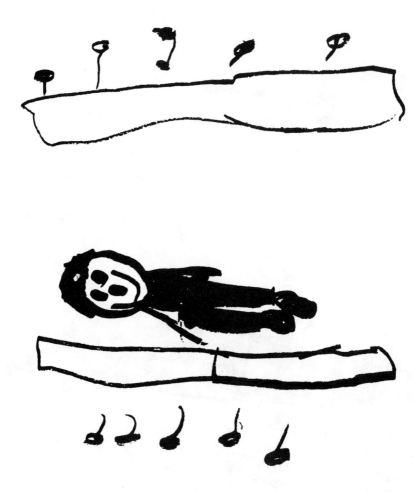

FIGURE 7.22 Tommy's art, May of kindergarten year (after new class assignment).

In the meantime, the school psychologist administered the Woodcock-Johnson Psycho-Educational Battery and Developmental Test of Visual Motor Integration (VMI) with the following results:

> Tommy scored overall in the average range of cognitive ability as measured by the early development scale of the Woodcock-Johnson Psycho-Educational Battery. He had significant problems with symbolic learning, visual tracking and visual motor skills. His strengths were in language, nonverbal reasoning and short term memory skills. He is having difficulty learning symbols in reading and mathematics. Tommy's behavior and self-concept were a concern during testing as he tends to be very hard on himself when he cannot produce a product he feels is correct. He was quite distractable during the testing and showed some inattentive behaviors when he felt threatened about the nature of the activity.

The psychologist's report made recommendations for instructional techniques based on the above-stated learning difficulties. However, Tommy's strengths such as word knowledge, auditory attention skill, common sense skills, social studies, and science were minimally addressed.

At this point the school was more receptive to the parent's request to move Tommy to another classroom setting. In January he was moved to a class where students were closer to his age and where the teacher was more sensitive to the child's needs. That is, she did not ostracize him for not being able to perform certain tasks. Instead, students in the new classroom setting were allowed to progress at a slower rate without recrimination. The internal change in Tommy is visibly reflected in his self-portrait (Figure 7.22) done in May at the end of the kindergarten year.

Tommy's unfortunate experience illustrates the very negative and damaging effects that an insensitive and perhaps unenlightened teacher can have upon a child's fragile self-concept, as well as upon the well-being of the child's entire family. The experience also illustrates the importance of children having ''defender(s) on the homefront against the onslaught of the school-induced erosion of their emerging sense of competence . . .'' (Segal and Yahraes, 1978, p. 221). As we mentioned before, a teacher who is immature as a human being, who is not striving to find himself or herself, and who has little faith in that self is not likely to benefit the young ones with whom he or she comes in touch.

Susan

Susan is a nine-year-old fourth grader who could not remember her last name the first two weeks of school. In the fall, she gave the following answers on an interest inventory.

What do you like to do when you have extra time of your own?	Read book go swimming
What do you like to play best?	games
What is your favorite work?	Building ArPlain
What things do you like to do in school?	Read Play speing bees Art music
What things don't you like to do in school?	math
What do you like to listen to on the radio?	tie a yellow ribin wound old Oak tRE
What are your favorite records?	western
What are your favorite TV shows?	TRuTH or concacences
How much TV do you watch each day?	lots
Do you like movies?	Yes
What are your favorites?	all kinds
What kinds of books do you like to read?	all kinds
Do you read newspapers and magazines?	Yes
What kind do you like best?	all kinds
Did you go on vacation this summer?	Yes
Where did you go?	califorgina
What was the best part of the summer?	summer
What three wishes would you make if you knew they would come true?	First: Ten Speed bycicle Second: shoe skates Third: Wish we could hav a longer summer

What are you really great at
   doing?   Art

Two teachers, a woman and a man, were jointly responsible for the class of sixty students. At the beginning of the school year, six eight-member and four three-member clean-up teams were formed on a self-assignment basis for various cleaning duties. An informal discussion among children preceded the actual grouping efforts, and later each team decided upon a captain and an assistant captain. Susan went with three girls to form an irregular, four-member team. There was another, anomalous team of two to balance this out. (On the March nominations for student representatives, these three other girls are to receive three, two, and zero votes. This places Susan's clean-up team at the bottom of the ten teams whose average spring nominations will be, respectively, 5.3, 5.0, 4.8, 4.0, 3.5, 3.0, 2.5, 2.5, 1.9, and 1.5.)

In October, Susan drew herself as in Figure 7.23. Whatever the reader's first impression from the above information might be, the female teacher admits to having harbored some suspicion of possible emotional problems when, on the very first encounter with the teacher, Susan was unable to come up with her family name. As it turned out, her mother had recently remarried and she was in the process of changing her legal name. The teacher also came to know that Susan lives with her mother and stepfather as an only child, but stays with her father, stepmother, stepbrother, and stepsisters every other weekend. During these weekend visits there seems to be a certain amount of rivalry between Susan and her stepbrother and stepsisters. From what Susan expressed, it seemed possible that the rivalry was more than the usual sibling squabbles, as the parents appeared to defend their own child(ren) in each situation.

Occasionally, the teachers found a private place with Susan to discuss such matters as her weekend visits with her other set of parents or her desire to stop sucking her thumb. During recess one day (in the spring), she made reference to the death of a younger brother. Following is a record of the conversation that afternoon in which the subject of her brother's death was pursued. (S stands for Susan, and T denotes the female teacher.)

S: I was four at the time. [The brother was two, then.]
T: What happened?
S: He drowned.

FIGURE 7.23 Susan in October.

T: Do you want to tell me about it? Was it in a swimming pool?

S: He got up on a garbage can and jumped in. Another girl who should have been watching him had the door shut and by the time she ran over to the swimming pool, he was on the bottom.

T: Where were you? Was this in your backyard?

S: It was at the babysitter's house. My mom and dad were at work. Had to call my mom at work. The police were called.

T: Did the police come and give mouth-to-mouth resuscitation?

S: I didn't know what happened until I got in the police car. I was still asleep. I was crying then.

T: How did you feel at the time?

S: I felt pretty bad.

T: How do you feel about it now?

S: It is like I never had one; I want one though.

T: You do?

S: I want a sister or brother or somebody to play with.

T: You're an only child? I thought you had several brothers and sisters.

S: I only see them when I go over to his house.

T: Where? Why do you say ''his'' house? Does your mom say ''his'' house?

S: No, she says, to Bob's.

T: Don't you call him your dad anymore?

S: Not anymore.

T: Does he still ask you what you are going to do when you are fourteen? Is that when you have to decide?

S: They are trying to beg me to go over there.

T: Your dad?

S: Yes.

T: Why do you suppose he is trying to beg you over there?

S: I don't know. He says he loves me more than my other dad, and that's baloney.

T: Why do you think that is baloney?

S: If he loved me he wouldn't blame me for what my dumb [step] brother did.

T: What kinds of things do you get blamed for?

S: [Susan explains a situation where her stepmother defends her own son in cases where Susan feels it is not her fault and that her brother should be reprimanded; Susan reports that the stepmother says the oldest child (i.e., Susan) should be punished more than the younger one, no matter who is right or wrong.] That isn't fair.

T: It sounds like your dad sticks up for you, though. [The two had discussed earlier situations where her father and stepmother would have arguments over which child should be punished.]

S: Kind of. Sometimes he doesn't. [She explains another situation.]

T: Do you enjoy going to visit your father? Do you enjoy playing with your brothers and sisters?

S: [She explains why she likes one of her sisters more than the other. It sounds as if both stepsisters make separate demands of Susan, such as cleaning up their rooms, and then yell at her for not doing both jobs.]

T: So how do you like your new dad? [She loves him and talks about him; this led into a conversation about when her father gets mad.]

T: What does he do when you make him mad or when you disobey him?

S: Spits nails.

T: Does he ever spank you?

S: Yah.

T: When does he spank you?

S: When I suck my thumb.

In the first parent-teacher conference, Susan's mother appeared to be adjusting to her new marriage. She spoke openly of her disapproval of Susan visiting her father. In addition, we discussed Susan's thumb-sucking with hopes that it could be stopped. At school Susan herself expressed the desire to stop sucking her thumb, and a sort of game developed to help remind her of this behavior. The teacher and Susan agreed that, on each occasion of her thumb-sucking, the teacher would wink at Susan, who would then suddenly realize and remove her thumb. Although this was a positive approach to stopping the habit, she was often absorbed in thumb-sucking and not receptive to signals from the teacher. Other attentive students soon caught on to the "secret game" between Susan and her teacher, thereby nudging Susan when the teacher winked. The actual decrease in thumb-sucking must have come from the adjustments Susan was making in school and at home.

Unfortunately, Susan's history has been one of ostracism from peers.

The teachers wanted to lessen this and find something of which Susan could feel proud and by which she could gain recognition. They encouraged her to bring in hobbies or pursue a special project that could be done with friends. This turned out to be rather frustrating as she ran into problems when she tried to develop an idea of her own or work with other children. In the spring clean-up formation, Susan teamed up with two other girls for a three-member group. These two girls happened to be those who did not receive any nominations of the spring ballot for student representatives. This put Susan's group again at the bottom of the ten teams with average nominations of, respectively, 7.3, 4.9, 4.1, 4.1, 3.7, 3.3, 3.3, 1.8, 1.5, and 0.3.

In the student representatives balloting in question, each child named two boys and two girls. Self-nomination was permissible. As for Susan, she received a single nomination out of the sixty children in the class. There were thirty-one girls and twenty-nine boys in the class and, of these, twenty-nine girls and twenty-four boys received at least one nomination. The top two girls got fourteen and eleven votes, respectively, while the top two boys had seventeen and twelve nominations.

The male teacher had organized a kickball intramural in which anyone can play. From those interested, teams were made with mixed boys and girls. This activity provided more growth for Susan than anything else at school. The team spirit had a great influence on her feeling of belonging to a group. With Susan's determination and experience, she improved her coordination, and her team seemed to realize this. Her captain had been a great leader and occasionally let Susan pitch, which, of course, meant a lot to her. Before the intramural began, Susan spent most of her recess time with adults but, increasingly, she was with peers much of the time, in the classroom as well as outside.

In the last conversation with Susan's mother, she indicated that both her husband and she had noticed a mature change in Susan. She also felt that they as a family had made progress in communication and closeness. At school teachers noticed that Susan's interaction with peers had become the source of some security rather than of frequent harassment. Her feelings of being accepted as a member of a team may have added to a certain amount of confidence. This, in turn, may have reduced the need for trying to gain attention from her peers in ways that were not reciprocated.

In the spring, Susan's answers on an incomplete sentences form were as follows:

I often wish I could . . .	Go RoLLer skating
My father sometimes . . .	Like to smoke
I am afraid when . . .	it is dark
I feel bad when . . .	I suck my thumB
The worst thing a person can do is . . .	Fight
I get excited when . . .	We got to my Grandmother hous
I hate . . .	(another girl's name given)
Most people don't know that I . . .	Like them
I like people who . . .	Like me
I feel proud when . . .	I Get my woRk DoNe
I get mad when . . .	I have to Go to Bed
I like to dream about . . .	people
I wish my family would . . .	Go to the movies
I do not like people who . . .	Fight otherR People
I am happy when . . .	I Go BowLing
I love . . .	my mom and Dad
Some day I will . . .	Get a tenspeed
I wish my father would . . .	Go swimming whith me
Someday I would most like to be like . . .	(a popular male singer's name given)
If I were an inventor, someday I would invent . . .	a caR
I wish I were ___ years old, because then I could . . .	20 have a husBand and Kids
Children would be better off if . . .	they wouldent Fight

Also in the spring (February), her self-portrait was the one in Figure 7.24, which far more resembled herself than the girl in her fall drawing (Figure 7.23).

All told, a variety of stabilizing and supportive factors seemed to have

FIGURE 7.24 Susan in February.

started working for Susan. In the beginning of the school year, her life was somewhat topsy-turvy. Her mother had recently remarried, thus bringing about yet another reconstituted family since her father had already remarried. In addition, the start of school is a major event for most children. The traumatic experience of the loss of a sibling six years earlier also added to the already sizeable stress for the nine-year-old girl. Given the fact that Susan sucked her thumb, the ostracism from peers did not help matters either. Yet, little by little she was making progress in the classroom environment created by the two sympathetic and attentive teachers and sixty classmates. By the end of the year, mother and daughter were speaking more positively about situations in the home also. Susan had gained a healthy respect from peers, and she had been able to share a very personal tragedy with a teacher who was willing to listen. In the relatively short span of the traditional nine-month school year, certain gains had definitely been made.

There remained signs that Susan's self-esteem was somewhat precarious in the face of cumulative or even multiplicative effects of traumatic early experiences. She still sucked her thumb from time to time. Given the complex dynamics of blended families, she would probably continue to have difficulty contending with step-sibling rivalries. After having demonstrated increased detachment from the teachers and more attachment to peers, Susan on the last day of school clung tenaciously to her favorite teacher, sobbing uncontrollably.

What chances and resources would such hurt children have in regaining (or gaining for the first time) their sense of self-worth? For Susan and many students like her, the school provides a greater anchor to the self than is often realized by teachers and parents. When families are experiencing important life transitions (e.g., a move, divorce, remarriage, or death, including that of pets), the classroom environment may be a stabilizing factor that plays a crucial role in support of children's self-esteem.

CHALLENGE FOR TEACHERS

Like anybody else, children are an organic whole. What takes place in one part of their lives immediately and unmistakably affects the rest. And the school *is* a vital part of their world, whether positive or negative in impact. Teachers *are* significant people, again whether positively or negatively. The challenge for teachers is to be there for children when needed — as a mature being who can and will support and guide the young. Wigginton (1986, p. 233), among others, has thrown down a gauntlet, saying, ''One alarming thing to me is the fact that so many teachers, given the power they have to affect young people's feelings about themselves, are often the more fragile and insecure adults I meet.'' Hopefully, we will take up the gauntlet to answer the challenge, both for children's sakes and for our own sake. In that struggle, Rabbi Liebman's observation (1946, p. 60) is truly worth remembering.

> It will help us to make peace with ourselves if we realize that in this battle for self-discovery we need not emerge either a genius or a saint. It will

be enough if we hang two comforting mottoes on the inner walls of our individual souls. First is "Respect thyself." The second, "Trust thyself." Respect yourself with all your shortcomings and achievements. Trust yourself to master the undesirable traits of your character and to achieve both relative inner decency and outer confidence. Such knowledge and trust will tend to eliminate our all-too-human tendency to self-contempt. They will be fertile sources of that true love of self which neither exaggerates its powers nor minimizes its worth.

REFERENCES

Adams, H. 1961. *The Education of Henry Adams: An Autobiography.* Boston: Houghton Mifflin.

Adorno, T. W., E. Frenkel-Brunswick, D. Levinson, Jr., and S. R. Nevitt. 1950. *The Authoritarian Personality.* New York, NY: Harper and Row.

Allport, G. W. 1958. *The Nature of Prejudice, Abridged Edition.* Garden City, NY: Doubleday.

Almy, M. and C. Genishi. 1979. *Ways of Studying Children, Revised Edition.* New York, NY: Teachers College Press.

Ashton-Warner, S. 1963. *Teacher.* New York, NY: Simon and Schuster.

Baruch, D. W. 1964. *One Little Boy.* New York, NY: Dell Publishing Co.

Beagle, C. W. and R. M. Brandt, editors. 1973. *Observational Methods in the Classroom.* Washington, D.C.: Association for Supervision and Curriculum Development.

Boehm, A. and R. A. Weinberg. 1977. *The Classroom Observer: A Guide for Developing Observational Skills.* New York, NY: Teachers College Press.

Bourisseau, W. 1972. "To Fathom the Self: Appraisal in School," in *The Child and His Image,* Kaoru Yamamoto, ed., Boston: Houghton-Mifflin, pp. 80–120.

Brandt, R. M. 1972. *Studying Behavior in Natural Settings.* New York, NY: Holt, Rinehart and Winston.

Buber, M. 1965. *Between Man and Man.* New York, NY: Macmillan.

Burt, C. 1963. As paraphrased in Harris, D. B., *Children's Drawings as Measures of Intellectual Maturity.* New York, NY: Harcourt, Brace and World.

Cadwalader, G. 1989. *Castaways.* New York, NY: Penguin Books.

Chukovsky, K. 1963. *From Two to Five.* Berkeley, CA: University of California Press.

Clark, K. B. 1965. *Dark Ghetto.* New York, NY: Harper and Row.

Cohen, D. H., V. Stern and N. Balaban. 1983. *Observing and Recording the Behavior of Young Children, Third Edition.* New York, NY: Teachers College Press.

Collins, M. and C. Tamarkin. 1982. *Marva Collins' Way.* Los Angeles: Jeremy P. Tarcher.

DiLeo, J. H. 1973. *Children's Drawings as Diagnostic Aids.* New York, NY: Brunner/Mazel.

Freedman, S. G. 1990. *Small Victories.* New York, NY: Harper & Row.

Goodman, M. 1964. *Race Awareness in Young Children, Revised Edition.* New York, NY: Collier Books.

Gordon, I. J. 1966. *Studying the Child in School.* New York, NY: John Wiley and Sons.

Gordon, J. W. 1970. *My Country School Diary.* New York, NY: Dell Publishing Co.

Hammer, E. F. 1980. *The Clinical Application of Projective Drawings.* Springfield, IL: Charles C. Thomas.

Harris, D. B. 1963. *Children's Drawings as Measures of Intellectual Maturity.* New York, NY: Harcourt, Brace and World.

Harris, D. B., J. Roberts and G. D. Pinder. 1970. *Intellectual Maturity of Children as Measured by the Goodenough-Harris Drawing Test* (DHEW Publication No. HSM-73-1267). Washington, D.C.: U.S. Department of Health, Education and Welfare.

Irwin, M. and M. Bushnell. 1980. *Observational Strategies for Child Study.* New York, NY: Holt, Rinehart and Winston.

Jourard, S. M. 1968. *Disclosing Man to Himself.* Princeton, NJ: Van Nostrand.

Kellogg, R. 1969. *Analyzing Children's Art.* Palo Alto, CA: National Press Books.

Koppitz, E. M. 1984. *Psychological Evaluation of Human Figure Drawings by Middle School Pupils.* New York, NY: Grune and Stratton.

Liebman, J. L. 1946. *Peace of Mind.* New York, NY: Simon and Schuster.

Machover, K. 1951. "Drawing of the Human Figure: A Method of Personality Investigation," in *An Introduction to Protective Techniques,* H. H. Anderson and G. L. Anderson, eds., Englewood Cliffs, NJ: Prentice-Hall, pp. 341–369.

Machover, K. 1960. "Sex Differences in the Developmental Pattern of Children as Seen in Human Figure Drawings," in *Projective Techniques with Children,* A. I. Rabin and M. R. Haworth, eds., New York, NY: Grune and Stratton, pp. 238–257.

Machover, K. 1980. *Personality Projection in the Drawing of the Human Figure.* Springfield, IL: Charles C. Thomas.

Marshall, S. 1963. *An Experiment in Education.* New York, NY: Cambridge University Press.

McCaslin, N., ed. 1986. *Children and Drama, 2nd Edition.* Washington, D.C.: University Press of America.

Medinnus, G. R. 1976. *Child Study and Observation Guide.* New York, NY: John Wiley and Sons.

Millard, C. V. and J. W. M. Rothney. 1957. *The Elementary School Child—A Book of Case Studies.* New York, NY: Dryden Press.

Moustakas, C. 1966. *The Authentic Teacher.* Cambridge, MA: Howard A. Doyle.

Oaklander, V. 1978. *Windows to Our Children.* Moab, UT: Real People Press.

Pratt, C. 1990. *I Learn from Children.* New York, NY: Harper and Row.

Rogers, C. R. 1983. *Freedom to Learn for the 80's.* Columbus, OH: Charles E. Merrill.

Rokeach, M. 1964. *The Three Christs of Ypsilanti.* New York, NY: Alfred A. Knopf.

Rosenberg, M. and R. G. Simmons. 1972. *Black and White Self-Esteem: The Urban School Child.* Washington, D.C.: American Sociological Association.

Rowen, B. 1973. *The Children We See.* New York, NY: Holt, Rinehart and Winston.

Segal, J. and H. Yahraes. 1978. *A Child's Journey.* New York, NY: McGraw-Hill Book Co.

Spring, L. W. 1946. "Socratic Yankee: Mark Hopkins," in *Great Teachers,* H. Peterson, ed., New York, NY: Random House, pp. 77–99.

Strang, R. 1959. *An Introduction to Child Study, Fourth Edition.* New York, NY: Macmillan.

Sutton-Smith, B. 1981. *The Folkstories of Children.* Philadelphia, PA: University of Pennsylvania Press.

Torgerson, T. L. 1947. *Studying Children.* New York, NY: Dryden Press.

Torrance, E. P. and R. E. Myers. 1972. *Creative Learning and Teaching.* New York, NY: Dodd, Mead.

Wagner, B. J. 1976. *Dorothy Heathcote: Drama as a Learning Medium.* Washington, D.C.: National Education Association.

Way, B. 1990. *Development through Drama.* Atlantic Highlands, NJ: Humanities Press.

Wigginton, E. 1986. *Sometimes a Shining Moment.* Garden City, NY: Anchor Books.

Wright, H. F. 1967. *Recording and Analyzing Child Behavior.* New York, NY: Harper and Row.

Yamamoto, K., ed. 1972. *The Child and His Image: Self Concept in the Early Years.* Boston, MA: Houghton-Mifflin.

Yamamoto, K. 1975. *Individuality: The Unique Learner.* Columbus, OH: Charles E. Merrill.

CHAPTER 8

Adolescent Self-Esteem in the Family and School Environments

GAIL McEACHRON-HIRSCH – *The College of William and Mary*
THOMAS J. WARD – *The College of William and Mary*

"SOMETIMES I wonder how my life would be different if I was raised by a father and a mother instead of just my mother," Janice contemplates as she examines where she is in life as a freshman in high school. "I know that I want to be a doctor, but my greatest interest now is hanging out at my brother's beach condo and surfing all day," shares Tim, a high achiever whose ambivalence has his mother very worried. "My father died when I was three," says Brent, ". . . and I sometimes think that I would have more self-discipline if he had been there all along."

These reflections from four case studies interviewed as a part of a four-year longitudinal study reveal the complex way adolescents contemplate an image of self in the face of what has taken place and what might happen in their lifetime. At any given time one's analysis of self is based upon the existing internal structure, which began at conception, the perception of ensuing events in one's life, and the anticipation of what the future might bring. Emerson's chambered nautilus is a useful metaphor for understanding this process. A cross section of the beautiful shell reveals inner chambers that have been formulated with the passage of time, an inner skeleton created and maintained to provide a foundation for the shell façade that faces the outer world.

Unlike shells, however, people not only have an inner skeleton and outer presentation, but have the ability to think about the past and, to a certain extent, chart their futures. One's self-esteem is that contemplative assessment of one's existence at a given point in time. So, in the case of the metaphor, one's inner skeleton is the sum total of one's experience – or self-concept; the outer shell is what the public responds to, thereby influencing the nature of one's experience – or self-concept; self-esteem is the judgment one makes of oneself based upon this interaction. The self is the complex combination of all the component parts.

This chapter is the first reporting of the data from the four-year study by Gail McEachron-Hirsch and Louis Messier; the study followed high school freshmen through their senior year.

It is perhaps easier, yet overly simplistic, to think of self-concept as a descriptive portrayal of one's life, "based on the roles one plays and the attributes one believes he or she possesses" (Beane and Lipka, 1984, p. 5). For example, in the case of Tim, quoted previously, one could say that his self-concept has been shaped by and formulated into the following characteristics: is White, male, and a high achiever; has grown up with two half-siblings, one sister, and both biological parents; wants to be a doctor; likes to surf; lives in Virginia. Yet, these descriptors do not reveal the sensitive feelings that represent expressions of self or one's self-esteem. For example, Tim's mother worries that he will neglect his studies and not pursue a long-term goal that he has had, whereas Tim is confident that he will still be able to go to medical school. Thus, one's assessment of self may be in sharp contrast to outside interpretations, thereby creating not only dissonance but feedback that can possibly bring about self-doubt or self-determination. In the case of Tim, at the end of his sophomore year, self-determination seems to be at the forefront.

Brent, by contrast, reveals an underlying streak of self-doubt. A look at the demographic descriptors that characterize Brent's identity will not automatically reveal clues to the nature of his self-doubt: White, average academic achievement, varsity wrestler (since freshman year), youngest of four boys, father (history of alcoholism) died when Brent was three, mother confined to a wheelchair. However, when interviewed, Brent revealed that he knew he had the potential to excel with his athletic ability in wrestling, but he had difficulty when it was necessary to muster the self-discipline required for training and practice. His older brother is a professional wrestler who, according to Brent, puts pressure on him to do well. With further discussion, Brent expressed that he missed having a father to discipline him and that he felt he had to grow up too soon after his mother had a stroke and became more sedentary.

The reports by Tim and Brent reveal the difficult task of trying to isolate and understand self-esteem on an individual basis, as well as in family and school environments. As a preview, however, the case studies already mentioned do suggest a range in levels of self-esteem. With scanty information one might predict that Tim has a more positive view of himself than does Brent. In fact, according to scores on the Rosenberg self-esteem scale, these predictions hold true. Tim's score on a scale of zero to six, with six being the highest self-esteem measure, was six and Brent scored two.

But what does it all mean? What do the scores of the four adolescents briefly described thus far contribute to our understanding of how adolescents integrate an image of self during their high school years? What role do the family and school play in influencing self-esteem? How do factors such as ethnicity, gender, parents' education levels, and family structure shape adolescent self-esteem? To investigate these questions, McEachron-Hirsch and Messier began a four-year longitudinal study, which followed high school freshmen through their senior year. The results of this study will be spotlighted by reporting the quantitative analyses generated from the 152 participants, as well as information collected from eight case studies. In Chapter Eleven, Messier and Ward will be comparing the findings reported here with self-esteem studies of juvenile delinquents.

DESCRIPTION OF LONGITUDINAL STUDY

The adolescents who participated in the study lived in a small community in Virginia with a population of about 50,000. The high school they attended has a total student enrollment of 1,658, which can be broken down into the following ethnic and gender compositions: Anglo, 72%; Black 27.5%; Asian, Hispanic, and Native American combined, .5%; 798 male and 860 female. From the freshman class, totaling approximately 400, including repeating freshmen, 152 agreed to participate. Of the 152 participants, 71 were male and 76 female; 5 did not report their gender. Ethnic composition included: 109 Anglos, 33 Blacks, 3 Asians, and 1 Native American; 6 did not report their ethnic background.

Four instruments were administered to students on two different occasions. In the fall, the Rosenberg Self-Esteem Scale (Rosenberg, 1965), the Family Environment Scale (Moos, 1974), and a demographic instrument designed for the study were administered. In the spring, the Classroom Environment Scale (Moos and Trickett, 1987) and Adjective Checklist (Gough and Heilbrun, 1983) were administered. These measures were repeated during the students' sophomore, junior, and senior years. The results of the Iowa Test of Basic Skills (ITBS) administered by the school during the students' sophomore year and grade point averages through the junior year were also made available to the researchers.[1]

What follows is a review of adolescent self-esteem studies and a description of the results of the McEachron-Hirsch and Messier study. Case study material will be interspersed in discussions of family and classroom environments. Fictitious names will be used for all case illustrations. McEachron-Hirsch and Messier formulated several hypotheses, primarily, that there would be no differences in self-esteem based on gender, ethnicity, and family structure (e.g., divorced or intact families), but that there would be significant differences in self-esteem based on academic achievement as well as levels of conflict and cohesion within the family. As indicated below, some of these hypotheses were accepted, while others were rejected.

SELF-ESTEEM IN RELATION TO FAMILY ENVIRONMENT

Family Environment

Family environment plays a key role in the development of adolescent growth and identity. A delicate balance is required if parents are to succeed in supporting a move toward independence while maintaining a strong family support network. The concept of individuation is expressed by this dual process wherein adolescents (1) gain increased independence from parental authority and (2) begin to construct a self that is separate from parental influence (Youniss and Smollar, 1985). Many psychological theories emphasize the adolescent's separation from parents to the extent that the parent's supportive role in the process is often clouded. However, family historians have recognized since the late nineteenth century that "the alliance that parents and offspring have on the matter of the latter's successful movement into society" is more important than the specific disagreements they have along the way (Youniss and Smollar, 1985, p. 78).

Before examining more closely the internal fabric of family life, it is helpful to place social characteristics of families in a broader context. In an in-depth study of adolescent self-esteem, Rosenberg (1965) considered two hypotheses—the stratification hypothesis and subcultural hypothesis. The stratification hypothesis suggests that religious groups, races, nationality groups, and social classes experience different levels of social prestige. Since personal feelings of worth, to a certain extent, depend upon the social evaluation of groups, one hypothesis is that the self-esteem of members within those groups may reflect the social prestige of particular groups. The subcultural hypothesis, on the other hand, states that members across broad social groups are seen as sharing certain interests, attitudes and values, e.g., child-rearing practices, regardless of their race, religion, and so on. Thus, if certain "child-rearing practices had a bearing upon self-esteem, then this differential treatment might create differences in levels of self-acceptance" (Rosenberg, 1965, p. 61). In his study, Rosenberg found more support for the subcultural hypothesis and concluded that "Among adolescents, subcultural norms, or other characteristic aspects of experience deriving from cultural factors are more important than general social prestige as determinants of self-esteem." An important contribution of Rosenberg's study was his finding that the adolescent subculture is more salient to self-esteem than the social classifications that appear to be operating in the larger society. In the next section, the McEachron-Hirsch and Messier findings of the relationship between self-esteem and the social classifications of gender, race, and socioeconomic status will be examined followed by the effects of family environments. Finally, an examination of the school environment as part of the adolescent subculture will be presented.

Social Norms

Rosenberg (1965) refers to social factors such as class and ethnicity as secondary groups or cultural groups sharing certain norms. In his sample of 4,600 students, he found that the social prestige of certain ethnic groups was generally unrelated to the self-acceptance of its members. With regard to social class, students from higher social classes were more likely to have high self-esteem, but the differences were small, varied between boys and girls, and appeared to be related to parent-child relationships.

A review of more recent studies focusing on ethnic background generally suggests that Blacks tend to have higher levels of self-esteem than Caucasians (Barnes and Farrier, 1985; Hoelter, 1983; Rust and McCraw, 1984), with some exceptions when socioeconomic levels were examined. For example, Jensen, White, and Galliher (1982) sought to defuse the myth that minorities have lower self-esteem by comparing self-esteem in non-Black minority groups with those based upon Black/White comparisons, concentrating on Chicano youth. Their findings suggest that when contextual variables (e.g., socioeconomic status, minority/majority status, etc.) are more constant, there is less likelihood for differences in self-esteem. Additional research suggests a slight tendency for Blacks and Whites to have higher levels of self-esteem when compared to Asians, Filipinos, and Indochinese, in a context where racial tension was the lowest for Blacks and Whites (Bowler et al., 1986). Jensen, White, and Galliher (1982) found no major differences between Anglos and Chicanos, arguing that previous studies comparing Whites and non-Whites have been limited due to the use of White comparison groups with unusually low self-esteem. Overall, the variation in self-esteem across ethnic groups has been attributed to the influence of socioeconomic status, length of time as a minority group within the American culture, and levels and opportunities for inter-ethnic contact.

When the self-esteem scores in the McEachron-Hirsch and Messier study were analyzed over a four-year period there was a significant interaction between measures of self-esteem and ethnicity. Figure 8.1 shows that minority students, primarily Blacks, had higher levels of self-esteem during their freshman and junior years, but their self-esteem scores dropped significantly during their sophomore year. The self-esteem of White students tended to remain stable over the four-year period with a slight upward trend. Overall, the self-esteem of both Whites and non-Whites ended up in the 1.5 range, which suggests middle to high self-esteem, but the path for non-Whites demonstrated greater variability. It is important to emphasize, however, that despite differences

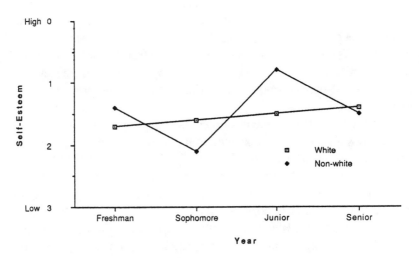

FIGURE 8.1 Self-esteem by race and year. (Rosenberg self-esteem scores range from 0 to 6; in this depiction lower scores indicate higher self-esteem.)

throughout the four years both Whites and non-Whites started and ended high school with relatively equivalent levels of self-esteem. In addition, all students' self-esteem levels showed a gradual increase by the senior year.

The ethnic disparity in terms of self-esteem stability puzzled the researchers. Attempts to explain the differences resulted in numerous speculations. One plausible hypothesis offered by school personnel was that an administrative change in assistant principals during the second year of the study affected self-esteem among minority students. Since the new assistant principal was responsible for detentions and in-school suspensions, and since there were a higher number of reported incidences for Black males, it was surmised that self-esteem scores may have been affected by the interaction between the Black males and the assistant principal, whose rapport with students has been criticized.

One parent of a minority student proposed that for her son the realization that success in sports was not a sufficient basis for graduation affected his self-perceptions and changing school performance. Another hypothesis given by a parent was that the success of Douglas Wilder in becoming the first African-American governor in the United States may have accounted for the surge in minority self-esteem during the junior year. Since most of the minorities in the study were in the middle to lower socioeconomic levels, this may have been a symbol for upward mobility, thereby enhancing self-esteem. When examined separately, however, socioeconomic status did not interact with self-esteem levels.

McEachron-Hirsch and Messier examined the effect of socio-economic levels on self-esteem by taking the father's educational level as an indicator of class. Statistical analysis indicated no significant differences in self-esteem between students' homes where fathers had a college education and homes where they did not. These findings support research claiming that class alone is not a sufficient determinant of variation in self-esteem scores.

The influence of class and ethnicity, which seem so pervasive in adult society may be perceived differently among adolescents. Rosenberg (1965, pp. 61−62) first raised this notion when he stated,

> . . . In the adult world, differential occupational achievement, dominance or submission, power or impotence, prestige or disesteem may influence one's self-esteem, whereas in the adolescent world, the reflected glory deriving from the occupational achievement of one's father may be less important. Nor does this mean that achievement is unimportant for the

adolescent. On the contrary, a successful school record or successful interpersonal relationships are . . . definitely related to self-esteem. But these reflect the adolescent's own achievements, whereas his class, religion and nationality are assigned to him by society. . . .

One Asian student revealed assimilation difficulties that he had encountered as a minority student who had recently emigrated to the United States from Hong Kong. Paul came to the United States the summer prior to his freshman year to live with grandparents for the purpose of increasing his career opportunities. His parents commended his uncle as a role model for Paul, because he had pursued medical school in England. When asked what things about his school stood out for him, Paul, as a sophomore, indicated that people at his school, with the exception of some of the girls, were not friendly toward him. He was not a member of any of the school clubs and associations but indicated that, if there had been a math club, he probably would have joined. These feelings stayed with Paul. During his senior year he remarked that throughout his high school years he had not made any good friends.

Paul's experience is consistent with findings by Bowler, Rauch, and Schwarzer (1986) who reported that the length of time minority students had lived in the United States and inter-ethnic contact were important factors to consider when interpreting self-esteem scores. With Paul, limited language proficiency and interest in activities such as math, which had not been sanctioned by way of being institutionalized as a separate school club, appeared to be factors that influenced his self-esteem and identity in the context of the school environment. Another important aspect of interpersonal relationships is the way adolescents perceive their roles as young men and women and whether or not their perception of these roles is supported by peers and teachers in the school environment.

Gender Relationships

An examination of the relationship between gender and self-esteem indicates that adolescent males tend to have higher levels of self-esteem than do adolescent females (Barnes and Farrier, 1985; Hoelter, 1983; Rosenberg, 1965). In particular, Caucasian adolescent females have been found to score lower than either Caucasian or Black males or Black females (Trent and McPartland, 1982). A further examination of the differences suggests that females, particularly Caucasian, appear to have a higher degree of anxiety over impulse control even though they describe their self-image as healthy (Leroux, 1986), higher levels of uncertainty over ascribed sexual roles (Rust and McCraw, 1984), and greater difficulty maintaining a positive self-image despite positive school adjustments (Trent and McPartland, 1982).

In the data collected from the adolescents in the Virginia study, there were no significant differences in self-esteem based upon gender, a finding that is incongruous with the studies reviewed above. Such findings suggest that female adolescents may not have the low self-esteem levels that they once had in the 1960s (Rosenberg, 1965). Perhaps the women's movement has had a positive effect on female adolescents. However, before suggesting that radical changes have taken place with regard to women's roles in American culture, it is important to consider the social and political backlash during the 1980s and 1990s (Faludi, 1991). A word of caution from Byrne adds perspective. Based upon the psychometric properties of self-esteem instruments, Byrne (1983) maintains that it is more appropriate to supplement global self-esteem measures with instruments that examine more specific facets of self, such as efficacy and self-perceptions of vocational potential.

While it is true that female adolescents may feel good about themselves in a general sense but not feel as efficacious about their roles within and beyond the school environment, the interviews with case studies reinforced the notion that gender roles and expectations may have changed for some individuals over time. Both male and female adolescents acknowledged that times had changed and certain assumptions about male/female role appropriateness were no longer as clearly defined. When asked, ''Do you think there are any important differences between women and men?'' (Belenky et al., 1986), the comments by the female adolescents expressed ''subtle conviction'' to the notion of womanhood, yet ambivalence regarding role expectations based upon age and context.

After several pensive moments, Sandra answered, ''I think that I am glad to be a woman. It has its definite advantages and I think that people might respect you more than they respect men . . . at this age, anyway.'' To Janice in her freshman year, the double standards she experienced while growing up created some ambivalence regarding gender roles. As a young child Janice played football ''with the guys'' but she was often told to come in the house and act like a young lady. Janice said that at first she didn't see why girls had to come in earlier than boys, but when she grew older she reflected, "Now with teenage pregnancies, there is a difference." Growing up with a mother and three older sisters since her parents divorced when she was five years old also influenced Janice's perception of her female identity: "Well, growing up with no brothers and no men in the house, we did what we had to do, there was no choice. . . . A girl can handle more responsibility than a guy."

For Debbie the presence of a half-brother has given her cause for reflection and reaction: "Some men are really self-centered. I am trying to think of the word—womanizers. My brother is a womanizer, big time. He will say something about women staying home. He thinks women shouldn't be out in the work force. I told him—yeah sure! I told him I was going into the Air Force. He said, 'No you aren't; you need to stay home and have 10 million kids!' "

The comments by Sandra, Janice, and Debbie suggest an awareness of socially imposed separate spheres (Gilligan, 1982) but do not imply an acquiescence to subservient roles. For all three there seemed to be a sense of strength and conviction in their identification with women. From Janice we glean a sense of confidence from having successfully maintained a family household without dependence upon men. Debbie's response to her half-brother acknowledges conflicting role expectations but an inclination to defend her own right to choose.

The comments by male adolescents who addressed the changing times and role differences revealed a wider range of perceptions—from no differences at all to changes that have resulted in confusion for both males and females. For example, when asked during their sophomore year, "Do you think there are any important differences between women and men?" Paul replied, "Nothing. [They're] treated the same. No different in Hong Kong either." Tim's distinctions centered around peer groups and social acceptance. He stated, "Girls think more about friends and are concerned about what they think. Girls are in bigger groups of friends, ten to twelve, guys have four to five. Guys are less concerned [about what others think]."

For Craig, men and women play hierarchical roles: "A man is supposed to have more authority than a woman. Men take care of the house and make sure everything is okay for everyone. Men and women could do the same, but they might try to be better than the other in keeping control." Brent acknowledged the changing times but seemed to be a little bewildered about the implications for male/female relationships and himself in particular. His comments also suggested that, in terms of being efficacious, his perceived social expectancies are fairly low for females. He claimed that males are expected to make something of themselves. Implicit in his remarks is the assumption that females are not expected to make "anything" of themselves.

> I act like a jerk sometimes. I wish I was brought up in the sixties and fifties. Cars and girls were great. Girls weren't easy back then but these days girls are outgoing, but a little bit. . . . They knew what they were doing [in the fifties and sixties]. If they wanted a career they could get one. These days girls don't know what they want—career, marriage, stay home; it's harder now. Men have one thing to do. They have to make something of themselves or they call you a bum. Men [are] not trying to be male chauvinist pigs, but they have it all planned for them. Now they're not depended on as much; you see both doing the same jobs. I'd hire 'em if they were qualified.

These interviews reveal the influences of cultural norms when formulating personal identities. Yet, as each personal account reveals, no two stories are the same. Each student reveals unique reactions to cultural norms and values based on personal experiences and perceptions. Even though cultural norms, what Rosenberg refers to as secondary classifications, may not be as strong as the influences on self-esteem by primary groups such as the family, we have seen from the case study interviews that these cultural norms affected the students' overall "fit" or comfort level within the adolescent subculture. Thus, while the degree of influence of cultural norms may be difficult to measure, the influence itself is more easily documented through the interview process.

Family Dynamics

According to the late British psychoanalyst, D. W. Winnicott, one's family is the foundation of a widening circle of influence as it mediates the development of the child through adolescence (Ianni, 1989). It is within the family that a growing child's perception of the accord or discord with the widening circle of social contexts is first experienced, thus setting the emotional tone for the development of self-esteem (Ianni, 1989). Stability and patterns of communication within the family have been targeted areas for research on the effects of family environment upon self-esteem. As a result, several competing theories have emerged within the broad rubric of family systems theory. Physical dissolution is a theory that has gained support by psychologists who argue that divorce is a major factor that adversely affects family lifestyle and family members. The mere act of physically splitting apart families, theorists maintain, creates psychological scars that have long-lasting effects into adulthood. According to supporters of the physical dissolution position, divorce brings about damaging effects to self-esteem in family members, especially children and youth.

Opposing psychological theories advocate the psychological wholeness position, claiming that divorce alone is not the cause of changes in self-esteem. Instead, events and family relationships that led to and followed divorce are the more crucial factors affecting self-esteem. For example, Wallerstein and Kelly (1980) and Wallerstein and Blakeslee (1989) conducted in-depth studies of families of divorce over a ten-year period. They found that the levels of conflict and cohesion in the family before and after the divorce itself were more crucial to adjustment than the mere act of divorce or physical dissolution of the family. In the 1950s, Nye (1957) was one of the first to examine the assumption that divorce has detrimental effects based on the physical dissolution of the family. Nye compared child adjustment in broken and in unhappy unbroken homes, finding that intact families, by structure alone, were not sufficiently distinguished to guarantee better adjustment in children. Since that time scholars have investigated the relationships between varying family structures (Burchinal, 1964; Kagel et al., 1978; Lutz, 1983; Marotz-Baden et al., 1979; McLanahan, 1983; Slater and Haber, 1984; Slater et al., 1983) and environments (Hirsch et al., 1985; Tyerman and Humphrey, 1983) and their influence upon child and adolescent self-esteem (Nelson, 1984; Raschke and Raschke, 1979), personality (Forman and Forman, 1981; Fowler, 1982; Hetherington, 1972; Prasinos and Tittler, 1981), academic achievement (Brown, 1980; Conyers, 1977), juvenile delinquency (Willie, 1967), and behavior (Hiltonsmith, 1985).

Based on this research it is possible to suggest that there is a significant relationship between high conflict and low levels of cohesion and self-esteem, regardless of the family structure. In other words, whether a child or adolescent is a member of an intact, blended, reconstituted, or single-parent family is less crucial than the incidence of conflict and degree of family cohesion. Family structure does appear, however, to have an impact on student truancy, absenteeism, suspension, and expulsion, in that adolescents from divorced families reveal higher incidences

Table 8.1. Family structure of entire sample.

Years	% Intact			% Reconstituted				
	Intact	Death of One Parent; Not Remarried	Separated; Not Divorced	Divorced; Not Remarried	Divorced; Remarried	Death of Parent; Remarried	Not Living with Parent	Missing Cases
1	63.6	2.1	0	9.3	12.9	7.9	4.3	7.9
2	62.7	1.6	1.6	9.5	13.5	7.1	4.0	17.1
3	64.7	3.4	2.6	6.9	13.8	5.2	3.4	23.7
4	62.8	4.3	0	8.5	14.9	5.3	4.3	38.2

of each of these than those from intact families (Brown, 1980). The impact of family structure upon self-esteem and related behaviors such as juvenile delinquency is also tied to socioeconomic conditions, whereby the preventive potential of two-parent households against juvenile delinquency tends to be impaired by poverty (Willie, 1967).

To assess the self-esteem/family structure relationship, comparisons between intact (including death of one parent) families and families that had experienced divorce, separation, remarriage, or living arrangements with other caregivers were made by McEachron-Hirsch and Messier. Table 8.1 portrays the family structures within the high school sample. Results indicated that there were no significant differences in self-esteem scores based on family structure. These findings help to defuse some of the stigma surrounding divorce and varying family patterns by demonstrating that family structure alone is not enough to categorically diminish self-esteem. However, there were significant differences in self-esteem when subscales of the Family Environment Scale were examined. In families where there were greater cohesiveness and a greater active recreational orientation, students had higher self-esteem levels. Table 8.2 displays the relationships between self-esteem and family environment.

Figure 8.2 shows the pattern of subscale scores on the FES for the freshman and senior years. The graph shows that the subscale pattern was stable over the four years studied. This graph also shows that the overall impression of these high school students was that they lived in normal families as indicated by their near normal mean scores (mean = 50).

These findings underscore the importance of psychological wholeness and stability within a family. In addition the findings also spotlight

Table 8.2. Self-esteem in relation to family environment.

Year	Multiple Regression	
1	$r = .43$ $r^2 = .19$	Cohesion and active recreational orientation
2	$r = .28$ $r^2 = .08$	Active recreational orientation
3	$r = .40$ $r^2 = .16$	Cohesion and active recreational orientation
4	$r = .27$ $r^2 = .08$	Cohesion and active recreational orientation

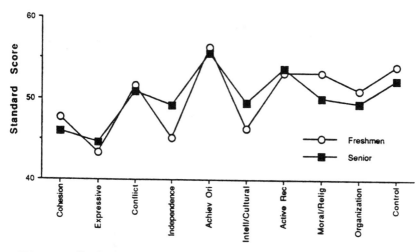

FIGURE 8.2 Freshman and senior year profiles on the Family Environment Scale.

another important dimension of family dynamics—active recreational orientation. The psychological bond within the family, paired with active recreation outside the immediate family environment, may be a combination previously underestimated in self-esteem research.

Adolescent Perceptions of Family Environment

The interviews conducted with four male and four female adolescents provided valuable insights into the importance of the family environment in contributing positively or negatively to self-esteem. Interviews were conducted by McEachron-Hirsch and Messier during the end of the freshman, sophomore, and senior years, each interview averaging approximately forty-five minutes to one hour. At the end of the interview, each case study was asked to draw a picture of himself or herself. For one interview, the case study participant was asked first to draw himself or herself, then to draw a picture of someone of the opposite sex. The portraits are presented in Figures 8.3 – 8.36. Their ethnic classifications are as follows: Anglo—Brent, Tim, Craig, Sandra, Debbie; African-American—Janice, Celeste; Asian-American—Paul. For now they serve as a means to introduce faces of individuals you will be reading about and allow the reader to formulate observations about adolescents. Additional interpretations will be made later in the chapter.

FIGURE 8.3 Janice, self-portrait, freshman year.

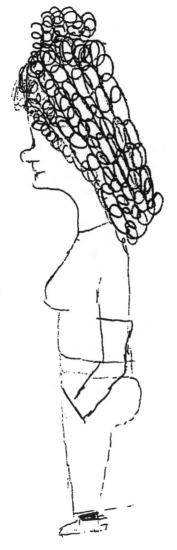

FIGURE 8.4 Janice, self-portrait, freshman year.

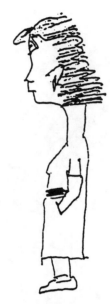

FIGURE 8.5 Janice, draw a person like yourself task, sophomore year.

FIGURE 8.6 Janice, draw a person of the opposite sex task, sophomore year.

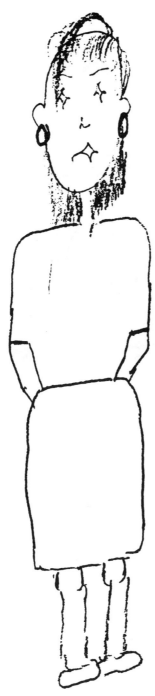

FIGURE 8.7 Janice, self-portrait, senior year.

FIGURE 8.8 Sandra, self-portrait, freshman year.

FIGURE 8.9 Sandra, draw a person like yourself task, sophomore year.

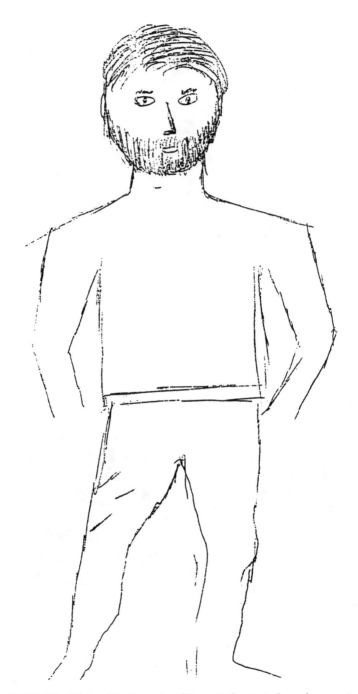

FIGURE 8.10 Sandra, draw a person of the opposite sex task, sophomore year.

FIGURE 8.11 Sandra, self-portrait, senior year.

FIGURE 8.12 Debbie, self-portrait, freshman year.

FIGURE 8.13 Debbie, draw a person like yourself task, sophomore year.

FIGURE 8.14 Debbie, draw a person of the opposite sex task, sophomore year.

French Braided hair

FIGURE 8.15 Celeste, self-portrait, freshman year.

FIGURE 8.16 Celeste, draw a person like yourself task, sophomore year.

FIGURE 8.17 Celeste, draw a person of the opposite sex task, sophomore year.

FIGURE 8.18 Celeste, self-portrait, senior year.

FIGURE 8.19 Craig, draw a person like yourself task, freshman year.

FIGURE 8.20 Craig, draw a person like yourself task, freshman year.

FIGURE 8.21 Craig, self-portrait, sophomore year.

FIGURE 8.22 Craig, draw a person like yourself task, senior year.

FIGURE 8.23 Craig, draw a person of the opposite sex task, senior year.

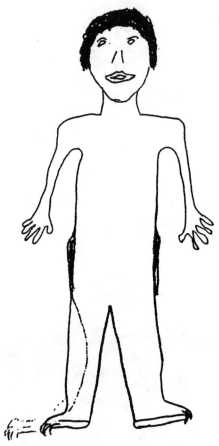

FIGURE 8.24 Brent, draw a person like yourself task, freshman year.

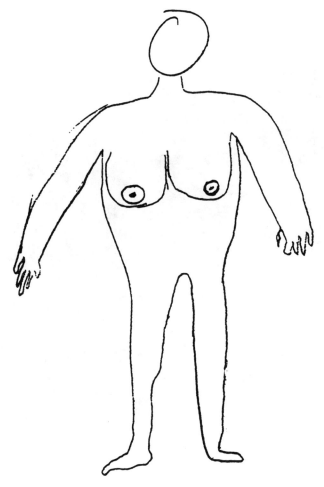

FIGURE 8.25 Brent, draw a person of the opposite sex task, freshman year.

FIGURE 8.26 Brent, self-portrait, sophomore year.

FIGURE 8.27 Brent, draw a person like yourself task, senior year.

FIGURE 8.28 Brent, draw a person of the opposite sex task, senior year.

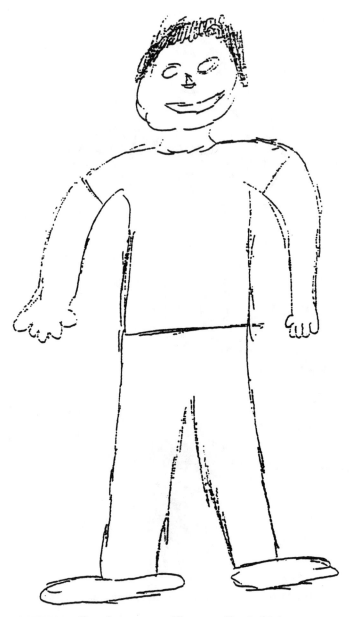

FIGURE 8.29 Tim, draw a person like yourself task, freshman year.

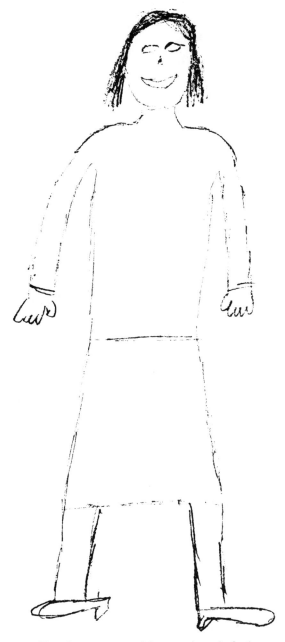

FIGURE 8.30 Tim, draw a person of the opposite task, freshman year.

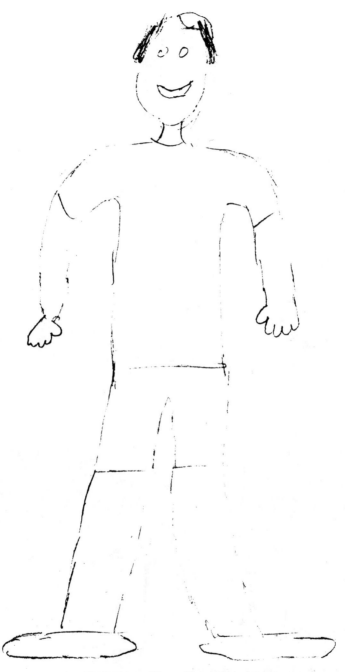

FIGURE 8.31 Tim, self-portrait, sophomore year.

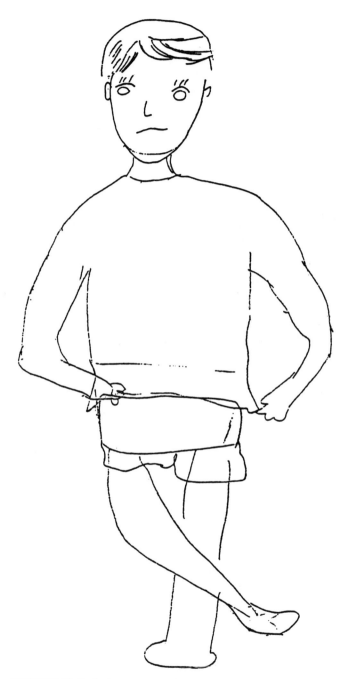

FIGURE 8.32 Paul, draw a person like yourself task, freshman year.

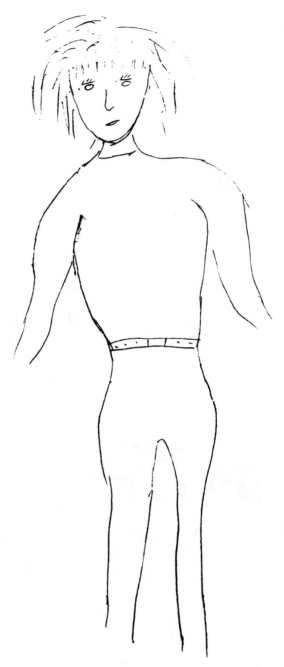

FIGURE 8.33 Paul, draw a person of the opposite sex task, freshman year.

FIGURE 8.34 Paul, self-portrait, sophomore year.

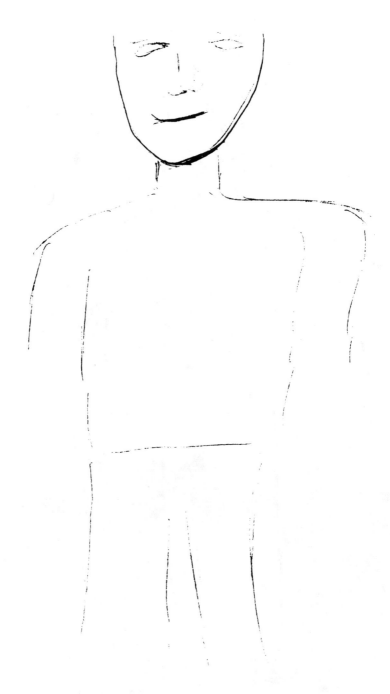

FIGURE 8.35 Paul, draw a person like yourself task, senior year.

240

FIGURE 8.36 Paul, draw a person of the opposite sex task, senior year.

Among the eight case studies, family structure proved to be as complex and variable as it was for the entire sample (see Table 8.3). From looking at the table, one might suspect that the four adolescents whose families had experienced divorce, remarriage, death, and estrangement from parents, but unification with grandparents, probably underwent difficult transitions when each of these events occurred. Long-lasting effects, both positive and negative, may still be operating. A glance at the table would also suggest that four of the families were spared these important events, thus precipitating the question relevant to the study of self-esteem, "In what ways have the dynamics within these families been conducive to positive growth for adolescents and what were the important mediating factors?" Family structure had less to do with psychological adjustment than did the nature of the relationships within the families, the perceptions of the adolescents toward their role within the family, the perceptions of the adolescents toward their peers, and the perceptions of adolescents toward themselves.

During the freshman year one female and three of the male case studies appeared to be having esteem problems either with themselves, their peers, or family members. Debbie, Brent, Paul, and Craig communicated certain discomforts that McEachron-Hirsch and Messier felt pervaded the mood of interview situations. Tim, Janice, Sandra, and Celeste, on the other hand, gave no impression that led the interviewers to believe they were experiencing stress or discomforts beyond a reasonable level of dissonance.

Among the four adolescents who were experiencing difficulties, there was a range in how those difficulties might be categorized. For example,

Table 8.3. Family structure of case studies.

Student	Intact	Death of One Parent; No Remarriage	Divorced and Remarried	Not Living with Parents
Brent		X		
Tim	X			
Paul				X
Craig	X			
Janice			X	
Sandra	X			
Debbie			X	
Celeste	X			

as described earlier, Brent, whose father had died when he was three and whose mother is confined to a wheelchair, appears to have long-lasting self-doubts and a lack of self-confidence and drive to pursue those goals that he feels he is capable of and "should" be accomplishing. He attributes some of his lack of motivation to the missing influence of a father who might have taught him more self-discipline. To the interviewers there was not only a sense of wanting to bolster Brent's confidence and sense of commitment, but also a feeling that Brent was at a stage of realistic self-reflection quite mature for his age. For with this self-appraisal there might be opportunities to make more deliberate choices about the future.

Paul, too, is facing challenges to his future course. Having been separated from his parents prior to his freshman year for the purpose of joining his grandparents in the United States, the pressure is there for him to be a high achiever and, thus, become upwardly mobile. When asked, "Looking back over your whole life, can you tell me about a really powerful learning experience that you've had, in or out of school?" (Belenky et al., 1986), Paul said, "Moving to the United States." He had some English instruction before coming but said that the instruction focused upon writing, not the spoken language. Paul said that the most helpful aspect of his school situation was the English as a Second Language course he was taking with two Vietnamese students. When asked how he and his life would be different fifteen years hence, Paul said that he would be a medical doctor, with a nice house and family, living in Canada or Australia. One cannot help but wonder about Paul's imminent sense of detachment, given his perception of schooling in the United States as an interlude to greener pastures.

For Paul and Brent, the anticipation and pursuit of specific goals are indeed powerful. Yet in comparison, living up to family expectations is clearly operating for Paul, whereas for Brent the need to muster up greater internal motivation is partially attributed to the lack of external push personified through a father figure. Brent seems to realize that it's up to him to move, or not move, in a particular direction, whereas Paul seems to have accepted his parents' goals as his own without question.

For Debbie and Craig, the mediating factors that influence their futures are more closely entwined with the interpersonal relationships of family members. In Debbie's first interview session at the end of her freshman year, she volunteered that her life was progressing on a more positive note since her suicide attempt while in junior high school. At the time of the interview, Debbie was living with her father and stepmother, sister, and two half-siblings. Her parents had divorced when she was seven, after which she lived with her mother, sister, brother, and half-sister (from her biological mother's first marriage). When those living arrangements didn't work out, Debbie lived with her grandmother for awhile before moving to Virginia to live with her father.

For Debbie, a freshman, there were obvious strains in her living arrangements, but they were discussed as minor compared to her mental health when she was about thirteen. Queries about individual family members revealed possible pressure points. When asked to describe her mother, Debbie said, ''That is kind of hard. I don't know; there isn't any way to describe her. She is nice . . . she is there . . . she is a mother.'' When asked to describe her stepmother Debbie said, ''Basically, the same.'' Are these the comments of a young adolescent trying to develop her own female identity, separate from the female role models surrounding her, or the voice of a young woman whose relationships with these women are tentative at best? More vivid descriptions came when Debbie was asked to describe her father:

> . . . Nice, caring, overprotective. [In what ways?] In all kinds of ways. He lets me date, but he has to meet the guy. I went out with (John Doe); my father made him tell where we were going, what we were going to do, when we were going to be back. [How old was your date?] He is a junior. He was going to ask me to the prom but he is afraid of my dad. My dad wouldn't let me go as a freshman.

Debbie continued discussing her dissatisfaction with her father's overprotectiveness by sharing the arrangements that she had to make for her date that evening. When asked if she had a curfew, Debbie said she didn't really have one but that she gets in trouble if she is not home by 3:30 A.M. Many high school freshmen would like to have the overprotectiveness of Debbie's father!

While upbeat about where her life was during her freshman year in contrast to how it was when she was thirteen, events during her sophomore year precipitated a recurrence of depression and family discord. Debbie's increased anger toward her father and stepmother was revealed during the sophomore year. According to Debbie, she did not feel as if her father cared about her as much as he cared about his new wife and their two young children. In addition, Debbie felt that her stepmother did not like the living arrangements either and that, as a result, relationships were strained between them. Given the escalating tensions in the home and the fact that Debbie admittedly was doing poorly in school and associating with a group of students who often found themselves getting in trouble, she shared that arrangements were underway for her to return to living with her biological mother. With the support of her high school guidance counselor and by her own initiative, Debbie had requested professional counseling. This proved to be an important step in seeking alternative living arrangements that would be acceptable to all parties. When it was clear that Debbie's mother welcomed her and that staying in Virginia would have meant repeating her sophomore year, Debbie felt that living with her mother was the best solution to a variety of adverse circumstances.

Based on the telephone interview conducted at the end of her senior year, the new family environment appeared to be a key factor in restoring Debbie's self-esteem. Although not shared during the sophomore year interview, Debbie admitted to having recurring suicidal tendencies when she was experiencing strained relations with family and peers as a sophomore. As a senior, however, Debbie remarked that she was a lot happier, her school performance had improved, and she was glad to be graduating on time. She felt that her present school environment was a lot more conducive to learning but admitted that she had been hanging out with a crowd in Virginia that was not academically motivated. Debbie was also looking forward to furthering her education by going to a junior college in the area, which would also make it possible for her to stay close to her boyfriend.

Debbie's adolescent years tell us a great deal about the significance of family and school environments in supporting healthy self-esteem. Family discord appeared to have definite repercussions, not only for Debbie's sense of her own self-importance, but with regard to the kind of peer group she maintained as well as school performance. The objective self-esteem scores of "4" during the freshman year and "2" during the sophomore year are inadequate measures for telling the entire story. In fact, one might expect the measures to be in the reverse order given the chronology of events. The variation in self-esteem scores and seemingly contradictory match to the events relayed during the interviews underscores the importance of using multiple measures. Multiple measures are important to add a broader perspective. As the present study demonstrated, differences that emerged in self-reports are covered up in the objective scales.

Another possible way to interpret the scores would be to suggest that they are consistent with the chronology of events. Perhaps at the beginning of the freshman year, Debbie was experiencing very low self-esteem given her family situation, even though at the end of the freshman year her remarks reflected an attempt to maintain a positive outlook. It is possible that the events during the summer months between the freshman and sophomore years became untenable in the home environment and that Debbie became rebellious, choosing a new peer group and refusing to put forth the necessary effort to maintain passing grades at the beginning of the sophomore year. Her sense of self may have been one of self-confidence, although with the hindsight that we now have, we might also suggest self-confidence marked by defiance. In other words, she may have had an "I'll do what I want" attitude, not caring about conforming to social expectations to do well in school and not wanting to acquiesce to parental expectations. For Debbie, self-esteem may have been perceived high based on empowerment she felt from her peer group, regardless of family discord. This points out the importance of placing self-esteem interpretations in a particular social context and underscores the importance of personal interviews to ascertain which factors may be more influential in affecting self-esteem.

Debbie's conceptions of self were very much influenced by family dynamics. In *Second Chances,* Wallerstein and Blakeslee (1989) describe the long-term process that their clients underwent in trying to develop an identity that was free of the emotional wounds that developed during the tumultuous years of divorce, remarriage, and, in some cases, divorce again. For some, the scars and resentful feelings endured, yet, for others resiliency persisted, resulting in strong feelings of self-acceptance. For Debbie, self-confidence had been restored. Less certain, however, is how the estranged relationship with her father will manifest itself as an unresolved conflict.

Troubled relationships are not unique to families of divorce, however. Self-esteem for an individual in an intact family is just as susceptible to stress and strain based upon interpersonal family dynamics. Craig, who has lived with both biological parents since birth, exemplifies the damaging effects on self-esteem based on family dynamics alone. Craig was interviewed as a freshman; he reported a history of depression, insecurity, and the fact that he had been referred to a private agency for thinking about suicide. When interviewed at the end of his sophomore year, however, the interviewer learned that there were alleged reports that Craig had sexually abused the children he had been babysitting and that Craig might be characterized as a perpetrator because he had been abused by his father. With the interviewer Craig did not openly discuss the activities that he had been accused of; however, he talked around them in such a way that implied he knew that the interviewer was aware of his history. Newspaper reports and admonishment by fellow students had made anonymity nearly impossible in such a small community. At the onset of the second interview, the interviewer said that she would be following an open-ended interview schedule, which had been used with the other case studies and that if there were questions that made him feel uncomfortable, he would not have to answer them.

When asked what kinds of things had been important to Craig over the last few years, he talked with great intensity about the close friendship he had developed recently with someone at school. In fact, most of his responses centered around his relationship with his friend and his desire to get help for his problem. For example, when asked, "Tell me something about what your life is like right now. What do you care about, think about?" Craig said, "I care about my friend . . . hoping to get off problem with court services; I'm on house arrest. Can't visit my friend but he can come over. He [friend] says 'Why don't you change?' I'm in a program and am trying to change my sexual behavior."

When the interviewer asked, "How did they [problems] come about in the first place?" Craig reported that he had been picked on in school when he was younger (third and fourth grade) and that he was frequently teased. Later in the conversation, Craig made reference again to difficulties with peers. He said that his new friend had been a powerful experience because he was learning to be with other people his own age. "In the past, I've spent a lot of time with younger kids, where I'm more in control. There's not as much competition as when I'm with kids my own age."

Further questioning revealed Craig's feelings about the regretful state of affairs that surrounded him. To the question, "Are there any other questions that I should have asked you, that would have thrown some light on these issues we are interested in . . . that is, your life and learning experiences with others?" (Belenky et al., 1986), Craig said, ". . . society. I got in trouble with two families; people are teasing; I got two mad families that didn't like what happened. I lost my job because the girl worked there. Families probably had reason to be mad, but I didn't do it to make them mad. If I had it to do over again, I wouldn't do it . . . wish I hadn't done it now that I see what trouble has come to me."

The harsh reality of public condemnation has hit Craig at a time when many adolescents are negotiating a gradual separation and heightened sense of independence from parental authority. For Craig, this process has been exacerbated by the fact that his parents, the people who were responsible for providing a foundation from which this separation could take place, are accountable for compromising Craig's transition into adulthood. One can only hope that the counseling services made available to Craig and his family will prevent further transgressions to him and other innocent victims. As a junior, Craig was transferred to a juvenile delinquent detention center. Coincidentally, he was identified for the Messier and Ward study presented in Chapter Eleven; therefore, his junior and senior years are presented in a different institutional and familial context.

Discussion

The findings from both the quantitative measures of 152 high school students, as well as the eight case studies, provide a multidimensional basis from which to better understand the relationship between self-esteem and family environment. The fact that family structure had no impact on levels of self-esteem provides support to the theory of psychological wholeness and discounts the notion of physical dissolution as a cause of low self-esteem. Higher levels of cohesion and active-recreational orientation, however, appeared to enhance self-esteem. Case study interviews reinforced the position that family dynamics were more salient to understanding self-esteem in adolescents than their family structure. Discussions with Janice and Debbie, for example, revealed contrasting interpretations of family environments long after parental divorce. Janice's self-esteem levels demonstrated an erratic pattern following her mother's remarriage, but her comments revealed no lingering hostility toward the events of divorce and remarriage. Self-esteem during the senior year decreased slightly, yet remained in the moderate range. Family environment subscales were stable and within the normal range for all four years with the exception of conflict, which was significantly below the norm for three years. Not apparent through the objective instruments, however, was the tremendous sense of loss that Janice felt as a result of six deaths in her family during her junior year. These events will be presented in the section on school environment because of the effect upon school performance and motivation.

Debbie's reactions to divorce and remarriage were considerably different, however. She experienced erratic levels of self-esteem, too, but family dynamics revealed possible pressure points. She experienced lower levels of independence, cohesion, and active-recreational orientation, and higher conflict levels.

Craig, whose self-esteem was the lowest of all the case studies, lived in an intact family with a father who had sexually abused him. Achievement orientation and conflict levels were high, cohesion levels very low the freshman year, and organization levels low for all three years. McEachron-Hirsch and Messier were unable to collect group administered data during the senior year because Craig had been moved to a detention center.

In sum, family dynamics, more than family structure or social characteristics (e.g., race, gender, socioeconomic status), play a key role in nurturing or debilitating self-esteem. Crucial to understanding the relationship of self-esteem to family environment has been the way in which individuals interpret their own family structure and environment. Further support for the collective data came from the case studies who were not experiencing high levels of family discord. Their scores on the family environment subscales as well as perceptions expressed during the interviews indicated higher levels of cohesion and active recreational orientation.

To return to our metaphor, the family environment is a continuous, yet changing spiral within one's inner chambers. When looking at a cross section of the chambered nautilus, we may be able to identify certain characteristics such as family structure and social characteristics but not necessarily know the individual's interpretation of those inner chambers, that is, one's self-esteem in relation to multidimensional aspects of self. Often secondary factors such as socioeconomic status, gender, and ethnicity are limited criteria for assessing self-esteem. Therefore, while the California Task Force on Self-Esteem may be correct in spotlighting the family as the primary factor in influencing self-esteem, it erroneously goes on to make a judgment about those factors that presumably cause low self-esteem, e.g., poverty, divorce, single-parent families, abuse, and teenage pregnancies. Our findings demonstrate the superficiality of such assumptions by emphasizing the importance of examining one's perceptions of one's own environment rather than the perceptions of others based upon social norms. Based on adolescents' self-reports, the more salient factors affecting self-esteem are cohesion within the family and the family's orientation toward recreational activities outside the home. This balance apparently provides adolescents with a firm foundation or anchoring point from which independence and participation in the larger community can be supported.

SELF-ESTEEM IN RELATION TO SCHOOL ENVIRONMENT

School Environment

The school environment has always emphasized the importance of academic achievement based upon a subject matter orientation. The underlying assumption has been that possession of a core body of knowledge creates an educated citizenry that, in turn, makes informed decisions about what is good for society. The subject matter tradition continues to this day but not without competing theories, which contest the passive nature of the learner. A more extensive treatment of the history of curriculum theory and practice can be found in Ornstein and Hunkins' (1988) *Curriculum: Foundations, Principles, and Issues* and Miller and Seller's (1985) *Curriculum: Perspectives and Practice.*

Curriculum theorists place the consideration of self-esteem as part of the phenomenological, or humanistic, curriculum orientation. The distinction between educational philosophies that address self-esteem and those that don't is artificial because it suggests that behavioral or interactive orientations need not be concerned with student self-esteem. Regardless of an educational institution's implicitly or explicitly stated philosophy of education, the possibility of affecting the self-esteem of its constituents cannot be denied. Educational institutions are designed to influence students' perceptions of self in relation to the broader society.

The longstanding emphasis upon a classic education is reflected in the amount of research devoted to subject matter and academic achievement. This large body of research has contributed greatly to our understanding of curricula, instructional strategies, and student performance documented by grades and standardized test scores. Less is known, however, about students' perceptions of their schooling experience and how individuals construct their own identity based upon those experiences.

In *A Place Called School,* Goodlad (1984) reported one of the most extensive studies of the school environment. His cross-national study examined students' perceptions of teachers, teaching strategies, classroom environment, and subject matter. Attitudes about the ideal, intended, and actual curriculum were obtained from teachers and parents. Although self-esteem was not assessed, the study reported that parents and teachers expressed concern about students' personal, social, vocational, and intellectual growth even though, in practice, intellectual activity is given the most attention.

The present study closes the gap between adolescent self-esteem studies, typically conducted in isolation, and the school environment by linking the two through the Rosenberg Self-Esteem Scale (Rosenberg, 1965) and the Classroom Environment Scale (Moos and Trickett, 1974). In addition, students' grade point averages, standardized test scores, and participation in extracurricular activities were investigated as a means to relate adolescent self-esteem to other school activities.

Classroom Environment

Few studies have investigated the relationship between classroom environment and adolescent self-esteem. Cheung and Lau (1985) utilized the Classroom Environment Scale, the Family Environment Scale, and the Self-Esteem Inventory (Coopersmith, 1967) in their assessment of 713 tenth-grade adolescents in Hong Kong. The highest correlations between the Self-Esteem Inventory (SEI) and the Family Environment Scale (FES) subscales were found between SEI and Cohesion (.44) and Conflict ($-.35$). Correlations between SEI and CES were low with five reaching levels of significance. The highest correlations with the CES subscales were found between SEI and Affiliation (.17), Teacher Support (.17), Order and Organization (.17), Involvement (.13), and Rule Clarity (.10). After dividing subjects into high and low groups according to their scores on the subscales separately, analysis of variance showed that five of the nine CES groupings yielded highly significant differences in self-esteem. Cheung and Lau found that groups high in Involvement, Affiliation, Teacher Support, Order and Organization, and Rule Clarity were also high in self-esteem. To examine the "importance of the effect of the family and classroom environments on self-esteem, regression analysis was also done with SEI as the criterion, and all of the FES and CES subscales as predictors" (Cheung and Lau, 1985, p. 448). The four most important predictors from the FES were Cohesion, Active-Recreational Orientation, and Conflict; from the CES the most important predictor was Teacher Support, all with betas greater than .10. The notion that the family is more strongly related to self-esteem than the classroom environment has been demonstrated by Cheung and Lau's findings. Also noteworthy is the finding that Teacher Support correlates with higher levels of self-esteem, a notion that will be discussed in greater detail in the context of academic achievement.

A similar study investigating self-esteem in relation to classroom and family environments was conducted with 196 seventh- and eighth-grade students in Canada (Nelson, 1984). Utilizing the CES, FES, and Self-

Appraisal Inventory (SAI), which measures self-concept in the areas of peer, scholastic, and general well-being, Nelson (1984, p. 286) found that scholastic self-concept was the one variable that was consistently related to both classroom and family environment dimensions, thereby concluding that "classroom and family environments which provide support and structure are clearly related to students' affective adaptation, but their relationship to students' achievement is less certain."

Research in the United States investigating self-esteem in relation to classroom environments has primarily focused on middle and elementary school students (Galluzzi et al., 1980). Analyses in the McEachron-Hirsch and Messier study make it possible to compare adolescent self-esteem in relation to family and school environments with the studies conducted with Chinese and Canadian students.

Moos and Trickett (1987) obtained separate norms for classrooms focusing on specific subjects. English and social studies classes were especially high on Teacher Support and more likely to try innovative teaching strategies. Math classes by contrast were lower in Teacher Support, Involvement, and Affiliation but demonstrated higher Task Orientation. Math classes were also very well organized and high in rule clarity. Science classes were high in Affiliation and low in Teacher Control but Teacher Control was still higher than in English and social studies classes. When administering the CES each spring semester, McEachron-Hirsch and Messier asked students to select a specific class to target for the questions on the CES. Year one students responded to their English classes, year two to math classes, year three to science classes, and year four to social studies classes. To investigate the relationship between classroom environment and self-esteem, measures from the CES were used to predict self-esteem. The results of the analyses indicated that classroom environment had a minor relationship with self-esteem in the freshman, junior, and senior years, and no relationship was found in the sophomore years. In the freshman year, the only CES factor that was predictive of self-esteem was Involvement $(-.22)$ and this relationship was modest. A similar relationship was found in the junior year with Competition $(-.29)$ being moderately predictive of self-esteem. During the senior year there was a correlation between self-esteem and Involvement $(-.22)$ as well as Affiliation $(-.20)$.

As freshmen there was no interaction between gender and race, and there were no differences in the CES based on gender and race. During the sophomore year, when students were evaluating their math classes, there was no interaction between gender and race, but there were differences when gender and race were examined separately. Non-Whites scored lower on Clarity, and females scored higher on Involvement, Affiliation, and Teacher Support. For the junior year, there was no interaction between gender and race, but there were differences based on gender. Females scored higher on the Affiliation subscale and lower on the Competition subscale. The Affiliation subscale assesses the level of friendship students feel for each other and the extent to which they enjoy working together. During the senior year there was no interaction and no gender effect. However, there was a race effect for Teacher Support and Competition. Non-Whites perceived their social studies classes to have less Teacher Support than did Whites; in addition, the classes were perceived by non-Whites as having a more competitive environment. Despite the significant demographic and self-esteem differences for given subscales during each year, no particular pattern emerged across all four years.

Further research is needed to assess student perceptions of subject matter and the various ways subject matter is presented. Goodlad's (1984) research provides a comprehensive record of students' subject-to-subject attitudes. He (p. 114) found that

> Regardless of subject, students liked to do activities that involved them actively or in which they worked with others. These included going on field trips, making films, building or drawing things, making collections, acting things out, and carrying out projects. These are the things which students reported doing the least and which we observed infrequently. They were observed more frequently in the arts, vocational education, and physical education as a group of subjects than in English, mathematics, social studies and science as a group.

Despite preferred learning activities, secondary students had different perceptions regarding the importance of specific subjects. They considered social studies "to be less important than English/language arts, mathematics, and vocational education, about as important as science, and more important than foreign language, the arts, and physical education" (Goodlad, 1984, p. 210). Goodlad attributes part of the differences between student perceptions of vocational and academic courses to disparity among educators about what constitutes a common general education. Furthermore, he maintains that students' self-esteem is "closely tied to their perception of which side of the separation they perceive themselves to be on" (p. 142).

A broader examination of the classroom and family environments illustrates dramatic contrasts in terms of intergroup dynamics. Assuming a relatively predictable home environment, the number of anticipated social transactions and role expectations are few in comparison to school environments. On a given day students change classes six to eight times, for six to eight different subjects, six to eight different teachers, and possibly hundreds of different classmates. After school, extracurricular activities create yet additional role expectations. It's no wonder that Cohesion as a dimension was not included when the Classroom Environment Scale was developed. Yet, Cohesion and an Active-Recreational Orientation were salient factors affecting self-esteem in family environments. While the schools may not be characterized as having an Active-Recreational Orientation, they certainly would seem to be actively shifting students in and out of various subject matter orientations. What seems to be more elusive, given this institutional pattern, is how patterns of cohesion are established, if at all, and what form of active roles are available to students within classes, not just when changing classes. In their current form, secondary schools apparently leave the cohesion issue up to the negotiating skills of individuals. One of the limitations of using only the Classroom Environment Scale is that the overall dynamics of the school environment are not assessed. While the present study attempted to go beyond the assessment of classrooms by investigating student involvement in extracurricular activities, further studies are needed to assess the overall school climate. While McEachron-Hirsch and Messier obtained glimpses of the overall school climate through case study interviews, more extensive studies are needed. See, for example, Peshkin (1991) and the initiative taken by secondary students reported in *Phi Delta Kappan* (Polakow-Suransky and Ulaby, 1990).

Extracurricular Activities

Social relationships in the school environment are another important dimension affecting the development of self-perceptions in adolescents. Youniss and Smollar (1985) identify the influence of peer relationships upon adolescent development as heretofore receiving minor attention by psychodynamic theorists. Although not a major thrust of the current study, McEachron-Hirsch and Messier investigated social involvement beyond the classroom environment by correlating the number of clubs the students joined with self-esteem. A hypothesis was put forth that students' self-esteem was affected by their increasing involvement in extracurricular activities from their freshman to senior years, thereby suggesting a relationship between global self-esteem and social affiliations. However, this hypothesis was not supported by the data. For all four years, there was no correlation between the number of clubs joined and self-esteem. There was a significant difference between males and females in the number of clubs joined for the third and fourth years, however, with females participating in more clubs. Affiliation, Involvement, and social networks appear to be more important to adolescent females than adolescent males, but in neither group does it appear to be related to self-esteem.

Academic Performance

Many self-esteem investigations have tried to examine a causal relation between achievement and self-esteem. These studies usually focus upon what Holly (1987, p. 14) refers to as global self-esteem: "how positive a person feels about himself or herself in general." Holly acknowledges the common belief that feeling good about oneself might enhance one's chances of academic and social success but cautions that simply knowing that a student has high global self-esteem tells us very little. More important is understanding how objective student self-esteem ratings coincide with personal attributes, perceptions, values, and social roles. The significance of these characteristics lies not in the external rewards associated with them, but rather in the importance attributed by the individual. Some students, for example, "are able to maintain high self-esteem even while acknowledging their academic incompetence, because they do not care about academic success" (Holly, 1987, p. 15). Conversely, individual students who know they are academically competent might have low self-esteem because they perceive failure in the area of popularity or personal appearance. Based on investigations of the relationship between academic achievement and self-esteem, Holly (1987, p. 31) concludes that self-esteem is an effect, not a cause, of academic achievement.

In contrast to Holly, Covington (1989) studied the relationship between self-esteem and failure in school in an attempt to establish a causal link between the two. Covington argues that the comprehensive reviews of studies over the past seventy-five years conducted by Purkey (1970), Walberg and Uguroglu (1980), and Wylie (1979) demonstrate a positive association between self-esteem variables and academic achievement.

However, Covington points out that because most of the studies are correlational, they "are of little more than circumstantial value in making a case for causation or for the direction of any causal relationship" (1989, p. 79). Citing recent advances in attribution theory, research on fear-of-failure and self-defensive motivation, Covington (1989, pp. 83–84) outlines several issues that make the relationship between self-esteem and performance seem counterintuitive:

> First, if high self-esteem favors achievement, and if noteworthy accomplishments increase esteem even more, then why should there be so little relationship between a sense of personal satisfaction in school and grade point average?
>
> Second, why do many students with low self-esteem perform at their best when the odds against succeeding are at their worst?
>
> Third, why should failure—which is known to elicit shame, guilt, and lowered self-esteem—actually mobilize some students to greater effort?
>
> Fourth, if success is so attractive and sought after, then why should students with low self-esteem reject success when it occurs?
>
> Fifth, if high self-regard is the product of numerous, accumulated past successes—as we generally assume—then why should some students' sense of confidence be devastated after only "one" failure? Shouldn't past successes count for something, compared to a single failure?

Based on the above complexities generated from a review of research Covington (p. 84) concludes that psychological resources such as "self-perception of ability, beliefs about the nature of the achievement process, and personal estimates of time and energy level" enter into the process of achievement in the form of causal attributions.

Students' conceptions of intelligence have been shown to play a key role in mediating academic performance. Laffoon, Jenkins-Friedman, and Tollefson (1989) found that underachieving students attributed success to ability and failure to external circumstances. By contrast, high achieving students attributed success to effort. Whether intelligence is perceived as a fixed statement of one's potential or a "cerebral muscle" that can be developed, student perception of ability appears to be salient to academic achievement and concerted efforts.

To investigate the relationship between academic performance and self-esteem, McEachron-Hirsch and Messier correlated self-esteem measures with students' scores on the Iowa Test of Basic Skills (ITBS) taken during their sophomore year. Although only moderate, these correlations support the previous research findings that there is some

Table 8.4. Correlations of subscales of the Iowa Test of Basic Skills and the Rosenberg Self-Esteem Scale.

Subject	Self-Esteem
Reading	.1357
Math	.1414
Social Studies	.1412
Writing	.1415
Science	.1410
Complete Composite	.1409

relationship. Table 8.4 shows that self-esteem correlated with all of the content area scores of the ITBS. All of the relationships indicated by these correlations are small in magnitude.

To further investigate the relationship between self-esteem and academic performance, McEachron-Hirsch and Messier correlated self-esteem measures during the junior and senior years with grade point averages through the junior year. No significant correlation emerged. It is difficult to generalize from these findings because of the variation in classes taken by students, grading procedures, and institutional guidelines. Given the standardization of the ITBS and its assessment of achievement in broad domains, the correlations obtained during the sophomore year are, perhaps, more reliable. Nevertheless, the influence of academic performance upon global self-esteem was very low in that, at best, it accounted for only 2% of the overall variability in self-esteem.

Adolescent Perceptions of Classroom and School Environments

The adolescents interviewed provided a variety of sentiments that shed light on the student-teacher-classroom triad. In response to the question, "What do you think will stay with you about your experiences here [in this school]?" Brent responded,

Kids will pay attention if something's interesting. Young teachers today are alright because they're young. I'd like to tell student teachers to listen to the students. If some kids fall asleep we're trying to tell them they're boring. Got to have fun in class. Tell a joke. Get the kids into the assignment. Kids lose interest. [Have you had any good teachers?] [After naming four teachers, he spotlights a fifth by saying] Mr. H. made you want to learn. He would blend reality with the course—physical science.

Mr. D. was boring. Some teachers don't care; others care too much. The school should be changed. If you took the teachers that are decent and split them apart that would be great. Once you get in the thirty-five-year-old range, they're OK, but twenty-five year olds are great.

To Brent, the variables that are important in a positive classroom environment center around teacher characteristics such as age, what Kounin (1970) refers to as "with-it-ness," and the extent to which a teacher can inspire one to learn.

When asked about valuable educational experiences as a sophomore, Tim discussed faculty professionalism as well as opportunities for freedom and responsibility. Tim spoke favorably of his teachers in accelerated classes, but he was disappointed in several teachers who taught in regular (nonaccelerated) classes. Tim felt positive about the overall school environment, reporting that there was "more freedom here than at other schools." When asked, "What has been most helpful about this school?" Tim said, "A lot of good teachers." He also appreciated the opportunities to do things where people, primarily peers, depended on his efforts or when peers worked together in preparation for school functions, such as the Ring Dance during his sophomore year. When asked if there were things that the school didn't provide that were important to him, Tim mentioned that there wasn't much help with college applications and information that would help in selecting a college or university. He felt that the guidance department was weak and stated, "They just make up things like 'you need to go to a middle [size-wise] school.' " Although Tim's perceptions reflected a slightly more serious tone than did Brent's, both highlighted the importance of teacher support and role competence in helping students achieve educational goals.

When interviewed at the end of their senior year, Tim and Brent summarized their attitudes toward their classroom experiences. Tim talked very positively about taking college-level classes as a junior and senior, stating that he liked challenging classes. He also felt that, during his senior year, teachers were more helpful with future plans—with the exception of English, that is. Tim was more reticent about saying anything positive about English as a field of study, or the English teachers more specifically.

Brent's negative associations with classroom experiences centered around feelings toward specific teachers. Several were perceived as "flat," "boring," "rigid," or "cold." English and government classes were characterized as "redundant work" and not related to real-life experiences. On the more positive side, Brent was more enthusiastic about his auto mechanics teacher stating that he was "one-of-a-kind" and that his teaching provided the best vocational preparation, e.g., "prepared me best for the world." Brent clearly excelled in the class, and as a result he was offered a scholarship for auto diesel mechanics and auto transmission training at a technical institute in Texas.

For Celeste, being inspired by a teacher did not come until late in her high school years. It wasn't until her senior year that a combination of motivational factors coalesced—Celeste was inspired by her teacher, excited about a topic, and confident in her own abilities. The previous years were perceived as testing ground, that is, Celeste felt as if teachers were just "seeing if you could do it." During her first three years of high school, she also didn't make, or feel that her teachers made, many connections between coursework and its relevance. In fact, Celeste did not perform well academically as a freshman, but with the help and encouragement of her parents, she improved her study habits, which resulted in better grades. Not until her senior year, however, did anything she was taking seem to have significance to her life or future.

Celeste's senior English teacher and, perhaps, her own maturity were instrumental in bringing about this positive growth. Celeste said that members of the class were assigned a research paper on a topic of their choice. She chose censorship, using the events surrounding Two Live Crew as a case illustration. Celeste said that her teacher helped her and made her believe that she was capable of doing a good job in completing the project. The combination of a high interest contemporary topic chosen by Celeste, with teacher support and Celeste's own motivation, brought about the most positive learning experiences throughout Celeste's high school years. Janice reiterated Celeste's sentiment, citing her English research paper on sexual harassment as one of her most rewarding and challenging classroom experiences. One cannot help but wonder why these did not occur until the last semester of four years of high school.

At the end of their freshman years, Janice and Sandra had quite different orientations toward their school experiences. For Janice, certain classes were definite favorites, whereas for Sandra interest in several classes made focusing difficult. Janice said that since she had been young, she was always a year ahead in math. As a high school student she continues to favor math and computers. As a result of her participation in a drill team, the Elks Club sponsored her participation in a computer camp. Janice spoke with fond memories of opportunities to meet students who lived throughout the United States and said that her career would most likely be in the field of math.

Unlike Janice, Sandra, at the end of her freshman year, left open many career options:

> Something gets in the way when somebody asks me what I want to be when I grow up. There are so many areas that I am interested in. I can imagine being any one of them—astronaut, chemical engineer, teacher, musician, sports player. I would like to be almost everything that I do. As times go on, I have to start narrowing everything. I really have no idea. I really get jealous of people who excel in one area and have everything planned out. They know what they are going to major in and they know what college they want to go to. They just know their whole lives.

When asked to talk about coaches and teachers, Sandra, like Tim and Brent, had obviously had some that she respected more than others.

> Well, some of them don't influence me at all and they don't motivate me to do anything. I like challenges and I like it when the teacher is really consistent and really organized and you know what is expected of you—you fulfill what they expect of you more easily. But if they're all scatterbrained and don't follow a program, I'm not as motivated to do my best. With the ones that are really good, you just feel, I don't want to say pressure, but you feel motivated.

Sandra contrasted two individuals, a Spanish teacher, and a field hockey and softball coach, to illustrate her feelings:

> This year I really liked Spanish and studying a foreign culture, but I didn't like the teacher. It's not my place to say, but I wish I were the teacher up there because it really bothered me. But anyhow I still like the subject and it's not like I'm going to drop Spanish. I just regret not having a teacher who was more enthusiastic about it.

By contrast, Sandra spoke highly about her field hockey and softball coach.

> She's really inspiring because she's older, over fifty I'd say, and she just has so much energy and self-sacrificing. She's always really a good coach. You can tell when people know what they are talking about or leading you off. She's not just a good coach, she's a good person, too. She has a sense of humor and she's fun to be around.

Evidently, Sandra's enthusiasm, ability, and love of learning was recognized by teachers early in her schooling experiences. During the freshman interview, Sandra related that one of her middle school teachers expressed confidence in Sandra's ability to become valedictorian of her senior class. At the sophomore interview and based on her grade point average by the end of her junior year, Sandra was well on her way to achieving the self-fulfilling prophecy.

When Janice was interviewed at the end of her senior year, it was clear that her interest in math had been maintained. Upon graduation, Janice was planning to go to a local community college and major in accounting for one year before transferring to a four-year college. The decision to wait before attending a four-year college was influenced by personal losses during Janice's junior year. She said, ''I didn't want to go far from home right now. I'm getting myself back together from last year.''

Janice experienced the deaths of *six* family members over the course of her junior year—two grandmothers, one step-grandmother, and three uncles. Most of the deaths were the result of cancer or not recovering from a series of operations. Janice had been very close to her grandmother and one uncle, who had been like a father figure. It is difficult to imagine the magnitude of such losses within such a short period of time, and for Janice the bereavement process admittedly was not over. She said that:

> After last year I didn't really want to go to college. This year [senior], I just did enough to get credit. Doing the minimum affected my GPA. I really haven't gotten back into work and study. I don't think I am on the same mental level as before.

In *Adolescent Psychology,* Nielson (1987, p. 694) captures some of the incongruities between social images of the adolescent experience and the everyday realities:

> Adolescence is a period associated with liveliness and longevity—a period during which death and dying are not assumed to be spectres on the immediate horizon. Yet, such visions of adolescent bliss do not represent the experiences of thousands of adolescents in our society for whom death or dying have become immediate realities.

For Janice and many other adolescents who experience the death of loved ones and close friends, little is known about reactions and coping strategies. In Janice's case, support came through a new boyfriend who encouraged her to pursue activities in which she excelled, such as accounting and basketball.

An examination of self-esteem measures reveals that Janice's self-esteem was highest during her junior and senior years. These findings raise several issues about the relationship between self-esteem, achievement motivation, and personal loss. Where achievement motivation is impaired and self-esteem remains high, depression over the death of loved ones may be the mediating factor affecting performance. Little is known about the accommodations that schools make during these stressful experiences. For Janice the statement, "I keep to myself" at home suggests that perhaps some in-school group therapy sessions would provide peer support for her sense of loss, manifested by an uncharacteristic tendency to withdraw.

At the end of Sandra's senior year, the interviewer was surprised to find out that recent events in her high school experience brought a series of disappointments and unfulfilled dreams. When asked which of her high school years was the most memorable, she said her senior year. What follows is an account of Sandra's most poignant, heartfelt discoveries regarding her own identity and self-esteem. Sandra's experience illustrates the competing motives faced by many adolescents; "the achievement motive often comes up against another strong human motive—the motive for affiliation, or the desire to be around other people" (Segal and Segal, 1985, pp. 140—141). To better understand Sandra's perspective the following schedule indicates one of her typical days:

6:00 A.M.	Get ready for school
8:00 A.M. —2:00 P.M.	School starts—Courses include four advanced placement courses, e.g., college-level courses in government, English, biology, calculus, in addition to a Spanish V course. Sandra also assumed leadership roles in student programs related to academic courses, e.g., Chair, Interact, joint projects with Model UN; Chair, Model United Nations Committee, Housing Partnerships; President, STAR (Student Academic Recognition). Sports Editor, *Ledger Issues*
3:00—5:30 P.M.	Field Hockey Practice, Captain of Team

6:30 – 9:00 P.M.   Play Practice, Student Director;
                                   Swimming Practice then started
                                   before Field Hockey ended;
                                   Co-Captain of Swim Team.

Interviewer: What year stands out as the most memorable?

This year [senior] you are realizing what a delicate balance it is
between school and your life. You have more independence than
ever before; you are on your own schedule but there are limits. I
am disappointed at my performance this year.

I experienced failure. I was Number One academically this year. I
stopped caring. . . . I think I got burnout. A lot of what burned me
out was that I was leading these things. For example, during play
practice, actors could do homework, but I couldn't take a break
because I had to watch everything. I stopped sitting with my friends
during lunch because I would use this time to get caught up; I
stopped wanting to be with these people. . . . My problem was that
. . . I volunteered for everything.

I am glad that I have a better sense of who I am. I can't get over it
. . . that I couldn't pull through at the end. There was so much
pressure. My mom was valedictorian. It was self-imposed pressure. I can't stand to let my teachers down. I became unreliable,
irresponsible, but not about group projects, only about things that
affected me. For example, I would never let the senior play go. I
loved doing that. I never let hockey go; we went to the State. I let
go what affected me. What I found was that it was selfishly
motivated. I think that a lot of the reason I am so competitive . . .
is insecurity. I had to prove that I could be Number One.

I would never trade the experiences. I think in the end, it was worth
all of that, but I can't get over these feelings that I have developed.
I am a real people person. I need mutual attention. I love social
contact. I like feeling as if I am an integral part of a working system.
Like, I am a pacemaker . . . I really like that. I learned about
professionalism, what is important, how to say "no." I said "no"
to softball this year.

Interviewer: Why do you think it took this long to say "no"?

Because of a lot of breakthroughs with my family. [Sandra relays the time when everything "came to a head" at swim practice one day in November.] My goggles snapped and it all came apart. . . . I knew I was failing academically [that is, losing the number one ranking]. I came home and couldn't stop crying. I have always been rebellious toward my father; he is critical of me. He didn't let me go to school for two days. I mostly stayed home. It was one of the first times we just talked. My mother and I are getting closer, too. I started having a boyfriend about that time, too. The way it should be is that you have a life! My whole life was school, instead of school being just a part of it.

I wonder if I will ever be able to do it again [regain the motivation to excel]. I have been depressed lately. Sometimes I am in the prime of life or I hate it. I am not stable. I can see that I am not stable now. Yesterday, I was really happy but today I had such dread. It is confusing to me because I don't see any cause in it. I question my motivation—do I have any for myself? Before I was doing it because I was just keeping the record.

Interviewer: How do you create privacy?

Lots of times I don't. It creeps up as an eruption. I do wasteful things, then I will get sick of it and then just walk off—more of an emergency need for privacy.

For a highly talented young woman such as Sandra, self-esteem issues are multifaceted. Teachers, counselors, parents, and peers perceive Sandra as a strong and capable person who experiences success in whatever she does. Yet, as Sandra has demonstrated, with success comes the recognition that one cannot be all things to all people and remain true to oneself. The danger of the "looking glass self" is that when peering into the mirror, one only sees the faces representing the demands of others rather than the likeness of oneself. Finding the balance between having a life enriched by others, rather than a life sapped by others, has proven to be one of the existential crises faced by Sandra for perhaps the first time.

Discussion

An examination of self-esteem in relation to the school and classroom environments is best understood when placed in a broader context. The research by Cheung and Lau (1985) and McEachron-Hirsch and Messier found low to moderate correlations with the following CES subscales: Affiliation, Teacher Support, Order and Organization, Involvement, Rule Clarity, and Competition. One possible explanation is that students who have higher levels of self-esteem also recognize and appreciate classrooms where the teacher is organized, gets students involved, and provides support to students.

In addition, the CES findings by McEachron-Hirsch and Messier supported those of Moos and Trickett (1987) with regard to finding higher Teacher Support in English and social studies classes. The race and gender differences in the McEachron-Hirsch and Messier study demonstrate the importance of examining the differential effects of subject matter and teaching strategies. If minorities and women are perceiving classroom environments differently, there also may be variation in academic performance based upon these perceptions. For example, since non-Whites scored lower on Clarity for math classes, lower on Teacher Support in social studies, and higher on Competition in social studies, these classroom environments may be perceived as presenting more performance problems than were experienced in English and science classes.

For females, the classroom environments in math and science were perceived differently from their male peers. Scoring higher on Affiliation in both, higher on Involvement and Teacher Support in Math, and lower on Competition in science suggests that females may respond differently to math and science settings. The traditional performances of females in these two subjects has been well documented (*The AAUW Report,* 1992), but further research is needed to examine the relationship between interactive styles, subject matter perceptions, academic performance, and gender. Beane and Lipka (1986) challenge educational institutions to include careful planning around student self-perceptions, as well as academic courses, so that schools can enhance student growth. Beane and Lipka outlined important factors affecting student self-esteem in the overall school environment, including climate, grouping, decision-making systems, and reward/punishment structures.

Interpreting growth of the self in relation to classroom environments and subject matter led Goodlad as well as Beane and Lipka to the teachings of John Dewey for insight and direction. When attempting to interpret a myriad of factors affecting self-esteem, it is perhaps wise to seek philosophical understanding for criticism toward secondary schools. For example, a significant amount of Goodlad's criticism toward the secondary schools' role in affecting self-esteem was attributed to the split between vocational and academic goals. Citing Dewey as one of the educational philosophers who espoused the importance of both manual and intellectual endeavors for developing the total person, Goodlad laments the artificial segregation between vocational and academically oriented students as a result of curriculum constraints. The social consequences of this split, Goodlad argues, is a disproportionately larger number of minorities and students from lower socioeconomic levels in vocational tracks. This relationship between curricular organization and self-esteem reveals the subtle ways that a hidden curriculum becomes operationalized by the overt curriculum. It also reveals the limitations of measures that assess global self-esteem. For example, a student may score in the average to high range in global self-concept, thereby revealing healthy self-perceptions. If the student is a minority with middle to lower socioeconomic status, there is a greater likelihood that he or she will be counseled into vocational tracks (Goodlad, 1984). The result is reduced aspirations and lower levels of vocational efficacy, despite average to high levels of global self-esteem and ability.

Relating school to life is the theme by which Beane and Lipka related self-esteem to Dewey's educational philosophy. Beane and Lipka (1986), along with Purkey (1970, 1978) and Combs, Avila, and Purkey (1971), emphasize the important role that teachers can play in helping learners understand themselves and their environment, thereby enhancing self-esteem. Beane and Lipka cited the results of the Eight-Year Study wherein 1,475 secondary students in experimental high school programs, which were designed to enhance self-perception, were compared to students in traditional subject-centered programs. High school students in the experimental groups "demonstrated the following characteristics relative to graduates of the control settings" (Beane and Lipka, 1986, p. 102):

1. A higher degree of intellectual curiosity and drive.
2. More clear and well-formulated ideas concerning the meaning of education.
3. A higher degree of resourcefulness in meeting new situations.
4. Greater effectiveness in approaching adjustment problems.
5. More frequent participation in student groups.
6. A more active concern for what was going on in the world.

Based on the research studies cited previously and interviews with case studies in the present study, secondary students are not fully active participants in their learning because of a curricular tradition that emphasizes subject matter as an entity not tied to their developing selves.

SUMMARY

Given the multidimensional nature of the investigations in self-esteem and variety of instruments used, a brief summary of the results will be presented. The original questions will serve as organizing themes for this summary.

First, how do factors such as ethnicity, gender, parents' educational levels, and family structure shape self-esteem?

(1) There were no differences in self-esteem based upon gender, parents' educational levels, socioeconomic status, or family structure.

(2) There were significant differences in self-esteem measures between Whites and non-Whites. During the sophomore year, nonWhites scored lower than Whites, and during the junior year non-Whites scored higher than Whites in self-esteem.

(3) Overall, both Whites and non-Whites started out with moderate to high self-esteem scores as freshmen. By the time they were seniors their scores converged at a higher point than when they had entered as freshmen, still in the moderate to high range.

Second, what role do the family and school play in influencing self-esteem?

Family and Self-Esteem

(1) Students who perceived their families as being more cohesive and having an active-recreational orientation had higher levels of self-esteem.

Classroom Environment and Self-Esteem

(1) As freshmen assessing English classes, students who scored higher on the Involvement subscale of the Classroom Environment Scale had higher levels of self-esteem.

(2) There was no relationship between self-esteem and sophomores' assessments of their math classes.

(3) As juniors assessing science classes, students who scored lower on

the Competition subscale of the Classroom Environment Scale had higher levels of self-esteem.

(4) As seniors assessing social studies classes, students who scored higher on the subscales of Involvement and Affiliation on the Classroom Environment Scale had higher levels of self-esteem.

Classroom Environment Based upon Race and Gender

(1) There was no interaction based on race and gender when freshmen assessed their English classes.

(2) When sophomores assessed their Math classes,
  (A) Non-Whites scored lower on Clarity.
  (B) Females scored higher on Involvement, Affiliation, and Teacher Support.

(3) When juniors assessed their Science classes,
  (A) Females scored higher on Affiliation and higher on Competition.

(4) When seniors assessed their Social Studies classes,
  (A) Non-Whites scored lower on Teacher Support and higher on Competition.

Extracurricular Activities

(1) There was no relationship between self-esteem and the number of extracurricular activities in which students participate.

(2) Females join a significantly higher number of clubs during their junior and senior years than do males.

Academic Achievement

(1) Sophomores who scored higher on the ITBS also had higher self-esteem levels.

(2) There was no correlation between grade point averages through the junior year and self-esteem levels during the junior and senior year.

Third, how do measures of general self-esteem, perceptions of family and classroom environments, and case study information further our understanding of how adolescents integrate an image of self during their high school years?

(1) Self-esteem levels increase from the time students enter as freshmen to the time they finish as seniors.

(2) Minorities experience greater variability in self-esteem throughout their high school years.

(3) Family dynamics, more than family structure, influence self-esteem levels; cohesion and recreation are key factors.

(4) Classroom environments are perceived differently by Whites, non-Whites, males, and females.

(5) The Relationship and Personal Growth Dimensions on Classroom Environment Scales correlate with self-esteem.

(6) Adolescents who seek or are given support from family members, peers, or significant others appear to be better adjusted despite no significant difference in objective measures of self-esteem.

(7) Sexual abuse impedes normal adolescent growth.

(8) The family and school support structures, as well as language proficiency, affect the overall adjustment of recent immigrants.

(9) Individual teachers play key roles in shaping the lives of students.

A fourth question should be added to the original list. That is, ''What insights into adolescent self-esteem were obtained but do not follow directly from the first three questions or the selected instrumentation?''

(1) A supportive family facilitates adolescent growth and enhances independence.

(2) Close friendships with members of the opposite sex are valuable growing experiences for adolescents.

(3) Experiencing the death of a loved one or close friend during adolescence can be a very alienating and sad experience, especially when there is little support during the bereavement process.

(4) What happens to adolescents' formal education when they become institutionalized as juvenile delinquents is not easily understood.

(5) The existence of racial tension and conflict can seriously affect the school climate and peer relations even though there may not be any documented differences based on race for general measures of self-esteem. That is, racial tension constitutes a separate construct and may not interact with individual measures of self-esteem.

(6) Adolescents have a very limited number of high school classroom

experiences that they recall as being intellectually or personally stimulating in some way.

(7) Adolescents have a difficult time identifying the relevance of what is learned in the earlier years of high school to real-life experiences.

(8) Some adolescents know at an early age the field of study or vocation they want to pursue as adults. Others who have not decided express a desire to learn more about the options and consequences of different professions earlier in their high school years; hence, more career counseling as part of the high school curriculum is desirable.

By now the reader has probably made a few observations about the case study self-portraits in conjunction with the vignettes contained in the chapters. McEachron-Hirsch and Messier hesitate to project too much into the meaning of these drawings. In fact, if the self-portraits had been provided anonymously, an attempt to match them to the case study anecdotes would have yielded incorrect placements. Like the ups and downs in their lives over the course of four years, the self-portraits displayed variability as well. Interestingly, the strongest self-portrait over the four-year period didn't always coincide with the year where events were more in sync. In other words, internal states, or the internal states as projected through artwork by observers, are not always consistent with information that is shared in an interview situation.

Nevertheless, the self-portraits provided both affirmation and contradiction for the observations made by the interviewers. In the case of Sandra, for example, the growing sense of self seems to nearly jump off the page in her senior self-portrait. Tim, on the other hand, had similar family and school experiences to Sandra but refused to draw a picture of himself during his senior year. One might think that Debbie's self-portrait demonstrated a significant regression during her sophomore year when she was experiencing a great deal of family discord, yet it is not uncommon for adolescents' drawings to revert to more simplified shapes or take on the appearance of caricatures. One would expect Craig's self-portrait to reveal a greater sense of inner turmoil, yet, when compared to Brent's portrait of a member of the opposite sex, one might be inclined to confuse sexual exploitation with budding sexuality. Given the inconsistencies revealed by the self-portraits, the researchers conclude that, for many of these adolescents, too many uncertainties and unanswered questions remain. It would be unfair to their evolving "sense of self" to place definitive judgments on the drawings. Instead, they serve as additional clues for scholars and researchers to attempt to unravel the mystery of adolescent identity formation.

CONCLUSION

Three themes emerged from the multidimensional investigations of the McEachron-Hirsch and Messier study: uniqueness of identity formation, a sense of awakening throughout adolescent growth, and an emphasis upon extrinsic versus intrinsic school orientations throughout the high school years. While it may not be possible to capture fully the uniqueness of how individual identity is formed, the three themes represent an attempt to portray the overriding significance of the high school years with regard to adolescent self-esteem.

Uniqueness of Identity Formation

By examining the collective data one gets the impression that adolescence is characterized by a gradual increase in self-esteem for White students and a more variable, yet overall increase, in self-esteem for minorities. From the case study interviews one gets nearly the opposite impression. That is, when talking to individuals one is impressed by the intensity of personal experiences and their poignancy with regard to perceptions of self. Even the objective measure of self-esteem for the case study participants generates a different picture; variability is much more apparent for individuals in comparison to collective trends.

In *At the Threshold: The Developing Adolescent,* Feldman and Elliot (1990) document the variability of adolescent experience, maintaining that adolescents are not the monolithic group that many researchers since the 1960s would have us believe (Carnegie Corporation of New York, 1990). Instead, they have different "backgrounds, life experiences, values, and aspirations . . . [and] differ enormously in their personalities, talents, growth patterns, and coping skills. . ." (Carnegie Corporation of New York, 1990, p. 4). In addition, the authors state that much of the research on adolescence, their own included, has neglected the

> subjective dimensions—the thoughts and feelings of adolescents themselves. There is little . . . that delves beneath the behavioral surface, or conveys the bittersweet feeling of adolescent life. There is little sense of

the urgency and intensity of passion in the young or the frustrations and anxieties involved in the fulfillment or failure of their aspirations and hopes (Carnegie Corporation of New York, 1990, p. 6).

The McEachron-Hirsch and Messier study adds further support to the literature that recognizes the uniqueness and variability of each adolescent's high school experience and provides valuable narratives about their individual challenges, successes, disappointments, and evolving identities.

Sense of Awakening

Developmental studies note that "among early adolescents, the cognitive shift from concrete thought to abstract reasoning is accompanied by a shift from concrete self-definition to more abstract self-portraiture that describes their psychological interior" (Carnegie Quarterly, 1990, p. 7). In the McEachron-Hirsch and Messier study, this pattern seemed to manifest itself as an awakening. Again, conversations with case studies revealed the depth of perception that adolescents express as early as their freshman years. Probing for deeper psychological meaning was revealed through discussions of divorce; the death of a close relative; sexual abuse; the desire for greater independence; self-discipline; heterosexual relationships; inter-racial heterosexual relationships; suicide; achievement motivation; and parental, sibling, and peer relationships, to mention only a sampling of the conversations. The act of contemplation and reflection about one's experiences and life stories seemed to characterize a dimension of adolescent development that heretofore has received minor attention, unless, of course, there has been an attempt to unravel some perceived psychological problem. While the presence of abstract reasoning in this age group has been well-documented with regard to cognitive levels of development (Piaget, 1955), the normal stages of psychological growth, perceptions of self, and their relationship to cognitive growth remains a relatively untapped area of research.

Extrinsic versus Intrinsic School Orientations

Noting the depth of perception with regard to an awakening inner life made the reverse pattern of school orientations all the more explicit. That is, while the case studies could function at a deeper psychological level when discussing meaningful life experiences, there seemed to be a void of complementary school-related experiences that generated a similar degree of poignancy. With one or two exceptions, the high school students were hard-pressed to identify specific classroom experiences that could sustain the intensity of a meaningful experience. School experiences were talked about as something one was required to "get through," almost like a series of hurdles.

Naturally, one would not want to place perceptions of selected classroom assignments on the same plane with personal crises such as attempted suicide or sexual abuse. There were classroom experiences that the adolescents clearly recognized as growth experiences, as opportunities to learn more about the world, themselves, and their capabilities. However, these identity expanding experiences were few and far between. In fact, most of the events referred to occurred during the senior year, such as working on a research paper for a senior English class, directing the school play, or becoming personally immersed in an auto mechanics class. When discussing these experiences, students described the greater sense of self-confidence they gained, as well as a sense of being "in one's element," that is, a greater sense of fit between self and the designated school experience.

Given the increase in psychological awareness of oneself, one's capabilities, interests, and aspirations, in combination with the adolescent's normal progression toward greater independence, perhaps the schools have underplayed their role in facilitating this move to adulthood. We know that parents play an important role in maintaining support while facilitating separation from the family. This role can be replicated in the school context. That is, adolescents need to be given more responsibility through classroom assignments and that responsibility should include a more personal investment. This personal investment in the educational process can create a greater sense of empowerment or intrinsic motivation and, therefore, enhance personal meaning. This, in no way, suggests minimizing the role of the classroom teacher; rather, it redefines the process whereby meaningful experiences can be gained from a joint commitment to personal and professional goals.

The growing desire to become a contributing and valued member of society begins when children and youth interact with adults who value them and value their adult role in fostering independent cognitive and psychological growth. Unfortunately, the roles of parents and teachers have often been dichotomized, whereby the family has been postured as the main source for creating a strong psychological predisposition for learning and the school has been portrayed as attending to mostly intellectual and cognitive needs. By emphasizing the primary responsibilities of the home and school as separate functions, an artificial split is made, which impedes our pedagogical practice and understanding of growth and development.

Reasons for the polarization of home and family roles lie in our educational tradition and in the history of psychology itself. Branches of the field of psychology have evolved from studies that examined the

FIGURE 8.37 High school student—female, first self-portrait.

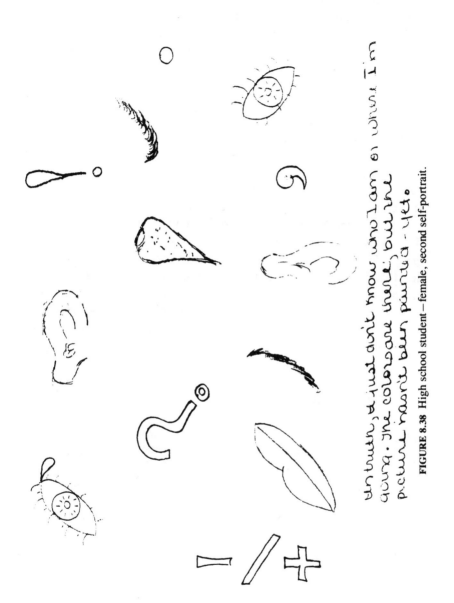

the truth, I just don't know who I am or who or what I'm going. The elements are there, but the picture hasn't been painted – yet.

FIGURE 8.38 High school student — female, second self-portrait.

problems of individuals in mostly clinical situations. Theories resulting from these studies may be characterized as having deficit orientations or deficit origins. Rhetoric from educational theories, on the other hand, emphasizes the "intellect" or "cognition" as if these are entities that can be cultivated apart from other functions of the mind and body.

As the present study has demonstrated, a more fruitful way of examining human growth and development for educational purposes is to study the psychological and cognitive development of normal individuals. From discovering how adolescents create an image of self by integrating multidimensional influences, it is possible to understand how self-esteem is enhanced when learning and growth, intellectual development, and psychic well-being, are perceived as interrelated. The more that educators and scholars articulate and document the ebb and flow of self-esteem, the more identity formation will be grounded in individual life stories, not rigid stages of development or social classifications. As one adolescent reflected (see Figures 8.37 and 8.38), "In truth, I just don't know who I am or where I'm going. The colors are there but the picture hasn't been painted—yet."[2] For children and adolescents, adult support should be manifested as encouraging a life-long process of discovery and re-creation. This, in turn, will reinforce the development of an identity that will be open to novel ways of viewing oneself, one's culture, and the ideas of others.

ENDNOTES

1 The Family Environment Scale (FES) has ninety true-false questions that assess three sets of dimensions: designated as the relationship dimensions (cohesion, expressiveness, and conflict), the personal growth dimensions (independence, achievement orientation, intellectual-cultural orientation, active-recreational orientation, and moral-religious emphasis), and the systems maintenance dimensions (organization and control). Internal consistencies for each of the ten FES subscales are all in an acceptable range of reliability, varying from moderate for Independence and Achievement to substantial for Cohesion, Organization, Intellectual-Cultural and Moral-Religious Emphasis. Normative data on FES Form R, used in the present study, were collected for 1,125 normal and 500 distressed families. The subsamples for normal families included families from throughout the United States, single-parent and multi-generational families representing all age groups.

The Classroom Environment Scale (CES) has ninety true-false questions that assess three sets of dimensions designated as the relationship dimensions (involvement, affiliation, teacher support), the personal growth/goal orientation dimensions (task orientation, competition), and the system maintenance and change dimensions (order and organization, rule clarity, teacher control, innovation). In addition to assessing the responsibility of the teacher to maintain conditions conducive to learning, the CES assesses student-student relationships. The Form R subscale internal consistencies are in an acceptable range of reliability, ranging from .67 for Competition to .86 for Teacher Control. Normative data was collected for students in 382 classrooms and teachers in 295 classrooms in a wide range of schools on both East and West coasts.

The Rosenberg Self-Esteem Scale (1965) is a ten-item scale that has been used extensively in self-esteem research. It is high in reliability and has yielded relationships supporting its construct validity. The reproducibility of the Rosenberg is 92% and its scalability is 72%. Sandra and Thomas Ward discuss the reliability of the subscales in Chapter Six.

2 This quote comes from an adolescent who was a case study for a classroom teacher completing a college course. Two of her self-portraits are provided in Figures 8.37 and 8.38. Presumably, the adolescent was anorexic and when asked to complete the self-portrait, she drew the mask in Figure 8.37. When asked to repeat the exercise she drew the self-portrait depicted in Figure 8.38.

REFERENCES

The AAUW Report: How Schools Shortchange Girls, A Study of Major Findings on Girls and Education. 1992. Commissioned by the American Association of University Women (AAUW) Educational Foundation; Researched by The Wellesley College Center for Research on Women. A joint publication of the AAUW Educational Foundation and National Education Association.

Barnes, M. E. and S. C. Farrier. 1985. "A Longitudinal Study of the Self-Concept of Low-Income Youth," *Adolescence,* 10(77):199–203.

Beane, J. A. and R. P. Lipka. 1986. *Self-Concept, Self-Esteem and the Curriculum.* New York, NY: Teachers College Press.

Belenky, M. F., B. M. Clincy, N. R. Goldberger, and J. M. Tarule. 1986. *Women's Ways of Knowing: The Development of Self, Voice, and Mind.* New York, NY: Basic Books.

Bowler, R., S. Rauch, and R. Schwarzer. 1986. "Self-Esteem and Inter-Racial Attitudes in Black High School Students: A Comparison with Five Other Ethnic Groups," *Urban Education,* 21(1):3–19.

Brown, B. F. 1980. "A Study of the School Needs of Children from One-Parent Families," *Phi Delta Kappan,* 61(8):537–540.

Burchinal, L. G. 1964. "Characteristics of Adolescents from Unbroken, Broken, and Reconstituted Families," *Journal of Marriage and the Family,* 26(1):44–51.

Byrne, B. M. 1983. "Investigating Measure of Self-Concept," *Measurement and Evaluation in Guidance,* 16(3):115–126.

"California Task Force to Promote Self-Esteem and Personal Social Responsibility: Toward a State of Self-Esteem, the Final Report." 1990. California Legislature.

Carnegie Corporation of New York. 1990. "Adolescence: Path to a Productive Life or a Diminished Future?" The Carnegie Council on Adolescent Development: Work in Progress, *Carnegie Quarterly,* 35(1 and 2).

Cheung, P. C. and S. Lau. 1985. "Self-Esteem: Its Relationship to the Family and School Social Environments among Chinese Adolescents," *Youth and Society,* 16:438–456.

Combs, A. W., D. L. Avila, and W. W. Purkey. 1971. *Helping Relationships: Basic Concepts for the Helping Professions.* Boston, MA: Allyn and Bacon.

Conyers, M. G. 1977. "Comparing School Success of Students from Conventional and Broken Homes," *Phi Delta Kappan,* 58(8):647.

Coopersmith, S. 1967. *The Antecedents of Self-Esteem.* San Francisco, CA: W. H. Freeman and Co.

Covington, M. 1989. "Self-Esteem and Failure in School: Analysis and Policy Implications in Mecca," in *The Social Importance of Self-Esteem.* A. Mecca, N. Smelser, and J. Vasconcellos, eds. Los Angeles, CA: University of California Press.

Faludi, S. 1991. *Backlash: An Undeclared War Against American Women.* New York, NY: Crown Publishers.

Feldman, S. S. and G. R. Elliot. 1990. *At the Threshold: The Developing Adolescent.* Cambridge, MA: Harvard University Press.

Forman, S. G. and B. D. Forman. 1981. "Family Environment and Its Relation to Adolescent Personality Factors," *J. of Personality Assessment,* 45(2):163–167.

Fowler, P. C. 1982. "Relationship of Family Environment and Personality Characteristics: Canonical Analyses of Self-Attributions," *J. of Clinical Psychology,* 33:804–810.

Galuzzi, E., E. Kirby, and K. Zuker. 1980. "Students' and Teachers' Perceptions of Classroom Environment and Self- and Others'-Concepts," *Psychological Reports,* 46:747–753.

Gilligan, C. 1982. *In a Different Voice: Psychological Theory and Women's Development.* Cambridge, MA: Harvard University Press.

Goodlad, J. I. 1984. *A Place Called School: Prospects for the Future.* New York, NY: McGraw-Hill.

Gough, H. G. and A. B. Heilbrun, Jr. 1983. *The Adjective Checklist Manual.* Palo Alto, CA: Consulting Psychologists Press.

Hetherington, E. M. 1972. "Effects of Father Absence on Personality Development in Adolescent Daughters," *Developmental Psychology,* 7:313–326.

Hiltonsmith, R. W. 1985. "Relationship between Perception of Family Social Climate and Behavior in the Home Setting," *Psychological Reports,* 56:979–983.

Hirsch, B. J., R. H. Moos, and T. M. Reischl. 1985. "Psychosocial Adjustment of Adolescent Children of a Depressed, Arthritic, or Normal Parent," *J. of Abnormal Psychology,* 94(2):154–164.

Hoelter, J. W. 1983. "Factorial Invariance and Self-Esteem: Reassessing Race and Sex Differences," *Social Forces,* 61:834–846.

Holly, W. 1987. *Student Self-Esteem and Academic Success.* Eugene, OR: University of Oregon.

Ianni, F. A. 1989. *The Search for Structure: A Report on American Youth Today.* New York, NY: The Free Press.

Jensen, G. F., C. S. White, and J. M. Galliher. 1982. "Ethnic Status and Adolescent Self-Evolutions: An Extension of Research on Minority Self-Esteem," *Social Problems,* 30(2):226–239.

Kagel, S. A., R. M. White, and J. C. Coyne. 1978. "Father-Absent and Father-Present Families of Disturbed and Non-Disturbed Adolescents," *American Journal of Orthopsychiatry,* 48(2):342–352.

Kounin, J. S. 1970. *Discipline and Group Management in Classrooms.* New York, NY: Holt, Rinehart and Winston.

Laffoon, K., R. Jenkins-Friedman, and N. Tollefson. 1989. "Causal Attributions of

Underachieving Gifted, Achieving Gifted, and Nongifted Students," *Journal for the Education of the Gifted,* 13(1):4−21.

Leroux, J. A. 1986. "Sex Differences Influencing Gifted Adolescents: An Enthnographic Study," Report No. EC 190 243, paper presented at the annual meeting of the *American Educational Research Association (70th, San Francisco, CA, April 16−20).* (ERIC Document Reproduction Service No. 1 ED 271934).

Lutz, P. 1983. "The Step-Family: An Adolescent Perspective," *Family Relations,* 32:367−375.

Marotz-Baden, R., G. R. Adams, N. Bueche, B. Munro, and G. Munro. 1979. "Family Form or Family Process? Reconsidering the Deficit Family Model Approach," *The Family Coordinator,* 28(1):5−14.

McLanahan, S. S. 1983. "Family Structure and Stress: A Longitudinal Comparison of Two-Parent and Female-Headed Families," *J. of Marriage and the Family,* 45(2):347−357.

Miller, J. P. and W. Seller. 1985. *Curriculum: Perspectives and Practice.* New York, NY: Longman.

Moos, R. H. 1974. *Family Environment Scale Preliminary Manual.* Stanford University, CA: Social Ecology Institute.

Moos, R. H. and E. G. Trickett. 1987. *Classroom Environment Scale Manual, Second Edition.* Palo Alto, CA: Consulting Psychologists Press.

Nelson, G. 1984. "The Relationship between Dimensions of Classroom and Family Environments and the Self-Concept, Satisfaction, and Achievement of Grade 7 and 8 Students," *J. of Community Psychology,* 12:276−287.

Nielson, L. 1987. *Adolescent Psychology.* New York, NY: Holt, Rinehart and Winston.

Nye, F. I. 1957. "Child Adjustment in Broken and in Unhappy Unbroken Homes," *Marriage and Family Living,* 19(4):356−361.

Ornstein, A. C. and F. P. Hunkins. 1988. *Curriculum: Foundations, Principles, and Issues.* Englewood Cliffs, NJ: Prentice Hall.

Peshkin, A. 1991. *The Color of Strangers, the Color of Friends: The Play of Ethnicity in School and Community.* Chicago, IL: The University of Chicago Press.

Piaget, J. 1955. *The Language and Thought of the Child.* New York, NY: New American Library; Kegan Paul, 1926.

Polakow-Suransky, S. and N. Ulaby. 1990. "Students Take Action to Combat Racism," *Phi Delta Kappan,* 71(8):601−606.

Purkey, W. W. 1970. *Self-Concept and School Achievement.* Englewood Cliffs, NJ: Prentice-Hall.

Purkey, W. W. 1978. *Inviting School Success: A Self-Concept Approach to Teaching and Learning.* Belmont, CA: Wadsworth Publishing Co.

Prasinos, S. and B. I. Tittler. 1981. "The Family Relationships of Humor-Oriented Adolescents," *J. of Personality,* 49(3):295−305.

Raschke, H. J. and V. J. Raschke. 1979. "Family Conflict and Children's Self-Concepts: A Comparison of Intact and Single-Parent Families. *J. of Marriage and the Family,* 41(2):367−374.

Rosenberg, M. 1965. *Society and the Adolescent Self-Image.* Princeton, NJ: Princeton University Press.

Rust, J. O. and A. McCraw. 1984. "Influence of Masculinity-Femininity on Adolescent Self-Esteem and Peer Acceptance," *Adolescence,* 19(74):359−366.

Segal, J. and Z. Segal. 1985. *Growing Up Smart and Happy.* New York, NY: McGraw-Hill Book Co.

Slater, E. J. and J. D. Haber. 1984. "Adolescent Adjustment Following Divorce as a Function of Familial Conflict," *J. of Consulting and Clinical Psychology,* 52:920−921.

Slater, E. J., K. J. Stewart, and M. W. Linn. 1983. "The Effects of Family Disruption on Adolescent Males and Females," *Adolescence,* 18(72):931−942.

Trent, W. T. and J. M. McPartland. 1982. "The Sense of Well-Being and Opportunity of America's Youth: Some Sources of Race and Sex Differences in Early Adolescence," Report No. UD 022775, (ERIC Document Reproduction Service NO. ED 242798).

Tyerman, A. and M. Humphrey. 1983. "Life Stress, Family Support and Adolescent Disturbance," *J. of Adolescence,* 6(1):1−12.

Walberg, H. J. and M. E. Uguroglu. 1980. "Motivation and Educational Productivity: Theories, Results, and Implications," in *Achievement Motivation: Recent Trends in Theory and Research,* L. J. Fyans, Jr., ed., New York, NY: Plenum.

Wallerstein, J. S. and S. Blakeslee. 1989. *Second Chances.* New York, NY: Ticknor and Fields.

Wallerstein, J. S. and J. B. Kelly. 1980. *Surviving the Breakup.* New York, NY: Basic Books.

Willie, C. V. 1967. "The Relative Contribution of Family Status and Economic Status to Juvenile Delinquency," *Social Problems,* 14(3):326−335.

Wylie, R. C. 1979. *The Self-Concept. Vol. 2, Theory and Research on Selected Topics. Revised Edition.* Lincoln, NE: University of Nebraska Press.

Youniss, J. and J. Smollar. 1985. *Adolescent Relations with Mothers, Fathers, and Friends.* Chicago, IL: The University of Chicago Press.

CHAPTER 9

Self-Esteem and Students with Special Needs

CHRISTINE WALTHER-THOMAS – *The College of William and Mary*

INTRODUCTION

STUDENTS with disabilities often experience academic and social problems that adversely affect their perceptions of themselves as competent and valuable learners. Because school constitutes such an important part of the daily work that children and youth do, a poor performance can negatively influence nearly every other dimension of their lives. Most parents and professionals recognize the potential damage that school failure can do to the emotional well-being of children and youth with disabilities. Despite these concerns, self-esteem is a rarely discussed topic in special education. Individualized Education Programs (IEPs) are annually formulated for special education students, yet few IEPs explicitly address the development of "self-esteem." Most IEP goals and objectives tend to focus on the development of "skills," "strategies," and/or "competencies" related to academics, interpersonal relationships, independent living, vocational preparation, and effective learning. Special educators have assumed that by improving performances in these areas, the overall effects upon self-esteem would be positive. Only recently have these assumptions been investigated.

This chapter will explore some of the philosophical, social, and political reasons that self-esteem is often neglected in special education planning and programming. First, an examination of some of the philosophical and psychological influences on special education will be presented. Second, a review of literature related to self-esteem and students with disabilities will be examined. Third, several significant social/political forces that have changed the focus of special education programming will be addressed: national concern for "academic excellence" and increasing student diversity. Finally, a collaborative model will be presented to help educators create supportive learning environments that are more attuned to the social-emotional needs of students.

281

THE INFLUENCE OF BEHAVIORAL AND COGNITIVE PSYCHOLOGY ON SPECIAL EDUCATION THINKING AND PROGRAM DEVELOPMENT

Recently a cover story in *Newsweek* (Adler et al., 1992) explored "what's wrong with the feel-good movement." The article criticized recent efforts by schools and families to enhance self-esteem in children and adolescents. These authors noted that, while many educators and parents believe that self-esteem develops from a genuine sense of achievement and self-worth, the 1990s interpretation of self-esteem enhancement has resulted in "an explosion of awards, gold stars, and accomplishments of childhood. Most children's sports teams now automatically give trophies just for showing up, with the result that the average 12 year-old's bedroom is as cluttered with honors as Bob Hope's den" (p. 49).

Adler and colleagues (1992) further contend that, given limited empirical data, professionals and parents want to believe that students will be happier and will perform more successfully if self-esteem is increased:

> As a theory of behavior, self-esteem has intuition on its side, if not necessarily a monopoly on convincing research . . . [It is] a matter less of scientific pedagogy than of faith — faith that positive thoughts can manifest the inherent goodness in anyone (Adler et al., pp. 48, 50).

To consider self-esteem and students with disabilities, it is important to first acknowledge how little is really known about this somewhat nebulous concept. Researchers and practitioners have had considerable difficulty determining what really constitutes self-esteem (Bracken, 1992). Is it a unidimensional concept? A multidimensional concept? Or perhaps both? Over the years self-esteem definitions have varied greatly. Researchers and theorists have had difficulty finding a universally accepted definition and reliably assessing potential dimensions of self-esteem (Adler et al., 1992; Bracken, 1992; Coopersmith, 1967, 1984; Harter, 1983; Marsh and Holmes, 1990; Piers, 1984).

These concerns are further compounded by the professional preparation that many educators receive. Behavioral (Skinner, 1990) and social-cognitive psychology (Bandura, 1986; Flavell, 1985; Meichenbaum, 1985) have been significant influences on the development of teacher thinking and behavior. This is particularly true for those teachers who work with students with disabilities. Most of special education researchers and practitioners are schooled in the basic tenets of behavioral and/or cognitive psychology. In general, most are firm believers in the fundamental principles associated with these two schools of thought. As a result, self-esteem has been either too vague or too unfamiliar for most special educators to consider when developing instructional programs.

The Impact of Behavioral Psychology

Skinner (1990) identified overt human behavior as the most important unit of psychological study. He contended that because the "self" cannot be seen, inferences about this concept can only be made by studying observable behaviors of individuals. Behavioral psychology maintains that clearly defined and systematic behavior can predict (1) future behaviors on the basis of past behaviors, (2) the likelihood of future responses on the basis of past reinforcers, (3) future behaviors occurring in certain environments on the basis of past performance in similar settings. It also states that individuals learn new behaviors through a process of observation and imitation.

Over the years special education has been strongly influenced by this school of thought. Behavioral intervention programs have proven effective in increasing performance levels among students in special education programs. This has been especially useful in programs designed for students with severe disabilities where behaviors often change very slowly. Using behavioral principles, special education researchers and practitioners have defined many valuable academic and social behaviors, have developed appropriate instructional sequences to teach students appropriate new behaviors, and have measured progress according to observable criteria. Special education literature in these areas reveals the significant influence behavioral psychology has had on the field of special education (e.g., Gaylord-Ross and Haring, 1987; Peterson and Haralick, 1977; Polsgrove and Nelson, 1982; Schulz et al., 1991; Smith and Luckinnson, 1992; Wallace and McLoughlin, 1988; Zins et al., 1988).

The Impact of Cognitive Psychology

During the past twenty years, cognitive psychology has become an increasingly important influence on the evolving field of special education (Reid, 1988). Many special educators became dissatisfied with purely behavioral approaches. They felt that behavioral approaches did not adequately help students with disabilities learn how to think more effectively. Farnham-Diggory (1977) noted, tongue in cheek, that pure behaviorism suggests that learning is simply a process whereby ''a stimulus goes in, a response comes out, and what happens in between is summarized by a hyphen'' (p. 128). Most special educators recognized that purely behavioral interventions did not adequately address many of the complex academic and social learning needs that persons with disabilities experience.

The weaknesses in behavioral approaches are especially apparent for the vast majority of students in special education. More than 90% of the students served in special education have disabilities that are mild to moderate [U.S. Department of Education (USDE), 1991]. These students frequently lack effective and efficient thinking skills that prevent them from performing satisfactorily in academic, social, and vocational settings. Many cognitive researchers and practitioners believe that students with disabilities need to understand more about thinking and learning. These students need to learn how to ''process'' new information more effectively (Flavell, 1985; Reid, 1988). Experts in this area believe that many students with disabilities are capable of learning more successfully if they use more effective strategies (Deshler and Schumaker, 1986; Meichenbaum, 1985; Swanson, 1987).

Behavioral-Cognitive Research: Defining Special Education's Role

Through behavioral and cognitive research, teaching strategies have been identified to modify behaviors effectively and foster more diverse thinking patterns of children and youth with disabilities. This research has significantly influenced special education theory and practice during the past thirty to forty years (Bandura, 1986; Farnham-Diggory, 1977; Flavell, 1986; Meichenbaum, 1985; Reid, 1988; Smith and Luckinnson, 1992). Furthermore, research findings have also influenced public policies that affect the lives of persons with disabilities. For example, legislative initiatives that have expanded the individual rights of persons with disabilities during the past twenty years include Section 504 of the Vocational Rehabilitation Act, 1973; Individuals with Disabilities Education Act (formerly known as The Education for All Handicapped Children Act, 1975),1990; and the Americans with Disabilities Act, 1990.

As a result of this legislation, notions such as least restrictive environment, educational mainstreaming, deinstitutionalization, normalization, and community-based employment have become common practice. These concepts are widely accepted, in large measure because behavioral-cognitive research has shown that most persons with disabilities can develop the fundamental skills needed to learn, live, and work in the same environments as their peers without disabilities when they are given appropriate educational opportunities to do so. For many special educators, social adjustment and self-sufficiency are key components for establishing a healthy self-image.

While the logical place to help students develop personal-social skills and participate in self-esteem enhancement is in the classroom, these goals receive minor attention in comparison to subject matter orientations. Vaughn (1985) noted several reasons why school administrators do not take an active role in promoting affective instruction in classrooms. First, many educators may not believe they have time to teach these skills to students. Second, they feel inadequately prepared to teach these skills to students. Third, they may not feel that direct instruction is necessary. They may assume that students without appropriate personal-social skills will develop them by exposure to others who are more skilled in these areas. Third, teachers may also assume that instruction is not needed because students will become more skilled as they mature. Fifth, they may believe that instruction in this domain is the responsibility of families and is not appropriate for classroom learning. Hazel and Schumaker (1988) also noted that some experts believe that fixed "personality" traits may limit the effectiveness of instructional efforts to change skills and/or coping strategies. Despite these concerns, researchers have begun to investigate the relationships between self-esteem, academic performance, and social interaction among special populations.

SELF-ESTEEM RESEARCH AND STUDENTS WITH DISABILITIES

Research has demonstrated that relationships exist between peer acceptance, self-concept, self-esteem, and school performance (Hansford and Hattie, 1982; Samuels, 1977). While students with disabilities follow the same stages of development as their peers without disabilities, their academic and social problems often complicate or impede their progress. It is not surprising that these problems can have a negative effect on the self-esteem of persons with disabilities. Repeated academic and social failure, feelings of inferiority, and concerns about being "different" increase the likelihood that children and youth with learning problems will experience low self-esteem on the basis of their own negative self-evaluations (Bingham, 1980; Kaslow and Cooper, 1978; Kistner et al., 1987; Winne et al., 1982).

Academic and Social Performance

Most of the research that has investigated possible relationships between disabilities and self-esteem have focused on students with mild disabilities, in particular those with learning disabilities or mental retardation, as these students constitute the majority of those served in special education programs (Schulz et al., 1991; USDE, 1991). Limited information is available regarding self-esteem and persons with severe disabilities.

While a number of studies have been conducted in this area, findings from these investigations need to be viewed cautiously. Many existing studies have utilized formal assessment instruments to assess the self-esteem of students with disabilities such as the Coopersmith Self-Esteem Inventory (Coopersmith, 1984) and the Self-Perception Profile for Children (Harter, 1985). Questions exist, however, regarding the reliability and validity of these tools (see Chapter Six). Methodological concerns also exist because many of these studies rely on findings based on informal measures (e.g., self-reports, teacher observations, parent reports), small numbers of participants, and inadequate comparison groups. In addition, these studies should be viewed cautiously because students with disabilities are recognized as poor test-takers. They also experience many receptive and expressive language problems and lack skills in assessing their own behaviors (Gresham and Elliott, 1987; Schulz et al., 1991; Smith and Luckinnson, 1992). Finally, many of these researchers have failed to define clearly what is meant by "self-esteem." Because their definitional parameters are so vague, it is difficult to assess the validity of many conclusions that are presented.

Relationships between self-esteem, academic performance, and expectations for school success have been established. For example, Gregory, Shanahan, and Walberg (1986) examined data on 26,147 twelfth graders who participated in the national High School and Beyond (HSB) investigation conducted by the National Opinion Research Center (NORC) under the direction of the National Center for Educational Statistics. Within this sample, 439 (1.7%) students indicated that they had a specific learning disability. In comparison with their peers, Gregory and colleagues (1986) found that students with disabilities scored significantly lower on all of the academic achievement measures and on most of the indices of motivation and self-esteem.

Children and youth view school in the same way that most adults view their jobs. We define ourselves, in large measure, by how successful we are at work. School is where students receive feedback about their skills, talents, abilities, and worth as individuals. If school is a daily experience filled with frustration, failure, disappointment, and embarrassment, it is easy to understand why many students with disabilities report negative feelings about their competence and worth as learners and choose to leave public schools as quickly as possible (Zigmond and Thornton, 1985; Edgar, 1987, 1988; USDE, 1991). During the 1989−90 school year 44% of all students with disabilities fourteen years of age or older left school (USDE, 1991). This is an alarming statistic and a sad commentary on the current state of services for these students. Post-school follow-up investigations of students with mild disabilities have shown that as many as 50% of these students leave school without earning a diploma (Edgar, 1987; Zigmond and Thornton, 1985). Many adolescents with mild to moderate disabilities fail to develop critical skills (e.g., academic, vocational, social, daily living, self-advocacy) and the self-confidence needed to live independently as young adults (Edgar, 1988; Wagner and Shaver, 1989). Consequently many of these young adults remain emotionally and financially dependent on their families long after their age mates have moved out on their own. This situation produces feelings of failure and financial and emotional stresses for all family members (Haring et al., 1990; Mithaug et al., 1985; Sitlington and Frank, 1990; USDE, 1991).

At the other end of the exceptional student continuum, Whitmore (1980) reported that gifted students, in particular those who are under-achieving in school environments, experience low self-esteem and low self-concept. Low self-esteem among gifted students may be the result of tension they experience in school environments where their actual potential is not recognized (Whitmore, 1980). This is common among students with disabilities who were also gifted (e.g., learning disabilities/gifted, emotional disturbance/gifted). Social-emotional problems may develop as the result of the exceptional abilities of these students going unnoticed while the problems associated with their disabilities are highlighted in academic and/or social situations. For example, in a review of self-esteem and self-concept studies related to LD and academic environments, Knoff (1983) reported that many students with LD find classroom environments so socially and emotionally punishing that they manifest many of the symptoms associated with emotional disturbance (e.g., acting out, withdrawal, verbal and/or physical aggression) during the six hours a day they attend school.

Comparing one's own performance against the performance of others is one mechanism by which students establish estimations of themselves (Harter, 1983; Omizo and Omizo, 1987). When students with disabilities compare themselves to their peers without disabilities, they frequently view themselves as less competent academically and socially (Biklen, 1985; Schulz et al., 1991; Zins et al., 1988). As a result, students may experience diminished feelings of self-esteem and self-worth (Mayberry, 1990). This finding has been reported in studies that have investigated self-esteem and self-concept across categories of exceptionality. It is frequently reported that students with orthopedic disabilities and chronic health problems (e.g., asthma, juvenile diabetes, sickle cell anemia, cystic fibrosis) have low self-esteem in contrast to their peers without disabilities (Walker and Jacobs, 1984). Additional studies of students with learning disabilities have reported social-emotional problems such as poor interpersonal relationships, low self-esteem, low self-concept, limited social skills, and withdrawal (Bryan, 1976; Hazel and Schumaker, 1988; Wallace and McLoughlin, 1988). The fact that these problems persist into adulthood suggests that a great portion of the responsibility lies within our educational institutions. In a national study of 600 adults with LD, Chesler (1982) found that low self-esteem was one of the five most frequently mentioned problems respondents noted. Problems related to academic work, often the source of many problems these students experience in schools, barely made the top ten.

Peer Relationships

The importance of peer relationships on the development of self-esteem cannot be minimized. In a study of adolescent boys, Newman (1976) found that they spent approximately 80% of their time interacting with peers and only about 20% of their time with adults. Peer group identification provides children and adolescents with a sense of security and helps them develop their self-confidence and self-esteem (Elkind, 1988). During elementary years most children strive to conform to behavior set by classmates or their own small group of friends, whereas during adolescence students become keenly aware of the larger community and its expectations regarding their behavior and appearance (Newman, 1976; Schulz et al., 1991).

A consistent finding in disabilities research is peer rejection of students with disabilities and/or feelings of alienation in general education classrooms (Schulz et al., 1991). Social rejection of students with mental retardation has been widely documented (e.g, Bruininks et al., 1974; Gottlieb and Switzky, 1982; Sandberg, 1982). In reviews of this research, Gottlieb (1975) and Gresham (1984) each concluded that students with mild retardation are generally accepted less and more likely to be reacted to negatively than are their peers without disabilities.

Similar findings are evident for students with LD. Wiener (1987) reviewed nineteen studies related to the peer status of students with LD. She found lower peer status was clearly evident in fifteen of these studies. The remaining four investigations had serious methodological flaws and could not be accurately interpreted. She hypothesized that lower peer acceptance is the result of the special education students' general lack of prosocial skills (e.g., turn-taking, conversation-maintaining skills, compliment-giving) and use of inappropriate social interaction strategies (e.g., negative remarks, physical aggression, inappropriate nonverbal communication).

LaGreca (1987) also compared peer relationships among students with LD and their peers without disabilities and found that some students with LD do not experience peer difficulties and appear to be well-liked by peers. Students with LD who do experience difficulties with peers, however, report problems related to poor conversation skills, limited social competence, and higher levels of negative interactions with peers and teachers. These students also appear to be more frequently ignored by their peers and by teachers.

Peer problems have also been documented with many other categories of disability. Schulz and colleagues (1991) noted that children with chronic health and/or orthopedic disabilities often experience embarrassment, insecurity, and social rejection by peers and adults. Negative interactions and experiences with peers and adults can adversely affect their confidence and self-esteem. Low self-esteem and social isolation are commonly reported problems among students with behavioral/emotional disabilities (Gaylord-Ross and Haring, 1987; Nelson, 1988). Antia (1985) reported similar concerns for students with hearing disabilities. Gifted students, particularly gifted underachievers and gifted students with disabilities, commonly experience problems of low self-esteem, frustration, and peer rejection (Gunderson et al., 1987; Weill, 1987; Whitmore, 1980).

Many students with disabilities experience language and speech problems (Donahue and Bryan, 1984). Difficulties with receptive and expressive language can result in peer rejection as a result of students' inability to understand and use popular slang expressions, metaphors, jokes, puns, and sarcastic remarks. Donahue and Bryan (1984) noted that language problems may present particular difficulties for adolescents. Frequently, they experience difficulty following dialogues with peers and are poor participants in rapid verbal exchanges. These problems may create feelings of loneliness, isolation, and misunderstanding.

Research has shown that peer rejection of students with disabilities happens early in children's social development (Brown et al., 1988, 1989; Jenkins et al., 1985; Levy and Gottlieb, 1984; Peterson and Haralick, 1977). These studies suggest that all young children, including preschoolers, need accurate information about disabilities, social skills training, and ongoing experience playing with children with disabilities. Existing research suggests that systematic interventions are often necessary for positive peer relationships to develop and social acceptance to occur among many students with disabilities and their peers without disabilities (Antia, 1985; Brown et al., 1988, 1989; Gresham and Elliott, 1987; Hazel and Schumacher, 1988; Schulz et al., 1991).

Teacher Acceptance

Teachers' attitudes toward students have long been recognized as powerful forces in determining the nature of their interactions. This, in turn, has a significant effect on students' level of achievement (Brophy and Good, 1974; Purkey, 1970; Rosenthal and Jacobson, 1968). Student achievement and behavior may suffer because of overindulgence or low expectations conveyed by teachers. Teachers are sometimes unaware of the hidden messages that they are communicating to their students. These messages convey the classroom teacher's views, conscious or unconscious, on a wide range of student-related topics and abilities to achieve, behavioral expectations, and their value as individuals. According to Schulz and colleagues (1991), students quickly learn if the teacher favors high or low achievers, feels respect or disgust for students with special needs, or is biased toward or against students who are different. Teacher attitudes frequently set the tone for acceptance or rejection of students with disabilities by their peers (Schulz et al., 1991).

A number of studies have found that teachers, as well as peers, are more likely to evaluate students with disabilities negatively (Bruininks, 1978; Chapman, 1988; Gresham, 1984; Pearl et al., 1983). Clark (1980) reviewed the research on teacher attitudes toward students with disabilities. She found that general education teachers are typically uncomfortable working with these students. Many expressed negative attitudes about the placement of these students in their classrooms. Similar findings have also been reported by other researchers (Idol-Maestas and Ritter, 1985; LaGreca, 1987; Margolis and McGettigan, 1988; Munson, 1987). Despite years of mainstreaming students with disabilities, many teachers do not feel well-prepared to teach students with disabilities and find that additional work is required to meet the needs of these students (Brown et al., 1988; Madden and Slavin, 1983). Given these negative feelings, it is not surprising that LaGreca (1987) found that classroom teachers were more likely to ignore students with LD than their peers without disabilities in classroom activities and discussions.

Locus of Control

External locus of control is noted as a common problem noted in studies related to self-esteem and students with disabilities (Basgall and Snyder, 1988; Gilmor and Reid, 1979). Frequently, students with disabilities feel that positive and negative experiences are the result of external factors beyond their control (e.g., good luck, fate, the behaviors of others). They may not recognize the value of their own efforts. They may not take credit for their own accomplishments and may have difficulty accepting responsibility for their own inappropriate actions. Students with a more internal locus of control achieve higher academically (Purkey, 1970), are more motivated (Mink, 1971), and are better adjusted socially (Bendell et al., 1980). Gilmor and Reid (1979) suggest, however, that this may actually be a valid coping strategy within the parameters of learning and behavior disabilities. Excuses may enable students to maintain their self-esteem and their willingness to continue to participate in social and academic activities in which they frequently experience failure.

Self-Esteem and Instructional Approaches

Students with mild to moderate disabilities need school environments that will nurture and enhance their self-esteem. In a time when the public school agenda is focused on academic excellence, self-esteem researchers recommend that schools also need to emphasize the benefits, in terms of learning and development, that can be derived from meaningful social experiences (Gresham and Elliott, 1987; Osman, 1987). Many researchers and practitioners suggest that students with disabilities can benefit from direct social-emotional skill instruction such as prosocial skills, self-talk, and relaxation training; peer and adult modeling; supervised skill practice; support and encouragement; and constructive feedback from adults and peers (Gresham and Elliott, 1987; Salend and Meddaugh, 1985).

While there may be some disagreement among educators and psychologists regarding the efficacy of intervention strategies specifically designed to build self-esteem, there is little disagreement among professionals that low self-esteem is a common problem for many students with disabilities. Teaching students to become more successful academically and socially can help build self-esteem (Biklen, 1985; Schulz et al., 1991; Zins et al., 1988). Unfortunately, many educators are reluctant to address the social-emotional needs of students. Few teachers and administrators feel adequately prepared to deal with complex social-emotional needs of poorly adjusted students (Madden and Slavin, 1983; Walker, 1986; Wehlage et al., 1989).

Many disabilities researchers contend that, without systematic interventions designed to build academic or social interaction skills, efforts to improve the self-esteem of students with disabilities are likely to fail (Gresham and Elliott, 1987; Hazel and Schumaker, 1988; Polsgrove and Nelson, 1982). Polsgrove and Nelson (1982) noted that students with disabilities who lack adequate social and academic skills will continue to experience failure and rejection from their peers and teachers, thus perpetuating self-esteem complications. Given special education's philosophical orientation, as well as a growing research base that supports cognitive-behavioral theories about learning, direct intervention to help students develop satisfactory academic and social skills is viewed as an effective way to help children and youth with disabilities acquire higher levels of self-esteem.

The research literature is far from conclusive regarding the impact that disabilities have on the development of self-esteem in students with disabilities. Methodologically sound investigations in this arena are limited. Many existing studies consist of small numbers of participants, inconsistent conceptual definitions, poorly defined populations, and questionable procedures regarding data collection and analysis. Clearly, more research is needed. Given these limitations, existing research suggests that students with disabilities frequently experience low self-esteem as a result of the academic and social problems commonly associated with disabilities. In general, it appears that the development of appropriate academic and social skills enables students with disabilities to perform more successfully, thus reducing failure experiences and enabling them to make more positive self-evaluations regarding their own worth.

BUILDING A CONTEXT FOR SELF-ESTEEM IN SPECIAL EDUCATION

During the past decade significant changes have occurred in public education. Changes in school environments and students' performance expectations have necessitated a critical review of current special education services for students with disabilities. Program planners and service delivery providers have begun to redefine their relationships with general educators and their roles in the development and delivery of services for low-achieving students. It is a time of unrest in special education, however, many professionals believe that, ultimately, improved services will emerge that will provide better mechanisms for addressing problems of all low achieving students – those with and those without clearly determined disabilities.

In this section we will examine key issues related to service delivery: concerns about current special education services, a changing mainstream population, and evolving academic expectations. An emerging model will be presented that emphasizes collaboration between special education and general education in program planning and service delivery. This model offers hope that, given a broad array of competing priorities, schools can more effectively utilize existing resources to meet the academic and social-emotional needs of students. This model offers hope that educators can critically assess the self-esteem needs of students and provide resources to meet those needs.

Concerns about Current Special Education Services

According to the *Thirteenth Annual Report to Congress on the Implementations of the Individuals with Disabilities Act* (USDE, 1991), approximately 4.5 million students participated in special education and/or Chapter I programs during the 1989–90 school year. This represents approximately 7% of the total school population. Ninety-four percent of these students have disabilities that are generally considered to be in the "mild to moderate" range on a disability continuum. High incidence disabilities include learning disabilities (49%), speech and language disorders (23%), mental retardation (13%), and emotional disturbance (9%).

During 1990 only 7% of students with identified disabilities received educational services outside traditional school buildings. In most cases these students are educated in the educational mainstream. The Individuals with Disabilities Education Act of 1990 (IDEA) as well as its legislative predecessor, the Education of All Handicapped Children Act (EHA), encourages schools to provide education for students with disabilities in the least restrictive environment where successful learning can take place. For most students with disabilities, this appears to be the general education classroom because educators and families recognize the importance of educating these students with their peers. Mainstream settings provide appropriate role models and facilitate academic growth and social interaction in natural environments. Active participation in these classes also increases the likelihood that students with disabilities will develop the content knowledge and performance skills needed to earn standard high school diplomas and prepare for post-secondary education and independent living.

Traditionally, most special education services are provided to students with disabilities through "pull-out" programs such as resource rooms. In these arrangements students with disabilities are assigned to general education classes for most of the school day. Currently, approximately 70% of all students with disabilities spend most of their school time in general education classrooms (USDE, 1991). These students leave their mainstream classrooms for one or more instructional periods each day to receive specialized academic, social, and compensatory instruction.

Resource programs provide students with disabilities greater opportunities for mainstream participation than do more restrictive service delivery options. Emerging data, however, suggest that pull-out models are not effective (Stainback and Stainback, 1990; Stainback et al., 1989). Linkage between special education and general education programs is often poor at best (Stainback and Stainback, 1990; Stainback et al., 1989). Consequently, students develop skills in resource programs that do not successfully transfer and/or generalize to mainstream settings (Reynolds et al., 1987; Stainback and Stainback, 1990; Stainback et al., 1989).

During the past decade research has challenged the value of many remedial programs (Will, 1986) and has resulted in concerns about the efficacy of current services. Questions have also surfaced regarding potential negative effects from the labeling process (Reynolds, 1989) and from continued emphasis in schools on remediating failure rather than preventing problems from developing (Stainback et al., 1989; Will, 1986).

A Changing Mainstream Population

Today, many educators find the nonacademic problems of their students staggering (e.g., AIDS, poverty, substance abuse, racial strife, violence, teen parenthood). For many teachers, it is virtually impossible to focus their students' attention on academic learning when the challenges they face from the outside world are so great. Students "at-risk" for academic and social failure perform poorly because of a complex combination of ethnic, social, cultural, environmental, and/or economic factors that permeate their lives (Helge, 1988; Hodgkinson, 1985; Kozol, 1990; Slavin et al., 1989; Spencer, 1985). For example, approximately one-fourth of all children in this country are born poor (Williams, 1992). Poverty is a serious concern to the educational system because a wide variety of factors associated with low income families (e.g., inadequate prenatal and postnatal health care, teenage pregnancy, low birth weight, poor nutrition, abuse and neglect, and limited intellectual stimulation) contribute to the school problems that many at-risk students experience (Hodgkinson, 1985; Kozol, 1990; Spencer, 1985; Wehlage et al.,1989).

Many of the academic and social-emotional problems of at-risk learners look like those of students with mild to moderate disabilities (Ornstein and Levine, 1989; Wehlage et al., 1989). Despite this, many at-risk students do not qualify for special education because it is assumed that their problems are environmentally based, not disability based. Because of inadequate assessment tools and vague procedural guidelines, many professionals find it difficult, if not impossible, to determine accurately which students have genuine disabilities that can qualify them for special education services (Ysseldyke et al., 1983a; Rosa, 1990). These inconsistencies have raised serious questions about current assessment procedures used to identify students with disabilities, especially for economically disadvantaged and/or minority students (Chinn and Hughes,1987; Ysseldyke et al., 1983b).

Williams (1992) estimated that 30−40% of the public school population is currently at-risk for school failure and that this figure will increase in coming years. If these figures are accurate, this means that special education students and at-risk students currently comprise approximately half of all students enrolled in schools. It is no wonder that many educators and families seriously question the capability of public schools to meet the complex needs of students.

Evolving Academic Expectations

In a time when many students are struggling with complex problems that are affecting their abilities to perform socially and academically, school performance standards are rising (Inman et al., 1990). Today, high school students must complete more rigorous math, science, reading, and foreign language requirements to earn standard diplomas than was the case a decade ago. During the past decade state and local boards have adopted higher academic standards and performance expectations for students in public schools (Inman et al., 1990). This has occurred in response to the 1980s educational reform movement, launched by the Reagan administration, that called for academic "excellence" in public education (National Committee on Excellence in Education, 1983).

Calls for higher student performance have put tremendous pressure on public education. In essence, educators are asked to meet the educational needs of an increasingly diverse and challenged student population and, simultaneously, to increase the academic standards. Advocates for students with disabilities and at-risk learners have stressed the need to maintain educational equity for low-achieving students as public education strives to create a standard of educational excellence [National Coalition of Advocates for Students (NCAS), 1985; Spencer, 1985; Kozol, 1990]. Unfortunately, few states have the economic resources to provide support programs to successfully help low-achieving students meet these higher goals. As a result many students with disabilities and at-risk learners drop out of the system before graduating (Slavin et al., 1989; USDE, 1991; Wehlage et al., 1989; Williams, 1992). Over one million students drop out of school annually (Anderson et al., 1988).

If support services exist in schools, they are usually offered on a very limited basis and focus almost exclusively on academic learning difficulties. In an era of academic "excellence," issues related to students' feelings of self-worth and self-esteem are not high priority items on the public education agenda. Consequently, students with disabilities and other at-risk learners find few sources for social-emotional development within public schools (Anderson et al., 1988; Wehlage et al.,1989).

THE COLLABORATIVE CLASSROOM: AN ORGANIZATIONAL MODEL TO FACILITATE SELF-ESTEEM DEVELOPMENT

Given the complex array of academic, social, and self-esteem needs that many students have today and the few resources available to address these concerns adequately, many schools have critically examined their programs and have found ways in which existing resources can be used more effectively. As a result of self-study and restructuring efforts, models have begun to emerge that focus on a more *collaborative* approach to program planning and service delivery.[1] Pooling human and material resources enables schools to provide students with more comprehensive and appropriate instruction and support. While most of these models have been designed specifically to meet needs of students with disabilities and other at-risk learners, it appears that many benefits also exist for normal-achieving students and for the professionals who provide these programs. Collaborative teams create more stimulating and supportive environments for students, while providing educators with ongoing sources of support, encouragement, and opportunities to learn from each other.

As these models have developed, many remedial and/or enrichment programs (e.g., special education, guidance, Chapter I, gifted) have moved away from traditional "pull-out" approaches to provide direct instruction and support within the context of mainstream classrooms. A number of innovative service delivery approaches have been demonstrated to provide students with disabilities and other at-risk learners with effective mainstream learning opportunities (Anderson et al., 1988; Johnson and Johnson, 1986; Laycock et al., 1991; White and White, 1992).

The primary purpose of these approaches is to facilitate the work of school-based teams so that they can utilize their resources more effectively to meet the needs of students experiencing academic and/or social failure. Most models emphasize the use of effective problem solving, communication skills, shared resources, and coordinated efforts. The fundamental tenets of these service delivery models are based on concepts used in educational consultation (Gresham and Kendall, 1987; Idol et al., 1986; Morsink et al., 1991; Phillips and McCullough, 1990; Sibley, 1986). In general, these concepts include active participation by all key stakeholders, professional trust, role parity, a sense of community, and respect for contributions of each team member (Friend and Cook, 1992; Lyon and Lyon, 1980; Morsink et al., 1991; Walther-Thomas, 1992). Other hallmarks include shared responsibility for problem solving and intervention implementation, monitoring and data-based decision making, scheduled follow-up, and commitment to the team process, as well as the team goals, pooled resources, professional accountability, and a more holistic view of student learning (Friend and Cook, 1992; Idol et al., 1986; Laycock et al., 1991).

Professional collaboration, cooperation, and teamwork are the philosophical cornerstones of these approaches. With this mindset in place, effective teams possess an orientation that enables them to think more broadly about dimensions of student growth and learning than is the case in more traditional classrooms. The organizational structure of collaborative models facilitates discussion of critical issues and provides ongoing opportunities to work together to maximize available resources. Cooperation and collaboration, coupled with regularly scheduled contact, enable participants to develop learning experiences and emotional support that can more effectively nurture and support the development of healthy self-esteem in ways that individuals working alone cannot.

Some collaborative models are more easily distinguished than others. While some differences exist in terms of the amount of direct classroom support provided, model goals, and key participants, many common features exist across models. Cooperative Teaching or Co-Teaching (Bauwens and Hourcade, 1991; Bauwens et al., 1989) will be described to illustrate both indirect and direct classroom support.

In co-teaching arrangements voluntary collaborators plan and instruct heterogeneous groups of students in mainstream classrooms. In general most co-teaching teams consist of two or three professionals working together (e.g., special educator, general educator, school counselor, school psychologist, speech-language therapist, and Chapter I reading specialist). Other school and community agency representatives such as the school nurse, vice principal, transition facilitator, vocational counselor, parent volunteers, and community college instructor may also be full-time or part-time members of the team. In general, most co-teachers teach together one or more instructional periods each day. In some cases, however, they arrange their schedules to teach together on a consistent, but less frequent, basis. This is frequently the case when guidance counselors, vocational specialists, or itinerant staff members are in-volved in co-teaching partnerships.

Planning classroom instruction is a critical part of their work together. Co-teachers meet regularly to plan and determine each person's respon-sibilities, discuss student progress, and make modifications as needed. General educators, recognized as the content specialists, frequently take primary responsibility for new material that is covered during class. The other co-teachers focus their attention on teaching students complemen-tary skills (e.g., learning strategies, social skills, self-advocacy skills, stress management, coping skills) and/or provide supplemental ac-tivities to help reinforce student learning (e.g., cooperative learning activities, peer tutoring, one-on-one instruction, small group review, project supervision, or computer-assisted activities).

Preliminary research findings suggest that collaborative approaches improve student attitudes and performance levels. Emerging research suggests that some of the student benefits include improvements in self-esteem, motivation, problem-solving and decision-making skills, peer relationships, achievement, and behavior (Chalfant and Pysh,, 1989; Evans, 1991; Glaser, 1986; Johnson and Johnson, 1986; Johnson et al., 1984; Villa and Thousand, 1990; Walther-Thomas, 1992). Low-achieving students perform more successfully in co-taught en-vironments than they do in individually taught classrooms (Walther-Thomas, 1992). Working in cooperative learning groups, many low-achieving students find themselves more skilled than they origin-ally believed. They also observe that "smart kids" frequently ex-perience learning problems similar to their own. Teachers report that normal-achieving students benefit from participation in these programs. They receive more individual attention and develop a greater respect for diversity among their peers (Walther-Thomas, 1992). It appears that collaborative approaches, emphasizing more unified and comprehensive program planning, facilitate academic and social-emotional growth for many students.

Walther-Thomas (1992) observed co-taught classroom sessions and individually interviewed team members. Consistently, co-teachers reported that the greatest benefit for students with disabilities and other low-achieving students was increased self-esteem. Successful participa-tion in mainstream settings enabled many of these students to see themselves as more capable learners as a result of increased teacher-student interactions, cooperative learning group experience, classroom modifications, and greater teacher understanding.

Teacher collaborators indicate that increased knowledge and use of effective instructional procedures enable them to be more attuned to a broader spectrum of student needs (Walther-Thomas, 1992). Working together, effective collaborators find successful approaches to classroom social and academic problems. As a result, fewer students are referred for help outside the classroom (Chalfant and Pysh, 1989). Collaborating teachers report greater tolerance for academic and behavioral problems and increased willingness and confidence to try to solve problems that exist in their classrooms (Pugach and Johnson, 1988).

For collaborative models to be long-lasting and effective, administrative leadership is an essential ingredient (Allington and Johnson, 1989; Fullan, 1991; Winget, 1988). Administrators need to be committed to the philosophy that academic learning and social-emotional development can best be addressed through collaborative and innovative approaches. They need to provide resources, moral support, and encouragement, and teams need to work together effectively (Fullan, 1991). In addition, they need to ensure that adequate planning time is provided to facilitate teams' efforts to develop new skills and to provide better learning opportunities and support services for their students (Evans, 1980; Idol-Maestas and Ritter, 1985). Administrators also provide important links with families, related services, division level leaders, and community representatives. Without administrative support, teachers find it difficult, if not impossible, to make significant changes in their current teaching practices (Fullan, 1991; Hord et al., 1987).

Student involvement ensures the appropriateness of new program initiatives. As primary stakeholders in public education programs, students are empowered by their participation on collaborative teams. Participation also provides students with opportunities to build their confidence and skills as self-advocates (Top and Osguthorpe, 1987; Villa and Thousand, 1990). Participation also enables the students to watch the interactions of the professional team members. As the professionals model collaboration and cooperation, students develop both skills and respect for the benefits found in the teaming process.

Family participation in programs for students with disabilities has been shown to be a powerful tool in facilitating student learning (Male, 1991). Active involvement by families in the development of goals, the design of programs, and the delivery of learning experiences helps ensure that schools and families are working together to provide students with the guidance, support, and encouragement they need to develop skills, confidence, and achieve important goals (Schulz et al., 1991). Family involvement helps educators teach families how to provide students with moral support and guidance. It helps ensure that smoother transitions are made from one learning environment to another. Schools need to offer families a variety of ways in which they can collaborate with school personnel. This increases the likelihood that families will feel more comfortable and confident in the helper role(s) they select.

Many collaborative models encourage community and business involvement. These partnerships that can provide schools with external support and resources that can stimulate new initiatives and sustain these efforts over time (Buffer, 1980; Cuninggim, 1980; Fullan, 1991). These partnerships can also provide indirect support to schools by putting more resources to bear on the nonschool problems many young people experience in their homes and neighborhoods (Wehlage et al., 1989). These arrangements also provide important ''real world'' links for students. The confidence and self-esteem of low-achieving students are often bolstered through successful experiences in recreation, employment, and volunteer experiences.

CONCLUSION

Educators and families recognize the important role that self-esteem plays in determining successful learning experiences for students with disabilities and other low-achieving students. Yet, many forces, such as competing priorities, growing problems in schools, and the limitations of traditional approaches, have infringed upon the time and attention given to self-esteem issues for these students. Despite the perception of these goals as being in competition with one another, a collaborative model is now in place that can facilitate more inclusive programming for students with disabilities and other low-achieving students (Ornstein and Levine, 1989).

Appropriate collaborative models for classrooms, schools, and school divisions depend largely upon program goals, student needs, professional beliefs regarding responsibility for students with complex academic and social-emotional needs, and the nature of existing interactions among possible collaborators. To create collaborative programs and build powerful networks of trust and support, key stakeholders need to work together in planning, implementing, and evaluating new col-

laborative initiatives. The success of these efforts hinges upon three key factors. First, program development/service delivery stakeholders must believe that self-esteem development is important. This philosophical orientation helps ensure that self-esteem is valued and recognized in a manner similar to support given to the development of fundamental academic skills. Second, participating stakeholders must possess appropriate process skills and content knowledge needed to foster the development of self-esteem. To accomplish this, schools must be willing to provide primary stakeholders with instruction and ongoing support to help them design and deliver effective programs for students. Finally, stakeholders must share a genuine commitment to a collaborative ethic. Participants need to value the perspectives and contributions of all team members. When role parity exists within teams and diversity is respected and thoughtfully considered as plans are formulated, collaborators will be more likely to develop programs that address self-esteem issues in a more comprehensive manner.

ENDNOTE

1 Some widely recognized collaborative service delivery models include: Collaborative Consultation (Idol et al., 1986), Behavioral Consultation (Gable et al., 1990), Peer Collaboration (Pugach and Johnson, 1988), Teacher Assistance Teams (Chalfant and Pysh, 1989; Chalfant et al., 1979; Hayek, 1987), and Cooperative Teaching (Bauwens and Hourcade, 1991; Bauwens et al., 1989; Reynolds,1989). Several well-known collaborative models emphasize the development of student-to-student relationships: Cooperative Learning (Johnson and Johnson, 1986; Johnson et al., 1984; Slavin et al., 1989) and Peer Tutoring (Haisley et al., 1981; Jenkins and Jenkins, 1985; Stainback et al., 1989).

REFERENCES

Adler, J., P. Wingert, L. Wright, P. Houston, H. Manly, and A. D. Cohen. 1992. "Hey, I'm Terrific," *Newsweek* (February 17):46−51.

Allington, R. L. and P. Johnson. 1989. "Coordination, Collaboration, and Consistency: The Redesign of Compensatory and Special Education Interventions," in *Effective Programs for Students at Risk,* R. E. Slavin, N. L. Karweit and N. A. Madden, eds., Needham, MA: Allyn and Bacon.

Anderson, M., L. R. Nelson, R. G. Fox, and S. E. Gruber. 1988. "Integrating Cooperative Learning and Structured Learning: Effective Approaches to Teaching Social Skills," *Focus on Exceptional Children,* 20(9):1−8.

Antia, S. 1985. "Social Integration of Hearing Impaired Children: Fact or Fiction?" *The Volta Review,* 87:279−289.

Bandura, A. 1986. *Social Foundations of Thought and Action: A Social-Cognitive Theory.* Englewood Cliffs, NJ: Prentice-Hall.

Basgall, J. A. and C. R. Snyder. 1988. "Excuses in Waiting: External Locus of Control and Reactions to Success-Failure Feedback," *Journal of Personality and Social Psychology,* 54:656–662.

Bauwens, J. and J. J. Hourcade. 1991. "Making Co-Teaching a Mainstreaming Strategy," *Preventing School Failure,* 35(4):19–24.

Bauwens, J., J. J. Hourcade, and M. Friend. 1989. "Cooperative Teaching: A Model for General and Special Education Integration," *Remedial and Special Education,"* 10(2):17–22.

Bendell, D., N. Tollefson, and M. Fine. 1980. "Interaction of Locus of Control Orientation and Performance of Learning Disabled Adolescents," *Journal of Learning Disabilities,* 13:82–85.

Biklen, D. 1985. *Achieving the Complete School: Strategies for Effective Mainstreaming.* New York, NY: Teachers College.

Bingham, G. 1980. "Self-Esteem among Boys with and without Specific Learning Disabilities," *Child Study Journal,* 10:41–47.

Bracken, B. A. 1992. *Multidimensional Self Concept Scale.* Austin, TX: PRO-ED.

Brophy, J. and T. Good. 1974. *Teacher-Student Relationships—Causes and Consequences.* New York, NY: Holt, Rinehart, and Winston.

Brown, W. H., E. U. Ragland, and N. Bishop. 1989. "A Naturalistic Teaching Strategy to Promote Young Children's Peer Interactions," *Teaching Exceptional Children,* 21(4):8–10.

Brown, W. H., E. U. Ragland, and J. J. Fox. 1988. "Effects of Group Socialization Procedures on the Social Behavior of Preschool Children," *Research in Developmental Disabilities,* 9:359–376.

Bruininks, R. H., J. E. Rynders, and T. C. Gross. 1974. "Social Acceptance of Mildly Retarded Pupils in Resource Rooms and Regular Classes," *American Journal of Mental Deficiency,* 78:377–383.

Bruininks, V. L. 1978. "Peer Status and Personality Characteristics of Learning Disabled and Nondisabled Students," *Journal of Learning Disabilities,* 11(8):29–34.

Bryan, T. 1976. "Peer Popularity of Learning Disabled Children, A Replication," *Journal of Learning Disabilities,* 9:307–311.

Buffer, L. C. 1980. "Recruit Retired Adults as Volunteers in Special Education," *Teaching Exceptional Children,* 12(3):113–115.

Chalfant, J. C. and M. Pysh. 1989. "Teacher Assistance Teams: Five Descriptive Studies on 96 Teams," *Remedial and Special Education,* 10(6):49–58.

Chapman, J. W. 1988. "Learning Disabled Children's Self-Concepts," *Review of Educational Research,* 58:347–371.

Chesler, B. 1982. "ACLD Committee Survey on LD Adults," *ACLD Newsbrief,* 145: 1, 5.

Chinn, P. C. and S. Hughes. 1987. "Representation of Minority Students in Special Education Classes," *Remedial and Special Education,* 8(4):4–46.

Clark, F. I. 1980. "The Development of Instrumentation to Measure Regular Classroom Teachers' Attitudes toward Mildly Handicapped Students," Doctoral dissertation, University of Kansas, Lawrence, KS.

Coopersmith, S. 1967. *The Antecedents of Self-Esteem.* San Francisco, CA: W. H. Freeman.

Coopersmith, S. 1984. *Coopersmith Self-Esteem Inventory.* Palo Alto, CA: Consulting Psychologists Press.

Cuninggim, W. 1980. "Citizen Volunteers: A Growing Resource for Teachers and Students," *Teaching Exceptional Children,* 12(3):108−112.

Deshler, D. D. and J. B. Schumaker. 1986. "Learning Strategies: An Instructional Alternative for Low-Achieving Adolescents," *Exceptional Children,* 52:583−590.

Donahue, M. and T. Bryan. 1984. "Communication Skills and Peer Relations of Learning Disabled Adolescents," *Topics in Language Disorders,* 4:10−21.

Edgar, E. 1987. "Secondary Programs in Special Education: Are Many of Them Justifiable?" *Exceptional Children,* 53:555−561.

Edgar, E. 1988. "Employment as an Outcome for Mildly Handicapped Students: Current Status and Future Directions," *Focus on Exceptional Students,* 21(1):1−8.

Elkind, D. 1988. "Peer Groups−Blessing or Curse?" *Parents Magazine,* 63:195.

Evans, S. 1980. "The Consultant Role of the Resource Teacher," *Exceptional Children,* 46:402−404.

Evans, S. 1991. "A Realistic Look at the Research Base for Collaboration in Special Education," *Preventing School Failure,* 35(4):10−13.

Farnham-Diggory, S. 1977. "The Cognitive Point of View," in *Handbook of Teaching Educational Psychology,* D. J. Trefinger, J. K. Davis and R. E. Ripple, eds., New York, NY: Academic Press.

Flavell, J. H. 1985. *Cognitive Development, 2nd Edition.* Englewood Cliffs, NJ: Prentice-Hall.

Friend, M. and L. Cook. 1992. *Interactions: Collaboration Skills for School Professionals.* New York, NY: Longman.

Fullan, M. 1991. *The New Meaning of Educational Change.* New York, NY: Teachers College Press.

Gable, R. A., M. Friend, V. K. Laycock, and J. M. Hendrickson. 1990. "Interview Skills for Problem Identification in School Consultation," *Preventing School Failure,* 35(1):5−10.

Gaylord-Ross, R. and T. Haring. 1987. "Social Interaction Research for Adolescents with Severe Handicaps," *Behavior Disorders,* 12:264−275.

Gilmor, T. M. and D. Reid. 1979. "Locus of Control for Positive and Negative Outcomes," *Journal of Research in Personality,* 13:154−160.

Glaser, W. 1986. *Control Theory in the Classroom.* New York, NY: Harper and Row.

Gottlieb, J. 1975. "Public, Peer, and Professional Attitudes toward Mentally Retarded Persons," In *The Mentally Retarded and Society: A Social Science Perspective,* M. J. Begab and S. A. Richardson, eds., Baltimore: University Park Press, pp. 99−125.

Gottlieb, J. and H. N. Switzky. 1982. "Development of School-Age Children's Stereotypic Attitudes toward Mentally Retarded Children," *American Journal of Mental Deficiency,* 86:596−600.

Gregory, J. F., T. Shanahan, and H. Walberg. 1986. "A Profile of Learning Disabled Twelfth-Graders in Regular Classes," *Learning Disabilities Quarterly,* 9:32−42.

Gresham, F. M. 1984. "Social Skills and Self-Efficacy for Exceptional Children," *Exceptional Children,* 51:253−261.

Gresham, F. M. and S. N. Elliott. 1987. "Social Skills Deficits of Learning Disabled Students: Issues of Definition, Classification, and Assessment," *Journal of Reading, Writing, and Learning Disabilities*, 3:131−148.

Gresham, F. M. and G. K. Kendall. 1987. "School Consultation Research: Methodological Critique and Future Research Directions," *School Psychology Review*, 16(3):209−225.

Gunderson, C. W., C. Maesch and J. W. Rees. 1987. "The Gifted/Learning Disabled Student," *Gifted Child Quarterly*, 31(4):158−160.

Haisley, F. B., A. T. Christine, and J. Andrews. 1981. "Peers as Tutors in Mainstream: Trained 'Teachers' of Handicapped Adolescents," *Journal of Learning Disabilities*, 14:224−226.

Hansford, B. C. and J. A. Hattie. 1982. "The Relationship between Self and Achievement/Performance Measures," *Review of Educational Research*, 55:123−142.

Haring, K. A., D. L. Lovett, and D. D. Smith. 1990. "A Follow-up Study of Recent Special Education Graduates of Learning Disabilities Programs," *Journal of Learning Disabilities*, 23(2):108−113.

Harter, S. 1983. "Developmental Perspectives on the Self-System," in *Handbook of Child Psychology, 4th Edition*, P. H. Mussen, ed., New York, NY: Wiley, pp. 275−385.

Harter, S. 1985. *Manual for the Self-Perception Profile for Children*. Denver: University of Denver.

Hayek, R. A. 1987. "The Teacher Assistance Team: A Prereferral Support System," *Focus on Exceptional Children*, 20(1):1−7.

Hazel, J. S. and J. B. Schumaker. 1988. "Social Skills and Learning Disabilities: Current Issues and Recommendations for Future Research," in *Learning Disabilities: Proceedings of the National Conference*, J. Kavanaugh and T. Truss, Jr., eds., Parkton, MD: York Press.

Helge, D. 1988. "Serving At-Risk Population in Rural America," *Teaching Exceptional Children*, 20(4):29−31.

Hodgkinson, H. L. 1985. "All One System: Demographics of Education−Kindergarten through Graduate School. Washington, D.C.: Institute for Educational Leadership.

Hord, S. M., W. L. Rutherford, L. Huling-Austin, and G. E. Hall. 1987. *Taking Charge of Change*. Alexandria, VA: Association for Supervision and Curriculum Development.

Idol, L., P. Paolucci-Whitcomb, and A. Nevin. 1986. *Collaborative Consultation*. Austin, TX: Pro-Ed.

Idol-Maestas, L. and S. Ritter. 1985. "A Follow-Up Study of Resource/Consulting Teachers," *Teacher Education and Special Education*, 8:121−131.

Inman, D., S. L. Pribesh, and L. H. Salganik. 1990. "Summary Profiles: State Education Indicators Systems," paper presented for the Special Study Panel on Educational Indicators. Washington, D.C.: Pelavin.

Jenkins, J. and L. Jenkins. 1985. "Peer Tutoring in Elementary and Secondary Programs," *Focus on Exceptional Children*, 17(6):1−12.

Jenkins, J. R., M. L. Speltz, and S. L. Odom. 1985. "Integrating Normal and Handicapped Preschoolers: Effects on Child Development and Social Interaction," *Exceptional Children*, 52:7−17.

Johnson, D. W. and R. T. Johnson. 1986. "Mainstreaming and Cooperative Learning Strategies," *Exceptional Children*, 52(6):553−561.

Johnson, D. W., R. T. Johnson, E. Holubec, and P. Roy. 1984. *Circles of Learning.* Arlington, VA: Association for Supervision and Curriculum Development.

Kaslow, F. and B. Cooper. 1978. "Family Therapy with the Learning Disabled Child and His/Her Family," *Journal of Marriage and Family Therapy,* 4(4):41–49.

Kistner, J., M. Haskett, K. White, and F. Robbins. 1987. "Perceived Competence and Self-Worth of LD and Normally Achieving Students, " *Journal of Learning Disabilities,* 10:37–44.

Knoff, H. M. 1983. "Learning Disabilities in the Junior High School: Creating a Six-Hour Emotionally Disturbed Adolescent?" *Adolescence,* 18:541–550.

Kozol, J. 1990. "The New Untouchables," *Newsweek,* 48–53.

LaGreca, A. M. 1987. "Children with Learning Disabilities: Interpersonal Skills and Social Competence," *Reading, Writing, and Learning Disabilities,* 3:167–185.

Laycock, V. K., L. Korinek, and R. A. Gable. 1991. "Alternative Structures for Collaboration in the Delivery of Special Services," *Preventing School Failure,* 35(4):15–18.

Levy, L. and J. Gottlieb. 1984. "Learning Disabled and Non-LD Children at Play," *Remedial and Special Education,* 5(6):43–50.

Lyon, S. and G. Lyon. 1980. "Team Functioning and Staff Development: A Role Release Approach to Providing Integrated Educational Services for Severely Handicapped Students," *Journal of the Association for the Severely Handicapped,* 5(3):250–263.

Madden, N. A. and R. E. Slavin. 1983. "Mainstreaming Students with Mild Handicaps: Academic and Social Outcomes," *Review of Educational Research,* 53(4):519–569.

Male, M. 1991. "Effective Team Participation," *Preventing School Failure,* 35(4):29–36.

Margolis, H. and J. McGettigan. 1988. "Managing Resistance Instructional Modifications to Mainstreamed Environments," *Remedial and Special Education,* 9(4):15–21.

Marsh, H. W. and I. W. Holmes. 1990. "Multidimensional Self-Concepts: Construct Validation of Responses by Children," *American Educational Research Journal,* 27:89–117.

Meichenbaum, D. 1985. "Teaching Thinking: A Cognitive-Behavioral Perspective," in *Thinking and Learning Skills: Research and Open Questions,* S. R. Chipman and J. W. Segal, eds., Hillsdale, NJ: Lawrence Erlbaum.

Mink, O. 1971. "Learner-Oriented Instruction," *Journal of Rehabilitation,* 37:25–27.

Mithaug, D., C. Horiuchi, and P. Fanning. 1985. "A Report on the Colorado Statewide Follow-Up Survey of Special Education Students," *Exceptional Children,* 51:397–404.

Morsink, C. V., C. C. Thomas, and V. I. Correa. 1991. *Interactive Teaming: Consultation and Collaboration in Special Programs.* New York, NY: MacMillan Publishing Company.

Munson, S. M. 1987. "Regular Education Teacher Modifications for Mainstreamed Mildly Handicapped Students," *Journal of Special Education,* 20:489–502.

National Coalition of Advocates for Students (NCAS). 1985. *Barriers to Excellence.* Boston, MA: NCAS.

National Committee on Excellence in Education. 1983. *A Nation at Risk: The Imperative for Educational Reform.* Washington, D.C.: U.S. Government Printing Office.

Nelson, C. M. 1988. "Social Skills Training for Handicapped Students," *Teaching Exceptional Children,* 20(4):19–23; *Educational and Psychological Consulting,* 1:41–67.

Newman, B. M. 1976. "The Study of Interpersonal Behavior in Adolescence," *Adolescence,* 11:127–142.

Omizo, M. M. and S. A. Omizo. 1987. "The Effects of Eliminating Self-Defeating Behavior of Learning-Disabled Children through Group Counseling," *The School Counselor,* (March):282–288.

Ornstein, A. and D. Levine. 1989. "Social Class, Race, and School Achievement: Problems and Prospects," *Journal of Teacher Education,* 40(5):17–23.

Osman, B. B. 1987. "Promoting Social Acceptance of Children with Learning Disabilities: An Educational Responsibility," *Journal of Reading, Writing, and Learning Disabilities,* 3:111–118.

Pearl, R., T. Bryan, and M. Donahue. 1983. "Social Behaviors of Learning Disabled Children: A Review," *Topics in Learning and Learning Disabilities,* 3:1–13.

Peterson, N. and J. Haralick. 1977. "Integration of Handicapped and Nonhandicapped Preschoolers. An Analysis of Play Behavior and Social Interaction," *Education and Training of the Mentally Retarded,* 12:235–245.

Phillips, V. and L. McCullough. 1990. "Consultation-Based Programming: Instituting the Collaborative Ethic in Schools," *Exceptional Children,* 56:291–304.

Piers, E. V. 1984. *Piers-Harris Children's Self-Concept Scale: Revised Manual.* Los Angeles, CA: Western Psychological Services.

Polsgrove, L. and C. M. Nelson. 1982. "Curriculum Intervention According to the Behavioral Model," in *Teaching Emotionally Disturbed Children,* R. L. McDowell, G. W. Adamson, and F. H. Wood, eds., Boston, MA: Little and Brown, pp. 196–205.

Pugach, M. C. and L. J. Johnson. 1988. "Rethinking the Relationship between Consultative and Collaborative Problem Solving," *Focus on Exceptional Children,* 21(4):1–8.

Purkey, W. 1970. *Self-Concept and School Achievement.* Englewood Cliffs, NJ: Prentice-Hall.

Reid, K. 1988. *Teaching the Learning Disabled: A Cognitive Developmental Approach.* Boston: Allyn and Bacon.

Reynolds, M. C. 1989. "An Historical Perspective: The Delivery of Special Education to Mildly Disabled and At-risk Students," *Remedial and Special Education,* 10(6):7–11.

Reynolds, M. C., M. C. Wang, and H. J. Walberg. 1987. "the Necessary Restructuring of Special and Regular Education," *Exceptional Children,* 53:391–398.

Rosa, C. 1990. "The Overrepresentation of Limited English Proficient in the Category of Learning Disabilities: A Review of the Literature," Unpublished manuscript, University of New Mexico, Albuquerque.

Rosenthal, R. and L. Jacobsen. 1968. *Pygmalion in the Classroom: Teacher Expectation and Pupils Intellectual Development.* New York, NY: Holt, Rinehart, and Winston.

Salend, S. J. and D. Meddaugh. 1985. "Using Peer-Mediated Procedure to Decrease Obscene Language," *Pointer,* 30:267–294.

Sandberg, L. D. 1982. "Attitudes of Nonhandicapped Elementary School Students toward School-Aged Trainable Mentally Retarded Students," *Education and Training of the Mentally Retarded,* 17:30–34.

Schulz, J. B., C. D. Carpenter, and A. P. Turnbull. 1991. *Mainstreaming Exceptional Students, 3rd Edition.* Boston: Allyn and Bacon.

Sibley, S. 1986. "A Meta-Analysis of School Consultation research," An unpublished doctoral dissertation, Texas Women's University, Denton, TX.

Sitlington, P. L. and A. R. Frank. 1990. "Are Adolescents with Learning Disabilities Successfully Crossing the Bridge into Adult Life?" *Learning Disability Quarterly,* 13:97 – 111.

Skinner, B. F. 1990. "Can Psychology Be a Science of Mind?" *American Psychologist,* 45:1206 – 1210.

Slavin, R. E., N. L. Karweit, and N. A. Madden, eds. 1989. *Effective Programs for Students at Risk.* Needham Heights, MA: Allyn and Bacon.

Spencer, C. M. 1985. *Children of Teenage Parents: A Review of the Literature.* Springfield: Illinois State Board of Education (ERIC Document Reproduction Service No. Ed 260 830).

Smith, D. D. and R. Luckinnson. 1992. *Introduction to Special Education: Teaching in an Age of Challenge.* Boston: Allyn and Bacon.

Stainback, S. and W. Stainback, eds. 1990. *Support Networks for Inclusive Schooling – Interdependent Integrated Education.* Baltimore, MD: Paul H. Brookes.

Stainback, S., W. Stainback, and M. Forest, eds. 1989. *Educating All Students in the Mainstream of Regular Education.* Baltimore, MD: Paul H. Brookes.

Swanson, H. L. 1987. "Information Processing Theory and Learning Disabilities: A Commentary and Future Perspectives," *Journal of Learning Disabilities,* 20:155 – 166.

Top, B. L. and R. T. Osguthorpe. 1987. "Reverse-Role Tutoring: The Effects of Handicapped Students Tutoring Regular Class Students," *The Elementary School Journal,* 87(4):413 – 423.

United States Department of Education (USDE). 1991. *Thirteenth Annual Report to Congress on the Implementation of the Individuals with Disabilities Act.* Washington, D.C.: U.S. Printing Office.

Vaugh, S. 1985. "Why Teach Social Skills to Learning Disabled Students?" *Journal of Learning Disabilities,* 18(10):588 – 591.

Villa, R. A. and J. S. Thousand. 1990. "The Power of Student Collaboration or Practicing for Life in the 21st Century," paper presented at the *68th Annual Council for Exceptional Children International Convention, Toronto, Canada.*

Wagner, M. & D. M. Shaver. 1989. *Educational Programs and Achievements of Secondary Special Education Students: Findings from the National Longitudinal Transition Study.* Menlo Park, CA: SRI International.

Walker, D. K. and F. H. Jacobs. 1984. "Chronically Ill Children in School," *Peabody Journal of Education,* 61(2):28 – 74.

Walker, H. 1986. "The Assessment for Integration into Mainstream Settings (AIMS) Assessment System: Rationale, Instruments, Procedures, and Outcomes," *Journal of Clinical Psychology,* 15(1):55 – 63.

Wallace, G. and J. A. McLoughlin. 1988. *Learning Disabilities: Concepts and Characteristics, 3rd Edition.* Columbus, OH: Merrill.

Walther-Thomas, C. S. 1990. "A Study of State-Mandated Outcomes Assessment," unpublished Doctoral dissertation, University of Kansas, Lawrence, KS.

Walther-Thomas, C. S. 1992. "Collaborating Teachers: Team Growth over Time," unpublished raw data.

Wehlage, G. G., R. A. Rutter, G. A. Smith, N. Lesko, and R. R. Fernandez. 1989. *Reducing the Risk: Schools as Communities of Support.* Philadelphia, PA: The Falmer Press.

Weill, M. P. 1987. "Gifted/Learning Disabled Students," *Clearing House,* 60(8):341−343.

White, A. E. and L. L. White. 1992. "A Collaborative Model for Students with Mild Disabilities in Middle Schools," *Focus on Exceptional Children,* 24(9):1−12.

Whitmore, J. 1980. *Giftedness, Conflict, and Underachievement.* Boston, MA: Allyn and Bacon.

Wiener, J. 1987. "Peer Status of Learning Disabled Children and Adolescents: A Review of the Literature," *Learning Disabilities Research,* 2:62−79.

Will, M. C. 1986. "Educating Children with Learning Problems: A Shared Responsibility," *Exceptional Children,* 52:411−415.

Williams, B. F. 1992. "Changing Demographics: Challenges for Educators," *Intervention in School and Clinic,* 27(3):157−163.

Winget, P. 1988. "Special Education/General Education Is a Team Effort," *The Special Edge,* 2(5):1, 6.

Winne, P. H., M. J. Woodlands, and B. Y. Wong. 1982. "Comparability of Self-Concept among Learning Disabled, Normal, and Gifted Students," *Journal of Learning Disabilities,* 15:470−475.

Ysseldyke, J. E., B. Algozzine, and S. Epps. 1983a. "A Logical and Empirical Analysis of Current Practice in Classifying Students as Handicapped," *Exceptional Children,* 50:160−165.

Ysseldyke, J. E., B. Algozzine, M. Shinn, and M. McGue. 1983b. "Similarities and Differences between Low Achievers and Students Classified as Handicapped," *Journal of Special Education,* 16:73−85.

Zigmond, N. and H. Thornton. 1985. "Follow-Up of Postsecondary-Age Learning Disabled Graduates and Drop-Outs," *Learning Disabilities Research,* 1:50−55.

Zins, J., M. Curtis, J. Graden, and C. Ponti. 1988. *Helping Students Succeed in the Regular Classroom.* San Francisco: Jossey-Bass.

CHAPTER 10

Developing Self-Concept in Gifted Individuals

JOYCE VANTASSEL-BASKA — *The College of William and Mary*

THE valuing of self is fundamental to human functioning. A healthy sense of self can positively affect relationships with others, provide the basis for appropriate life and educational choices, and frame useful perspectives on a career. Thus, it is a topic of interest to educators who study gifted students because this population represents the potential for high-level performance in a variety of human endeavors. If self-esteem of such individuals is impaired in some way, it can severely inhibit their capacity to unleash their potential in the most productive channels. It does a person little good to be extremely gifted and yet be too emotionally impaired to harness the ability toward a positive personal or social end. Key questions of interest come to mind regarding the role of self-concept and self-esteem in the development of high-level ability. Does the perception of self affect, in a significant way, how gifted individuals behave in a society? Does self-concept change appreciably in these individuals over their lifespan? Does self-esteem function as an important factor for making important decisions about educational and career attainment? This chapter will present a review of the literature on self-concept and self-esteem as the concepts pertain to gifted individuals; present a study comparing various domains of self-concept among gifted students according to gender, race, and class; and provide commentary on promising directions for educational practice.

REVIEW OF RELEVANT LITERATURE

Tannenbaum (1983) summarized the literature on self-concept and the gifted by stating, ''The quality of performance influences self-image and the self-image of the performer affects performance.'' The assumption is often made that students with more potential will perform better and therefore feel better about themselves. This important issue has been studied comparing gifted students to nonidentified gifted groups and comparing gifted students among themselves based on gender, race, and class differences. Results suggest that, while the assumption of positive self-concept is generally accurate, the relationship is complex. Some factors to be considered are

(1) The issue of different forms of self-concept — Some gifted students are high in academic self-concept yet lower in social self-concept or, as was found with gifted middle school girls, lower in their perception of physical appearance (VanTassel-Baska and Olszewski-Kubilius, 1989).

(2) The way in which self-esteem and performance are related — For example, does high performance guarantee a high self-perception of competence?

(3) The way in which school programs affect self-concept and self-esteem

(4) The type of guidance provided to children to foster both self-esteem and performance

Several inconsistent findings have emerged from studies directed at the self-concept of the gifted. Studies of gifted children, usually identified as children with IQs over 120, show that they typically score significantly higher than the mean on self-concept inventories (Coleman and Fults, 1983; Coleman and Fults, 1982; Karnes and Wherry, 1981; Kelly and Colangelo, 1984; Ketcham and Snyder, 1977; Tidwell, 1980). Yet within the gifted populations, those higher in IQ do not necessarily score higher in self-concept than less-gifted peers (Ketcham and Snyder, 1977). Bracken (1980) found no significant difference in self-concept between gifted and nongifted groups. Little difference has been suggested in level of self-concept between gifted girls and boys at elementary levels (Coleman and Fults, 1983; Karnes and Wherry, 1981; Ketcham and Snyder, 1977). More recent work, however, has found gifted boys to outperform gifted girls on a measure of global self-concept and physical self-concept (Schneider et al., 1989). None of the studies noted [except Tidwell (1980)] included sizeable numbers of minority or disadvantaged students. Also, while a connection between academic performance and self-concept has been established by Trowbridge (1972), some question exists about the influence of achievement as opposed to ability on the self-concept of gifted students. For example, Ketcham and Snyder (1977) found that students identified as academically weak by teachers did not earn significantly lower scores on the Piers-Harris Children's Self-Concept Scale. Reading achievement also showed little relationship to self-concept in this study.

One possible factor complicating the achievement/self-concept connection is the impact of the environment. Brophy (1983) notes that teacher variables such as communicating higher expectations or differential treatment can affect academic self-concept favorably for the gifted. Yet special program placement may affect gifted students in the opposite way. Social comparison theory would suggest, for example, that gifted students' self-concept should decline when placed with other students equally able since such a situation would create a view of self as less competent in relation to the relevant peer group. It has also been hypothesized that it is not the social milieu but achievement that is the major vehicle for judging academic competence (Franks and Dolan, 1982); presumably, a lower level of mastery of more challenging work might produce a weaker feeling of competence than full mastery of easier work.

Coleman and Fults (1982) found that students of higher IQ who participated in a special gifted program one day per week increased self-concept scores over time, but lower IQ students showed some decline. These same researchers and others (Maddux et al., 1982) found substantially lower self-concept scores for gifted program participants when compared to nonprogram participants. Moreover, in a study of talent search students attending a summer program, Olszewski, Kulieke, and Willis (1987) found that a change in self-concept was discernible but not significant between the beginning and the end of the program experience. Gifted students showed higher self-concept scores after the program than before, a finding attributed by the authors to anxiety at the beginning about being with other highly talented students in a high-powered academic environment, but a reaffirmation of ability occurring by the end of the program. Kulik and Kulik (1982) conducted a meta-analysis of fifteen studies that investigated the self-concept of gifted students in different school settings. They concluded that the effect of special programming on the self-concept of the gifted was minor.

Other authors have separated social and academic self-concept and have found gifted students to score higher than the general population in both areas (Kelly and Colangelo, 1984). Intra-group differences among gifted children also have been reported. Janos, Fung, and Robinson (1985) found that 37% of their sample of high IQ elementary school age children reported feeling different from peers. Although they described their difference in positive ways, they still scored lower on the Piers-Harris Children's Self-Concept Scale than did those in the group who did not report feeling different.

Stipek and Mac Iver (1989) have reviewed the developmental literature on children's assessment of intellectual competence. They found a consistent decline with age in self-perceived level of competence, with a shift from an early stage in which children are most affected by praise for their own accomplishments, through a stage in which effort, social reinforcement, and mastery are the prominent criteria, to a final stage in which normative information and a wide set of objective criteria are employed.

In a comprehensive review of the literature on the social-emotional development of the gifted, Janos and Robinson (1985) found that studies have demonstrated three important aspects of self-esteem in the gifted: (1) the gifted exhibit greater psychosocial maturity than nonidentified groups as seen by their play interests, choice of older children as friends, perspective-taking and their social knowledge; (2) the gifted demonstrate average or superior psychosocial adjustment at preadolescent ages compared to nongifted groups as seen by studies that document such diverse qualities as trustworthiness under stress, sociability, reduced antisocial tendencies, fewer aggressive and withdrawal tendencies, and higher ratings on courtesy, cooperation, and self assurance; and (3) the gifted generally exhibit higher self-esteem than other groups on self-report inventories.

Overall, the literature suggests that gifted students, in general, have strong self-concepts in both academic and social areas as measured by self-concept inventories, although there is some evidence that highly gifted learners and gifted girls may have less positive self-esteem than other gifted students. There also appears to be some temporary reduction in self-esteem for students who relate most often with peers of equal or superior ability in special programs. Yet the overall diminished effect on self-esteem has not been demonstrated.

A set of problems accompanies much of the research on self-concept and the gifted, including the study reported in this chapter. One of these problems is related to the absence of an overall theoretical framework that posits what healthy development of gifted individuals is in social-emotional areas as they grow and develop. Instead, the field has been dominated by theories of cognitive development, reflecting trends in education generally. A second problem in existing studies is the varying definitional construct of giftedness that has been used. Since many studies use students identified for school-based gifted programs as their sample and since the definitions of giftedness in this country are relative to a local district rather than absolute, the resulting gifted samples are likely not to be comparable. Finally, researchers have used control groups poorly matched on variables other than intelligence. Many of the studies have used comparisons of gifted students to the normative groups on whom a measure was standardized or used accessible groups of children presumed to be of normal ability but not matched for other background variables.

Clearly, better focused studies are needed to clarify important distinctions about self-concept within gifted populations. The lack of precision in existing studies on the criterion of giftedness is particularly problematic. A 120 IQ cutoff on a group test is an arbitrary basis for applying the label gifted to a given group of students. Thus, findings from such studies that report differences should be viewed with caution, since both false positives and negatives would abound in the sample.

SPECIAL POPULATIONS

Among special populations of gifted learners, including gifted girls, students from low-income backgrounds, and minority students, some research has been conducted regarding perceptions of social support and work orientation. Studies have attempted to discern discriminating personality factors between successful Black children and those who were underachievers. Hirsch and Costello (1970) compared Black inner-city children who were achievers and underachievers to explore personality attributes. Achievers exhibited the following characteristics: organized in learning task approach, high degree of interpersonal skills, intense relationships with caretaking figures, greater capacity for individual initiative, reasonable goal-setting, task completion, higher mental health ratings, and stimulation by failure to greater effort and subsequent success. Glaser and Ross (1970) attempted to discern personality traits that would differentiate economically disadvantaged achievers from disadvantaged nonachievers. The differentiating traits favoring disadvantaged achievers were a strong sense of identity, some degree of alienation, supportive inspiring relationships, identification models, a questioning orientation, awareness of alternative paths, existential crisis, effective channeling of rage, risk-taking capacity, and perception of rewards for change.

While low socioeconomic status is frequently entangled with cultural group membership, it appears to be a powerful variable in its own right affecting personality development. Frierson (1965) investigated the difference in personality characteristics between gifted students who came from lower socioeconomic status to those from a more advantageous environment. He found a trend for the advantaged gifted to show superiority in superego development, that is, possessing greater conscience and self-discipline. The advantaged gifted were also superior to the disadvantaged gifted on measures of creative thinking.

Self-esteem has been extensively studied in relation to achievement patterns in females. Academic self-concept consistently has been shown to influence academic success, career choice, and test performance (Eccles, 1987). Some studies on gifted girls and women have also supported this general thesis. Olshen and Matthews (1987) studied the proposition that "the view of self determines achievement." They hypothesized that increasing gifted girls' awareness of conflicts related to being female and gifted would result in a higher self-esteem. An increase in self-esteem should then increase the likelihood of achievement of potential. The authors propose that such enhancement could reverse the significant downward trend in school achievement for girls from grade six onward.

Several studies have examined important antecedents of personality dimensions, such as self-concept. Parsons et al. (1982) conducted a study of the effect that parental beliefs and expectations have on their children. First, the sex of the child had a significant effect on the parents' assessments of the child's ability in mathematics. Although the boys and girls had performed equally well in math the previous year, as well as on a recent math test, parents of daughters believed their daughters had to exert more effort to do well in math than did the parents of sons. Perhaps more significant is the finding that the children's beliefs about their abilities in math were more strongly influenced by their parents' expectations than by their own past performance.

Farmer (1985) studied the aspiration motivation of young women and found that high aspiration was caused by perceived support for women working and by teacher support. She also found the effect of environment on females was much stronger than for males. In respect to gifted girls achieving the highest level of education, home environment would appear to be very influential. Callahan and Cornell (1989) found that the quality of parent-adolescent communication is consistently associated with young women's self-esteem. Daughters who enjoy more positive and open communication with their parents have higher perceptions of their competence in a wide range of areas.

Fear of success may cause some females to believe that they may be rejected by their peers or appear undesirable to the opposite sex if they are too competent or successful (Horner, 1972; Lavach and Lanier, 1975). Although more current research suggests that fear of success can be eliminated with age and experience (Birnbaum, 1975; Hoffman, 1977), preliminary findings in a study of high school valedictorians found that female students who had done well in high school lose confidence in their ability after a few years of college (Arnold and Denny, 1985).

Other research on gender differences has revealed related areas of concern for gifted girls. Dweck (1986) noted a tendency toward low expectancies, challenge avoidance, attributing failure to lack of ability, and debilitation under failure as characteristics of bright girls when compared to boys. Dweck (1986) also reported that measures of children's actual competence do not strongly predict their confidence in future attainment. In a qualitative study, Kramer (1985) found that gifted adolescent females used social interaction to determine the quality and acceptability of their achievement and to determine, through social comparison, the extent of their own abilities. Thus, sex differences in motivational and personality patterns emerge as central issues to consider in explaining achievement patterns.

THE CASE OF THE UNDERACHIEVING GIFTED

Underachievement among the gifted population has plagued educators for the last seventy years. What causes able children to fail in utilizing their high-level abilities in productive ways? What can parents and educators do to curb this condition? How might the ability of these learners be productively channeled to enhance their own sense of self? These questions are as open to debate today as they were in Terman's day. Yet a sizeable amount of research has been conducted on this issue, and we have reason to speculate that unrealized potential among gifted children has a very high incidence rate. Generally, about half of the gifted children who score in the top 5 % of intellectual ability on individualized IQ tests have been reported not to match their ability with comparable school achievement (Gallagher, 1975; Gowan, 1955; Laycock, 1979; Perkins, 1969; Pringle, 1970; Raph et al., 1966; Terman and Oden, 1947; Wolfe, 1954).

Gifted underachievers compared to achievers manifest particular patterns of behavior: social immaturity, emotional problems, antisocial behavior, and low self-concept. Studies also have indicated that it is primarily a male phenomenon. Families of underachievers are more likely to be unstable, lower income, single-parented, and offering fewer social/educational opportunities (Bricklin and Bricklin, 1967; Colangelo, 1979; Hecht, 1975; Newman et al., 1973; Saurenman and Michael, 1980; Wellington and Wellington, 1965; Whitmore, 1980).

Several studies have compared gifted students who achieve and those who do not achieve on personality measures. Davis and Connell (1985) report that high IQ, high-achieving fourth through sixth graders were higher on internal control and lower on control by powerful others compared to low-achieving students of equal ability. Ringness (1967) compared high IQ eighth-grade achievers and nonachievers. Low-achievers were lower on achievement motivation and higher on affiliation motivation than the high-achieving, talented students. Davids and Sidman (1962) compared high- and low-achieving gifted high school students on the Adjective Check List. High achievers were higher on self-control compared to low-achieving groups. These researchers also found that high achievers were higher than the low achievers on self-assurance, socialization, maturity, achievement potential, and intellectual efficiency. In a recent study, Laffoon, Jenkins-Friedman, and Tollefson (1989) found that high-achieving gifted learners attributed success and failure to effort, while underachievers attributed success to ability and failure to luck, fate, or other people.

Purkey (1970) noted that underachievers often lack self-confidence and perseverance, fail to express themselves adequately, have a poorly organized belief system, and are unable to establish good social relationships. Zilli (1971) pointed to inadequate motivation, social pressure or maladjustment, poor educational stimulation, and problems in the home environment as some of the reasons that gifted children fail to measure up to expectations. Janos, Sanfilippo, and Robinson (1986) studied the underachievement of fourteen-year-old early college entrance program students. Underachieving males appeared less psychologically mature than achieving males, but underachieving females evidenced greater maturity than their achieving counterparts, engaging in pragmatic activities like varsity sports and employment.

Other studies reported by Gallagher (1966) continue to contribute to our understanding of the personalities of underachieving gifted students. Morgan (1952) compared a group of college achievers with underachievers, all of whom had scored in the top 10% of their freshman class in academic aptitude tests. The major differences found between the two groups on tests of personality and interest were that (1) the nonachievers tended to score high on the Psychopathic Deviate Scale while the achievers scored higher in the areas of dominance and social responsibility and (2) more achievers were interested in social service and welfare occupations, while the nonachievers had interest patterns that resembled those of persons in business or sales occupations.

Upon examination of the desire to achieve, Pierce (1959) found in a study of tenth and twelfth graders that both high-achieving girls and boys valued achievement more highly than did the low-achieving students, with the exception of the twelfth-grade boys. The high-achieving students valued the concepts of school, work, and imagination more than did their low-achieving peers and also rated the concepts of self, student, and competition higher. As one might predict, the low-achieving students scored higher on both aggressive and withdrawal maladjustment, while the high-achieving students were more active in school-related activities and leadership activities. In the general area of emotional adjustment, the high achievers also were better adjusted as measured by tests of personality. Haggard (1957) also found in a longitudinal study of personality attributes that the high achievers at the upper grade levels had largely accepted adult values and were striving to live up to adult expectations.

The results of several studies strongly suggest that underachievement becomes a life pattern for some gifted individuals. McCall and Evahn (1987) compared underachievers and achievers thirteen years after high school. Underachievers pursued further schooling and took jobs consistent with their grades, not with their abilities. Further, underachievers had a substantially lower likelihood of completing four years of college and a greater likelihood of divorce than did achieving students. Some underachievers ultimately did catch up to their abilities: those who, as high school students, had high educational and occupational experiences, those who had high self-esteem and perceived competence, those who participated in activities (especially true of females), and those whose parents were well-educated. However, serious underachievers of medium to high mental ability did not catch up. They attained very little relative to other groups. Students from less educated families were less likely to achieve levels commensurate with their ability than students from better educated families.

Most of the early work on gifted underachievers was done by Terman in his longitudinal study on the characteristics of gifted individuals. He and his associates (Terman and Oden, 1947) compared 150 men who, as determined by judges, made the most success out of their lives in achieving their tested potential. He found that the key difference between these two groups of gifted men lay not so much in IQ scores as in the area of personality characteristics.

On rating scales that the men and their wives and parents completed, four areas were found that differentiated the successful and unsuccessful men. The same four areas were found on the self-ratings and on the ratings of wives and parents. These were lack of self-confidence, the inability to persevere, lack of integration of goals, all of which show the presence of inferiority feelings. It would appear that the life pattern of underachievement and self-esteem is set fairly early in life for many individuals and persists in problematic ways through adulthood, negatively affecting relationships as well as work habits.

Thus, given a lack of research on differential intrapersonal dimensions among special populations of gifted learners, the focus of this study was to investigate variations in selected personality dimensions based on race, gender, and class among gifted junior high school students. The study was developed to ascertain a better understanding of the role of self-concept and related factors in the academic achievement pattern of gifted adolescents.

The Sample

The sample consisted of 147 gifted junior high students who live in the midwestern region of the United States and attend junior high in either a large city or a suburban school district. There were seventy-six males and seventy-one females in the study. There were ninety-seven students who were considered middle socioeconomic status (SES) and above and fifty students who were of low socioeconomic status. Socioeconomic status level was based on free or reduced lunch designations made by the schools. Thus, low SES students in the study came from families with incomes below $22,000 with four children. A sliding scale based on household size determined lower income requirements for smaller households. All students designated middle SES and above came from families where the income level was above that required to access the free or reduced lunch program in schools. There were fifty-six Black students in the study and ninety-one Caucasian students. All students in the sample were enrolled in a self-contained gifted program where curriculum expectations and standards were high in all subject areas. Classes in the program were taught at honors levels, and homework was a nightly staple in each class. All students were selected for the program in their school district based on ability and achievement indicators. Group intelligence test indicators placed students in the range of 120 and above. In-grade achievement test levels were at or above the ninety-fifth percentile in either mathematical or verbal areas. The age of the sample was in the range of thirteen to fourteen years. All of the students in the sample were considered high achieving by educational personnel working with them, as evidenced by grades of "B" or better in all classes in the program.

Procedure

Four instruments were administered to these seventh and eighth grade gifted students during two group testing administrations in their classrooms: the Rosenberg Self-Esteem Scale, People in My Life, Work Orientation, and the Harter Perceived Self-Competence Scale (What Am I Like). These scales examined self-esteem, perceptions of social support, conditions of work, and perception of self-competence, respectively.[1]

Data Analysis

Multifactored analysis of variance (ANOVAs) was computed to ascertain differences among the subpopulations of gifted students based on gender, race, and socioeconomic status. Where interaction effects were significant, t-tests were run to determine the locus of differences. Effect sizes were also calculated to determine the relative magnitude of differences.

Results

No significant effects of SES or gender were found on the Rosenberg Self-Esteem Scale. However, significant differences were found between Black and Caucasian gifted students. Black gifted students evidenced higher self-esteem ($p < .05$) than Caucasian gifted students. Table 10.1 summarizes the significant ANOVA results. Tables 10.2 – 10.4 report the relevant means, standard deviations, and effect sizes for each group comparison.

Table 10.1. *Summary of significant results of ANOVAs.*

Variable	Race	Gender	SES	Race by Gender	Gender by SES	Race by SES	Gender by Race by SES
People in my life							
Classmates		M > F**	A > D**				
Friends		M > F**	A > D†				
Parents			A > D**				
Teachers			A > D**				
Work orientation							
Work							
Mastery							
Competition		F > M*					B > C*
Personal unconcern							FA > FD
							MD > MA
Self-perceptions of competence							
Physical appearance							
Athletic ability							
Scholastic competence			A > D†				
Social competence	B > C*	M > F*					
Behavioral conduct		M > F**					A > D*
							B > C
							M > F
Global self-worth							
Self-esteem	B > C*						

*p < .05. **p < .01. †p < .001. F = Female; M = Male; C = Caucasian; B = Black; A = Advantaged; D = Disadvantaged.

Table 10.2. Means and standard deviations by SES groups.

Measure	Construct	Group	m	sd	Effect Size
People in my life	Classmates	A	18.07	4.02	.30
		D	16.48	5.84	
	Friends	A	19.92	4.66	.61
		D	16.70	6.52	
	Parents	A	20.05	4.15	.49
		D	17.44	6.42	
	Teachers	A	18.25	4.45	.42
		D	16.03	5.81	
				$x = 5.23$	
What I am like	Scholastic	A	19.48	2.85	.57
		D	17.11	3.96	
	Social	A	16.59	4.10	-.11
		D	17.05	4.92	
	Athletic	A	16.07	3.95	-.03
		D	16.21	5.14	
	Physical appearance	A	15.78	4.12	.01
		D	15.73	4.74	
	Behavioral conduct	A	18.32	3.41	.50
		D	16.24	4.92	
	Global self-worth	A	18.68	3.55	.007
		D	18.65	3.82	
				$x = 4.12$	

(continued)

Table 10.2. (continued).

Measure	Construct	Group	m	sd	Effect Size
Rosenberg self-esteem	Self-esteem	A	15.68	2.84	.12
		D	15.29	3.59	
				x = 3.21	
Work orientation	Mastery	A	16.89	3.89	-.17
		D	17.51	3.98	
	Work	A	20.15	4.10	-.05
		D	20.32	3.34	
	Competition	A	17.37	3.99	.79
		D	17.59	3.76	
	Personal unconcern	A	12.84	3.33	-.24
		D	13.75	3.61	
				x = 3.75	

A = Advantaged (N = 118).
D = Disadvantaged (N = 63).

Table 10.3. Means and standard deviations by race.

Measure	Construct	Group	m	sd	Effect Size
People in my life	Classmates	C	17.55	4.30	-.05
		B	17.82	5.46	
	Friends	C	19.42	5.21	.30
		B	17.84	6.13	
	Parents	C	19.89	4.53	.28
		B	18.45	6.02	
	Teachers	C	17.85	4.72	.28
		B	16.36	5.49	
				x̄ = 5.23	
What I am like	Scholastic	C	19.05	3.38	.29
		B	17.88	3.48	
	Social	C	16.04	4.56	-.32
		B	18.13	4.15	
	Athletic	C	15.95	4.61	-.30
		B	17.14	3.95	
	Physical appearance	C	15.41	4.41	-.20
		B	16.21	4.33	
	Behavioral conduct	C	17.76	4.31	.13
		B	17.25	4.09	
	Global self-worth	C	18.27	3.95	-.22
		B	19.18	3.10	
				x̄ = 4.03	

(continued)

325

Table 10.3. (continued).

Measure	Construct	Group	m	sd	Effect Size
Rosenberg self-esteem	Self-esteem	C	15.45	3.17	-.22
		B	16.13	2.98	
				x̄ = 3.08	
Work orientation	Mastery	C	17.00	3.98	-.05
		B	17.20	3.79	
	Work	C	19.46	4.17	-.34
		B	20.77	3.56	
	Competition	C	17.64	4.05	.23
		B	16.77	4.07	
	Personal unconcern	C	12.83	3.37	-.31
		B	14.02	3.75	
				x̄ = 3.84	

C = Caucasian (*N* = 92).
B = Black (*N* = 56).

Table 10.4. Means and standard deviations by gender.

Measure	Construct	Group	m	sd	Effect Size
People in my life	Classmates	M	18.28	4.32	.32
		F	16.64	5.15	
	Friends	M	19.91	4.99	.47
		F	17.53	5.91	
	Parents	M	19.62	4.90	.19
		F	18.63	5.49	
	Teachers	M	17.80	4.67	.14
		F	17.09	5.48	
				x = 5.11	
What I am like	Scholastic	M	18.66	3.30	.005
		F	18.64	3.68	
	Social	M	17.50	3.59	.38
		F	15.95	5.05	
	Athletic	M	15.85	3.84	−.14
		F	16.43	4.92	
	Physical appearance	M	15.53	4.29	−.17
		F	16.08	4.43	
	Behavioral conduct	M	18.61	3.84	.50
		F	16.63	4.21	
	Global self-worth	M	18.70	3.19	.01
		F	18.66	4.07	
				x = 4.03	

(continued)

Table 10.4. (continued).

Measure	Construct	Group	m	sd	Effect Size
Rosenberg self-esteem	Self-esteem	M	15.64	3.10	.04
		F	15.52	3.28	
				x = 3.19	
Work orientation	Mastery	M	17.13	3.62	−.03
		F	17.24	3.77	
	Work	M	20.55	3.51	.19
		F	19.88	3.75	
	Competition	M	16.69	3.77	−.48
		F	18.40	3.48	
	Personal unconcern	M	13.30	3.56	.06
		F	13.08	3.11	
				x = 3.57	

M = Male (N = 94).
F = Female (N = 86).

The multiple ANOVAs revealed significant effects on all four sub-scales of People in My Life, the instrument designed to measure perceptions of social support. A significant effect of gender was found on the Friends subscale, with males scoring significantly higher than females in perceiving their friends to be supportive ($p < .01$). Significant effects for SES were found on all four subscales ($p < .01$). Consistently, higher SES gifted students found classmates, friends, parents, and teachers more supportive of them than did lower SES gifted students. While overall effect sizes were modest for the dimension of classmate support (.30), they were moderate to high for the other constructs, with the highest effect size evident for the Friends subscale (.61). No significant differences were found on ethnicity for social support variables.

On the Work Orientation Questionnaire, the ANOVAs revealed no significant effects for the Mastery or Work subscale. However, there was a trend for Black gifted students to score higher than Caucasian gifted students on the Work subscale. A significant effect of gender was found for the Competition subscale ($p < .05$). Females scored higher than males on this dimension. There was a three-way interaction effect among race, gender, and SES on the Personal Unconcern scale, a set of questions that taps into a student's perception of how others might view his or her achievements. Blacks scored significantly higher than Caucasians on this scale ($p < .05$) with Black low-SES males and Black high-SES females outperforming all other groups. These findings indicate that the construct of Personal Unconcern appears to differ within the Black population by both gender and class, meaning that identifiable subgroups of Black gifted students are less affected by perceived social rejection from others based on achievement than White gifted students.

On the Harter Perceived Self-Competence Scale, there were no significant effects of race, gender, or SES on the scales measuring self-perceptions of Physical Appearance, Athletic Ability, or Global Self-Worth. However, a significant effect of SES was found on perceived scholastic competence, favoring higher SES gifted students ($p < .001$). A significant main effect of gender and race was found for perceived social competence; males scored significantly higher than females ($p < .05$), and Blacks scored significantly higher than Caucasians ($p < .05$). For Behavioral Conduct there was a main effect of SES ($p < .05$) and a three-way interaction of race, gender, and SES. Post hoc analyses revealed that Black advantaged males scored significantly higher than other groups of males, while Caucasian advantaged females scored significantly higher than all other groups of females. Mean scores for

Black disadvantaged males were 17.35 compared to 17.64 for Caucasian advantaged females. All groupings of males scored better on this subscale than any group of females except the Caucasian advantaged group.

Discussion

The findings of this study help confirm studies cited earlier in this chapter (e.g., Coleman and Fults, 1983) that, among gifted students regardless of race, gender, or class, self-esteem tends to be high. Even where significant differences were found within the gifted group in the study, the lower band of scores was typically within the standardization group for the measure used.

One interesting finding pertained to racial differences favoring Blacks. Black gifted students appeared to have higher self-esteem than did Caucasian gifted students. These findings are inconsistent with studies of minority students that show lower self-esteem when compared to the majority group (Marsh and Shavelson, 1985). Moreover, while the study found higher perceived scholastic competence among Caucasian gifted students, higher perceived social competence was found among Black gifted students. Black gifted students also appeared to manifest a stronger work ethic and less concern for personal interests in work-related settings than did Caucasian gifted students.

However, the greatest number and the strongest effects found in the study were between advantaged and disadvantaged groups, thus supporting to some extent the notion that class may be a more significant variable than race in impeding the achievement of disadvantaged gifted students. Even given high levels of gifted program support, the disadvantaged students in this study still showed significantly lower perceived academic and social self-competence than their more advantaged peers. They also expressed feeling less support by significant others in their environment. Specifically the study suggested that disadvantaged students perceived that they have less support from classmates, friends, parents, and teachers than do advantaged students. They also perceived themselves as less scholastically competent and less correct in social/behavioral conduct than advantaged gifted students did.

Gender differences were also noted in the study. The findings suggested that female gifted students perceived less support from classmates and friends than did their male counterparts; they also perceived themselves as socially less competent and behaviorally less correct. However, they perceived themselves as manifesting a higher degree of competition in work situations than gifted males. These findings lend support to the contention of several researchers that gifted girls may receive less support from their social environment than males and that the lack of support makes them feel less competent in social contexts and that, perhaps as a result of feeling less competent, they have to try harder, hence feeling more competitive (Eccles et al., 1983; Kramer, 1985).

Overall, the findings suggest that key differences may exist among subpopulations of gifted students at junior high age on dimensions of self-esteem; perceived social support; perceived scholastic, social, and behavioral conduct; and work orientation that may affect our understanding of their needs at a critical stage of development, namely early adolescence. Moreover, the findings challenge the use of general self-esteem measures as being sufficiently targeted to pick up domain-specific issues. For example, students who have high academic self-concept may not have an equally high social or behavioral profile. Thus, at the level of practice, it may be important to focus on targeted areas where perceptions of competence are less strong and provide those experiences that may optimally benefit students in such contexts.

Special Issues

Given our understanding of the research on self-concept, self-esteem, and the gifted, what are the implications for educators who are in positions to influence this population? Since studies have demonstrated a relationship between positive self-concept in childhood and enhanced school achievement, and studies of gifted individuals have demonstrated that social and family adjustment during childhood were predictive of family satisfaction and success in marriage, it is reasonable to assume that optimal development of potential in school and in life is dependent on a healthy perception of self. Thus, the task is to attend to the maintenance of positive self-concept in gifted individuals and the enhancement of it in special populations of gifted learners in need of additional assistance.

Self-perception may act as a catalyst or impediment to adult achievement, accounting for attrition at advanced levels of education and professions for special populations of gifted individuals (see Figure 10.1). Even among top students from special populations, their own perceptions about ability have been shown to affect aspirations for achievement. A longitudinal study of high school valedictorians in Illinois found that two-thirds of female valedictorians who achieved at

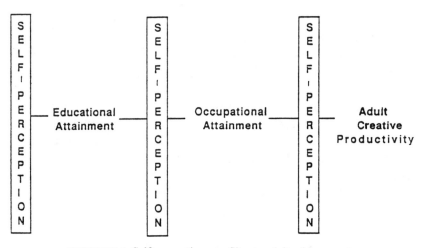

FIGURE 10.1 Self-perception as a filter to adult achievement.

honors level settled for careers significantly lower than their educational attainment, while fewer than 10% of the males did. In another related study, minority students and students from poor families reported problems with lack of support in college environments, finding the social context inimical to them and affecting their sense of potential for academic success (Arnold and Denny, 1985; Arnold, 1991). A longitudinal investigation of Study for Mathematically Precocious Youth (SMPY) graduates also showed that, of the top 1% of women in math ability only 3% stayed in the math/science pipeline compared to 32% of their male counterparts (Benbow, 1992).

There appears to be, among gifted individuals who experience difficulties with self-concept, a persistent psychic battle of the self going on. This is particularly true for special populations who must master successful coping mechanisms if they are to succeed in the larger social context. Handicapped individuals, for example, learn to compensate for physical and other weaknesses through coping mechanisms idiosyncratic to the individual and the nature of the handicap. Stephen Hawking's capacity to speak through a voice box and ''write'' by typing with an object in his mouth demonstrates the compensatory power of a brilliant individual with severe cerebral palsy. Disadvantaged individuals learn to use their deprivation of circumstances of birth as a catalyst for catching up, yet being ever mindful of their limited repertoire of experience. Culturally diverse groups battle a dual value system message: one that calls for subgroup loyalty and adherence to tribal, family, and cultural traditions and the other that calls for individual excellence in a mainstream world. The psychic battle for gifted girls and women is one of pursuing career fulfillment and yet satisfying social responsibility and personal standards around home and family.

In order for such individuals to succeed in these internal wars, they must be armed with a strong sense of self as resourceful individuals capable of assuming new challenges. Their identity is shaped and influenced greatly by these adversities. Not only do such gifted individuals need a set of goals, they also need a philosophy of life that allows for the evolution of a healthy self-concept to emerge over time. Gifted students may experience self-concept difficulties for a variety of reasons. One reason may relate to the same stressful life events and circumstances that beset other students, such as poverty, child abuse, divorce, and so on. Another reason may relate to their lack of fit in a particular social or academic situation where they may be denied appropriate educational programs or lack regular contact with peers of comparable ability. A third reason may be their negative response to parental pressure or expectations for high achievement. A fourth theory recently proposed suggests that parental appraisal has a powerful impact on the self-concept of children (Phillips, 1987). Another reason that has been suggested by the literature that may affect short-term drops in self-concept is placement in gifted programs where students encounter for the first time others who are as bright if not brighter than themselves (Olszewski, Kulieke, and Willis, 1987). These are all important reasons to consider when deciding how to approach students experiencing such difficulties.

Positively affecting the self-concept of any child would seem to be a tricky business. For gifted learners and especially those from special populations, the issues are compounded by all of the factors in their psychological and sociological context that may affect self-perception. What are these related factors and issues that need to be considered in educational settings? There are at least three that need some discussion. They are underachievement, individual attention, and intra-personal resources.

Underachievement needs to be viewed as a key problem associated with low self-esteem among gifted students and one that should be prevented through positive intervention at early stages of development. Research has shown that underachievement is a vast problem among the gifted population, which tends to haunt them throughout life (Terman and Oden, 1959; Dowdall and Colangelo, 1982). One of the key patterns in the profile of these underachieving gifted individuals is a persistent low self-esteem, with reported feelings of inferiority, lack of goal integration, social and emotional difficulties, and lack of persistence. And this pattern that emerges by age ten frequently persists throughout life. Clearly then, we have strong evidence that low self-esteem among the gifted has a debilitating effect on their achievement, not only in societal terms but also in personal ones. Such individuals report lower life satisfaction than do high achieving gifted individuals and are more likely to take jobs commensurate with their perceptions of ability, more likely to divorce, and more likely to encounter unsatisfactory life experiences.

Underachievement among the gifted frequently is an undetected problem, in that a student may be meeting or exceeding the expectations of a particular context and still not be optimizing her potential as a learner. Since the norms of behavior in some intellectual contexts typically require so little of individuals, the gifted can "look gifted" without really expending any intellectual energy on a topic, issue, or problem. This "covering up" of intellectual power to suit the social circumstance can easily become the standard for such individuals at all ages who wish to function well in their context. Consequently, a more subtle form of underachievement begins to be actualized where daily performance is found to be laudatory yet consistently represents below-potential functioning. This condition is particularly profound among gifted girls whose expectations for social behavior are more overriding than considerations of intellectual challenge.

Examples of the enhancement of self-concept among the gifted are primarily found in case studies of eminent individuals (see Goertzel and Goertzel, 1962). A persistent theme of these studies is the role of an individual in the lives of these eminent people who became a friend, a mentor, or a collaborator. As a result of such a relationship at a critical stage of development, these individuals, many of whom came from adverse circumstances, were able to use their energies in creative and productive ways. Consequently, it may be most useful to consider how individuals who come in contact with gifted students on a regular basis might work with them toward the enhancement of self-esteem and self-concept. Thus, innovations through mentorships, internships, or tutorials might focus on positively affecting the multidimensional view of self as a primary goal rather than a more narrowly defined academic one. The need for individual attention and nurturance to the perception of self then becomes a major factor in the development of gifted individuals whose self-concept may be at risk.

Strategies for Practice

Since the nature of self-concept can best be understood as a reciprocal relationship between the individual's behavior and the impact of that behavior on the social world filtered back to the individual through self-perception, any recommendations to professionals who work with the gifted must be tentative and suggestive (not prescriptive) and take into account the highly idiosyncratic nature of many gifted students. Moreover, our recognition of different aspects of self-concept and how gifted populations differ in respect to these aspects is another important grounding needed for successful interventions. How one enhances academic self-concept may differ considerably from strategies to heighten social self-concept or behavioral or physical self-concept.

Given these factors and issues associated with enhancing self-concept and self-esteem among the gifted, what general practices might we adopt to ameliorate problems among this population? The following points are offered as working ideas for counselors, teachers, parents, and others who influence the lives of these students.

Developing Self-Knowledge

The gifted student tends to adopt a highly analytical approach to life that results in earlier self-analysis, which in turn feeds a tendency towards perfectionism both in self and others. An overlay of inappropriate adult expectations, such as being number one in the class or winning specialized competitions, can further affect, in a negative manner, the opportunity for such students to develop healthy identity formation. Thus, assisting gifted students with an understanding of the difference between perfection and the pursuit of excellence, for example, may be a first step in helping them mediate their world.

A gifted student must appreciate the role of competition in breeding excellence when raising one's own personal standard in a given area is often based on the performance of others. Olympic figure skaters, for example, now must perform intricate triple toe loops not required ten years ago in competition because the world-class standard has been raised through a single performance of excellence by one skater. This standard then becomes the basis for the "pursuit of excellence" in figure skating at world-class levels. More generally speaking, competition that focuses on individual improvement and goal attainment is healthy. This may be contrasted, however, with competition where the total focus is on winning, with performance taking precedence over learning and self-growth.

There is an unfortunate perception by many gifted adolescents that the more able one is, the less effort one should have to invest in attaining goals or earning grades. In the adolescent culture it becomes important not to be a "nerd" or "bookworm" but, rather, the person to whom academic attainment seems effortless. Although some bright adolescents view giftedness not as a trait but as a "performance" requiring sustained effort (Kerr et al., 1988), other bright students view ability as an entity that translates into turning away from challenging opportunities such as honors or advanced placement classes in favor of those requiring minimal effort (Stipek, 1988). These adolescent perceptions underscore the importance of finding out more about the relationship between self-knowledge, perceptions of self, and selected achievement patterns.

Developing Self-Acceptance

Gifted students tend to exhibit intense sensitivity and internal responsiveness to the actions of others, which can lead to feelings of alienation and rejection where none was intended. By the same token, however, this very characteristic can lead to peer ridicule and social rejection because of the overreaction to a trivial incident, leaving the gifted feeling unaccepted by peers. This condition can adversely affect self-esteem (Janos and Robinson, 1985). Providing gifted students with concrete examples of behavioral incidents that illustrate how these perceptions of difference are formed through role-playing, scenarios, and bibliotherapy may help ameliorate such occurrences and assist with self-acceptance.

Developing Relationships

The characteristics of popular children, such as friendliness, peer dependency, conformity to peer rules and routines (Coleman, 1980), are not typical among the gifted. They frequently have fewer opportunities for positive recognition from peers and fewer friendships, and their friendship patterns more frequently involve older children and adults. In a study of concerns of gifted middle school students (VanTassel-Baska and Olszewski-Kubilius, 1989), developing relationships was the most cited concern of the students. Thus, providing gifted students with strategies for developing new peer relationships and improving existing ones is an important way to assist their self-concept development.

Developing Appropriate Expectations of Self

Since gifted students have a propensity for expecting more of themselves than is warranted given a particular set of circumstances, they are often more critical of self than others would ever be and feel many times a conflict between internal drives for excellence and external pushes for performance, resulting in stress, impatience, and a lowered tolerance for ambiguity (Delisle, 1985). Helping such students negotiate a healthy balance between inner and outer expectations, as well as reasonable expectations for performance based on ability, interest, and personality factors, is critical to the development of self.

Developing Risk-Taking Behaviors in Intellectual Contexts

Sometimes gifted students exhibit behaviors that are antithetical to intellectual risk-taking. They insist on finding the one right answer, they refuse to take on new challenges unless they are assured of the outcome reward (a grade, credit, or recognition of some kind), and they abhor being wrong. All of these risk-taking behaviors are critical in the development of the intellectual inquiry process because students will encounter serious challenges to their ideas, may find intellectual work demanding in some contexts, and discover that authentic learning occurs from making mistakes. Thus, if students do not develop these traits as a normal part of their earlier education, the assault on their self-concept at a later time can be devastating. Creating task demands for the gifted that require intellectual risk-taking is crucial to their affective, as well as cognitive, development.

Developing Self-Concept and Self-Esteem

These guidelines should serve as a starting point in thinking through ways to enhance self-concept and self-esteem among those gifted students who particularly need it. In addition, following these guidelines for all gifted students as a preventive measure may prove useful since there is sufficient evidence to suggest the malleability of self-concept based on a given stage of development and situational context (Briggs, 1975). Thus, working on self-concept development with gifted students throughout the school years is a worthy program goal.

Misinterpretations about gifted students can impair their evolving sense of self. School personnel must be sensitive to individual differences among gifted students. The more gifted the student, the less generalizations may apply about a healthy self-concept. Personality patterns in many highly gifted students may run counter to the norm. They may suffer from others' perceptions of an "inflated" self-concept because of a preference to work alone, which appears as aloofness from the group. Such behavior may be more indicative of strong self-direction, nonconformity, and a concentrated personal intent and effort. Feeling different can create a dissonance in the gifted that impairs self-esteem. Being too gifted or too creative can be internalized as detrimental, depending on the peer group. Sometimes a student's own behavior exacerbates the problem by appearing too critical of self and others or hiding talents just to get along in a social setting. School problems can also affect self-concept. Poor study habits, difficulty with accepting criticism, refusal to do routine tasks, and resistance to authority constitute behaviors that would alienate teachers and peers, leading to negative appraisals of student work and potentially instilling a sense of incompetence.

Finally, the importance of a gifted student's connection to another student cannot be overstated. Many problems of self-concept for these students is rooted in their sense of separation from peers and alienation from social worlds in which they feel unwelcome. Empathic adults cannot control social worlds, but they can facilitate the discovery of positive peer relationships with at least one other person in the student's environment. Again, as with other programs, the importance of an optimal match between the aptitude and interest of the student should be a foremost consideration.

The context for focusing on these broad approaches to self-concept development in the gifted may, in some instances, be the counselor's office, the home, or the classroom itself. Within the context of the classroom, several specific strategies have been used with individual students and shown to be helpful when augmented with outside support. These school-based strategies include a consideration for changing the student's school program to respond better to his or her individual needs. Labeled "academic therapy" (Baska, 1990), this approach is grounded in the conception that self-concept problems can arise from the mismatch between a student and the social context in which he or she is asked to function. These problems can be ameliorated by adjusting the nature and level of classroom work, changing teachers, providing a more appropriate peer group, or offering curricular experiences to the student that provide an optimal match between learning potential and interests.

A second strategy that has been used widely with gifted students is bibliotherapy, a technique that views books as intellectual tools to be applied to understanding affective issues and problems. Books are selected that have a character experiencing the same types of problems as the gifted student. The gifted student then identifies with the characters, experiences empathic emotional reactions to the character, and sees the path to resolution experienced by the character. Sensitive discussions about such books in the classroom, school, or home with the gifted students in a small group are typically productive. Resource books for use in bibliotherapy are available in many materials, and methods for application are also numerous (see Boyce et al., 1990).

Creative problem-solving models are also useful heuristics to apply with gifted students on a regular basis. The premise of creative problem solving is to study a problem in a systematic way that leads to a plan of action. Since perseverance and a preference for complexity are characteristics of many gifted students, using a model that demands positive action is helpful in working through personal problems with self-esteem, which are caused or exacerbated by social contexts.

Gifted education along with general education has engaged in some questionable practices in the area of self-concept development. Educators have focused on "self-esteem" activities once a week with all students in a given class; they have also treated self-concept development as the same for all students; and they have viewed self-concept development as a process separate from other areas of development, particularly academic. We need to know much more about the idiosyncratic process of self-concept development in the gifted individual before we can hope to apply workable strategies in any systematic way. Particularly, we need to know more about the kinds of situational contexts over the lifespan that can have both a positive and a negative impact on self-concept and self-esteem at critical stages of development. While we understand that parents can play a negative role in the self-concept development of their children, we need to know more about those parenting procedures that would be ameliorative. We also need to know what, if any, curricular and instructional strategies would strengthen self-concept in the gifted so that educational personnel might be more effective.

CONCLUSION

This chapter has provided a review of the literature on self-concept, self-esteem, and related social support issues of gifted individuals. It has focused particularly on the special problems in self-concept development among special populations of gifted students—the disadvantaged, minority students, the handicapped, gifted girls, and the underachiever. Moreover, the chapter presented a study that examined social support issues including self-concept among junior high school age students. Findings from that study indicated a need for a more refined view of self-concept enhancement with the gifted based on race, class, and gender considerations. Major issues such as underachievement, need for individual attention, and struggles of the self were described as a prelude to offering some intervention guidelines for practitioners.

ENDNOTE

1 The specific instruments used were as follows: The Rosenberg Self-Esteem Scale (Rosenberg, 1965) is a five-item, self-report questionnaire that measures general self-esteem. Reported reliability is .76. The People in My Life questionnaire is a twenty-four-item forced choice response form that assesses self-perceptions about the support provided by classmates, friends, parents, and teachers to students in both academic and nonacademic contexts. Reliabilities for the four subscales range from .83 to .89. The Work Orientation Questionnaire is a nineteen-item self-report scale that examines four constructs related to mastery, work, competition, and personal unconcern. Reliabilities for the subscales range from .59 to .75. The People in My Life and Work Orientation Questionnaire are available from Joyce VanTassel-Baska. The What I Am Like self-report instrument is a thirty-six-item forced choice questionnaire designed to measure perceived competence across the following areas: scholastic, social, athletic, physical appearance, behavioral conduct, and global self-worth (Harter, 1985). Reliabilities for the subscales range from .75 to .82; internal consistencies range from .73 to .86 (Harter, 1982).

REFERENCES

Arnold, K. 1991. ''Case Studies of Minority Valedictorians,'' paper presented at the annual meeting of the American Educational Research Association, Chicago, IL.

Arnold, K. and T. Denny. 1985. "The Lives of Academic Achievers: The Career Aspirations of Male and Female High School Valedictorians and Salutatorians," paper presented at the annual meeting of the American Educational Research Association, Chicago, IL.

Baska, L. K. 1990. "Educational Therapy for the Gifted: The Chicago Approach," in *A Practical Guide to Counseling the Gifted, Second Edition,* J. VanTassel-Baska, ed., Reston, VA: Council for Exceptional Children, pp. 47–52.

Benbow, C. 1992. Presentation of paper on outcome-based education, Colorado Educators of the Gifted, Denver, CO.

Birnbaum, J. A. 1975. "Life Patterns and Self-Esteem in Gifted Family-Oriented and Career-Committed Women," in *Women and Achievement,* M. T. S. Mednick, S. S. Tangri, and L. W. Hoffman, eds., New York, NY: John Wiley, pp. 396–419.

Boyce, L. N., J. Bailey, and J. VanTassel-Baska. 1990. *Libraries Link Learning Resource Manual.* Williamsburg, VA: Center for Gifted Education.

Bracken, B. A. 1980. "Comparison of Self-Attitudes of Gifted Children and Children in a Non-Gifted Normative Group," *Psychological Reports,* 47:715–718.

Bricklin, B. and P. Bricklin. 1967. *Bright Child, Poor Grades.* New York, NY: Delacourt Press.

Briggs, D. 1975. *Your Child's Self-Esteem.* Garden City, NY: Doubleday and Company, Inc.

Brophy, J. E. 1983. "Research on the Self-Prophesy and Teacher Expectations," *J. of Educational Psychology,* 71:733–750.

Callahan, C. M. and D. G. Cornell. 1989. "Gifted Girls' Self-Concept and Their Communication with Parents," *Understanding Our Gifted,* 2(2):12–14.

Colangelo, N. 1979. "Myths and Stereotypes of Gifted Students: Awareness for the Classroom Teacher," in *Multicultural Nonsexist Education,* N. Colangelo, C. C. Foxley, and D. Dustin, eds., Dubuque, IA: Kendall/Hunt, pp. 458–464.

Coleman, J. 1980. "Friendship and the Peer Group in Adolescence," in *Handbook of Adolescent Psychology,* J. Adelson, ed., New York, NY: Wiley, pp. 408–431.

Coleman, J. M. and B. A. Fults. 1982. "Self-Concept and the Gifted Classroom: The Role of Social Comparisons," *Gifted Child Quarterly,* 26(3):116–120.

Coleman, J. M. and B. A. Fults. 1983. "Self-Concept and the Gifted Child," *Roeper Review,* 5(4):44–47.

Davids, A. and J. Sidman. 1962. "A Pilot Study–Impulsivity, Time Orientation, and Delayed Gratification in Future Scientists and in Underachieving High School Students," *Exceptional Children,* 29:170–174.

Davis, H. B. and J. P. Connell. 1985. "The Effect of Aptitude and Achievement Status on the Self-System," *Gifted Child Quarterly,* 29(3):131–136.

Delisle, J. 1985. "Vocational Problems," in *The Psychology of Gifted Children,* J. Freeman, ed., London, England: Wiley, pp. 367–378.

Dowdall, C. B. and N. Colangelo. 1982. "Underachieving Gifted Students: Review and Implications," *Gifted Child Quarterly,* 25(1):179–181.

Dweck, C. 1986. "Motivational Processes Affecting Learning," *American Psychologist,* 41(10):1040–1048.

Eccles, J. 1987. "Gender Roles and Women's Achievement-Related Decisions," *Psychology of Women Quarterly,* VII(2):135–137.

Eccles (Parsons), J., T. F. Adler, R. Futterman, S. B. Goff, C. M. Kaczala, J. L. Meece, and C. Midgley. 1983. "Expectations, Values, and Academic Behaviors," in

342 DEVELOPING SELF-CONCEPT IN GIFTED INDIVIDUALS

Achievement and Achievement Motivation, J. T. Spence, ed., San Francisco, CA: W. H. Freeman, pp. 75–146.

Farmer, H. 1985. "Model of Career and Achievement Motivation for Women and Men," *J. of Counseling Psychology,* 32:363–390.

Franks, B. and L. Dolan. 1982. "Affective Characteristics of Gifted Children: Educational Implications," *Gifted Child Quarterly,* 26:172–178.

Frierson, E. 1965. "Upper and Lower Status Gifted Children: A Study of Differences," *Exceptional Children,* 32(2):83–90.

Gallagher, J. J. 1966. Research Summary on Gifted Child Education. Department for Exceptional Children: Gifted Program, State of Illinois, Office of the Superintendent of Public Instruction.

Gallagher, J. J. 1975. *Teaching the Gifted Child.* Boston, MA: Allyn and Bacon.

Glaser, E. M. and H. L. Ross. 1970. "A Study of Successful Persons from Seriously Disadvantaged Backgrounds: Final Report," Washington, DC: Department of Labor Office or Special Manpower Programs (Contract No. 82-05-68-03).

Goertzel, V. and M. A. Goertzel. 1962. *Cradles of Eminence.* Boston, MA: Little, Brown Company.

Gowan, J. C. 1955. "The Underachieving Gifted Child. A Problem for Everyone," *Exceptional Children,* 21:247–249.

Haggard, E. A. 1957. "Socialization and Academic Achievement in Gifted Children," *School Review,* 55:388–414.

Harter, S. 1982. "The Perceived Competence Scale for Children," *Child Development,* 53:87–97.

Harter, S. 1985. *Manual for the Self-Perception Profile for Children.* Denver, CO: University of Denver.

Hecht, K. A. 1975. "Teacher Ratings of Potential Dropouts and Academically Gifted Children: Are They Related?" *J. of Teacher Education,* 26:172–175.

Hirsch, J. G. and J. Costello. 1970. "School Achievers and Underachievers in an Urban Ghetto," *Elementary School Journal,* 71(2):78–85.

Hoffman, L. W. 1977. "Fear of Success in 1965 and 1974: A Follow-Up Study," *J. of Consulting and Clinical Psychology,* 45:310–321.

Horner, M. S. 1972. "Toward an Understanding of Achievement Related Conflicts of Women," *J. of Social Issues,* 28:157–175.

Janos, P. and N. Robinson. 1985. "Psychological Development in Intellectually Gifted Children," in *The Gifted and Talented: Developmental Perspectives,* F. Horowitz and M. O'Brien, eds., Washington, D.C.: American Psychological Association, pp. 180–187.

Janos, P. M., H. C. Fung, and N. M. Robinson. 1985. "Self-Concept, Self-Esteem, and Peer Relations among Gifted Children Who Feel 'Different,' " *Gifted Child Quarterly,* 28(2):78–82.

Janos, P. M., S. M. Sanfilippo, and N. M. Robinson. 1986. " 'Underachievement' among Markedly Accelerated College Students," *J. of Youth and Adolescence,* 15(1):303–313.

Karnes, F. A. and J. N. Wherry. 1981. "Wishes of Fourth- through Seventh-Grade Gifted Students," *Psychology of the Schools,* 18(2):235–239.

Kelly, K. R. and N. Colangelo. 1984. "Academic and Social Self-Concept of Gifted, General, and Special Students," *Exceptional Children,* 50(6):551–554.

Kerr, B., N. Colangelo, and J. Gaeth. 1988. "Gifted Adolescents' Attitudes towards Their Giftedness," *Gifted Child Quarterly,* 32:245–247.

Ketcham, B. and R. T. Snyder. 1977. "Self-Attitudes of the Intellectually and Socially Advantaged Student: Normative Study of the Piers-Harris Children's Self-Concept Scale," *Psychological Reports,* 40(1):111–116.

Kramer, L. 1985. "Social Interaction and Perceptions of Ability: A Study of Gifted Adolescent Females," paper presented at the annual meeting of the American Educational Research Association, Chicago, IL.

Kulik, C. C. and J. A. Kulik. 1982. "Effects of Ability Grouping on Secondary School Students: A Meta-Analysis of Evaluation Findings," *American Educational Research Journal,* 19:415–428.

Laffoon, K., R. Jenkins-Friedman, and N. Tollefson. 1989. "Causal Attributions of Underachieving Gifted, Achieving Gifted, and Nongifted Students," *J. for the Education of the Gifted,* 13(1):4–21.

Lavach, J. F. and H. B. Lanier. 1975. "The Motive to Avoid Success in 7th, 8th, 9th, and 10th Grade High-Achieving Girls," *The J. of Educational Research,* 68:216–218.

Laycock, F. 1979. *Gifted Children.* Glenview, IL: Scott and Foresman.

Maddux, C. D., L. M. Scheiber, and J. E. Bass. 1982. "Self-Concept and Social Distance in Gifted Children," *Gifted Child Quarterly,* 26:77–81.

Marsh, H. W. and R. J. Shavelson. 1985. "Self-Concept: Its Multifaced Hierarchical Structure," *Educational Psychologist,* 20:107–123.

McCall, R. B. and C. Evahn. 1987. "The Adult Educational and Occupational Status of Chronic High School Underachievers," paper presented at the annual meeting of the American Educational Research Association, Washington, DC.

Morgan, H. H. 1952. "A Psychometric Comparison of Achieving and Nonachieving College Students of High Ability," *J. of Consulting Psychology,* 16:292–298.

Newman, J., C. Dember, and O. Krug. 1973. "He Can but He Won't," *Psychoanalytic Study of the Child,* 28:83–129.

Olshen, S. R. and D. J. Matthews. 1987. "The Disappearance of Giftedness in Girls: An Intervention Strategy," *Roeper Review,* 9(4):251–254.

Olszewski, P., M. Kulicke, and G. Willis. 1987. "Changes in the Self-Perceptions of Gifted Students Who Participate in Rigorous Academic Programs," *J. for the Education of the Gifted,* 10(4):287–303.

Parsons, J., T. Adler, and C. Kaczala. 1982. "Socialization of Achievement Attitudes and Beliefs: Parental Influences," *Child Development,* 53(4):310–321.

Perkins, H. V. 1969. *Human Development and Learning.* Belmont, CA: Wadsworth Publishing.

Phillips, D. A. 1987. "Socialization of Perceived Academic Competence among Highly Competent Children," *Child Development,* 58(5):1308–1320.

Pierce, J. V. 1959. "The Educational Motivation Patterns of Superior Students Who Do and Do Not Achieve in High School," Mimeograph report, University of Chicago.

Pringle, M. L. 1970. *Able Misfits.* London: Longman Group Ltd.

Purkey, W. W. 1970. *Self-Concept and School Achievement.* Englewood Cliffs, NJ: Prentice-Hall.

Raph, J. B., M. L. Goldberg, and A. H. Passow. 1966. *Bright Underachievers.* New York, NY: Teachers College Press, Columbia University.

Ringness, T. A. 1967. *Mental Health in the Schools.* New York, NY: Random House.

Rosenberg, M. 1965. *Society and the Adolescent Self Image.* Princeton, NJ: Princeton University Press.

Saurenman, D. and W. Michael. 1980. "Differential Placement of High-Achieving and Low-Achieving Gifted Pupils in Grades 4, 5, & 6 on Measures of Field Dependence-Field Dependence, Creativity, and Self-Concept," *Gifted Child Quarterly,* 24:81–85.

Schneider, B., M. Clegg, B. Byrne, J. Ledingham, and G. Combie. 1989. "Social Relations of Gifted Children as a Function of Age and School Program," *J. of Educational Psychology,* 81(1):48–56.

Stipek, D. 1988. *Motivation to Learn: From Theory to Practice.* Englewood Cliffs, NJ: Prentice-Hall.

Stipek, D. and D. Mac Iver. 1989. "Developmental Change in Children's Assessment of Intellectual Competence," *Child Development,* 60:521–538.

Tannenbaum, A. J. 1983. *Gifted Children: Psychological and Educational Perspectives.* New York, NY: Macmillan.

Terman, L. M. and M. Oden. 1947. *Genetic Studies of Genius—IV. The Gifted Child Grows Up.* Stanford, CA: Stanford University Press.

Terman, L. M. and M. H. Oden. 1959. *The Gifted Group at Mid-Life.* Stanford, CA: Stanford University Press.

Tidwell, R. 1980. "A Psycho-Educational Profile of 1,593 Gifted High School Students," *Gifted Child Quarterly,* 24(2):63–68.

Trowbridge, N. 1972. "Self-Concept and Socio-Economic Status in Elementary School Children," *American Educational Research Journal,* 9(4):525–537.

VanTassel-Baska, J. 1989. "Case Studies of Disadvantaged Gifted Students," *J. for the Education of the Gifted,* 13(1):22–36.

VanTassel-Baska, J. 1989. "The Role of the Family in the Success of Disadvantaged Gifted Learners," in *Patterns of Influence: The Home, The Self, and The School,* J. VanTassel-Baska and P. Olszewski, eds., New York, NY: Teachers College Press, pp. 66–80.

VanTassel-Baska, J. and P. Olszewski-Kublius, eds. 1989. *Patterns of Influence on Gifted Learners.* New York, NY: Teachers College Press.

VanTassel-Baska, J., J. Patton, and D. Prillaman. 1991. *Gifted Youth At-Risk.* Reston, VA: Council for Exceptional Children.

Wellington, C. and J. Wellington. 1965. *The Underachiever: Challenges and Guidelines.* Chicago, IL: Rand McNally.

Whitmore, J. R. 1980. *Giftedness, Conflict, and Underachievement.* Boston, MA: Allyn and Bacon.

Wolfe, D. L. 1954. *America's Resources of Specialized Talent.* New York, NY: Harper and Row.

Zilli, M. C. 1971. "Reasons Why the Gifted Adolescent Underachieves and Some of the Implications of Guidance and Counseling to this Problem," *Gifted Child Quarterly,* 15:279–292.

CHAPTER 11

Self-Esteem among Juvenile Delinquents

LOUIS P. MESSIER – *The College of William and Mary*
THOMAS J. WARD – *The College of William and Mary*

JUVENILE delinquents account for a disproportionate percentage of the nation's crime. According to studies based on the United States Uniform Crime Report, 27% of all major crimes are committed by juveniles under the age of eighteen (Achenbach, 1982; Nelson et al., 1987; Uniform Crime Report, 1989). While approximately one-third of all recorded crimes are committed by juveniles, there is almost universal agreement that these figures are but the tip of the iceberg (Snarr and Walford, 1983). Unreported or undetected crimes by juveniles are thought to actually approach 50% of all index crime arrests. Five percent of all persons arrested nationally in 1989 were under the age of fifteen, while those under the age of eighteen accounted for 15% of arrests, with juveniles showing an overall increase of 3% over the five-year period from 1985 (Uniform Crime Report, 1989). Index crimes are the crimes of murder, non-negligent manslaughter, forcible rape, and robbery. Even though some 60% of serious offenders cease involvement in delinquency within one year (Elliot, 1988), from these data one could hypothesize that significant numbers of unreported delinquent acts occur and that the juvenile perpetrators remain unidentified.

A commonly asked question is what predisposes these youths to commit delinquent acts? The following variables have been suggested as possible at-risk indicators: low school achievement, low verbal intelligence, parental alcoholism, parental arrest, dysfunctional home, contradictory parental attitudes on discipline, substance abuse by parent or juvenile, ethnic identity, and mental health (Bayrakal and Kope, 1990; Lehr and Harris, 1988; Loeber and Stouthamer-Loeber, 1986). In this chapter delinquent youths will be compared to other youths to determine where differences exist. The assumption that delinquent youths were different from other youths had been totally accepted. At the very least, we expected to find differences in the areas of self-esteem, family functioning, intelligence, and mental health. Overall, the comparative findings were much different than anticipated.

SELF-ESTEEM AND DELINQUENCY

The literature on delinquency has long alluded to and shown a variable and tantalizing relationship between aspects of self-esteem and adolescent problems including depression, alcohol abuse, drug abuse, and social alienation (Harper and Marshall, 1991; Downs and Rose, 1991). Typical of the literature are findings reported by Leung and Lau (1989) indicating that poor parental relationships and poor self-concept are related to higher frequencies of delinquent behavior. While strained parent-child relationships have been considered a source of delinquency for some time (Kavaraceus, 1966), contemporary research continues to document a relationship between low levels of family support and higher levels of depression and delinquency (Windle, 1991; Steinberg et al., 1991).

The intricacies of the self-esteem delinquency relationship continue to unfold with a complexity that is seemingly paradoxical. Low self-esteem fosters delinquent behavior, as many have long suspected (Kaplan, 1980), yet delinquency has the effect also of enhancing self-esteem for some delinquents (Rosenberg et al., 1989). The relationship of low self-esteem as directly causal for delinquency is less challenged than the idea that delinquency enhances self-esteem. However, Wells (1989) found that delinquent behavior enhanced self-esteem in those adolescents whose self-esteem was extremely low. Wells unexpectedly found that some adolescent youths whose self-esteem was exceedingly high apparently engaged in delinquent acts for its self-enhancing effect. Thus, one may see delinquency as enhancing to the self-esteem of those engaged in the behavior, but low self-esteem is not a universal prerequisite for delinquency.

Ethnic identification has also been investigated as a factor of low self-esteem and as a predictor of delinquency in youth. Leung and Drasgow (1986) tested Kaplan's theory of deviant behavior across White, Black, and Hispanic ethnic groups and concluded that, while all three groups reported low self-esteem (Hispanics reported the lowest of the three), only the low self-esteem levels of the White group could be seen to be related to delinquent behavior. However, Calhoun, Connley, and Bolton (1984) found no differences in self-esteem and delinquency between Black and White delinquents and nondelinquents. They did find that low self-esteem correlated with more delinquent behaviors for Mexican-Americans and that Black and Mexican-American delinquents tended to be middle-born children from large families.

Thus, while there emerges an apparent pattern of low self-esteem promoting delinquent behaviors in many youths—especially Whites—high self-esteem is present in some delinquent youths. Delinquent behavior apparently provides enhanced self-esteem for many youths, but self-esteem among incarcerated youths is lowered by the negative effects of being labeled delinquent or deviant (Chassin and Stager, 1984). Incarcerated delinquents in the Chassin and Stager study had differentiated self-esteem based upon their own valuation of delinquency. Both peer and adult valuations had negative effects upon the youths' self-esteem in proportion to their own impressions of delinquent behavior. The less valued the delinquent behavior as perceived by adults and the greater the delinquent's identity with that negative behavior, the lower their self-esteem (Stager et al., 1983).

A variation in the direction of the self-esteem—delinquency dynamic is also offered by McCarthy and Hoge (1984), which retains the hypothesis that delinquency is related to low self-esteem but with a twist: that self-esteem is reduced subsequent to delinquency. In this view, the more serious the delinquent behavior, the lower the self-esteem. The authors demonstrate the point by stating that subjects with low self-esteem prior to their delinquent behaviors showed little change in self-esteem level subsequent to their delinquency. However, subjects high in self-esteem initially had reduced self-esteem subsequent to their delinquency. Yet McCarthy and Hoge (1984, p. 396) maintain the correlation to be very weak and exhort other researchers to discontinue the search for a linkage between self-esteem and delinquency and to "look elsewhere than self-esteem for a fuller understanding of delinquency."

One alternative area of inquiry lies in school practices that are presumed to lower self-esteem. For example, some educators believed that curriculum tracking had a deleterious effect upon self-esteem and, while that is not evident in research (Wiatrowski et al., 1982), it is an example of a potential focal point for the enhancement of self-esteem. It seems logical to think, however, that the lack of ability grouping may potentially reduce self-esteem for some gifted or high-ability students since it is becoming evident "that gifted students exist in the populations of antisocial youth" (Harvey and Seely, 1984, p. 78). Gifted or high-ability youths might, in fact, experience reduced self-esteem if their curriculum is regarded by themselves and others as unstimulating or unproductive.

Self-esteem enhancement programs are ubiquitous in programs offered by public schools, public recreation programs, and public and private residential treatment programs. In general, the rationale for such social intervention programs is that by enhancing the youths' self-esteem through experiences that engender feelings of accomplishment and acceptance, one will interrupt the low self-esteem—delinquency process. However, Wells and Rankin (1983) dispute the existence of a causal relationship between delinquency and low self-esteem. In a four-year nationwide study of 2,277 high school youths, The Youth in Transition Study, no statistical relationship between delinquency and self-esteem was found (Bachman, 1978). Thus, it is possible that raising self-esteem levels may have no effect upon delinquency.

Even when studies find no support for deflated self-esteem as a predictor for delinquency, there still are differences in levels of self-esteem that are unexplained. For example, Thompson and Dodder (1983) investigated Kaplan's (1980) hypothesis that a personality factor exists, which provides containment or protection from involvement in delinquency. They found no support for less favorable self-concept as predictive of delinquency, despite slightly lower levels of favorable self-concept in both Black and White institutionalized males and Black females. Furthermore, they noted higher favorable self-concepts among institutionalized delinquent White females. Thus, except for institutionalized delinquent White females, lower favorable self-concept scores are evident but at less than significant levels.

There has been considerable frustration in attempts to analyze devalued self-concept as either a precursor to or a corollary of delinquent behavior. Some researchers have lamented the lack of research progress and interest in the area of self-esteem and delinquency. While Dinitz and Pflau-Vincent (1982) advocate more research on the etiology of deviant and delinquent behavior, they acknowledge considerable difficulty in operationally defining self-concept so that it may be measured. Despite the ambiguity of the concept, Dinitz and Pflau-Vincent are satisfied that negative self-concept, influenced principally by familial experiences, is inextricably involved in delinquent behaviors but that the mechanism of that process defies intervention and measurement.

Tannenbaum (1982) takes issue with Dinitz and Pflau-Vincent's characterization of a developmentally fixed self-concept that later insulates or fails to insulate a rising adolescent from delinquency. He postulates instead that self-esteem and delinquency are situational. That is, some delinquents, due to social and other factors, may devalue themselves, while other delinquents with similar backgrounds do not devalue themselves. Tannenbaum questions the utility of adopting a construct of the self-concept as a fixed trait and also the assumption by some researchers that damaging socialization and familial experiences were present only in the devalued selves of confirmed delinquents. According to Tannenbaum, research should identify victims of damaging familial/social experiences and prospectively follow them to their current status in life. The implication is that following such a course of research would yield persons with similar experiential backgrounds but with differentiated delinquent versus nondelinquent outcomes. Difficult as such a study would be, it could shed light on the presupposed universality of self-devaluation as a consequence of untoward familial/social experiences, as well as the presumption that such devaluation is exorably related to seeking relief in delinquent behavior.

One must be mindful that any study dealing with self-concept and its purported relationship to delinquency relies upon a variety of definitions by numerous authors and measurements by instruments, which may or may not provide valid measures for the elusive construct. Hoffman and Davis (1988), for example, conducted a factor analysis of the commonly used Tennessee Self-Concept Scale (TSCS). They concluded that while the TSCS does provide a general, overall index of the delinquents' self-esteem, multifactorial scoring for delinquents on the TSCS is not warranted and that more study of nondelinquent adolescents' responses is required before making delinquent versus nondelinquent comparisons. Thus, ultimately, the relationship of self-esteem to delinquency may be more artificial than causal.

Concerns about the construct validity of the multitudes of self-esteem measures notwithstanding, the evidence continues to accumulate that delinquents, in general, yield less favorable self-valuations than nondelinquents (recalling that a small percentage of delinquents rate themselves quite highly and appear to have quite high valuations of self). Cole, Chan, and Lytton (1989) found delinquents to have a differentiated perceived competence when compared to three nondelinquent groups of high achievers, low achievers, and behavior disordered students. One might expect that delinquents, behavior disordered youths, and low achievers would have lower self-competence valuations. Yet the delinquents scored themselves lower on cognitive, social, and general self-worth domains. However, on the physical competence subscale, the delinquents valued themselves as equal to all three nondelinquent groups. The authors speculate that in physical competence, delinquents could demonstrate prowess in what otherwise could be esteem deflating environments for them, such as schools and secure detention centers.

Cole, Chan, and Lytton (1989) also found that delinquents are less able to see themselves as competent in the spheres of cognition, social, and general self-worth. Noting the findings of McCarthy and Hoge discussed above, Cole and colleagues reiterated that, once incarcerated for delinquency and becoming aware of negative societal reactions, the delinquent begins to feel less effective and more inferior to nondelinquents. The confounding aspect of this view is that, as discussed earlier, one must consider that negative self-valuation and self-esteem may be a consequence of delinquency rather than a precursor to it.

In perhaps an enlightened expansion of the self-valuation relationship to delinquency, Oyserman and Markus (1990) offer the view that "possible selves" rather than self-esteem should be the focus of research and that self-esteem alone is not an adequate predictor of delinquency. What one believes one might become, that is, "possible selves" serves to show what motivates someone to be what they are. Thus, an adolescent who is confused about what he/she could be, wants to be, or fears being may resort to delinquency to create a self that is seen as tough and adventurous. Oyserman and Markus hypothesize and demonstrate that the most delinquent youths are those who lack balance between their expected selves (someday I'll be married) and their feared selves (I could fail in school or go to jail). They postulate that it is this lack of balance that predicts delinquency better than low self-esteem. Examples of delinquent responses to the Oyserman and Markus questionnaire for expected possible selves were "depressed," "alone," or "a junkie," and little mention of achievement or school-related activities. In contrast, nondelinquents responded with achievement-related responses and school and social concerns and anticipated successful outcomes.

Overall, nondelinquent youths showed significantly more balance between fears and expectations than their delinquent counterparts. Since high or low self-esteem has been variable if not unreliable in predicting delinquency, as our own data show, the possible selves approach may provide a useful, enhanced construct to apply to this issue. The new element of the Oyserman-Markus (1990) self-concept paradigm is the element of future. Oyserman and Markus believe that self-concept research, until now, has focused entirely upon past and present while ignoring the effects of expected futures. The youth's possible self of the future is believed to serve as a motivating energy and a stabilizing force as one traverses the vicissitudes of adolescent development. Without a sense of future and accompanying sense of possible future self, the adolescent succumbs to delinquent activity "simply because as opportunities for delinquent activities arise, these adolescents can find no compelling reasons to resist them'' (Oyserman and Markus, 1990, p. 147). Thus, delinquent youths frequently just "drift" into delinquency without the stabilizing benefit of a sense of future self. Even though more males (30%) than females (10%) are involved as delinquents in serious violent crime, one would assume that there are similarities in the threatened balance between expected identities and present choices for both males and females (Oyserman and Markus, 1990, p. 142).

DEPRESSION WITHIN THE DELINQUENT POPULATION

An astounding 30 to 60% of incarcerated juveniles (Murphy, 1986) are estimated to be handicapped as defined by Public Law 94-142, The Education of All Handicapped Act of 1975 (EHA), now the Individuals with Disabilities Act of 1990 (IDEA). The majority of those handicaps are manifested as learning disabilities (LD), emotional disturbances (ED), and mental retardation (MR). We wondered what numbers we would actually find in the area of psychological depression and high mental ability. Depression as currently defined by state and federal school regulations does not stand alone as a handicapping condition; it is but one requirement for the category "seriously emotionally disturbed." Likewise, high mental ability is not a handicapping condition, yet both depression and high mental ability may be generally regarded as exceptionalities. Exacerbating the dearth of knowledge about the prevalence of depression and giftedness within the incarcerated delinquent population is the serious opposition to the basic idea that high mental ability may coexist to any significant degree within the delinquent population (Hirschi and Hindelang, 1977; Harvey and Seeley, 1984; Delisle, 1990; Lajoie, 1981). The more prevalent assumption is the linkage between delinquency and problems with performance in school. That there is a link between learning disabilities and delinquency has for years been a concern for apprehensive parents of learning disabled youth. In fact, if a youth is learning disabled, there is a 220% greater chance of that youth becoming delinquent than for a nonlearning disabled peer (Keilitz and Dunivant, 1986).

While no significant dispute exists today regarding the existence of psychological depression in children and youth, there is disagreement over how it is manifested (Beck, 1967; Carlson and Cantwell, 1982; Achenbach, 1982; Nelson et al., 1987; Farrington, 1991; Willerman and Cohen, 1990). Studies indicating its prevalence within youth detention and correctional centers are lacking. Knowing the prevalence of depression within this population is critical from a mental health and crime prevention perspective since it is well-known that depression correlates highly with suicide (Kendel and Davies, 1982; Tishler et al., 1981) and, though less strongly, with its counterpart homicide (Cornell, 1987).

Implicated in many behavioral aspects of academic life, depression may also block the appearance of high mental ability or intellectually gifted behaviors in traditional school settings. Certainly, it is recognized that unidentified intellectually gifted youth present many discipline and behavior problems for schools (Deslisle, 1990; Farrell, 1989; Page, 1991; Leroux, 1986; Weisse, 1990). The more prominent of these untoward behaviors may be masked depression manifested as delinquency and/or learning disabilities.

Hyperactivity may also serve to mask depression. While that idea has limits in terms of symptom expression or diagnosis (Achenbach, 1982; Kauffman, 1989), it remains an intriguing concept. Heightened motor activity is at times a correlate of depression, and such activity has been thought to actually lead depressed youths to impulsive, acting-out, delinquent behaviors (Weston, 1958). Certainly the depressed, acting-out youngster is no stranger to child development researchers (Lief and Zarin-Ackerman, 1980). However, when these students are referred for services in the context of schooling, it is not always the case that the relationship between intelligence and depression is investigated as an underlying factor in the heightened motor activity.

HIGH-ABILITY YOUTHS WITHIN THE DELINQUENT POPULATION

It is generally, and we think erroneously, assumed that high IQ offenders are not included in significant numbers in the delinquent population (Hirschi and Hindelang, 1990). How could it be that a high-ability student could be unrecognized or overlooked? The reasons are varied and may include choice of tests selected and used in the screening or assessment process. A majority of delinquents are thought to be language deficient, as shown on verbal components of IQ tests (Glueck and Glueck, 1950). Thus, traditional measures of intelligence or academic achievement relying upon verbal or performance components would not adequately identify high-ability and potentially gifted students.

The intellectually gifted, in addition to being under-recognized for intellectual qualities, are also the victims of pervasive myths about their supposed invulnerability to the effects of depression among other life stresses. The myths are based upon presumptions that gifted students are better able to manage these stressors because of their superior abilities. In fact, while sensitivity, awareness, and intellectual ability would seem to offer better coping potential, in the gifted such attributes may well be associated with loneliness, alienation, rage, mistrust, self-deprecation, and intense feelings of being different (Leroux, 1986; Farrell, 1989; Weisse, 1990; Delisle, 1990; Page, 1991), all of which are associated with depression. Of course, the correlated danger of suicidal ideation with the associated potential for self-injurious and even death-producing acts may then become more intense. While some gifted do show themselves to be vulnerable to depression for the reasons cited, there is also evidence that they are not necessarily any more vulnerable (Bartell and Reynolds, 1986) than their nongifted peers.

Harvey and Seeley (1984) investigated the prevalence of intellectually gifted delinquents in a Colorado detention center. Of 268 delinquents assessed, forty-eight (18%) qualified as intellectually gifted. This finding is much higher than one would have expected when the literature typically continues to say that "it is difficult to imagine the proportion of gifted among delinquents being found to be over-represented, except perhaps in rural populations" (Lajoie, 1981, p. 141). A more recent study by Cornell (1992) reached different conclusions using psychometrically similar tests of intelligence. As Cornell (1992, p. 235) states, his results show "that high intelligence is not associated with severe delinquency." Our contention is, as Cornell also says, that delinquents are known to do less well on tests with verbal response requirements. Thus, we would not expect to find high-ability or gifted delinquents by using tests of intelligence based in significant part on verbal processing.

Not only are high-ability children and youth difficult to identify under optimal circumstances, they may use the fluid aspect of their intelligence to engage in "the masking misadventures" (Klumb, 1983) of delinquency. While this is largely an underconfirmed but very popular notion held by many public school and detention personnel, our data lend considerable support to the notion that a significant number in the detention population are in fact undetected and undiagnosed gifted or depressed.

Our numerous questions about delinquent youths and their nondelinquent counterparts are synthesized as follows. First, would delinquents describe themselves less favorably than nondelinquents? Second, would delinquents have less well functioning families than nondelinquents? Third, would delinquents show significant degrees of depression? The three questions were posed in the null hypotheses mode. Thus, we assumed we would find no difference in descriptions of self- and family functioning between delinquents and their nondelinquent peers. On the contrary, the prevalence of depression and the presence of high-ability youths was evident among incarcerated adolescents.

THE SAMPLE

The comparative data for this chapter come from the compilation of the samples of three separate studies that we conducted. Each of the samples consisted of thirteen- to eighteen-year-old juveniles who reside in the southeastern portion of the mid-Atlantic United States. Two of the groups were involved in the juvenile justice system, and the third group was a comparison group of high school students.

The comparison group comes from a study of 125 youths studied for four years from their freshman through senior years. These students attended a small urban high school and were approximately evenly distributed on socioeconomic status from low to high. Ethnic breakdown was 72% Anglo, 27% Black, and .5% combined Hispanic, Asian, and Native American. Gender make-up consists of 48% male and 51% female. This sample is the same sample discussed by McEachron-Hirsch and Ward in Chapter Eight.

The first delinquent group comes from a study of youths in secure detention centers. Youths in secure detention have been detained by police and are awaiting disposition by juvenile court on charges of misdemeanor and felony crimes such as trespassing, breaking and entering, simple and aggravated assault and battery, maiming, larceny, attempted murder, conspiracy to murder, and murder. These youths are ultimately found not innocent or innocent and handled accordingly. Our group consisted of 120 youths, of which 90% were male. We are unaware how many were found innocent and returned to home, community, and school.

The second delinquent group comes from a study of youths incarcerated in five learning centers as adjudicated youthful offenders. All of these youths were found by juvenile court judges to be "not innocent" (a juvenile court term used to reduce the stigma of delinquency associated with the term "guilty") and were sentenced to a learning center for a period of time. It is technically possible for a sentencing disposition to be as brief as three months or to be imposed to continue until the youth's twenty-first birthday. Our sample consisted of 105 youths, of which 89% were male.

PROCEDURE

For the nondelinquent high school group, four instruments were administered during each school year. In the fall, the Rosenberg Self-Esteem Scale (Rosenberg, 1965) and the Family Environment Scale (Moos and Moos, 1986) were administered, and in the spring, the Classroom Environment Scale (Moos and Trickett, 1987) and the Adjective Checklist (Gough and Heilbrun, 1983) were administered.

Both of the delinquent groups received a one-time administration of four instruments: the Family Environment Scale (FES), Children's Depression Inventory (CDI), Raven's Advanced Progressive Matrices, and the Adjective Checklist (ACL). The juveniles in these groups were tested in small group sessions as participants became available. The data for these two groups were collected over a two-year period.

The Adjective Checklist (ACL)

The Adjective Checklist (ACL) has 300 descriptive adjectives from which the subject chooses those most appropriately describing him/herself, and produces thirty-seven subscales that describe the individual on several domains. Normative data on the ACL is based upon 9,382 subjects from high school, college, law school, graduate school, medical school, delinquency, and psychiatric settings from throughout the United States. Figure 11.1 presents the ACL profiles for our three groups. The first characteristic that one may notice is the consistency of the three profiles, which indicates that the three groups are very similar. The notion that delinquent youths are grossly different from nondelinquent youths is clearly not justified by the current results. Statistical comparisons among the groups did reveal some differences between the groups. The groups were distinguishable on fifteen of the subscales. Although the group profiles do indicate some differences, they are more similar than dissimilar.

None of the subscales of the Adjective Checklist directly measures self-esteem; however, the subscales of Favorable, Unfavorable, Abase-

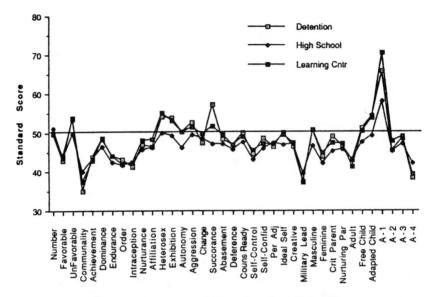

FIGURE 11.1 Group profiles on the adjective checklist.

ment, Self-Confidence, Personal Adjustment, and Ideal Self are sub-scales with close ties to self-esteem and will be used to discuss the self-esteem of the groups. Three of these subscales are among those where differences between the groups were detected and are depicted in Figure 11.2 to clarify the association between self-esteem and delinquency.

More detailed descriptions of selected subscales will be provided in the tables. The Favorable subscale (Table 11.1) indicates the degree to which the individual feels positively about him/herself. Those that score high on this subscale see themselves as adaptable, cheerful, and productive (Gough and Heilbrun, 1983). Favorable feelings about one's self is an indication of positive self-esteem. Our groups scored close to each other and close to the norm for high school students, indicating that they were average in their favorable self-ratings.

The Unfavorable subscale (Table 11.2) is an indicator of how negatively an individual feels about one's self. High scores on the Unfavorable scale indicate low self-esteem. Our analysis showed that the two delinquent groups scored identically and significantly higher than the nondelinquent high school group. In comparing the scores of our groups to the norms, our nondelinquent group scored somewhat lower than expected while the delinquent group scored higher than the ACL norms for delinquents. Thus, our nondelinquent group appears less negative about themselves than other, similar juveniles, and our delinquent groups appear more negative than expected when compared to other delinquents.

The subscale of Abasement (Table 11.3) indicates the degree to which the individual expresses inferiority through self-criticism, guilt, or social impotence (Gough and Heilbrun, 1983). High scores on this subscale would seem to indicate a lack of self-esteem, and one would expect group scores to be similar to the Unfavorable scale. Our analysis showed the three groups scoring equally on the Abasement scale, and all of the groups scored close to the norm for high school students indicating that our groups were typical.

Scores on the Self-Confidence (Table 11.4) scale differed between the groups with the delinquent groups expressing more self-confidence. On first examination it would appear that those with higher self-esteem, as shown by the Unfavorable scale, should also score higher on this subscale. Following this argument, it would seem that the delinquent groups should score lower than the nondelinquent group. However, low scorers on the Self-Confidence scale are seen as shy, inhibited, and withdrawn, descriptors that are clearly not typical of delinquent youths. The pattern observed in our sample also matches the pattern described by the norm samples of delinquent and high school youth. One presumes

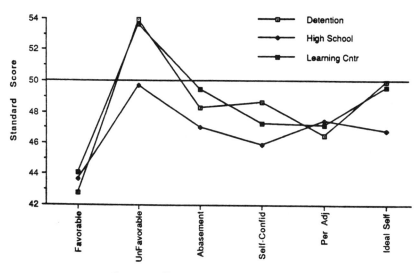

FIGURE 11.2 Group profiles on ACL subscales related to self-esteem.

Table 11.1. ACL subscale descriptors.

Scale and Definition	High Score	Low Score
Favorable: the number of favorable items checked by the respondent.	Adaptable, outgoing, protective, and cheerful in the face of adversity. These are productive workers.	Dispirited, self-denying and fearful of the future. Rarely, low scorers may also be skeptical and quick to point out shortcomings of others; more typical is the low scorer who sees himself as deficient in socially desirable attributes.

Table 11.2. ACL subscale descriptors.

Scale and Definition	High Score	Low Score
Unfavorable: The number of negative, unfavorable self-descriptors checked by a respondent.	A disbeliever, pessimistic of future, headstrong, quick to take offense, self doubt, bitter, hostile toward others.	More dependable, more tactful, less judgmental, less easily offended.

Table 11.3. ACL subscale descriptors.

Scale and Definition	High Score	Low Score
Abasement: To express feelings of inferiority through self-criticism, guilt or social impotence.	Ask for little, submit to the wishes and demands of others and avoid conflicts at all costs. Interpersonal world is worrisome and others seen as stronger and more effective and more deserving.	More self-confident and respond quickly in obtaining what they feel to be their just rewards.

Table 11.4. ACL subscale descriptors.

Scale and Definition	High Score	Low Score
Self-confidence: The degree to which the respondents feel assertive, outgoing, confident, and can mobilize their resources.	Initiators, may cut corners to make a good impression. Are assertive, enterprising.	Inhibited, shy, withdrawn. Have difficulty taking action.

that striving for favorable impressions among a delinquent peer group partially motivates the propensity for delinquent acts. In any event, the delinquent group displays more Self-Confidence than their nondelinquent peers.

The Personal Adjustment subscale (Table 11.5) is a measure of one's attitude toward life. High scorers on this scale have positive attitudes towards life and are self-confident. The scores of our three groups were equivalent and slightly below the norm for high school students. To the extent that a positive attitude toward life can be seen as relating to positive self-esteem, the indication is that our groups were less positive toward life than average and expressing lower self-esteem.

The subscale for Ideal Self (Table 11.6) presents another of the many seeming paradoxes as one compares the three groups. One might have entered such a comparison assuming that higher Ideal Self statements would have been ascribed to the nondelinquent group (Reckless et al., 1957), but instead we found the lower scores to be our nondelinquents.

Table 11.5. ACL subscale descriptors.

Scale and Definition	High Score	Low Score
Personal adjustment: The degree of self-satisfaction.	Positive attitudes toward life and enjoys the company of others. Feels capable of initiating activities and carrying them to conclusion. Possess the ability to love and to work.	Anxious, high-strung, moody, and avoids close relationships. Worries about their ability to deal with stresses and strains of their lives. Seen by others as being defensive, preoccupied, and easily distracted.

Table 11.6. ACL subscale descriptors.

Scale and Definition	High Score	Low Score
Ideal Self: The degree of congruence between the self and ideal self indicates a corresponding degree of personal adjustment.	Effective in interpersonal relations, effective goal attaining, well-adjusted but not well-liked.	Poor morale, feel defeated by life, difficult to set and attain goals. Are seen as kind, modest, and considerate of rights and wishes of others.

High scores on Ideal Self are those who are characterized by personal effectiveness and goal attaining abilities. While high scorers are not as well-liked by others, they are rated by others as well adjusted. Low scorers on Ideal Self, our nondelinquents, are those thought to have poor morale and who feel defeated by life. They also have difficulty attaining goals. One important redeeming quality is associated with low scorers on the scale; they tend to display qualities of kindness, modesty, and consideration for others. These latter attributes are consistent with the "good Samaritan" or "nice guy" qualities found in nondelinquents by Gillis and Hagan (1990). The paradox, then, is that higher goal attainment scores in Ideal Self values may be predictive of delinquency. At least those qualities are not productively utilized by our delinquent groups. The lower scores produced by the nondelinquents then may be seen as more realistic views of self-capabilities and self-aspirations.

The significantly higher scores of the two delinquent groups on the Unfavorable scale lend support to the notion that self-esteem is related to delinquency. The apparent pattern of low self-esteem promoting delinquent behaviors found in other studies appears to be upheld (Calhoun et al., 1984; Kaplan, 1980; Leung and Drasgow, 1986; Leung and Lau, 1989). At the least, delinquent youths, as a group, appear to have lower self-esteem than do nondelinquent youths. The question that remains is whether these youths had lower self-esteem prior to their entry into the juvenile justice system or had their self-esteem lowered as a result of their entry into the system.

Although not directly tested, it is possible to make some inferences about the effect of delinquency on self-esteem. The detention center youths had recently entered the juvenile justice system and should represent a group that has had little time to change their self-esteem. The learning center youths have been in the system for some time and have had time to evaluate the effects of their delinquent acts as well as the valuations of those acts by others. Since there was no difference between the two delinquent groups on the Unfavorable scale, there seems to be evidence that self-esteem is not changed by the delinquent act.

This finding is contrary to the positions of those that indicate delinquency is self-esteem enhancing (Rosenberg et al., 1989; Wells, 1989) and those that indicate that it is self-esteem limiting (McCarthy and Hoge, 1984). The position of Chassin and Stager (1984), that some juveniles have their self-esteem enhanced and others have theirs lessened after delinquent acts, is tenable based on these data. A balance of enhancements and detractions in self-esteem would produce no mean difference between the groups we examined. Since we do not have data that follow large groups from prior to arrest through placement in a learning center, caution is necessary in making interpretations based on separate groups. However, the data available to us indicate that group shifts in self-esteem do not occur after delinquent acts.

Several ACL subscales, used in the three-group comparison, may seem somewhat removed from the sphere of self-esteem. However, the scales of Exhibition, Aggression, and Succorance are, we argue, scales indicating behavior driven by an individual's levels of self-esteem (Figure 11.3). According to the tenets of self-psychology (Kohut, 1973), an

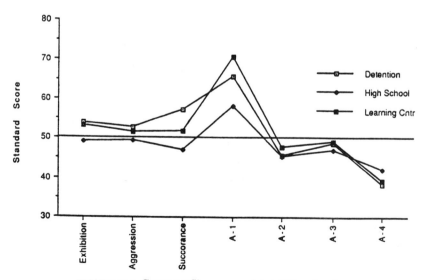

FIGURE 11.3 Group profiles on associated ACL subscales.

individual develops a sense of competence and self-value by internalizing feelings from experiences supported by mothers and fathers or other significant caregivers. The experiences of *mirroring* (parent shows delight and pride in child's accomplishment), *idealizing* (parent provides assurance and comfort after child experiences disappointment or injury), and *twinship* (child works with parent and feels sense of alikeness) (Wolf, 1988) contribute to a state of well-being and a healthy sense of self and self-esteem.

By virtue of hostility within the family or antagonisms directed by parents and significant others toward the child, the sense of well-being would be replaced by feelings of emptiness, depression, anxiety, or worthlessness (Klonoff and Lage, 1991). It is these feelings of low self-worth and related anxiety that cause the subject to seek relief in attention-getting behaviors (Exhibition) (Table 11.7), and to solicit sympathy, affection, or emotional support from others (Succorance) (Table 11.8). The exhibition and succorance scores for both delinquent groups is quite high, demonstrating low esteem.

If the individual's self-esteem is sufficiently low to threaten the individual's sense of well-being or sense of value, a sense of shame could result eventuating anger or "narcissistic rage" (Terman, 1975). A consequence of unmitigated narcissistic rage would be aggression (Table 11.9) directed toward the external world. Both delinquent groups scored high on aggression and significantly higher than the nondelinquent group.

As can be seen in Figure 11.3, all three groups scored quite high while maintaining significant differences between delinquent and nondelinquent groups. Thus, all three tend toward adventuresome, merry-making, creative paths, but the learning center group scored a full standard deviation above the expected mean of comparable delinquent peers. Clearly, this suggests a group with atypical high-activity levels and one with little interest in societal rules. Furthermore, impulses are not well-controlled for this group.

The four remaining ACL scales, High Origence − Low Intellectance (A-1), High Origence − High Intellectance (A-2), Low Origence − Low Intellectance (A-3), and Low Origence − High Intellectance (A-4) show interesting alignments among the groups. The most remarkable scores in Figure 11.3 are those for the A-1 scale of High Origence (creativity) and Low Intellectance (cognitive). On this scale (Table 11.10), one demonstrates attraction to creative, freewheeling interests versus intellectual cognitive interests. All three of the groups are imaginative,

Table 11.7. ACL subscale descriptors.

Scale and Definition	High Score	Low Score
Exhibition: To behave in such a way as to elicit the immediate attention of others.	Forceful, obtrusive, even bombastic. Insists on winning attention, impatient with opposition and delay. Willing to coerce and manipulate to gain cooperation.	Cautious, holds back, avoids conflict, gives in to escape interpersonal stress or controversy. Lacks confidence, shrinks away from limelight.

Table 11.8. ACL subscale descriptors.

Scale and Definition	High Score	Low Score
Succorance: To solicit sympathy, affection, or emotional support from others.	Feels inadequate in coping with stress and crisis, avoids confrontation, and tends to retreat to fantasy. Others are seen as stronger and more effective and their support is solicited.	Independent, relatively unbothered by self-doubt. Is effective in setting and attaining goals.

Table 11.9. ACL subscale descriptors.

Scale and Definition	High Score	Low Score
Aggression: To engage in behaviors that attack or hurt others.	Aggressive, competitive, and sees others as rivals to be vanquished. Has strong impulses, undercontrolled, and little regard for courtesies of conventional society.	Is patient, avoids conflict, makes few if any demands on others, and is conciliatory.

Table 11.10. ACL subscale descriptors.

Scale and Definition	High Score	Low Score
Intellectance = Intelligence, Origence = Creativity A-1 High Origence – Low Intellectance.	Adventurous, easy-going, relaxed, sophisticated but underachievers in academic settings. They score high on vocational interest scales for real estate and life insurance sales. They are merrymakers, distractible, accepting of self or others. They score high on anxiety and activity level.	Prudent, vigilant, and programmed. They plan ahead and are not impulsive. Take firm stand on ethical issues and look askance at those who violate societies' rules.

intuitive, and analytical, but are differentiated by degrees of attraction to more creative than conventional lifestyles. On the A-2 scale, High Origence – High Intellectance (Table 11.11), the learning center delinquents scored highest showing more self-sufficiency, more originality in thought, more aesthetic sensitivity, yet more indifference to convention. While all three groups are below the mean, the difference between the learning center group and the detention and nondelinquent groups is statistically significant. Thus, while all are close to the low side of the mean, the detention and nondelinquent groups are distinctly conventional, practical, predictable, and tolerant.

The A-3 scale, Low Origence – High Intellectance (Table 11.12), also shows the three groups close to and slightly below the mean and this time with a new alignment; both delinquent groups are the higher scorers and differ significantly from the nondelinquent group. Both delinquent groups are described as less complicated and more unpretentious, while the significantly lower scoring nondelinquents are intelligent and inventive, yet anxious, ill-at-ease, and tend to keep people at a distance. The lower scoring nondelinquents are skeptical of others and tend to feel alienated.

On A-4, Low Origence – High Intellectance (Table 11.13), two remarkable things are observable; while all three groups scored low, the

Table 11.11. *ACL subscale descriptors.*

Scale and Definition	High Score	Low Score
A-2 High Origence – High Intellectance: Intellectance = Intelligence, Origence = Creativity.	Self-sufficient, strong-willed, original in thought and perception. Aesthetically sensitive, indifferent to convention and annoyed by those who are uninsightful, intellectually maladroit, or lacking in perspicacity. In spite of many talents, the high scorer is scarcely more comfortable with his/her own reactions than with those of others. Intimacy and shared emotional feelings are threatening and are avoided.	More practical and mundane. A more ordinary individual. Less temperamental, more predictable, and less likely to lash out at others for their ineptitude or intellectual blunders.

Table 11.12. *ACL subscale descriptors.*

Scale and Definition	High Score	Low Score
A-3 Low Origence – Low Intellectance: Intellectance = Intelligence, Origence = Creativity.	Unpretentious, uncomplicated, protective of close friends. Rule-respecting and content with his/her role in life.	Intelligent and inventive, but anxious, ill-at-ease, and preoccupied with keeping people at a distance. Is skeptical about intentions of others and tends to feel alienated.

Table 11.13. ACL subscale descriptors.

Scale and Definition	High Score	Low Score
A-4 Low Origence – High Intellectance: Intellectance = Intelligence, Origence = Creativity.	Analytical, logical, astute, intellectually capable, and self-disciplined. Prepared to undertake planning and hard work for attainment of rational goals. Finds it hard to unbend and give in to whim and impulse.	Less controlled, more changeable and more easily influenced by illogical concerns.

two delinquent groups scored more than one standard deviation below the mean and are significantly different from the nondelinquent high school group. While all three groups must be seen as more changeable, less controlled, and easily influenced, the degree to which those descriptors apply to the delinquents is profound. The delinquents stand out as more easily influenced by illogical concerns and perfectly willing to let go and give in to impulse. These are exactly the kinds of descriptors confirmed by delinquents on many of the other ACL scales described above.

GROUP COMPARISONS ON THE FAMILY ENVIRONMENT SCALE (FES)

As we compare descriptions of delinquents on the FES with the nondelinquents from the McEachron-Hirsch and Messier data in Chapter Eight, the reader will note parallels in patterns and direction for each FES scale (Figure 11.4). In the normative samples for the FES, those described as distressed families were those scoring lower on Cohesion, Expressiveness, Independence, Intellectual-Cultural Orientation, and Active-Recreational Orientation. Dysfunctional families are also higher on Conflict and Control scales. In their description of the data, McEachron-Hirsch and Ward note high correlations between self-esteem scores and the FES scales for Cohesion and Active-Recreational Orientation. Thus, the detention center delinquents, who scored lowest on these scales, would be expected to have significantly lower self-esteem than either their learning center and nondelinquent counterparts. This was not the case. Interestingly, the detention center delinquents scored lowest, also, on Conflict, and thus, would be expected to be higher on self-esteem than either of the other groups. This was not the case according to the seven ACL subscales that are related to self-esteem.

By examining the Relationship Dimension, which includes Cohesion, Expressiveness, and Conflict, the similar but still divergent patterns between the groups first became apparent. It is notable that on Cohesion (the degree of family support and family commitment to its members), all three groups scored below the mean, thus pointing out a general pattern of low cohesion within all three group's families. Yet it is the two delinquent groups that scored lowest, with the detention center population being closest to a standard deviation below the mean. If juvenile incarceration for alleged and confirmed serious crimes would serve as one indicator of family dysfunction, one could conclude then that the least supportive families had the most dysfunctional children. The detention center group scored even lower than the learning center (not innocent) group, suggesting that those youths already having spent more time out of the family in learning centers have less intense recollections of lack of family support or view it as less important. It is also conceivable that incarceration in a learning center may increase perceptions of

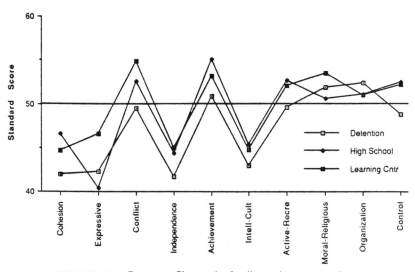

FIGURE 11.4 Group profiles on the family environment scale.

family support. Family members must agree to certain supervisory conditions if delinquent learning center youths are to be allowed home visits or, ultimately, released to the family when sentences have been served. In fact, Craig, first introduced as a nondelinquent in Chapter Eight, has intensified his relationship with his family and has enjoyed weekly visits from his parents during the sixteen months of incarceration in a learning center. One could also suspect that the detention center youth has most recently experienced the greatest turmoil and has yet to sense what, if any, new family cohesion will develop. In any event, it is clear that while the nondelinquent high school youths showed the most family cohesion, all three groups were below the mean but in what must be regarded as the normal range, even if leaning toward the distressed family side. The delinquent groups, scoring lowest on Cohesion are those lower also on self-esteem.

On the Expressiveness scale, a seeming paradox appears. The nondelinquent high school group scored the lowest and is but an eye-blink from being one full standard deviation below the mean indicating severe limits on expressiveness within the family. Such a low score matches the low scores of quite distressed families in the FES protocols. On the face of it, the nondelinquent group appears more distressed than either delinquent group and certainly that is possible. This finding does run contrary to most expectations, and thus, one seeks to make better sense of it. Is it possible that expressiveness, in the nondelinquent families, who also scored highest in Achievement Orientation, leaves no room for discussion on issues of school achievement and socialization issues? Or that the more expressive, and perhaps argumentative, learning center youths were less conforming, thus, more vocal in resisting expectations than their nondelinquent counterparts?

The third member of the Relationship triad is the Conflict subscale, which appears to differentiate between the three groups significantly. The detention group perceives less conflict than either the learning center or nondelinquent high school groups. Yet the three groups are all close to the mean. Still, as might be expected, the learning center group does report the greatest amount of family conflict. Once again, one could conclude that the group most conflicted, on issues ranging from family values to childrearing and discipline, would be the group most distressed as indicated by convictions and incarceration for crimes and, as discussed by McEachron-Hirsch and Ward, the most likely to have low self-esteem.

It is in the Personal Growth dimension of Independence, Achievement

Orientations, Intellectual-Cultural Orientation, Active-Recreational Orientation, and Moral-Religious Orientation subscales that showed the detention group to be generally lower than either the learning center and nondelinquent high school groups. Two subscales in particular, Independence and Intellectual-Cultural Orientation expectations, are clearly oriented toward distressed family profiles. Yet the remarkable finding here is the overall profile of each groups' score, which serves to strengthen the notion that, in almost all FES subscales, the delinquent versus nondelinquent differences are not predictive of delinquency.

Each of our study groups' families showed typical expectations and family practices for themselves and their children on Moral-Religious Orientations and Recreational aspects of their lives. Interestingly, all three groups were above the mean on the Moral-Religious subscale, and, surprisingly, the highest values were reported by learning center groups. Obvious contradictions emerge when considering the relationship between moral-religious orientations and moral and ethical behavior. Again, a contrast is evident between the ideal or possible selves and real selves.

The subscale for Organization shows the three groups to be above the mean with the detention group being highest. On the Control subscale, while the three groups approximate each other, the detention center group does score lower, though without statistical significance.

As one considers that the American family is still changing rapidly and dramatically [as evidenced by an approximately 50% divorce rate, (Robertson, 1988); an increasing dysmorphous family structure (Zigler, 1989), accompanied by intensifying family violence; and the related dysfunctional outcomes (Gelles and Strauss, 1988)], the sameness of delinquent and nondelinquent scores on the FES must be considered in a new light. While the delinquents scored slightly closer to the distressed FES family profiles than nondelinquents, overall FES family environment dynamics do not meaningfully discriminate between delinquent and nondelinquent families. Thus, nondelinquent families are more similar to delinquent families than dissimilar. Since the FES findings offer no discriminatory or predictive values, one is left to conclude that, except for charges filed by police for delinquent acts, there are no statistically significant differences between the families of these youths. However, one cannot ignore the more extreme pattern within the learning center group regarding lower levels of cohesion and higher levels of conflict. This pattern was also identified in studies reviewed in Chapter Eight.

THE PREVALENCE OF DEPRESSION AND HIGH-ABILITY YOUTHS WITHIN THE DETENTION AND LEARNING CENTER POPULATION

Earlier, we discussed the significant potential for adolescent depression to obscure a host of performance capabilities, to contribute to delinquency, and to affect high-ability youths. There is widespread agreement that too little is known about depression in the general adolescent population as well as the care of depressed adolescents in delinquent populations (Ehrenberg et al., 1990; Lajoie and Shore, 1981). Also, we pointed out that one needs to be aware of the presence of depression from a mental health standpoint in an effort to prevent suicidal acts by any adolescent. Since it is widely recognized that a universally common disorder in the suicidal adolescent is depression (Farrell, 1989) and, as demonstrated earlier, that depression correlates so strongly with low self-esteem as a precursor to suicide, we measured the prevalence both of depression and high-ability levels in our delinquent population. The test used for the determination of high mental ability is The Raven's Advanced Progressive Matrices, the third most widely used test of mental ability in the United States. Table 11.14 shows cutoff levels in percentiles for inclusion in the high-ability groups. There are some stunning findings. Table 11.15 displays the number in each group, the mean ages, and breakdown of percentages by gender. The number of detained delinquent males significantly exceeds the number of females.

Comparing the prevalence of depressed and high-ability youths in the one detention center and five learning centers produced higher than expected numbers of each, as shown in Table 11.16.

These data show remarkable consistency between the two groups. It is noteworthy that there is minimally less depression reported in the learning centers than in the detention center. While one might expect this since the initial incarceration in the detention center could, in itself, cause depression, the level of depression remains quite high once the

Table 11.14. Descriptive information for the two delinquent groups studied.

Group	N	Mean Age	Percent Male
Learning center	102	15.7	89%
Detention center	105	15.7	86%

Table 11.15. Prevalence of high ability and depression – detention center.

	Non-Depressed	Depressed	Total
Low and average ability	50.0%	35.7%	85.7%
High ability	7.1%	7.1%	14.3%
Total	57.1%	42.9%	

youths have been placed in learning centers (Table 11.17), and this suggests chronicity.

The coincidence of high ability and depressed versus nondepressed is initially the same for both groups with 7.1% for each in the detention center and 6.1% depressed in the learning center group. The total number of high-ability detainees, with depression or without, is remarkable with 14.3% appearing in the detention center and 13.2% in the learning center. The reader is reminded that we were able to recruit only a small fraction of the approximately 800 learning center detainees, thus the 14.2% and 13.2% respectively, represent a significant finding of previously unidentified high-ability youths and, in fact, may be the tip of the iceberg.

SUMMARY/CONCLUSION

This chapter compares three groups from three separate studies. Two groups were involved in the juvenile justice system and the third group was a comparison group of high school students. Our initial assumptions were that delinquent youths would differ from nondelinquent youths on the instruments used in the study.

Outcomes on the Adjective Checklist (ACL) are distributed over thirty-seven subscales. Of particular interest at this time are the outcomes on several scales showing critical differences on Favorable,

Table 11.16. Incidence of high ability and depression – learning center.

	Non-Depressed	Depressed	Total
Low and average ability	57.6%	29.3%	87.5%
High ability	7.1%	6.1%	13.2%
Total	64.6%	35.4%	

Table 11.17. Performance levels on the Raven's Advanced
Progressive Matrices.

Level of Performance	Detention Center	Learning Center
Below fiftieth percentile	56.0%	63.6%
Above seventy-fifth percentile	44.0%	36.3%
Above ninetieth percentile	14.2%	13.1%
Above ninety-fifth percentile	7.1%	4.0%

Unfavorable, Abasement, Self-Confidence, Personal Adjustment, Ideal Self, Succorance, Aggression, Exhibition, High Origence – Low Intellectance (A-1), High Origence – High Intellectance (A-2), Low Origence – Low Intellectance (A-3) and Low Origence – High Intellectance (A-4).

All three groups scored within the normal range of scores on Favorable, indicating similar favorable feelings about themselves. On the Unfavorable scale, the delinquents scored higher and significantly different from the nondelinquent high school group and higher than other comparable delinquents.

The Abasement scale, indicating inferiority through self-criticism, guilt, or social impotence, was one on which the three groups again scored equally and typically of age peers; thus, one could not differentiate the groups on the basis of these scores. Interestingly, though without statistical significance, the nondelinquent group scored lower than the two delinquent groups.

On Self-Confidence, the two delinquent groups expressed the greatest degree of self-confidence and outscored the nondelinquent group. All three groups were slightly below the mean on Personal Adjustment, but all within the normal range. Although, again, there were no differences between groups, the nondelinquent groups scored lowest, indicating a less positive attitude toward life and the lowest self-esteem level.

The scores on Ideal Self again present a seeming paradox with delinquents scoring highest. High scores on the Ideal Self scale with delinquents higher than nondelinquents raises many questions regarding the perceived well-being of all three groups. It may well be that the delinquents have abandoned traditional goal attainment and thus have higher morale, albeit from what is ultimately a counterproductive lifestyle.

We argued that self-esteem can be linked to Exhibition, Aggression, and Succorance. Our delinquent group scored higher on Aggression than the nondelinquent group and significantly higher on Succorance and Exhibition, indicating lower self-esteem in each instance.

These data, overall, appear to uphold the literature, which supports the low self-esteem/delinquency relationship. The question remains whether the delinquent youths had lower self-esteem prior to entry into the juvenile justice system; however, it appears that self-esteem is not impacted by the delinquent act.

Some quite remarkable findings are shown on the Origence (creativity) – Intellectance (intelligence) scales A-1, A-2, A-3, and A-4. High origence – low intellectance in the high school group was high and significantly higher in the delinquent group. By degree then, one can see the delinquents rejecting conventional lifestyles and adopting a more freewheeling style with a delinquent twist.

On A-2 and A-3, the three are quite closely grouped: with the nondelinquents more on the side of mundaneness, tolerance, and predictability – delinquents being more self-sufficient, original in thought, indifferent to convention, and, in many ways, less complicated than their nondelinquent peers. The A-4 scale clearly differentiates delinquents who scored significantly below the mean and are thus shown to be given to illogical concerns and impulsiveness. These delinquents see themselves as self-serving, impulsive, recognition-seeking, and aggressive and are recognized as such by juvenile justice authorities.

Our findings on the FES scales are parallel with those of the McEachron-Hirsch and Ward data described in Chapter Eight. That is, the nature of family dynamics was influential in determining self-esteem levels. Also, the delinquent groups who were lowest on Cohesion were the ones lowest on self-esteem. The learning center and high school groups who were highest on the FES Conflict scale, were those lowest on self-esteem. In addition, learning center and high school groups demonstrated higher self-esteem in relation to higher scores on the FES Active-Recreational Scale.

The learning center group, in particular, came from families with lower Cohesiveness, lower Cooperation, lower Intellectual-Cultural Orientation, and significantly lower sense of Control within the family. What differentiates the three groups from one another, who appear generally similar, is the contrast in scores by the detention group on Cohesiveness, Confidence, Intellectual-Cultural Orientation, and especially a greatly different score on Control. These low score areas are similar to what one finds in the dysfunctional family.

The Raven's Advanced Progressive Matrices, a nonverbal test of mental ability, shows high-ability youths in the detention center to represent 14.2% of the sample while the learning center population shows 13.1% scoring as high-ability subjects. The cutoff for inclusion as high-ability scorers was set at the eighty-fifth percentile. It is notable that 14.2% of the detention center youths scored above the ninetieth percentile. Clearly, these are significant scores given the low expectations for finding such youths in these settings.

Scores on the Children's Depression Inventory are remarkable for the numbers of delinquent youths in the detention center (42.9%) and learning centers (35.4%) who are positive for psychological depression. The Children's Depression Inventory, regarded as a reliable instrument, points out alarming and consistently high numbers of depressed youths in this survey.

The trend for the prevalence of delinquent youths who were found to score at significant levels for high ability and psychological depression is at least surprising. They were not expected, and none of these characteristics had been previously identified by the public schools from which they came. If we view high ability as an important attribute to be nourished and depression as a mental health problem—particularly for the delinquent population—then, clearly, we need to know more about the extent and depth of the prevalence of both conditions. The implications for social, educational, and mental health professionals deserve serious attention given the previously underestimated relationships between high ability and depression.

We have shown some typical and expected outcomes for the delinquent versus nondelinquent comparison, as well as some clearly unexpected. On the expected side, the less supportive and higher levels of conflict within the family, the more likely one is to see delinquency. Conversely, members of more cohesive families have higher self-esteem, and delinquents, surprisingly, also have high self-esteem in relation to the degree of cohesiveness and conflict. The numbers of undetected high-ability and depressed youths in the delinquent population is truly startling and unexpected. Also noteworthy is the high percentage of males involved in the juvenile justice system.

REFERENCES

Achenbach, T. M. 1982. *Developmental Psychopathology, Second Edition.* New York, NY: John Wiley and Sons.

Bachman, J., P. O'Malley, and J. Johnson. 1978. *Youth in Transition: Vol. VI, Adolescence to Adulthood – Change and Stability in the Lives of Young Men.* Ann Arbor, MI: Institute for Social Research.

Bartell, N. P. and W. M. Reynolds. 1986. "Depression in Self-Esteem in Academically Gifted and Non-Gifted Children: A Comparison Study," *Journal of School Psychology,* 24:55–61.

Bayrakal, S. and T. Kope. 1990. "Dysfunction in the Single-Parent and Only Child Family," *Adolescence,* 25:1–7.

Beck, A. T. 1967. *Depression: Clinical Experimental and Theoretical Aspects.* New York, NY: Harper and Row.

Calhoun, G., Jr., S. Connley, and J. A. Bolton. 1984. "Comparison of Delinquents and Non-Delinquents in Ethnicity, Ordinal Position and Self-Perception," *Journal of Clinical Psychology,* 40(1):323–328.

Carlson, G. A. and D. P. Cantwell. 1982. "Suicidal Behavior and Depression in Children and Adolescents," *American Academy of Child Psychiatry,* 21:361–368.

Chassin, L. and S. Stager. 1984. "Determinants of Self-Esteem among Incarcerated Delinquents," *Social Psychology Quarterly,* 47(4):382–390.

Cole, P. G., L. K. S. Chan, and L. Lytton. 1989. "Perceived Competence of Juvenile Delinquents and Non-Delinquents," *Journal of Special Education,* 23(3): 294–302.

Cornell, D. G. 1992. "High Intelligence and Severe Delinquency: Evidence Disputing the Connection," *Roeper Review,* 14(4):233–236.

Cornell, D. G., M. D. Benedek, and B. A. Benedek. 1987. "Juvenile Homicide: Prior Adjustment and a Proposed Typology," *American Orthopsychiatric Association,* 57(3):383–393.

Delisle, J. R. 1990. "The Gifted Adolescent at Risk: Strategies and Resources for Suicide Prevention among Gifted Youth," *Journal for the Education of the Gifted,* 13:212–229.

Dinitz, S. and B. A. Pflau-Vincent. 1982. "Self-Concept and Juvenile Delinquency: An Update," *Youth and Society,* 14(2):133–158.

Downs, W. and S. Rose. 1991. "The Relationship of Adolescent Peer Groups to the Incidence of Psychosocial Problems," *Adolescence,* 26(102):473–492.

Ehrenberg, M. F., D. N. Cox, and R. Koopman. 1990. "The Prevalence of Depression in High School Students," *Adolescence,* 25:905–912.

Elliott, D. S., D. Huizinga, and B. Morse. 1988. *A Career Analysis of Serious Violent Offenders: Violent Crime.* Ann Arbor, MI: Center for the Study of Youth Policy.

Farrell, D. M. 1989. "Suicide among Gifted Students," *Roeper Review,* 11(3): 135–138.

Farrington, D. 1991. "Psychological Factors in the Explanation and Reduction of Delinquency: Today's Delinquent," in *Juvenile Delinquency: Theory, Practice and Law,* L. J. Siegel and J. J. Senna, eds., New York, NY: West Publishing.

Gelles, R. and M. Strauss. 1988. *Intimate Violence.* New York, NY: Simon & Schuster, p. 27.

Gillis, A. R. and J. Hagan. 1990. "Delinquent Samaritans, Network Structure, Social Conflict, and Willingness to Intervene," *Journal of Research in Crime and Delinquency,* 27:30–51.

Glueck, S. and E. Glueck. 1950. *Unraveling Juvenile Delinquency.* New York, NY: Commonwealth Foundation.

Gone, W. 1985. "The Effect of Age and Gender on Deviant Behavior: A Biopsychoso-cial Perspective," in *Gender and Life Course*, A. S. Rossi, ed., New York, NY: Adline, pp. 115–144.

Gough, H. G. and A. B. Heilbrun. 1983. *The Adjective Checklist: Manual*. Palo Alto, CA: Consulting Psychologists Press.

Harper, J. and E. Marshall. 1991. "Adolescents' Problems and Their Relationship to Self-Esteem," *Adolescence*, 26(104):799–808.

Harvey, S. and K. Seeley. 1984. "An Investigation of the Relationships among Intellec-tual and Creative Abilities, Extracurricular Activities, Achievement and Giftedness in a Delinquent Population," *Gifted Child Quarterly*, 28(2):73–78.

Hirschi, T. and M. Hindelang. 1977. "Intelligence and Delinquency: A Revisionist Review," *American Sociological Review*, 42:571–586.

Hoffman, R. G. and G. L. Davis. 1988. "Factor Analysis of the Tennessee Self-Concept Scale in an Adolescent Sample," *Educational and Psychological Measurement*, 48:407–417.

Kaplan, H. 1980. *Deviant Behavior in Defense of Self*. New York, NY: Academic Press.

Kaplan, H. B. 1982. "Self Attitudes and Deviant Behavior: New Directions for Theory and Research," *Youth and Society*, 14(2):185–211.

Kauffman, J. M. 1989. *Characteristics of Behavior Disorders of Children and Youth*. New York, NY: Merrill.

Kavaraceus, W. C. 1966. "Programs of Early Identification and Prevention of Delin-quency," in *Social Deviancy among Youth: The Sixty-Fifth Yearbook of the National Society of the Study of Education*, W. W. Wattenberg, ed., Chicago: University of Chicago Press.

Keilitz, I. and N. Dunivant. 1986. "The Relationship between Learning Disability and Juvenile Delinquency: Current State of Knowledge," *Remedial and Special Educa-tion*, 7(3):18–26.

Kendall, D. B. and M. Davies. 1982. "Epidemiology of Depressive Mood in Adoles-cents," *Archives of General Psychiatry*, 39:1205–1212.

Klonoff, R. S. and G. A. Lage. 1991. "Narcissistic Injury in Patients with Traumatic Brain Injury," *Journal of Head Trauma Rehabilitation*, 6(4):11–21.

Klumb, K. J. 1983. "Some Characteristics of Mentally Gifted Children Who Are Difficult to Identify as Such," University of California at Berkeley, CA: Dissertation Abstract International.

Kohut, H. S. 1973. "Thoughts on Narcissistic Rage," *Psychoanalytic Study of the Child*, 27:360–399.

Lajoie, S. P. and B. M. Shore. 1981. "Three Myths? The Over-Representation of the Gifted among Dropouts, Delinquents, and Suicides," *Gifted Child Quarterly*, 25(3):138–141.

Lehr, J. B. and H. W. Harris. 1988. *At Risk, Low Achieving Students in the Classroom*. Washington, D.C.: National Education Association.

Leroux, J. A. 1986. "Suicidal Behavior and Gifted Adolescents," *Roeper Review*, 9(2):77–79.

Leung, K. and F. Drasgow. 1986. "Relation between Self-Esteem and Delinquent Behavior in Three Ethnic Groups: An Application of Item Response Theory," *Journal of Cross-Cultural Psychology*, 17(2):151–167.

Leung, K. and S. Lau. 1989. "Effects of Self-Concept and Perceived Disapproval of

Delinquent Behavior in School Children;' *Journal of Youth and Adolescence,* 18(4):345 – 357.

Lief, N. P. and J. Zarin-Ackerman. 1980. "Sociocultural Deprivation and Its Effects upon the Development of the Child;' in *Child Development in Normality and Psychopathology,* J. R. Bemporad, ed., New York, NY: Bruner-Mezel.

Loeber, R. and M. Stouthamer-Loeber. 1986. "Family Factors as Correlates and Predictors of Juvenile Conduct Problems and Delinquency;' in *Crime and Justice: An Annual Review of Research, Vol. 7,* M. Tonry and N. Morris, eds., Chicago, IL: University of Chicago Press, pp. 29 – 151.

McCarthy, J. and D. Hoge. 1984. "The Dynamics of Self-Esteem and Delinquency;' *American Journal of Sociology,* 90(2):396 – 405.

Moos, R. H. and B. S. Moos. 1986. *Family Environment Scale (FES): A Social Climate.* Palo Alto, CA: Consulting Psychologists Press, Inc.

Moos, R. H. and E. G. Trickett. 1987. Classroom Environment Scale Manual, Second Edition. Palo Alto, CA: Consulting Psychologists Press.

Murphy, D. M. 1986. "The Prevalence of Handicapping Conditions among Juvenile Delinquents;' *Remedial and Special Education,* 7:7 – 17.

Nelson, W. M., III, P. M. Politano, A. J. Finch, Jr., N. Wendel, and C. Mayhall. 1987. "Inventory: Normative Data and Utility with Emotionally Disturbed Children;' *American Academy of Child and Adolescent Psychiatry,* 26:43 – 48.

Oyserman, D. and H. R. Markus. 1990. "Possible Selves and Delinquency;' *Journal of Personality and Social Psychology,* 59(1):112 – 125.

Oyserman, D. and H. R. Markus. 1990. "Possible Selves in Balance: Implications for Delinquency;' *Journal of Social Issues,* 46(2):141 – 157.

Page, R. A. 1991. "Loneliness as a Risk Factor in Adolescent Hopelessness;' *Journal of Research in Personality,* 25:195 – 198.

Reckless, W., S. Dinits, and B. Kay. 1957. "The Self-Component in Potential Delinquency and Potential Non-Delinquency;' *American Sociological Review,* 22:556 – 570.

Robertson, I. 1988. *Sociology.* New York, NY: Worth.

Rosenberg, M. 1965. *Society and the Adolescent Self-Image.* Princeton, NJ: Princeton University Press.

Rosenberg, M., C. Schooler, and C. Schoenbach. 1989. "Self-Esteem and Adolescent Problems: Modeling Reciprocal Effects;' *American Sociological Review,* 54:1004 – 1018.

Snarr, R. W. and B. I. Walford. 1985. *Introduction to Corrections.* Dubuque, IA: William. C. Brown.

Stager, S., L. Chassin, and R. D. Young. 1983. "Determinants of Self-Esteem among Labeled Adolescents;' *Social Psychology Quarterly,* 46(1):3 – 10.

Steinberg, L., N. Mounts, and S. Lamborn. 1991. *Journal of Research on Adolescence,* 1(1):19 – 36.

Tannenbaum, S. 1982. "The Self and Youthful Deviance: Some Comparative Notes;' *Youth and Society,* 14(2):235 – 254.

Terman, D. M. 1975. "Aggression and Narcissistic Rage: A Clinical Elaboration;' *Annual of Psychoanalysis,* 3:239 – 255.

Thompson, W. E. and R. A. Dodder. 1983. "Juvenile Delinquency Explained? A Test of Containment Theory;' *Youth and Society,* 15(2):171 – 194.

Tishler, C. L., P. C. McHenry, and K. C. Morgan. 1981. "Adolescent Suicide Attempts: Some Significant Factors," *Suicide and Life Threatening Behaviors*, 11:86−92.

Weisse, D. E. 1990. "Gifted Adolescents and Suicide," *The School Counselor*, 37:351−357.

Wells, L. E. 1989. "Self Enhancement through Delinquency: A Conditional Test of Self Derogation Theory," *Journal of Research in Crime and Delinquency*, 26(3): 226−252.

Wells, E. L. and J. H. Rankin. 1983. "Self-Concept as a Mediating Factor in Delinquency," *School Psychology Quarterly*, 46(1):11−22.

Weston, D. L. 1958. "Motor Activity and Depression in Juvenile Delinquents," *Boston University Dissertation Abstracts International*.

Wiatrowski, M. D., S. Hansell, C. Massey, and D. Wilson. 1982. "Curriculum Tracking and Delinquency," *American Sociological Review*, 47:151−160.

Willerman, L. and D. B. Cohen. 1990. *Psychopathology*. New York, NY: McGraw Hill.

Windle, M. 1991. "The Difficult Temperament in Adolescence: Associations with Substance Use, Family Support and Problem Behaviors," *Journal of Clinical Psychology*, 47(2):310−315.

Wolf, E. S. 1988. *Treating the Self Elements of Clinical Self Psychology*. Guilford Press.

Zigler, E. 1989. "Addressing the Nations Child Care Crisis: The School of the Twenty-First Century," *American Journal of Orthopsychiatry*, 59:484−491.

CHAPTER 12

The Resilient Ones: Stress and Coping

KAORU YAMAMOTO — *University of Colorado at Denver*

EVEN though most grownups tend to remember childhood as carefree days of fun and laughter, it has actually never been easy for anyone to be young and small anywhere anytime. The particulars may vary, but many experiences give rise in the young to a strong sense of helplessness, worthlessness, and hopelessness. Feelings of fear, anger, guilt, sadness, and loneliness are companions to the child, as familiar as those of pleasure, joy, and happiness. Indeed, some (e.g., Klein, 1977) even argue that our cultural "obsession with happiness slaps masks not only on children but on ourselves as well" (p. 9), and youngsters, "very early in life, long before they learn to read, . . . begin learning the scripts of what they perceive as being 'acceptable' expression of self" (p. 8). Most adults want and expect children to be happy all the time and try to shield them from threatening events, disturbing experiences, and, most of all, their (i.e., children's) own unsettling feelings. However, a more helpful approach is to assist youngsters to prepare better for inevitable eventualities of life and to provide support and guidance whenever and wherever needed.

WINDS AND WAVES OF LIFE

The concept of "stress" was borrowed from physical sciences by a medical researcher, Hans Selye (born in Vienna in 1907 and died in Canada in 1982), and introduced into medical and human sciences. In his usage, an external "stressor," such as shock, injury, illness, crowding, and isolation, triggers the general stress syndrome in the organism, including hormonal and other biological changes. The reaction is uniform regardless of the specific nature of the stressor, as the body mobilizes itself to adapt to any of life's major demands. Because of that, "stress cannot and should not be avoided" (Selye, 1978, p. 63). However, some stress, called eustress, is more pleasant and much less damaging than the other, unpleasant variety, namely, distress.

Over the years, the cumulative effects of both categories of stress cause inevitable wear and tear in a person. In fact, it was Selye's opinion that each individual is born with a fixed amount of "adaptation energy" according to his or her genetic givens. There is only so much of it, and how that person spends it, lavishly or frugally, will make a difference in the style and duration of life itself. Although some people have more adaptation energy than others, the total for any person is limited over the life span, just as the maximum capacity of a particular reservoir.

A better analogy appears to be a shallow well that must periodically replenish itself from the groundwater. Here, what is fixed is not only the maximum total water supply over the life of the well, but also the amount of immediately available supply at any one time (i.e., for a given interval of shorter duration). For that specific interval, therefore, water may be quickly exhausted unless reasonably husbanded. This sort of analogy seems to fit the results of studies conducted by some medical researchers like Rahe and Holmes (see, e.g., Dohrenwend and Dohrenwend, 1984; Gunderson and Rahe, 1974), who developed the idea of the Life Change Unit (LCU), or an index of the amount of change involved in differing life events and the extent of the required readjustment. These experiences touch upon all sorts of personal, social, and work aspects of adult life, including both typically desirable "eustress" events (e.g., marriage, outstanding personal achievement, and vacation) and undesirable "distress" ones (e.g., death of spouse, detention in jail, and being fired from work). Using marriage as the arbitrary standard that represents fifty life change units, each experience was assigned a value proportionate to the *perceived* intensity of needed adjustment and the time it takes for accommodation. Predictably, experiences like the death of spouse (100 LCUs), divorce (73), jail terms (63), and personal injury or illness (53) were judged high in their demand on adaptation energy, but, in agreement with Selye's idea, some of the more joyous and pleasant occurrences were also seen as being not without stress. Some examples in this category were marriage (50 LCUs), retirement (45), gain of new family member (39), outstanding personal achievement (28), vacation (13), and Christmas (12).

A fascinating result of this research with adults has been that, irrespective of the particular combination, the more LCUs people accumulate through various life events, the more likely they have certain major health changes within a couple of years following those experiences. The health changes in question include such varied illnesses as heart disease, tuberculosis, skin disease, severe tonsillitis, depression, and hernia. The greater the life change, the greater the vulnerability and the more serious the disease. In other words, to return to my preferred analogy, when the water in the well has been drained for whatever reasons, no additional supply can be obtained in short order. The less the reserve at any given moment (and, of course, the less the remaining total supply for the life of the well), the more at risk the user of the well.

Needless to say, what may hold true for a large number of people, seen from the outside, does not necessarily apply to given individuals. In fact, no single person in the flesh and blood enacts any descriptions of the typical or the average. Exceptions to the rule and deviations from the norm are always to be expected, since everyone lives in his or her own world and behaves in view of that singular reality. An individual remains more or less unpredictable precisely because one can, and does, show variations even within oneself across time and space—that is to say, variations according to the contexts perceived and defined from the inside.

View from the Inside

How, then, do youngsters themselves look at the winds and waves in their lives? For a few years now, my associates and I have been studying the question by asking children about certain familiar experiences that are likely to be upsetting to them. Naturally, there had been several earlier studies on the subject of disturbing experiences among youngsters. Interestingly, however, all of them had decided on the possible stressfulness to children *by first asking adults* like pediatricians, psychiatrists, social workers, teachers, and mothers. In contrast, our inquiry was motivated by the suspicion that what grownups see and judge from the outside might not be the same as what children feel and think inside. So, we simply described twenty events in the family, school, and general contexts to children and asked for them to rate how upsetting each was to them, individually. The scale for the rating ranged in value from "the most upsetting" (rated 7) to "the least upsetting" (rated 1).

Initially, there were still some reservations in our mind as to whether children really know themselves well enough to be able to give us dependable responses. However, the results of our studies with youngsters mostly of the primary-elementary ages suggested that their judgments are both discriminating and stable over time. Not only that, there appeared to be a rather close agreement among children in spite of some variations in ratings according to their sex, grade, social class, and ethnic group. Such differences were small in contrast with the remarkable, overall similarity among all children, amounting to about 95% overlap in response variance (Yamamoto, 1979; Yamamoto and Byrnes, 1984, 1987).

Typically, and perhaps predictably, ..ie loss of parent turned out to be the most upsetting experience, closely followed by such events as the loss of sight and parental fights, all suggestive of concerns with one's fundamental security, in the sense of both individual welfare and the stability of the family. At the other end were found, somewhat surprisingly, such events as the arrival of a new baby sibling and a visit to the dentist. Of course, this does *not* necessarily mean that these experiences are not upsetting in themselves, only that, among the particular twenty events considered one by one at a given point in the young life, some others would be seen as more serious in children's minds.

By now, the scope of our study has expanded to include several thousand children of preschool to junior high school ages in such diverse countries as the U.S., Canada, England, Egypt, Japan, the Philippines, Australia, Iceland, Poland, and South Africa. The characteristic results are shown in Table 12.1, summarizing findings from six countries (Yamamoto et al., 1987). Here again, in spite of some variations in detail among children of these widely separate nations, what has stood out in the findings is the remarkably close, overall agreement in their assessments of the selected life events in terms of how upsetting an experience each event is (see Table 12.2 from the same source).

In fact, the extent of the accord revealed is such that we may seriously consider the possibility that there exists what can be called the culture of childhood, which overlaps rather little with the prevalent adult life circle. Because all these youngsters are children in a contemporary world, their perceptions and experiences of more or less upsetting everyday events seem to reveal much that is common, regardless of specifically where and how they are growing up. It was revealing to learn in another study (Yamamoto and Felsenthal, 1982) that, while children showed themselves to be of one mind in judging the stressfulness of these experiences, their assessments were not well second-guessed by even knowledgeable adults such as clinicians and teachers. The overlap between these children's views and the adult opinions was only about 46%. The irony is that the different subgroups of adults, whether specialists or not, were themselves nicely in agreement with each other.

Table 12.1. Scale values of children's ratings on stressfulness of life events.[1]

Life Event	Egypt	Canada	Australia	Japan	Philippines	USA(a)	USA(b)
Losing parent	6.88	6.88	6.92	6.90	6.76	6.90	6.76
Going blind	6.83	6.75	6.83	6.68	6.70	6.86	6.58
Academic retainment	6.83	6.32	5.94	6.78	6.21	6.82	6.30
Wetting in class	6.73	6.17	6.58	6.73	5.43	6.74	5.78
Parental fights	6.83	5.57	6.16	6.23	6.32	6.71	6.54
Caught in theft	6.62	5.71	6.08	6.73	4.29	6.63	5.20
Suspected of lying	6.62	5.58	6.04	6.73	5.88	6.53	5.86
A poor report card	6.69	5.46	5.69	6.61	5.57	6.23	5.52
Sent to principal	6.63	4.45	5.11	6.63	3.22	5.75	4.68
Having an operation	6.55	4.35	4.58	5.82	4.28	5.51	4.80
Getting lost	6.52	4.22	5.22	5.01	3.90	5.49	4.52
Ridiculed in class	6.63	4.25	4.67	6.11	6.26	5.28	4.65
Move to a new school	6.52	3.41	4.17	5.21	2.55	4.60	4.09
Scary dream	6.59	3.69	4.63	5.07	4.80	4.08	4.06
Not making 100 on test	6.46	2.94	2.94	5.04	3.15	3.75	4.05
Picked last on team	4.73	3.94	2.40	5.92	3.45	3.30	3.30
Losing in game	5.68	2.79	2.23	4.48	3.33	3.16	2.75
Going to dentist	4.87	2.42	1.43	3.05	2.30	2.73	2.54
Giving class report	3.08	2.98	1.53	2.75	1.78	2.58	2.79
New baby sibling	1.20	1.42	1.18	1.43	1.25	1.27	1.46
N	296	283	191	248	156	367	273
Grade	3–6	7–9	3–8	4–6	5–6	4–6	4–6

Reprinted from Journal of Child Psychology and Psychiatry, 28(6); Kaoru Yamamoto, Abdalla Soliman, James Parsons, and O. L. Davis, Jr., "Voices in Unison: Stressful Events in the Lives of Children in Six Countries," pp. 855–864, 1987, with permission from Pergamon Press Ltd., Headlington Hill Hall, Oxford OX3 OBW, U.K.

383

Table 12.2. Correlations among scale values.

	Egypt	Canada	Australia	Japan	Philippines	USA(a)	USA(b)
Egypt	—	0.70*	0.79*	0.87*	0.73*	0.83*	0.80*
Canada		—	0.93*	0.88*	0.88*	0.95*	0.96*
Australia			—	0.87*	0.86*	0.98*	0.96*
Japan				—	0.81*	0.91*	0.88*
Philippines					—	0.85*	0.90*
USA(a)						—	0.97*
USA(b)							—

*$p < 0.01$.

Reprinted from *Journal of Child Psychology and Psychiatry*, 28(6); Kaoru Yamamoto, Abdalla Soliman, James Parsons, and O. L. Davis, Jr., "Voices in Unison: Stressful Events in the Lives of Children in Six Countries," pp. 855–864, 1987, with permission from Pergamon Press Ltd., Headington Hill Hall, Oxford OX3 OBW, U.K.

These findings supported Anthony's comments (1974, p. 106) that stress as experienced by the child may be of quite a different order than stress as estimated by the watching adult.

In other words, an outside-in view of a person's world often does not coincide with an inside-out view by the same person. When seen from the inside, children's life among the giants is not the mirror image of the adult life or what grownups have come to depict out of their selective memories and romanticizing tendencies.

Being Abandoned

As noted above, certain events were rather uniformly perceived to be quite upsetting, regardless of whether being actually experienced by a given child and also irrespective of how prevalent such an experience is in a particular group. The loss of parent was obviously one such event, being rated no less than 6.76 (out of the maximum 7) by any group of children, thus being invariably at the top in stressfulness on the list of twenty life events. What needs to be recognized, however, is that the core experience of loss itself is the source of stress, notwithstanding the specific form that a particular loss may take, e.g., parental death, separation, divorce, desertion, or sickness. Indeed, much more routine situations, like an unintended neglect due to a chronic parental illness or a preoccupation with work, may rival or even surpass in psychological impact such dramatic instances or loss as a sudden death or bitter divorce. Another prevalent, yet mostly hidden, form of losing a parent would be a typically unconscious parental rejection of the child.

From the child's perspective, what appears to be a major, underlying concern is being abandoned and all alone in an unknown, rather frightening world. Even among preschool-age children, this potential source of distress was readily detectable (Dibrell and Yamamoto, 1988). When we stop to think about it, children are, for both physical and social reasons, so very dependent upon grownups that this pervasive concern should come as no surprise.

This feeling of being isolated and helpless in a potentially hostile world constitutes one's "basic anxiety" (Horney, 1937), and that is what underlies much of our inner conflicts and interactional difficulties. For a long time in the course of human development, a person's fundamental sense of security hinges upon the ready availability of benign, caregiving adults, particularly parents. To most children, therefore, "hearing [one's] parents quarrel and fight" would understandably be a very unsettling experience, and their responses indeed bore that out.

The basic anxiety is pervasive and touches upon every facet of one's life, connecting all the experiences big and small, remote and immediate. As Fromm observed (1970, p. 104), while as an animal *Homo sapiens* is most afraid of dying, as a human being he or she is most afraid of being totally alone. That ordeal of being utterly alone does not necessarily have to be abstract and existential in nature. Among children, the experience can be quite literal as in "getting lost in some strange place."

Another event that often has negative impact on the child's sense of security is "moving to a new school." The fact that this experience typically found itself in the midrange on the scale of 1 to 7 should not lull us to underestimate its potential to make children's lives miserable. Many go through a difficult time before, during, and after a move, and quite a few believe that their development has been deeply affected ever since. Yet another study of ours, on the "invisible" children in the classroom (Byrnes and Yamamoto, 1983), gave indications of such long-range effects. These youngsters are ignored by their classmates and often forgotten even by their own teachers. They are a part of the so-called social isolates but, unlike their more vocal, defiant, and disruptive buddies who are clearly noticed and actively rejected, the invisible ones are simply overlooked and neglected by everybody. They are typically quiet, shy, passive, and compliant. Inconspicuous in many ways, and having few friends, these children are seldom troublemakers. As a matter of fact, even their isolation is not clearly seen.

One of the striking findings of the study was that many of these children had moved about quite a bit since beginning school. The group as a whole averaged one move every year and eight months, while close to one-quarter of them attended as many schools as their years in school (e.g., a fifth grader having attended five or more schools). There are other research results suggesting that changes of school early in a child's life, say, during the kindergarten and primary years, can pose difficulties for the young pupil in his or her later personal-social adjustment and academic progress. The point is that the experience of moving to a new school may spell quite complex dynamics for a youngster with potentially detrimental effects in many ways.

Being Disgraced

Children also fear and detest humiliation as much as any honorable adults. Their ratings of such experiences as "telling the truth, but no one believing me," "wetting pants in class," "being caught stealing something," "receiving a poor report card," and "being laughed at in front of the class" made this quite clear. Meanwhile, another event of which the significance frequently escapes adults is "being kept in the same grade next year." To begin with, the bulk of available research suggests that academic retainment *as such* does not help students to improve upon their school knowledge or learning skills. However, a far more sensitive, and often damaging, factor is the way in which the practice of keeping back a child has been handled by adults involved. Some extra and carefully planned guidance, which is seldom made available to the repeaters in the typical school setting, is obviously needed for any real benefits from retention.

In our study on the "invisible children" (Byrnes and Yamamoto, 1983), we have discovered that, in addition to changes in schools and several other events of early stress, quite a few of these forgotten ones had undergone the trauma of academic retainment. At least 35% of them had repeated grades, the first time usually being early in primary years. Thus, while 25% of the third-grade invisibles were repeaters, the proportion went up to 70% among those in the fifth and sixth grades.

In subsequent studies on retainment (Byrnes and Yamamoto, 1985, 1986), we learned something more about the school dynamics behind this practice. First of all, when we inquired of the parents, teachers, and principals their views on grade repetition, an interesting difference surfaced among the three adult groups. In answering a question about who should have the final say on whether or not a child is to be kept back for another year, 48% of parents said the teacher, and 20% said the parent. In contrasts, 66% of teachers named the teacher, followed by 13% who said the teacher and principal. Of course, principals had their own opinion, and 54% of them said the principal, and 23% named the teacher. While, apparently, many parents kept their faith in teachers, school professionals did not see much use for parents in the decision on nonpromotion. Only about three teachers out of 100 were of the view that the parent should have the final say, and the proportion among principals was lower still.

The most sobering finding, however, was that all adults, regardless of their particular relationship to the child, virtually ignored the young themselves in consideration of retention decision. Thus, *none* of the teachers and *none* of the principals even remotely entertained the idea that perhaps the child in question should be the one who makes the final judgment. Even among the parents, only four out of one thousand would give a voice to the child as the ultimate decision maker. This sort of result brings to the fore the issue of every person's right to decide the matters that most directly affect them. And it is undoubtedly the children who are directly and deeply affected by the experience of retention.

In our studies, we did interview children who had been kept back in the first, third, and sixth grades and also the teachers involved. The topic of conversation was introduced by saying to children: "Some students who need more time to learn spend another year in the same grade. Have you or any of the students in your class ever had that happen?" Interestingly, only 57% of the girls included themselves in the answer, whereas 81% of boys mentioned their own names. While the first-grade girls were the most reticent, there was a general feeling of discomfort in sharing this information.

When asked how they felt about being retained, 84% of these children used such expressions as "sad," "bad," and "upset"; 3% explicitly used the word "embarrassed." To the question of what they felt to be the worst thing about not being promoted, their responses included "being laughed at and teased" (22%), "not being with friends" (16%), "being punished" (14%), "being sad" (10%) and "getting bad grades" (8%). As for how their parents felt about their repeating a grade, 46% replied "mad," 28% said "sad," and 8% felt their parents to be indifferent.

We also inquired how these children had found out that they were going to be retained. The majority (42%) learned their fate only when they saw it on their report card, not when some familiar adults like parents (21%) or the teacher (20%) personally explained to them. The most disturbing were a few instances in which children had not discovered the decision, which surely affects them most directly and deeply, until the following fall when they were turned away from the new classroom full of their old friends!

Unfortunately, interviews with teachers tended to confirm children's perceptions of how academic retainment is typically handled in the school. To be fair, it did not appear to be the case that any such decisions were lightly made. Among the adults concerned, certain procedures were being recognized and followed; however, the care tended to break down where the adult world touches the child world. When asked, "How do you let the children know that they will be repeating a grade?" 60% of teachers said they would leave that, either directly or indirectly, up to the parents. The general assumption seemed to be that the parents naturally know how to explain things and handle emotions, where teachers themselves felt quite uncomfortable. Teachers of younger children were particularly squeamish in discussing nonpromotion with those to be retained and often waited until the very last week of school to bring up the matter. Varied explanations were given to soften the blow, both to the child and to the teacher: "It is only because you missed a lot of school"; "After all, you are much younger than others"; "Oh, you will be the best in the class next year"; "You know how hard second grade work is—you want to do well, don't you?"; and so on.

The same kind of sensitivity was shown in the fall by teachers in their dealings with the repeating students, making a point of concealing the fact of retention and treating the child as anybody else in the class. One unhappy side effect of such well-meaning efforts was that little new or different was done with the nonpromoted ones who are crying out for assorted guidance and help, ranging from a thorough physical-sensory examination, the development of appropriate study skills, the introduction of a different curriculum, the nurturance of motivation to learn, the cultivation of expanded peer relations, a proper resolution of the trauma, to a new sense-making about the whole experience.

Of course, parents are often left in the dark on how to proceed with the parallel tasks at home. In a culture where even a first grader explains retention by saying, "Oh, you mean, flunking?!" and where many children equate nonpromotion with punishment, parents typically end up taking out their own confusion and frustration upon the children, rather than providing support and comfort to the youngsters in their hour of need. In fact, many parents add to the stress of the situation by punishing the child for failing to get promoted—they see their own failure in this shocking, and even unpardonable, act on the part of their offspring. They are hurt, embarrassed, and angry. As humanly understandable as such reactions are, we need to remind ourselves that, if adults felt that way, how much deeper children's pain, humiliation, or anger must be. Their sense of pride and honor has been profoundly affected, and that is indeed a major crisis in their young lives, requiring our full attention and care.

Security and Honor

Even as the general mobility of the American population has increased over the past decades, as the distinctness and stability of communities have decreased, as the average size of the family has shrunk, as more of the parents of both sexes have begun working outside the home, and as the proportion of single-parent families has increased over the past decades, the school has been willy-nilly entrusted with more and more things to do, which were once performed by the family. As a result, the role school plays in children's lives has increased and what takes place in the classroom, in the playground, and on the way to and from school has come to carry more significance in the lives of youngsters.

Unfortunately, in the face of all this, the school experience is a trying one that casts a long shadow on the lives of many children. For one thing, our culture places so much emphasis upon what a person allegedly has in, and does with, her or his brains that any indication, real or supposed, of one's inability to achieve in the academic arena represents a hard blow to the whole sense of personhood. For another, where so much importance is attached to social success, any event that gives rise to the feelings of shame and embarrassment in relation to one's peers has quite negative meanings to the individual, no matter who and how old or young, he or she may be.

In a broader sense, the young are apprehensive of being left isolated, powerless, and helpless. Like adults, children wish to have a basic sense of security in their lives, which, fundamentally, should not be chaotic, arbitrary, or malevolent. They would like to be autonomous, being in reasonable control of their own lives, and, to a certain extent, to be able to foresee the future course of events. Just as grownups, children want to be respectable among, and respected by, their fellow beings. For all its fragility, their sense of personal honor and integrity is of no less import than it is among adults.

It was Sinclair Lewis who remarked that "there are two insults which no human being will endure: the assertion that he hasn't a sense of humor, and the doubly impertinent assertion that he has never known trouble . . ." (1961, p. 358). Similar statements may be validly made of children—it would indeed be an insult if we insisted that they do not understand what goes on in and around them or, more rudely, that they do not know any real trouble in their own realities.

WEATHERING THE STORM

In general, the effects of stressful experience seem to depend upon three things: (1) the duration of the stressor, (2) the intensity of the stressor, and (3) the state of the organism (Torrance, 1965). Regardless of the specific source, a suddenly encountered stressor brings shock to anyone. If the individual quickly and appropriately sizes up the situation, her or his mobilization for handling it would be faster, first by expending much effort until, in time, "a handle on life" has been regained. The duration of stress reaction could accordingly be shorter. However, if the stressor persists so as to bring forth fatigue in the person, an ultimate collapse of some sort may result.

Now, in the unfortunate development towards such a breakdown, the persistence of a stressor may be a result more of what the person has *not* done than of the nature of the stressor itself. There are two forms of such inaction. One is the case of insufficient mobilization where a maximum effort has not been put in at the early stage. When the individual is unable or unwilling to go all out in order to meet the requirement of the situation at the very outset, the challenge remains and continues to drain the person's adaptation energy so that any later major efforts become increasingly more difficult. Things, in other words, get out of hand.

The other form of inaction, closely related to the first, stems from a delay in recognizing the seriousness of the situation. This tendency to ignore signs of trouble and remain inactive has frequently been noted as the major contributor to the magnitude of damage in disasters of all sorts. Regrettably, for example, we can point to many children whose lives have been marred by our delay in noticing and handling early indications of academic, emotional, or behavioral difficulties. Youngsters themselves are unlikely to recognize the sources and nature of their afflictions, but it is nevertheless they who must pay for the cumulative negative effects of such conditions. As time goes on, those who found themselves behind or astray at the outset will see the distance or deviation grow more and more, to make even intensive remedial efforts ineffective.

The same kind of disbelief and denial may be more clearly seen in the typical reaction of parents who are suddenly told that their child has just been injured or killed in an accident. Usually, it takes quite a bit of time before anyone acknowledges the possible veracity of that sort of news, and, even after the whole thing started sinking in, a person is prone to be in a daze, either being apathetic or acting erratically. Such response is a quite natural and acceptable way of dealing with unpleasant and painful situations, since it serves a definite protective purpose in a crisis, buffering the person against the immediate shock and allowing time for proper mobilization. Nevertheless, a medicine in small doses can be a poison in larger amounts. If an individual lingers too long in the reactive (i.e., past-oriented) frame of mind, she or he cannot get into action to take the steps necessary for adaptation, thereby damaging one's own chances for successful reconstruction of life.

One variant of the denial-inaction behavior is the belief in personal immunity or the "not to me" orientation rather common in youngsters — "That may be true for anybody else, but it can *never* happen to *me!*" One often hears this disclaimer of invincibility or omnipotence in relation to the preventive practices against known or potential dangers to health and life. For instance, quite a few people, especially preadolescents to young adults, make light of the possibility of becoming pregnant or contracting venereal diseases or the acquired immunodeficiency syndrome (AIDS) by engaging in sexual acts without taking any precautions. In all such instances, one is inclined to hurt oneself, as well as those close to him or her, by not adopting a proactive (i.e., future-oriented) perspective.

Shape of the Storm

The first factor in how a stressor affects people is its duration. The second is its intensity. Again, there are great variations among individuals and situations, but it is generally known that the experience of mild stress has more of a stimulating influence on performance, while extreme stress typically results in degeneration and collapse. In between, however, the potential effects of stressor intensity seem to be related to its duration. Accordingly, a moderate, yet protracted, stressor may be more damaging than an intense but brief stressor. The continuous highway noise or a loud, all-night party at a neighbor's can be much harder for a studying child to take than occasional blasts of an air hammer or the roar of an overflying jet.

Of course, the prolonged mild stressor may take many different forms in young lives. For instance, *under certain circumstances,* continuous quarrels and fights between parents and the accompanying uncertainty and tension can become harder for growing children to handle than a clear dissolution of the unhappy union. Of course, there is the expected range of views among the young people, since the life context of each individual is different by nature. Still, most who have had first-hand experience with parental divorce could see it coming for a long time. While, looking back, some deplore a lack of reconciliatory efforts on the parts of parents, many prefer not to have seen their beloved parents become increasingly bitter, cantankerous, or warped. Understandably, deep anger and resentment tend to remain for a long time over the major disruption in their lives and so does a strong yearning for the lost love and harmony in the home. As incisively put by an experienced adolescent, one of the key considerations in the whole experience may be that divorcing "parents should be careful not to divorce themselves from their children" (Grollman, 1972, p. 235).

Another example of the potentially unbearable effects of a less intense, yet protracted, stressor may be found in the dread of children, who have sufficiently developed their conscience, of a delayed parental sanction. Both the guilt over the committed, unsavory act itself and the interminable anticipation for the fateful retribution make many children cringe and shake in their boots, wishing for a swift, if severe, justice.

Finally, it should be added that little, if any, stress can be quite tough to take: "It seems that the absence of stress is itself a kind of stress" (Tanner, 1976, p. 25). This has been shown in studies on sensory deprivation in people of all ages, ranging from newborns to older individuals, from survivors of mine disasters to prisoners of war. Even though they would surely complain about their "fussing" parents and protest against "meddling" teachers, youngsters would rather have the bother of such solicitous attention from concerned, "interfering" adults than have nothing but a complete neglect by totally indifferent adults. In fact, if it is of the right kind within certain reasonable bounds, such a stressor may be a welcome sign of adult concern and caring.

State of the Individual

The third, and probably the most critical, factor in how a stressor affects a person is in what state she or he is. Some people crumble in a little crisis, others thrive under a considerable amount of stress, while still others withstand even an extremely harrowing condition. As the magnitude of stress increases, so also does the variation among individuals in ego strength (i.e., the capacity for inner-integration and considered action). With some people, the center holds even in a severe storm, and the person continues to perform appropriately and satisfactorily, staying aware of ever-changing life situations and their varied requirements, and of the available resources within and without himself or herself.

When difficulties arise in facing a storm, there is always some sense of being adrift or of the "loss of anchor" in one's life. The individual does not feel in control any longer. Several conditions appear to be there that commonly give rise to such a debilitating state of affairs. First, there is isolation, or lack of social contact. Since even our notions of who we are and how we are doing depend heavily on social definitions, our reality becomes quite tenuous when we are cut off from others. We certainly feel lonesome, and that is hard enough. Over and beyond that, however, isolation cripples us because we cannot continue to take a bearing for our course of action in the absence of other people's responses. That is why children who withdraw to a marked extent should cause concern in adults. That is also why, as shown in many studies, child abuse tends to be associated with socially isolated parents who are cut off (or who have cut themselves off) from family and community resources and support.

Second, there is confusion. What is missing in this condition is a structure in life—sufficient information organized in a familiar, understandable way. Where established channels do not inform and clarify and where known routines do not work, a person finds himself or herself quite confused and threatened with the situation. Children behave in the same way in the absence of adequate information and guidance given in a manner intelligible to them. For that reason, clear, simple explanations and directions are almost always preferable to a silence or a repeated admonition merely to "Be quiet!" or "Wait!"

Finally, there is the matter of changes in time perspective—in one of two forms. If time is stretched out, the psychological effect would be monotony and boredom, nothing much happening or the same old thing repeating itself with little change. Such sameness dulls one's judgment and induces fatigue. In that way, many children are "bored stiff" with school and looking for some, indeed any, form of excitement.

On the other hand, if time is condensed, the effect would be a feeling of too much, too fast—in other words, overloading. One rushes about frantically, being overwhelmed, never having the gratification of taking time and pursuing a project at one's own pace to some satisfactory closure. Both in and out of school, many children are flitting from one activity to another, and the perpetual spinning wears them down.

Facing Winds and Waves

As hard as we might try, to recall Selye, "Stress cannot and should not be avoided." In the final analysis, an effective functioning of a person hinges upon how well she or he faces and manages life's stresses. To that end, a major portion of adults' assistance should be aimed at better equipping and preparing children to handle daily pressures, frustrations, and conflicts. It is convenient in discussing such adaptive efforts to identify three tiers: (1) defense, (2) coping, and (3) mastery.

The first tier is the mechanism of defense in the face of some outside events or inner conflicts, which are sensed as an imminent danger to oneself. Defense consists mostly of subconscious efforts at self-protection and subsumes quite an array – displacement, rationalization, projection, suppression, repression, regression, identification, compensation, reaction formation, sublimation, etc.

Although typically thought of in unfavorable terms, these mechanisms indeed defend one's self against hurt, anxiety, and disorganization. They are therefore helpful devices, and there is nothing inherently abnormal or harmful about them. However, because of the immediate threat felt by the person, many of these defense approaches have a somewhat desperate, "fight or flight" flavor to them. Perhaps for that very reason, they tend to be rather blindly applied to any and all situations regardless of the timeliness or appropriateness. What starts out to be nice protective efforts may thus end up hurting the self when so used in a rigid, indiscriminate manner. In fact, that is when people start talking about neurotic or psychotic patterns of life.

In contrast, when we speak of the second tier of adaptation, i.e., coping, the element of intentional choice of approach(es) becomes more apparent. Rather than an automatic, knee-jerk response typical in defense, a more problem-solving orientation emerges in coping. In view of the nature of the specific challenge, the particular circumstances, and the resources (both internal and external) at one's disposal, the child may simply elect to face only certain challenges at the time and also choose where, when, and how to handle them. Meanwhile, he or she might avoid, evade, or postpone other difficult tasks or unpleasant confrontations through sleep, apathy, denial, fantasy, fainting, illness, and other ways. The youngster can also reduce the pressure by simply forgetting; by tolerating or changing the situation (e.g., physically restructuring it or mentally redefining one's needs, desires, and roles); by crying, blowing up, doing hard physical exercises, or otherwise venting one's emotions; or by coming to terms with oneself. Naturally, she or he can also work hard at the particular task, striving for a quick solution; find suitable alternatives and devise options; pace oneself for persevering until the right time and resolution come; or give up, either momentarily or for good.

The point is that, in coping, there is an element of novelty in one's approach, required by a situation that defies an application of habitual, reflex-like behavior for solution. Some defense mechanisms may naturally be put to use, but their mobilization is not routine and reactive. Another way of putting this is to say that, in coping, a certain strategic-tactical perspective, a more forward-looking orientation, is in evidence.

In facing a difficult, unpleasant, or boring experience, people often change it into a game or contest of some sort. Also, humor has always been an effective way to change a harrowing or socially awkward situation into something manageable. Similarly, diversion of one sort or another helps, not only as a way of brief escape and recuperation but also as a means of changing pace and varying outlook.

Often some ingenious ideas come out of distancing oneself from a preoccupation with a problem and trying out something different. A reassessment of the situation and of oneself is helpful most of the time — we may not actually need what we thought indispensable, since there is usually more than one way to reach a destination. No child has to be a success or ''number one'' all the time. Most everybody can be a leader in certain matters, if not in all. The child does not have to do everything by himself or herself either. As a matter of fact, working with and through others frequently brings better results. Sometimes, meanwhile, a simple retreat may be both necessary and desirable. Each context is different and, thus, demands a somewhat novel way of coping. What should be remembered is that no single approach is in and of itself right or wrong, superior or inferior — it all depends.

Interestingly, but not surprisingly, many of these same coping approaches have helped people handle even very drastic circumstances such as the Nazi death camps. For example, Frankl (1978) has incorporated in his ''logotherapy'' some relevant ideas from his survival experience at Auschwitz. One is self-detachment, which is a uniquely human capacity to detach oneself not only from a particular life situation but also from oneself. This distancing, so to speak, may be seen in some heroic conduct under even the worst conditions, but it can also reveal itself equally in simple, everyday humor. Closely related is the notion of self-transcendence, in which one gets deeply concerned with somebody other than oneself. This, obviously, is the opposite of self-absorption, and even young children have often shown this quality in crises. Self-transcendence may be thought of as lifting oneself up above the mundane level of existence with which one tends to be preoccupied.

This image brings us to the third tier of adaptive efforts, namely, that of mastery. When the distancing (self-detachment) is coupled with the lifting (self-transcendence), a person finds himself or herself on a higher plane looking back and down upon the particular life scene as if she or he were somebody else who is not so deeply absorbed in its immediate demands and concerns. That higher perch gives the person a clearer view of the whole situation and allows an opportunity to approach the tasks and challenges more thoughtfully and to deal with them better. Again, even youngsters can reveal this mature perspective.

In mastery, the strategic orientation becomes even more salient than in coping. One becomes increasingly more autonomous, thus not merely reacting to external demands as they arise but also acting upon life's circumstances on one's own accord. The person stays in touch with what goes on in the surroundings, anticipates and even initiates changes, monitors the course of events, and strives for a gradual movement towards virtuosity in the handling of life situations and towards higher and higher levels of human maturity. Even as the individual carries a heavy burden herself or himself, the person's sphere of concern encompasses the fate of her or his fellow travelers. Even in the darkest moments, such a person reveals much will, hope, faith, and compassion, reaching out to others, making order out of chaos, and grasping the big picture spanning the past, present, and future.

It is important to keep in mind that, just as coping does not simply mean executing more defenses well, mastery does not mean mobilizing more coping approaches and applying them better. It is not merely a matter of doing the same coping more skillfully, but also, and more critically, that of climbing to a higher viewpoint and seeing farther. Any action here reflects that broader perspective and reveals a keener and deeper sense of what it means to be human. Over and beyond defense and coping, which are anchored more in the past and present, mastery adds something of a "seeing into the future" dimension. In grasping the whole picture, one transcends the here and now, as well as one's self and group (of all sizes and varieties), so that his or her caring now touches a far broader circle, even the whole of humanity. One becomes aware of immortality and senses the ultimate meaning of life.

Needless to say, such mastery does not come easily to most of us, even as we learn and practice every day the exquisite, creative art of living. Fortunately, nevertheless, there have been enough good artists of life among us, though mostly unsung, to show that the feat is within reach of all, young and old. The loftiest deeds of human valor and compassion have also been frequently revealed in the midst of some of the starkest events, the worst storms, in human history to give us courage and inspiration.

BEING COMPETENT AND PREPARED

Styles of adaptation developed early in life, even during the first six months, continue to be used for a long time. Approaches learned in early childhood tend to play a dominant role in emergencies, while those stemming from later experiences play a stronger role in handling stress over time. Although it is probable that differences exist among people in their genetic endowment (e.g., the adaptation energy, physiological capacity, and temperamental dispositions), most of the contrasts in how they approach and manage stress are likely to be a result of learning in the course of development within a given sociocultural environment. "Child-rearing then is not just a matter of taking care of the baby and the young child . . . but of supporting the child's efforts to take care of himself" (Murphy and Moriarty, 1976, p. 348). The sense of competence, as well as a sufficiently large repertoire of coping approaches, cannot be built overnight. No adaptive action, big or small, can suddenly take place without the necessary spadework by adults and children together in anticipation of stressful occurrences. It is probable that, even more acutely than in adults, unnamed perils and unseen dangers aggravate the fear of young children. Without careful guidance and support from concerned grown-ups, the familiar apprehension can easily give way to all sorts of mistaken beliefs and interpretations, unbearable anxiety and dread, and even out and out panic.

To Be Prepared

It helps everyone to be prepared, both emotionally and cognitively, for what is (or might be) coming his or her way. The preparation does not have to be (and probably should not be) full of details—after all, one does not need to know all there is to know about disasters to be duly warned of them and informed of what to do just in case. It has more to do with giving a child a general notion of the lay of the land, so to speak, or a suitable frame of reference for an unknown occurrence or a rough idea of what the experience is like, what it is about. That goes a long way in preventing the individual from feeling lost and overwhelmed when the event arrives and, thus, his or her coping mobilization can be so much quicker and more appropriate.

An interesting example of the application of this sort of outlook can be seen in new preparatory efforts in France, Canada, and elsewhere. In a Marseille hospital, for instance, children who are expecting a surgery will first witness their beloved teddy bear undergo a similar operation under the scalpel of real doctors. The youngsters themselves are no mere bystanders. Wearing paper surgical masks and boots, they actually ''assist'' surgeons in many of the relevant medical procedures. This arrangement not only provides children with an opportunity to form a rough idea of what is to come and why, but also allows them to reveal their emotions and allay their anxieties. Moreover, when the little patient reaches the recovery room after her or his own operation, the trusted bear, who courageously went ahead and is now fully recovered, will be waiting there for the child.

To be effective, obviously, any preparation must be based upon the steady foundation of a close child-adult relationship, built over time upon countless interactions of a sensitive and satisfying nature. Ironically, no ''crisis'' reactions and no ''emergency'' measures can manage real crises and emergencies well. What is needed is an ongoing education, in which proper cognitive skills and knowledge are integrated with deep and secure effect. Most children are understandably afraid of being alone, apprehensive of what lies ahead, and uncertain of what they can do. They remain fundamentally dependent upon grownups for a long time, and find themselves vulnerable in the face of upsetting events and unpredictable developments. Often they wait—wait until something happens, wait until an adult intervenes. They think of dire possibilities, realistic or otherwise. Too often, they must persevere and persist alone in the face of the unknown and overwhelming.

Adults can render assistance by providing an anchor so as not to leave children at the mercy of the waves of powerlessness, helplessness, and hopelessness. They can shed a light in the darkness of the young's struggle by offering some suitable explanations of ongoing or anticipated events so as to give them some ideas, some ''handles.'' Likewise, they can clarify and accept the accompanying emotions so as to assure children that there is nothing wrong about feeling scared, sad, lonely, or angry, and even about crying a bit.

Grown-ups can also help by suggesting some concrete things to do, and practicing them with the child, for such common circumstances of real or potential danger as when lost, when hurt, when trapped in an elevator, when power (electricity) goes out, when caught in a house fire, and when parent falls ill or gets hurt. It would, of course, be the best if everybody knew exactly the right thing to do in dire situations, but, even short of that, it is much better for people, young and old alike, to have some simple thing(s) to do other than standing around idle, feeling lost,

powerless, and helpless. In addition to any practical benefits that may
or may not follow, such actions give the young something definite and
familiar to do and help focus their minds on the task(s) and off the straits
they are in. The principle is very simple — so long as a child, or anybody
else, can *act,* can do something, in no matter how limited a manner, the
person feels more the master of his or her fate than a slave, and that sense
of self-control and self-confidence serves as a good antidote for fright,
panic, and chaos.

Against the supportive and orienting backdrop of security offered by
grown-ups, children may further develop and try out their own skills of
understanding and coping. A thoughtful preparation needs to become a
continuous way of life, a general style of living. The whole thing begins
in the family, to be expanded and sustained in the school, community,
and other social groups and institutions. The basic tenet remains the same
everywhere: "Children all over the world, living in their own sea of
troubles, can find a true haven only in these institutions [the family,
school, hospital, etc.] that treat their concerns about life and death as
both real and manageable" (Schwartz, 1982, p. 419). Like anyone else,
youngsters want to be taken seriously, and they indeed deserve to be so
treated with basic respect.

The Resilient Ones

Of course, no one handles every situation equally well, and there are
also wide variations among children, as well as in adults, in the proficiency of adaptation. Some appear to be more adept than others at coping
with life's demands, and have the capability not only to succeed better
but also to fail better, in the sense that they turn bad things into good
things. In recent years, some studies have been done with such children
often called invulnerable, invincible, undefeated, resilient, or stress-
resistant. A question of obvious interest is, "What makes them that
way?" Needless to say, no simple, single answer is likely to be found,
and little is to be gained by debating how much is due nature (the
biological-genetic givens) and how much is due nurture (the childrearing
and other cultural influences). The child grows and develops in the
complex interactions of both, and adults' help has to be applied where
it can.

Some pertinent observations on parental attitudes may be gleaned
from a couple of research projects: "The parents of good copers neither

indulged their children nor overprotected them. They respected their children's capacities, encouraged and rewarded their efforts, and offered reassurance in times of frustration and failure'' (Murphy and Moriarty, 1976, p. 349). Another says, ''The parents of the invulnerable child are not less protective, but less anxious, than average parents and more likely to leave matters to the child himself. . . . The parents of the invulnerable child are not less loving, but less possessive, than the average and more likely to allow the child his own territorial imperatives in which he can operate fairly autonomously'' (Anthony, 1974, pp. 541−542).

Not surprisingly, the influence of any disturbing events at the moment needs to be looked at in relation to the long background of a person's life. Some experiences and arrangements in that background (the protective factors) may serve to buffer or reduce the negative effects of stressor. While others (the vulnerability factors) may aggravate such effects. A family climate of support, stability, and cohesion can, in fact, be an example of protective factor. According to Rutter (1988, p. 24), ''Good personal relationships and social supports may mitigate the effects of stressful life events, and . . . a lack of such intimate relationships increases the adverse effects of stressors.'' Garmezy (1987) adds that children with greater ''assets'' like higher intelligence, higher socioeconomic class, and family attributes of stability and cohesion appear to be more competent and, when under pressure, less disruptive in the classroom and better socially engaged with their peers.

Now, a study that began in 1954 followed the development of close to 650 children born during the year 1955 on the island of Kauai, Hawaii, for the following three decades. The majority were of Asian and Polynesian heritage, and more than half came from poor homes. Due to unfavorable conditions and complications before and around birth, family instability and chronic lack of resources, low parental schooling level, psychiatric problems in some parents (about 4%), and the rapid social changes on the island, the group of children as a whole was regarded to be at risk at birth and long thereafter. Predictably, one out of every five youngsters revealed serious behavioral or mental health difficulties at some time during the second decade of life.

Nevertheless, one in ten ''managed to develop into competent and autonomous young adults who 'worked well, played well, loved well, and expected well,' '' in the words of Werner and Smith (1989, p. 153). These authors pointed to three clusters of factors that may account for the resiliency of these invincible ones: (1) positive disposition of the child (active, good-natured, responsive, autonomous, etc.) and adequate intellectual and communication skills; (2) supportive family environment (smaller family size, close parent-child relationship, additional family caregivers besides mother, clear household structures and rules, a sense of family cohesion, etc.); and (3) external ties with wider community (close peers, supportive neighbors and elders, trusting and trusted teachers, coaches, and ministers, access to social services, etc.).

Among the family environmental factors mentioned, the significance of the availability of extra caregivers was underscored by Werner and Smith (1989, pp. 76–77) as follows: "When other adults (than the primary caregiver) are present in the household as child-rearing agents, children the world over tend to receive a fair amount of warmth. . . . Accepted children, throughout the world, tended to be more self-reliant than rejected children . . . a trend we observed among the resilient children in our own study." Further, they noted that the resilient girls themselves had "tended to assume the care of yet younger children, and with it a greater sense of responsibility and competence" (p.78) and added that "child caretaking appears to be an important antecedent to nurturant and responsible behavior that leads to strong bonds" (p. 160).

The warmth and responsiveness of early life setting are thus related to the nurturing of a sense of competence and self-reliance. That, in turn, helps develop a critical perspective in adolescence, as noted by Werner and Smith (1989, pp. 88–89) of their eighteen year olds: "Achievement and psychological well-being appeared to be closely related to what the youth [especially girls] believed about their environment—whether they believed, as the resilient ones did, that the environment would respond to reasonable efforts, or whether they believed as the youth with serious coping problems did, that it was random and immovable." Finally, one sees the same orientation and capability persisting into young adulthood at age thirty-two: "Most resilient individuals who had coped successfully with adversity in childhood and adolescence are also competent in coping with their adult responsibilities" (Werner, 1989, p. 78).

Literally and figuratively, therefore, it appears that a solid foundation laid early in life can sustain a person well through numerous tempests of life. Some of these storms have been extreme in their ferocity to push the test of endurance to the limit. Thankfully, some people have not only survived but, indeed prevailed over such ordeals to give credence to the human qualities we all desire. A hopeful thing is that we can help children prepare themselves properly for the winds and waves of life they should expect to face. That is our opportunity, and that is our challenge.

ENDNOTE

1 The first group of youngsters (a) numbered 367 in total – 84 in the fourth grade, 143 in the fifth, and 140 in the sixth. There was a half-and-half split between girls and boys, and 83% were non-Hispanic white, 9% Hispanic, and 7% black. These children were mostly of middle-class families, living in a Southwestern metropolis of one million population. The second group (b) had 273 in it, 49% being girls – 91 in the fourth grade, 81 in the fifth, and 101 in the sixth. They were from middle- and working-class homes in a Southcentral city of 50,000, and three-fifths were of Hispanic heritage.

REFERENCES

Anthony, E. J. 1974. "The Syndrome of the Psychologically Invulnerable Child," in *The Child in His Family, Vol. 3*, E. J. Anthony and C. Koupernik, eds., New York, NY: John Wiley and Sons, pp. 529 – 544.

Byrnes, D. A. and K. Yamamoto. 1985. "Academic Retention of Elementary Pupils: An Inside Look," *Education*, 106:208 – 214.

Byrnes, D. A. and K. Yamamoto. 1983. "Invisible Children: A Descriptive Study of Social Isolates," *Journal of Research and Development in Education*, 16:15 – 25.

Byrnes, D. A. and K. Yamamoto. 1986. "Views on Grade Repetition," *Journal of Research and Development in Education*, 20:14 – 20.

Dibrell, L. L. and K. Yamamoto. 1988. "In Their Own Words: Concerns of Young Children," *Child Psychiatry and Human Development*, 19:14 – 25.

Dohrenwend, B. S. and B. P. Dohrenwend. 1984. *Stressful Life Events and Their Contexts*. New Brunswick, NJ: Rutgers University Press.

Frankl, V. E. 1978. *The Unheard Cry for Meaning*. New York, NY: Simon and Schuster.

Fromm, E. 1970. "Psychoanalysis and Zen Buddhism," in *Zen Buddhism and Psychoanalysis*, E. Fromm., D. T. Suzuki and R. de Martino. New York, NY: Harper Colophon Books, pp. 77 – 141.

Garmezy, N. 1987. "Stress, Competence, and Development," *American Journal of Orthopsychiatry*, 57:159 – 174.

Grollman, E. 1972. *Explaining Divorce to Children*. Boston, MA: Beacon Press.

Gunderson, E. K. E. and R. H. Rahe. 1974. *Life Stress and Illness*. Springfield, IL: Charles C. Thomas.

Horney, K. 1937. *The Neurotic Personality of Our Time*. New York, NY. W. W. Norton.

Klein, C. 1977. *How It Feels to Be a Child*. New York, NY: Harper Colophon Books.

Lewis, S. 1961. *Main Street*. New York, NY: New American Library.

Murphy, L. B. and A. E. Moriarty. 1976. *Vulnerability, Coping, and Growth*. New Haven, CT: Yale University Press.

Rutter, M. 1988. "Stress, Coping, and Development: Some Issues and Some Questions," in *Stress Coping, and Development in Children*, N. Garmezy and M. Rutter, eds., Baltimore, MD: The Johns Hopkins University Press, pp. 1 – 41.

Schwartz, R. E. 1982. "Children under Fire: The Role of Schools," *American Journal of Orthopsychiatry*, 52:409 – 419.

Selye, H. 1978. *The Stress of Life, Revised Edition*. New York, NY: McGraw-Hill.

Tanner, O. 1976. *Stress.* New York, NY: Time-Life Books.

Torrance, E. P. 1965. *Constructive Behavior.* Belmont, CA: Wadsworth.

Werner, E. E. 1989. "High-Risk Children in Young Adulthood: A Longitudinal Study from Birth to 32 Years," *American Journal of Orthopsychiatry,* 59:72 – 81.

Werner, E. E. and R. S. Smith. 1989. *Vulnerable but Invincible.* New York, NY: Adams, Bannister, Cox.

Yamamoto, K. 1979. "Children's Ratings of the Stressfulness of Experiences," *Developmental Psychology,* 15(5):581 – 582.

Yamamoto, K. and D. A. Byrnes. 1984. "Classroom Social Status, Ethnicity, and Rating of Stressful Events," *Journal of Educational Research,* 77:283 – 286.

Yamamoto, K. and D. A. Byrnes. 1987. "Primary Children's Ratings of the Stressfulness of Experiences," *Journal of Research in Childhood Education,* 2:117 – 121.

Yamamoto, K. and H. M. Felsenthal. 1982. "Stressful Experiences of Children: Professional Judgements," Psychological Reports, 50:1087 – 1093.

Yamamoto, K., A. Soliman, J. Parsons, and O. L. Davis, Jr. 1987. "Voices in Unison: Stressful Events in the Lives of Children in Six Countries," *Journal of Child Psychology and Psychiatry,* 28:855 – 864.

CHAPTER 13

Future Directions in Self-Esteem Research: Debunking Myths and Charting New Territory

GAIL McEACHRON-HIRSCH — *The College of William and Mary*

OVER the past few years, when discussing self-esteem research in my college classes, I have occasionally asked students to predict whether certain subgroups, e.g., minorities, women, or individuals in lower socioeconomic levels, might score lower on self-esteem measures. Students surmised that women, minorities, and the poor were inclined to have lower self-esteem given their lower social status. Students are often surprised to find out that empirical studies are inconclusive, making it impossible to make such generalizations, despite the fact that social rankings of racial, religious, and ethnic groups have remained consistent over decades (Rosenberg, 1979).

The tendency to link social norms with personal identities has contributed to the perpetuation of certain myths about the way individuals construct their identities. Eight of these myths were presented in Chapter One as a means to set the stage for the authors' dismantling of the myths, or so-called conventional wisdom. This chapter will illuminate the authors' premises, which debunk the myths and enlighten our understanding of self-esteem and identity formation. In closing, a series of continuing and unanswered questions will be presented, as well as initial steps that may be taken to address them.

MYTH #1: SELF-ESTEEM CAN BE ISOLATED AND MEASURED IN WAYS SIMILAR TO INTELLIGENCE TESTING

In Chapter Six, the Wards critique investigative procedures that purport to measure self-esteem or self-concept without fully explaining or defining the concepts. Their review of the self-esteem literature revealed that there are no consistent or universally accepted definitions of terms, a condition that adversely affects current practice in the helping professions. Without reliable and valid assessment procedures, professionals make treatment plans for children and youth based on insufficient and unreliable assessments.

Likewise, the empirical studies reviewed in other chapters throughout the book revealed many inconsistencies between social expectations, measures of self-esteem and self-concept, collective performances and individual case studies. For example, children's self-portraits revealed developmental patterns, including emotional development, but these normal, healthy, developmental patterns could be disrupted by relationships with parents and teachers. Among adolescents, gradual increases in self-esteem were documented throughout the high school years for large numbers of students, but individual case studies and minorities demonstrated more erratic patterns depending upon events taking place in their homes or classrooms. Self-esteem and self-concept measures in special populations, such as the gifted or juvenile delinquents, for example, defied stereotypical interpretations that the gifted would have higher self-esteem than juvenile delinquents or even that these were mutually exclusive groups.

For the Wards and other authors in the book, the notion that a single measure of self-esteem can be isolated to reflect the essence of one's total Self is a myth. More inclusive frameworks and theories of Self are needed to fully appreciate the meaning of singular and multidimensional assessments. Through their behavioral assessment model the Wards have sought to remove some of the restraints of traditional psychological approaches. Their approach underscores the importance of contextual influences, reflecting what Bruner (1990, p. 106) refers to as a contextual revolution occurring in psychology today. Analyzing notions of Self in the new transactional contextualism, Bruner (1990, pp. 99, 105) proposes that both mind and Self are presented as part of the social world rather than as "a substance or an essence that preexisted our effort to describe it." Bruner proposes that the field of psychology's persistence in converting ontological issues into the nature of knowing resulted in a reliance upon standardized research paradigms to define its own concepts. In time, the paradigms became the operations that defined the concept being studied and tested, whether it was intelligence or Self (Bruner, 1990). According to Bruner (1990, p. 102) each test created "its own disconnected module of research, each to be taken as an 'aspect' of some larger notion of Self that is left unspecified." For Bruner, the initial progress that was being made by psychologists who were formulating more general theories of Self soon became too procedurally limited and insulated.

MYTH #2: WOMEN, MINORITIES, AND THE POOR HAVE LOWER SELF-ESTEEM THAN DO MEN, NONMINORITIES, AND THE AFFLUENT

Results of empirical studies presented throughout the book provided mixed messages regarding the self-esteem of women, minorities, and those in lower socioeconomic levels. The McEachron-Hirsch and Messier longitudinal study, for example, demonstrated no significant differences in self-esteem among male and female adolescents, using the Rosenberg Scale, which assessed global self-esteem. Yet case study interviews revealed that male and female adolescents, and minorities and nonminorities, acknowledged that their identities were differentially created and shaped.

Similar incongruities were found in studies of gifted junior high students. VanTassel-Baska discovered that when the Harter Perceived Self-Competence Scale was administered to junior high students, there were no significant differences in global self-worth, but differences based on gender, race, and socioeconomic status were found on subscales tied to scholastic competence, social competence, and behavior. Again, individual global perceptions of self become more differentiated when self is described in a particular social context.

When social context is also examined on the basis of developmental stages, additional patterns emerge. In studies of psychological adjustment in young children, Yamamoto reported that stress and coping in the lives of children were remarkably similar across six countries in spite of some variations based on gender, social class, and ethnicity. Such findings raise important questions about the traditional approaches to studying self-esteem. Classical sociological approaches that define groups on the basis of social class, roles, and so on need to be balanced by the social, political, and psychological distinctions that people make in their daily lives (Bruner, 1990). Yet attempts to separate the two approaches create perpetual challenges for scholars throughout the social sciences when individual perceptions mask social realities or when social realities mask individual potentialities.

For example, collective measures of global self-esteem may be useful if they reveal important patterns among subgroups, such as those based on gender, age, social class, and ethnicity. When significant differences occur, the results may signify stress or potential problems when scores are exceedingly low, even though the nature of the stress cannot be derived from a global self-esteem instrument. Multidimensional self-esteem instruments, on the other hand, may generate insights into more specific social contexts of well-being, confidence, or feelings of inadequacy but, examined in a compartmentalized fashion, may reveal little about an individual's overall feelings of self-worth and very little still about how the individual perceives societal support for his or her identity formulation. Taken together, measures of global self-esteem and measures of multidimensional self-esteem, in their current conceptualizations, are not sufficiently linked to the processes of social and cultural constructions of identity.

Rosenberg (1979, p. 13) distinguishes between social status and personal identity in *Conceiving the Self,* maintaining that ''one cannot assume a direct conversion of social identity evaluation into self-evaluation . . . [but] one can assume that people *respond* in various ways to the social evaluation of their identity elements.'' Rosenberg's analysis would be considered understated by scholars and feminists such as Catherine MacKinnon who probe further into the interactive forces between social and personal views of the world.

For MacKinnon, an individual's freedom of choice to directly convert or not convert social identification into self-evaluation is more limited than Rosenberg would suggest. In *Toward a Feminist Theory of the State,* MacKinnon (1989, p. 51) criticized Gilligan's (1982) work on gender differences in moral reasoning for failure to situate thought in social reality.

> By establishing that women reason differently from men on moral questions, she [Gilligan] revalues that which has accurately distinguished women from men by making it seem as though women's moral reasoning is somehow women's, rather than what male supremacy has attributed to women for its own use. When difference means dominance as it does with gender, for women to affirm differences is to affirm the qualities and characteristics of powerlessness. Women may have an approach to moral reasoning, but it is an approach made both of what is and of what is not allowed to be. To the extent materialism means anything at all, it means that what women have been and thought is what they have been permitted to be and think. Whatever this is, it is not women's possessive. To treat it as if it were is to leap over the social world to analyze women's situation *as if* equality, in spite of everything, already ineluctably existed.

MacKinnon's critique is not only relevant to any member of society whose identity includes membership in social groups characterized by lower status, but has implications for those who enjoy membership in higher status groups as well. For an identity shaped by power or dominant status over others cannot be denied, however unconscious those factors remain.

When instruments used to measure self-esteem reveal no differences among subgroups such as minorities, women, and the poor, there is a potential for shortsightedness and continued inequality if gender and ethnic discriminatory practices are ignored because individuals within those groups score in the same range as those in positions of power. Yet the fact that there are no differences in self-esteem among minorities, women, and the poor should not be taken lightly either, for the results, assuming the use of valid instruments, refute misinformed claims that members of these groups are lacking in feelings of self-worth. Equally important to achieving individual or subgroup self-worth, however, is the attainment of self-worth in a social context that values equality.

MYTH #3: CHILDREN WHO GROW UP IN INTACT FAMILIES HAVE HIGHER SELF-ESTEEM

Having spent my early years growing up in the 1950s, the image of an Ozzie and Harriet family seemed to hold true for my family and most of the families on the block. My mother and father never divorced, I had an older brother, and I can't remember a time when we didn't have a dog and a cat. When divorce became more commonplace during the 1960s and 1970s, there still seemed to be an aura around the notion of the nuclear family, thus perpetuating certain stigmas toward adults and children who had experienced divorce. When I married into a blended family and attended stepfamily support groups, it became obvious that divorce and remarriage affected individual members in a multitude of ways and that the stigma of divorce masked the underlying crux of family relationships.

In Chapter Eight, the longitudinal study by McEachron-Hirsch and Messier investigated adolescent self-esteem in relation to family structure, concluding that whether students came from an intact, single-parent, foster-parent, blended, or extended family was less of a factor influencing self-esteem than the dynamics within each of the family variations. More important than family structure was whether or not the families were cohesive and experienced an active-recreational orientation. The adolescent case studies, as well as the experience of Susan, an elementary-aged student presented in Chapter Seven, revealed that levels of conflict and cohesion within the family, as well as the nature of parent/stepparent and stepsibling relationships, were salient factors affecting self-esteem and a sense of fit with one's "family."

The importance of family dynamics over family structure is described in the systems theory analyses presented by Gallas and Hardinge in Chapter Five. By delineating the alliances and coalitions that emerge in family systems, largely as a means to compensate for hierarchical confusions, guilt feelings, or a variety of other psychological dispositions, members of families are in a better position to deal with factors that may be influencing self-esteem. One of the benefits of having strong working relationships between families and schools is that factors that may be inhibiting healthy self-esteem in one context may manifest themselves in the other context, thus creating an opportunity for shared reflection and problem solving.

The significance of refuting Myth #3 lies not only in removing the stigma of divorce, but in the importance of understanding how problems that emerge in the classroom may be the result, not only of family dynamics, but a lack of fit between an individual student and family or school systems. Attributing problems to superficial causes, such as family structure, merely reflects the teacher's or the parent's unwillingness to tackle the tough conditions of shared responsibility. In the words of Bruner (1990, p. 47), "The viability of a culture inheres in its capacity for resolving conflicts, for explicating differences and renegotiating communal meanings."

MYTH #4: SMARTER STUDENTS HAVE HIGHER SELF-ESTEEM

Being smart, being valued for being smart, and valuing one's own intelligence are three different conditions. The conditions are shaped by the same social factors that define being average or below average. The social factors are closely tied to three values that have been espoused throughout our educational history, namely pluralism, equality, and individualism, yet the realization of these values has been uneven throughout the American educational system (Bowles and Gintis, 1976; Spring, 1972; Apple, 1986). Social and political response to these disparities has often led to debates that depict the values of pluralism, equality, and individualism as mutually exclusive (Welsh, 1990), prompting educators to defend the viability of attaining several values simultaneously (Greer, 1972; Slavin, 1990). Caught in these debates are the students whose identities are shaped by a system that compartmentalizes and labels them on the basis of what sometimes appears to be social benefits or liabilities. As Hofstadter (1963, p. 305) pointed out in *Anti-Intellectualism in American Life,* ''The American educational creed itself needs further scrutiny.'' Hofstadter maintains that our educational system ''was not founded primarily upon a passion for the development of mind, or upon pride in learning and culture for their own sakes, but rather upon the supposed political and economic benefits of education'' (p. 305).

For example, Harvard psychologist David McClelland proposed in 1969 that a nation's economic prosperity depended upon the predominance of ''personality types characterized as high in *achievement motivation*'' (Gergen, 1991, p. 46). According to Gergen (1991, p. 46), ''McClelland and his colleagues mounted programs to assist economically disadvantaged nations, such as India, in developing this economically essential personality trait.'' Most of the rhetoric in the 1980s, starting with *A Nation at Risk: The Imperatives for Educational Reform,* and the Education for Excellence Movement continuing into the 1990s reflects the same instrumental mentality. Federal funding for selected educational programs has been maintained, in part, by the expressed need to have a competent workforce to compete in the international marketplace. When funding for educational programs is overshadowed by political rhetoric, it is questionable that the educational benefits are completely understood or appreciated. When this happens, programs that are vital to differentiating curricula become vulnerable to the ebb and flow of political platforms.

Similar economic and political motivations can be identified at the state level. When John Vasconcellos (Mecca et al., 1989, p. xv) became head of the California State Assembly's Ways and Means Committee in 1980, he was disheartened to find out that ''billions of tax dollars were spent to contain destructive behaviors, to compensate for human failures after the fact—more than a billion dollars each year for building prisons and two billion for operating them, as well as substantial sums for programs to address alcoholism, drug abuse, teenage pregnancy, child abuse, welfare dependency, and school dropouts.'' After talking with practitioners who cited self-esteem as a factor central to these problems, Vasconcellos spent several years trying to get a bill passed that would legislate money to investigate self-esteem issues. Convincing the governor necessitated that Vasconcellos appeal to his wise sense of fiscal spending: ". . . Think of it this way: By spending a few tax dollars, we can collect the information and get it out. If that helps even a few persons appreciate and understand self-esteem and how they can live their lives and raise their kids better, we may have less welfare, crime, violence, and drugs—and that's a very conservative use of taxpayers' money" (Mecca et al., p. xvii). The governor was convinced and signed the bill that led to the California Task Force on Self-Esteem. The political reality was such that before self-esteem and individual identities could be placed at the forefront to understand better the interrelated factors affecting psychosocial development, a case for economic gain had to be made more explicit. As Losito pointed out in Chapter Two, many contemporary educational goals do not directly address the fundamental problems of individual and social existential anxiety.

Yet the results of a nationwide study indicated that many parents and educators agree that a comprehensive education includes the pursuit of personal, social, intellectual, and vocational development, not strictly academic achievement (Goodlad, 1984). Nearly all of the chapters in this book have demonstrated the inseparability between these various aspects of identity development, despite many of the classifications used by educational institutions. For example, analyses of the populations of gifted students and juvenile delinquents in Chapters Ten and Eleven revealed the superficial polarization between these two groups. The assumption that brighter students will automatically demonstrate higher levels of achievement was questioned by the research conducted by VanTassel-Baska, Messier, and Ward. Students who were expected to perform well in school based upon traditional intelligence measures sometimes became depressed, underachievers, dissatisfied achievers, or juvenile delinquents.

The limitations of responding to students on the basis of only one dimension of their identity, e.g., gifted, delinquent, and so on, can also be seen in the institutional expectations placed on students in special education classes. As Walther-Thomas pointed out in Chapter Nine, bringing the academic performance of special education students in line with the average grade level performance is practically the singular goal of most individual education plans (IEPs). To do otherwise, to examine something as vague as self-esteem when such students have been identified for special education because of specific academic weaknesses, would be perceived as a misuse of taxpayers' money. Again, funding patterns and the structure of educational institutions dictate which aspects of the student will be spotlighted—in some cases individual strengths, in other cases individual weaknesses. Those not singled out seem to represent what society defines as "normal." The assumptions are that the gifted do not have weaknesses, those in special education do not have strengths, and those who are normal have neither strengths or weaknesses. The role that these distinctions play is further complicated by the tradition that minorities are overrepresented in juvenile detention centers and special education classes and underrepresented in gifted classes.

Solutions to the perpetuation of narrowly defined identities based on educational structures lie not in the abandonment of specialized programs, but in finding ways to differentiate the curriculum without creating rigid grouping patterns. Professionals traditionally defined as gifted, general, and special educators have begun to bridge the barriers within their profession so that the ideals of pluralism, equality, and individualism can be attained (Laycock et al., 1991; Laycock, 1992; Korinek, 1992; VanTassel-Baska, 1992; Donovan, 1992; McEachron-Hirsch, 1992). The pursuit of these longstanding educational goals will come to greater fruition; however, when educational and political leadership recognizes the limitation of economic gain as the underlying motive for educational excellence.

MYTH #5: SELF-ESTEEM IS FORMED PRIMARILY IN THE FIRST FIVE YEARS OF LIFE AND REMAINS STABLE THROUGHOUT ONE'S LIFETIME

Psychoanalysis has shown us the importance of parent-child relations during the highly dependent period of a young person's life. Extreme and even mild cases of abuse and neglect during the first five years of life certainly contribute to an uphill battle against debilitating perceptions of self. The mirroring effects of the treatment by caregivers are reflected in the words of Dorothy Briggs (1975, p. 14): "Children value themselves to the degree that they have been valued." The devastating effects upon children who have not been valued or cared for in appropriate ways have been well-documented (Bettelheim, 1950), yet, even in the most extreme cases, there is hope for creating a sense of trust in others that might lead to trust in oneself (Clarke and Clarke, 1978). Not all children lack trust in themselves as a result of damage incurred by others in infancy. Some children may lose their grip on whatever foundation was nurtured in their early years because of changing family dynamics and their unique way of perceiving themselves in relation to these patterns of interaction (Jersild, 1952). And still other children may hold together an identity that functions well in most social settings throughout adolescence, only to discover when reaching adulthood that one's precarious identity was shaped largely by a world of pretense and deception (Parker, 1972).

Understanding why the early years are important yet not totally irreversible, why the effects of childhood and adolescent experiences may not surface until adulthood, why children respond to seemingly positive environments in negative or antisocial ways, and why children respond to seemingly negative environments in positive or socially rewarded ways represent just some of the parameters that make the study of identity formation and self-esteem seem almost elusive. Once you think it is safe to make a definitive statement, exceptions soon become more commonplace than imagined.

The studies conducted and reviewed by Yamamoto clarified the stressful factors that influence self-esteem during the early years. Yamamoto points out in Chapter Twelve that even though children experience a basic anxiety that underlies a basic state of human conflict (Horney, 1937), the feelings of abandonment and aloneness that this state represents are felt differently among children, adolescents, and adults. Parents and professionals must become better informed not only about how to prevent stress caused from social and cultural conditions (e.g., poverty, abuse, neglect, discrimination), but in how to distinguish between healthy stress and unhealthy stress, and how adults can help themselves and young people become more self-sufficient in coping and mastering life's existential quest.

Three factors Yamamoto noted as salient to the individual's healthy development of self were a positive disposition, a supportive family environment, and external ties with the wider community. Two of these factors were also found to be salient in the McEachron-Hirsch and Messier study of adolescents presented in Chapter Eight. As you may recall, self-esteem correlated positively with the subscales of Cohesion and Active-Recreational Orientation. These similar findings based on a comparison of separate age groups and completely separate investigations reinforce the notion that the enhancement of well-being depends on the dynamic interaction between the individual's personality, family support, significant others in the extended family or community, and how significant life events are negotiated based upon developmental stages.

Yamamoto's claim that understanding the individual from the "inside out" is echoed by Kegan (1982) in *The Evolving Self.* Kegan (p. 113) maintains that, "If you want to understand another person in some fundamental way, you must know where the person is in his or her evolution . . . that a lifelong process of evolution or adaptation is the master motion in personality. . . ." For Kegan, adaptation is not synonymous with coping or adjusting to things as they are, but "in the sense of an active process of increasingly organizing the relationship of the self to the environment" (Kegan, 1982, p. 113). The process takes place not just inside oneself but also as a result of the person's imbeddedness in culture throughout developmental stages.

Studies of child and adolescent perceptions of self throughout the schooling years assist parents and professionals in separating their own self-esteem issues from the individuals for whom they are responsible. For although it is reasonable to expect that people will look for harmony between their self-image, their place of work, and their relationships to others (Nias, 1989), it cannot be assumed that adults will understand where others are in their stages of identity formation. The goal to understand the nature of individual member's developmental stages is a significant challenge to family members, but in an elementary classroom of twenty-five to thirty students or in a secondary school where teachers see twenty-five different students six times a day, the challenge is severely inhibited by numbers alone. Nevertheless, studies of effective schools have documented that a supportive school environment shares many of the characteristics of caring family environments.

Taking a point of departure from the "pathology" model of research, which traditionally examines maladaptation, Bernard (1992, p. 3) reviews studies of resiliency in children and adolescents using a "transactional-ecological model in which human personality is viewed as a self-righting mechanism that is engaged in active, ongoing adaptation to its environment." She concludes that successful families, schools, and communities have three common characteristics that contribute positively to the development of healthy self-esteem in children and youth — caring and support, high expectations, and opportunities for young people to participate with adults in family, school, or community activities. Many of the studies Bernard reviewed offered hope not just for those families, schools, and communities who experienced numerous adverse circumstances, but demonstrated the effective ways in which the three constituents can assist each other to affect the lives of children and youth in positive ways.

MYTH #6: PEOPLE WHO HAVE HIGH SELF-ESTEEM ARE VALUED MEMBERS OF SOCIETY

Being valued by others is a necessary condition for self-acceptance, as we have seen in the previous discussion of Myth #5. One's acceptance through a circle of friends, parents, teachers, and immediate neighborhood or community may provide the ideal combination of factors to nurture a positive self-esteem. However, the effect of such factors should not be confused with general notions of being valued by society. Being a valued member of society requires an examination of the individual's social, economic, and political positions within the larger social structure. High levels of self-esteem within a subgroup that experiences either economic, political, or social inequalities could represent a number of possibilities.

First, the individual might deny those aspects of identity that have been shaped by inequality. Second, individuals in subgroups that experience various forms of discrimination may reject those conditions. In fighting against the discrimination, they may experience a heightened sense of self-worth. Third, individuals may experience moderate to high self-esteem because they accept their identity in a social structure of inequality. And fourth, individuals may experience moderate to high levels of self-esteem because they do not feel that their identity has been shaped by inequality.

Global and multidimensional self-esteem measures typically do not assess perceptions of one's social surroundings or how one thinks he or she is perceived by others. Nor do they balance such perceptions with social assessments of specific cultural subgroups. Yet the influence of these social contexts has a continuous effect upon identity formation. Case study interviews of adolescents presented in Chapter Eight revealed the tenuous relationship between individual identities and social climate.

Three of the females whose self-esteem levels were in the medium or high range talked about the racial tension they felt in the school environment. The study assessed individual self-esteem, classroom and family environments, and personality, but racial tension was not investigated directly with all 152 students. Nevertheless, the effects of racial tensions shared by one female minority student during an interview are noteworthy.

When discussing school climate, Janice recounted several incidents of fighting among Black and White male students during her sophomore year. When asked about the impact these racial conflicts had on her,

Janice elaborated upon her efforts through the Black Student Organization (recounted in Chapter Eight), as well as her relationship with her boyfriend who is White. Janice spoke positively about the way in which both families accepted the interracial relationship, but references to peers foreshadowed more ambivalent feelings. While Janice maintains some of the same friendships, these friendships seem more marginalized. Although Janice claims the teasing from her Black male and female friends is all in fun, there has been an increased aloofness on her part as well, as indicated by her remarks, "I don't talk to anyone much anymore." Janice's ambivalence may be attributed to a combination of factors—death of family members, new relationship with boyfriend, and changing social relationships with peers, all of which should be considered important to Janice's identity formation. The willingness to take political action on sensitive racial issues in the Black Student Organization and make a personal choice that may have marginalized her relationships among peers demonstrates a great deal of strength and personal commitment. The teasing that Janice encountered, however, suggests that race relations continue to be a formidable hurdle in negotiating one's identity in a small Virginia town, regardless of what one's global measures of self-esteem might be.

As this case study has illustrated, having high self-esteem is not always linked to being generally valued. Being liked by selected peers and family members is not the same as being accepted on the basis of sanctioned political, economic, and social norms. Being a valued member of society implies a certain level of support. When individuals attempt to step out of those norms or establish an identity that doesn't conform to social expectations, the support networks are tested. The experiences of minorities, women, and the poor are typically presented to illustrate these discriminatory practices, but the experience can occur in many intragroup configurations.

The relationship between self-esteem and feeling different has received minor attention. The relationship is important, however, because perceiving oneself as different from others has the potential to define positive aspects of a unique identity. Perceiving unique qualities in a positive light is closely tied to how accepting society is of individual differences. In Chapter Ten, VanTassel-Baska reported a study of intragroup differences among gifted children, finding that children perceived their own qualities of differentness in positive ways, but "they still scored lower on the Piers-Harris Children's Self-Concept Scale than did those in the group who did not report feeling different." Social expectations were also manifest in the views of gifted females. The belief that peer rejection would result from competent levels of performance may be linked to socially created "fear of success." These perceptions by gifted students may be reflecting the more generalized ways in which American society encourages and discourages differentiation. Certain social patterns may serve to hold back the expression of individual differences, while others, as exemplified in the case of Nazi Germany, may serve to perpetuate differences beyond what was thought to be humanly possible.

In Chapter Four, Hirsch discussed the extreme ways in which political leaders sanction discriminatory practices, thus affecting who is generally accepted in society. He pointed out that such extremes evolved from a complex network with varying degrees of discriminatory treatment of selected groups of people. This process of political socialization "is the same as the psychological processes of learning, but the content of what is transmitted and learned differs markedly from culture to culture, from state to state" (Chapter Four). Each cultural context "involves questions of power, which are tied closely to the dominant or subordinate positions to which groups within a society are assigned . . ." (Chapter Four).

In order for self-esteem research to progress, it will be necessary to develop theories of identity formation that integrate both social and individual perceptions of self and others. In so doing, theoretical formulations of identity will encompass how the Self is created by the interplay between individual choices and social conditions. Attending only to individual choices keeps the study of Self in a vacuum, whereas examining only cultural norms masks the efforts of individuals to change the status quo.

Enhancing self-esteem is a worthy goal for those who are concerned with individual feelings of self-worth, but encouraging individuals to be self-assured in an oppressive state of affairs is shortsighted. Self-enhancement requires more than a psychological adjustment to a problematic social environment; it requires an examination of Self embedded in a cultural context that may be supportive or debilitating. Identifying what those supportive and debilitating factors are is an important goal for future self-esteem research.

MYTH #7: PEOPLE WHO ARE WELL-LIKED BY OTHERS HAVE HIGH SELF-ESTEEM

When discussing Myth #5, the importance of being valued by others was linked to healthy self-esteem. As Yamamoto pointed out in Chapter

Twelve, the goal is not to condition children and youth to become completely dependent upon external assessments of self, but to equip children so that they will have the resourcefulness to tackle the challenges in living. Yet thinking about where one's self-assured identity stops and socially defined identity begins can be a mindboggling enterprise. While one cannot deny that identity is shaped by the decisions one makes along the lifespan, the influences of the social and cultural context in setting the parameters for those decisions cannot be denied either. Furthermore, it is not always easy to ascertain when a decision is right for oneself but wrong from the perspective of the social other, whether that other represents a sibling, spouse, co-worker or classmate. Nor is it easy to determine when a decision is right in the social context but wrong for the welfare of the individual.

As we saw in Chapter Eight, being overextended in social networks can reinforce a genuine condition of being well-liked and respected for one's capabilities from the perspective of others, but it can also take one so far in diffusing the multidimensional self that the forces of continuity and stability which hold Self together become almost shattered. When this happens, as in the case of Sandra, the limitations of overextension have a tailspin effect, bringing the entire organism into a sense of disequilibrium. The individual may reflect upon the circumstances and make appropriate adjustments to reinstate well-being, but if not, the pattern repeats itself, thus creating another cycle of stress and self-doubt.

Both Losito and Matthews discuss the ways in which aspects of western culture encourage the abdication of intrinsic motivations for the sake of social reward. Losito's recollection of his son Daniel's frenzy to check off activities for his Wolf Badge exemplified how one's ''performance'' in a particular activity can be rewarded socially despite the meaningless void it perpetuates. As Losito indicated, these social rewards that foster ''addictive self-centering attachments to power, symbols to prestige, and material goods'' may be intended to make people feel good about themselves, but they fail ''miserably to engender a permanent sense of well-being . . .'' (Chapter Two). Instead, the pattern of attachments ''facilitates an even greater psycho-cultural climate of ontological anxiety, guilt, and feelings of being dislocated'' (Chapter Two).

Matthews also exposes the mythological elements of linking popularity to self-esteem through Wilber's transpersonal analysis. That is, when one's self-esteem has been shaped by the notion that happiness must come from outside the person rather than created from one's unity with Self and others, "The 'self' in 'self-esteem' is an illusion" (Chapter Three). For Matthews, the key to enhancing self-esteem lies not in teaching children and youth to please others nor in teaching them to please their own egos, but in aligning one's self-esteem with the Self or the All. For both Losito and Matthews, self-transcendence is the key to resolving this conflict between culturally sanctioned and individual well-being.

Alignment with the All or the cosmos, however, should not be mistaken for a fanatical religious or political quest. The set of symbols through which one transcends self-absorption or individual alienation from the collective can be manipulated by religious, political, or social leaders or virtually any significant other, including one's teacher, partner, or institutional superior, as a means to serve the ends of those in positions of power.

In Chapter Four, Hirsch explains how the boundary between self and others is permeable. He states that even if the individual does not personally experience acts of political oppression, he or she cannot escape knowing such facts and this knowledge influences one's identity. "Politics now intrudes on all aspects of life and there are no more bystanders. The personal has been transformed into the political and the disintegration of the boundary between them has left the modern individual face to face with the power of the modern state" (Hirsch, Chapter Four). Given these complicating factors, Hirsch argues that self-esteem should be analyzed at both the individual and societal level. The relationship between the two is crucial, however, for as Hirsch points out, "Both high and low self-esteem may lead to visions of superiority or inferiority and could conceivably provide a justification for hostility toward other groups" (Chapter Four). Furthermore, dependency upon the group for support for one's enhanced self-esteem leads to the likelihood that one will follow what the group decides. Herein lies the irony in identity formation, according to Hirsch (Chapter Four, pp. 62–63):

> The more atomized and disconnected the person, the easier time they have coping with community crises and the less connected they may feel to the community. At the same time, the more disconnected they are, the more likely they will be unconcerned about members of their own community. The great puzzle is: How does one maintain both a feeling of belonging and connection without becoming a person willing to follow the leaders or the group in the pursuit of negative action such as violence?

In the end, one's transpersonal and transcendent identities cannot be transpolitical as well because such a state would entail the denial of the way in which identity is embedded in culture. Nevertheless, attempts to alter the locus of political power or social constraints that threaten individual identity can be self-enhancing.

MYTH #8: MORE PROGRESS IN SELF-ESTEEM RESEARCH CAN BE MADE ONCE HUMANISTIC PSYCHOLOGY GAINS THE RECOGNITION IT DESERVES

When internal states such as motivation, desire, and self-esteem are identified as important considerations for theories of learning, they are typically relegated by curriculum theories and psychologists to the realm of humanistic psychology (Ornstein and Hunkins, 1988; Miller and Seller, 1985). In this narrow conception, perceptions of self are virtually ignored in more traditional behavioristic and cognitive-developmentalist interpretations. While giving more credence to the works of Carl Rogers (1969), Abraham Maslow (1962), and other humanistic psychologists would definitely enlighten rigid behavioral interpretations of teaching and learning, Matthews argued in Chapter Three that humanistic psychology does not go far enough in trying to encourage actualization through transcendence. For Matthews, self-esteem and self-concept, as defined in humanistic psychology, are concepts that deal primarily with the fragmented self because they represent perceptions shaped by social expectations rather than an understanding of the self as an embodiment of the collective.

Losito also identified transcendence as an important goal in one's existential quest to relieve ontological anxiety. Losito explained in Chapter Two that a transcendent purpose imbues human actions with a greater sense of significance. The arguments by Matthews and Losito necessitate an analysis of self-esteem in relation to more fundamental questions about the spiritual nature and purpose of human beings.

In an attempt to reconcile differences and similarities between Eastern and Western notions of transcendence, Fromm examined Western trends in psychoanalysis and the eastern principles of Zen Buddhism. Fromm's selection of psychoanalysis as a source of spiritual transcendence deserves an explanation. Fromm (Fromm et al., 1970, p. 92) maintains that a spiritual crisis exists for all individuals who evade the existential question brought on by the very nature of their human existence—"that of being in nature and at the same time of transcending nature by the fact that [one] is life aware of itself." Regardless of one's cultural tradition, Fromm and colleagues (1970, p. 92) suggest that

> Any man who listens to this question posed to him, and who makes it a matter of "ultimate concern" to answer this question, and to answer it as a whole man and not only by thoughts, is a "religious" man; and all systems that try to give, teach, and transmit such answers are "religions."

For Fromm (p. 87) there are only two possible answers to this question; the first is regression to the state of unity that existed before humanity, and the second, and more desirable response, is "to be fully born, to develop one's awareness, one's reason, one's capacity to love to such a point that one transcends one's own egocentric involvement, and arrives at a new harmony, at a new oneness with the world."

Fromm feels that many people who seek psychoanalysis today suffer from alienation "from oneself, from one's fellow man and from nature . . ." (p. 86). He suggests that help through psychoanalysis for those who suffer from this twentieth century malaise is different from a cure characterized by the removal of anti-social symptoms. "For those who suffer from alienation, cure does not consist in the 'absence of illness,' but in the 'presence of well-being' " (p. 86).

Through this rejection of the negative orientation advanced by Freud, Fromm formulates a common ground between psychoanalysis and Zen Buddhist thought. The key parallel between Zen Buddhism and psychoanalysis for Fromm is the attempt to reach wholeness by merging the unconscious with the conscious, in the case of psychoanalysis, and merging the subject and the object, in the case of Zen Buddhism. In *Zen Buddhism and Psychoanalysis,* Fromm, Suzuki, and DeMartino (1970) elaborate on the importance of making the unconscious conscious and merging the subject with the object as a means to enhance well-being and achieve transcendence. One of the important ideas that comes out of their argument is the universal existential quest and the inseparability of the spiritual quest from the rest of identity formation. Recognizing Spinoza's argument that " 'intellectual' knowledge is conducive to change only inasmuch as it is also 'affective' knowledge," Fromm and colleagues (pp. 110, 111) delineate the importance of this proposition for human growth:

> It became apparent that intellectual knowledge as such does not produce any change, except perhaps in the sense that by intellectual knowledge of

his unconscious strivings a person may be better able to control them—
which, however, is the aim of traditional ethics, rather than that of
psychoanalysis. . . . Discovering one's unconscious is, precisely, "not"
an intellectual act, but an affective experience, which can hardly be put
into words, if at all. . . . The importance of this kind of "experiential
knowledge" lies in the fact that it transcends the kind of knowledge and
awareness in which the subject-intellect observes himself as an object,
and thus that it transcends the Western, rationalistic concept of knowing.

American educational discourse has not given serious consideration to
the philosophical tenets found in eastern thought or the ways in which
linkages might be made to Western culture. As Matthews, Losito, and
Hirsch have suggested, concern for one's fellow humans requires
greater understanding of the meaning-making and symbol systems that
have the potential to unite or destroy us.

CONCLUSION

Appearing almost elusive at times, self-esteem is tied to dynamic
family, school, and social contexts, which makes it difficult to make
generalizations about individuals. However, in debunking the eight
myths, overlapping principles emerged, which help to delineate a more
comprehensive analysis of Self, of which self-esteem plays an important
role. The social principles will be presented first, followed by relevant
family and school contextual considerations.

Self-Esteem in the Social Context

(1) Individuals behave differently when social context changes. The
    individual's creation of Self is generated from perceptions of
    self-esteem within several social contexts, but in any given social
    context, self-esteem may vary considerably. The intent of global
    self-esteem instruments is to capture one's overall self-assessment;
    the intent of multidimensional self-esteem instruments is to capture
    self-assessment in a variety of social contexts.

(2) Global and multidimensional assessments of self-esteem need to be
    supplemented by differentiated assessments of social factors im-
    pinging upon individual identity. Such assessments provide insight
    into how supportive a given social structure is for differentiation.
    An analysis of the ethnic, religious, racial, gender, class, handicap,

age, and other social distinctions require examination along with the social dynamics that define family and school interpersonal relationships. These variables in conjunction with one's multidimensional and global assessments will provide a more comprehensive configuration of Self. Future directions in self-esteem research should include the refinement of global and multidimensional self-esteem instruments and the development of instruments that assess the social climate for various subgroups within one's cultural environment. Thus far, self-esteem research has concentrated on the individual's global and multidimensional perception without linking them to the cultural factors in which identity is embedded.

(3) Self-esteem research has been overshadowed by a Western psychological tradition, which emphasizes individual weaknesses rather than strengths. This tradition is reflected in educational institutions whose learning theories are based largely on deficit orientations and conforming to environmental stimuli. Theories that recognize the important link between the individual's natural meaning-making efforts, self-actualization, and learning reflect a belief in the positive nature of human beings.

(4) Theories of Self have ignored the importance of individual connectedness with a collective consciousness that encompasses more than just immediate family, school, and community environments. Existential and spiritual transcendence, transpersonal psychology, and altruistic and genocidal behavior are all notions that have been presented to address dimensions of identity that are crucial to the survival of the human species. As we have seen, identity is culturally constructed and culture is maintained or destroyed by these competing or compatible cultural constructions.

Self-Esteem in the Family Context

(1) A child learns to value himself or herself if he or she is valued by a caring adult, especially during one's early stages of development. The logical place for this to occur is within one's primary family environment, the people with whom one lives. When children get older, they and caring adults may create or expand upon such bonds through other relationships, e.g., grandparents, teachers, significant others in community organizations, etc.

(2) Self-esteem is enhanced by support from family members in a variety of ways: high expectations; a cohesive living environment; opportunities to be a contributing member of the family environment; opportunities for family members to be involved in activities outside the home, e.g., recreational, cultural, etc.; low levels of conflict; and the absence of physical or sexual abuse.

(3) Healthy and unhealthy stress occurs throughout one's lifetime. The self-esteem of children and youth is enhanced when the unhealthy stress is of short duration and when adults teach children to become successful and self-sufficient in developing ways to cope with stress.

(4) The self-esteem of family members is affected by the dynamics within the family rather than the structure of the family. Family systems theory and studies of blended, single-parent, intact, foster, and extended family arrangements have demonstrated that the way family members treat each other is more salient to self-esteem than family structure.

(5) The relationship between one's self-esteem and one's social standing, given family demographic characteristics, e.g., race, ethnicity, class, gender, and religion, is inconclusive. More research is needed to explicate this relationship. It is possible that, (1) the individual does not ascribe to the social standings as represented by social surveys or, (2) self-esteem may reflect social standings represented by social surveys. A social context that perpetuates unequal opportunities among subgroups should be challenged regardless of the self-esteem levels within those subgroups because of the potential for damaging identity formation.

Self-Esteem in the School Context

(1) A teacher plays a very valuable role in the development of positive self-esteem in children and youth. Given the amount of time students spend in classrooms, the potential for damage or support to a growing child's self-esteem is dependent upon a number of factors that are within the teacher's primary control. Being overly critical and negative can create an atmosphere of condemnation and hostility; inappropriate expectations that are either too high or too low can send students a message of rejection. The students' feelings of rejection stem from perceiving that their teacher (or educational

institution) either does not care enough to find out their various levels of performance or interest or the teacher (or institution) knows what the performance levels are and does not think they should be at that level, based on some social standard or bias. Conversely, teachers and educational institutions that are sensitive to the varying developmental differences among individuals and support the individual differences through their manner and curricula can demonstrate that they value each student for the unique qualities and cultural backgrounds he or she brings to the classroom.

(2) Like families, educational institutions can create a climate that is cohesive and cooperative or divided and lacking in trust. Students need adult role models who can create an environment that involves them in such a way that going to school becomes a personal commitment. Taking pride in one's student body requires more than just team spirit at sporting events. The schools that have been effective in reducing the drop-out rate are those where the students feel a part of the school environment, where they do not feel alienated from each other or from the overall goals of the educational institution, and where their educational abilities and interests are recognized. Wearing the school colors will do little to create this ''collective whole'' if the internal systems of the school are characterized by territorial infighting as a result of programmatic or social issues. Like families, school districts are comprised of key players—school board members, superintendents, principals, and teachers who are all responsible for the effective functioning of school environments.

(3) The effectiveness of schools in enhancing self-esteem depends on how well they work in tandem with parents and members of the community. When teachers work at odds with parents and vice versa, the student is caught in the middle. Teachers, parents, and guardians working together create a supportive bond with the student. If working cooperatively, teachers may be able to offer a supportive anchor during times when families may be experiencing stress. On the other hand, if teachers are experiencing rough times, students and their families can provide certain supports. If these notions sound somewhat romantic or idealistic, it is partially because the strong working relationship that characterizes effective schools may sound like a bygone era. As more students have either

both parents or a single parent working, the opportunities for establishing stronger working relationships have become more difficult. The solution to this predicament lies not in parents and teachers blaming each other, but in finding ways to make the responsibilities of work, school, and parenting more compatible.

SUMMARY

Educators and many others in the helping professions know that their work is not always held in high esteem in American society. In fact, one of the favorite topics of conversation among teachers is the inverse proportion between how hard they work and how little they are valued. In a recent class, I asked students, some of whom were experienced teachers and others aspiring teachers, to share an incident in a working relationship with children where they felt they had already made a difference. One woman's experience was particularly memorable. In relating her story I will refer to her as Ms. Rene.

Ms. Rene had a student in her class who had not been well-liked by any of his previous teachers. But as the school year progressed, Ms. Rene and the boy struck up a challenging but compatible relationship. Ms. Rene had an open disposition and I could appreciate how the boy might respond to her straightforward manner. Toward the end of the year a tragic accident occurred and the boy was killed. All of us in the class were in tears as Ms. Rene recounted a conversation with the boy's mother weeks after the funeral. The boy's mother told Ms. Rene how grateful she was that her son had been in her class. She knew that his last year was a happy one and that he felt good about himself knowing that Ms. Rene cared about him.

Not all anecdotes about the importance of classroom teachers in developing positive self-esteem are this poignant. But the story illustrates an important lesson. When children and youth feel that adults care about their well-being, they learn to value themselves in the same way when they know instinctively that they are loved by parents and guardians. In the best of circumstances, this unconditional feeling of acceptance would be communicated throughout classrooms and families. But escalating social and psychological problems suggest that American society has lost some of the more traditional values of human respect and concern for the community.

While this may be the case, it is possible to think about the current state of affairs as a reaction to historical events that have perpetuated discrimination and inequality. Many long for the "good old days," but I shudder to think of the rigid social boundaries that helped to maintain that genteel community spirit. What we are now seeing in the form of drug abuse, violence, and family discord is more the result of the need to change the underlying structure of American society, a structure that has perpetuated notions of democracy amidst an economy based upon powerful elites. Through education, more individuals who have traditionally been excluded from these power bases have become less willing to assume subservient roles. Many of the manifestations we refer to as social problems actually mask more deep-seated social and psychological issues. Yet, as we have seen, many confuse the social manifestations with low individual self-esteem. Others argue that these social problems represent a form of self-esteem enhancement because they demonstrate rebellion against submission to a culture that has historically rewarded others. Both hypotheses are far too simplistic.

In closing, self-esteem research has been limited by its inattention to the influence of one's cultural context, a context that is highly specialized for each individual. To examine self-esteem issues, one cannot capture the essence of individuality by relying on such sweeping analogs as personality, on the one hand, or American culture, on the other hand. Rather, the individual's identity and self-esteem is influenced by layers and layers of contextual differences, starting with family and school dynamics, but including the ever-present influences of the nation-state, religion, ethnicity, and gender, to mention only a few. Identifying the values of caring, support, and participation in the community, as building blocks for self-esteem enhancement is an important step, but the significance of these values must be embedded in a culture whose structure also reinforces the values of individualism, pluralism, and equality.

REFERENCES

Apple, M. W. 1986. *Teachers & Texts*. New York, NY: Routledge & Kegan Paul.

Benard, B. 1992. "Fostering Resiliency in Kids: Protective Factors in the Family, School and Community" in *Prevention Forum*, J. Daumen, ed., Vol. 12, Issue 3, Summer, Illinois Prevention Resource Center, 822 South College Street, Springfield IL, 62704.

Bettelheim, Bruno. 1950. *Love Is Not Enough*. New York, NY: Macmillan Company.

Bowles, S. and H. Gintis. 1976. *Schooling in Capitalist America*. New York, NY: Basic Books, Incorporated.

Briggs, D. 1975. *Your Child's Self-Esteem: The Key to Life.* Garden City, NY: Dolphin Books.

Bruner, J. 1990. *Acts of Meaning.* Cambridge, MA: Harvard University Press.

Clarke, A. M. and A. Clarke, eds. 1978. *Early Experience.* New York, NY: W. W. Norton.

Donovan, A. 1992. "Bridging Family and School: A School Psychologist Perspective," in *Planning Effective Curriculum for Gifted Learners,* J. VanTassel-Baska, ed., Denver, CO: Love.

Fromm, E., D. J. Suzuki, and R. DeMartino. 1970. *Zen Buddhism and Psychoanalysis.* New York, NY: Harper Colophon Books.

Gergen, K. 1991. *The Saturated Self: Dilemmas of Identity in Contemporary Life.* New York, NY: Basic Books.

Gilligan, C. 1982. *In a Different Voice.* Cambridge, MA: Harvard University Press.

Goodlad, J.I. 1984. *A Place Called School: Prospects for the Future.* New York, NY: McGraw-Hill.

Greer, C. 1972. *The Great School Legend.* New York, NY: Viking Press.

Hofstadter, R. 1963. *Anti-Intellectualism in American Life.* New York, NY: Vintage Books.

Horney, K. 1937. *The Neurotic Personality of Our Time.* New York, NY: W. W. Norton.

Jersild, A. 1952. *In Search of Self; An Exploration of the Role of the School in Promoting Self Understanding.* New York, NY: Bureau of Publications, Teachers College, Columbia University.

Kegan, R. 1982. *The Evolving Self: Problem and Process in Human Development.* Cambridge, MA: Harvard University Press.

Korinek, L. 1992. "Gifted Children with Specific Learning Disabilities," in *Planning Effective Curriculum for Gifted Learners,* J. VanTassel-Baska, ed., Denver, CO: Love.

Laycock, V. 1992. "Curricula for Exceptional Children: A Special Education Perspective," in *Planning Effective Curriculum for Gifted Learners,* J. VanTassel-Baska, ed., Denver, CO: Love.

Laycock, V. K., R. A. Gable, and L. Korinek. 1991. "Alternative Structures for Collaboration in the Delivery of Special Services," *Preventing School Failure,* 35(4):15–18.

MacKinnon, C. 1989. *Toward a Feminist Theory of the State.* Cambridge, MA: Harvard University Press.

Maslow, A. 1962. *Toward a Psychology of Being.* New York, NY: Van Nostrand Reinhold.

McEachron-Hirsch, G. 1992. "A Perspective on Curriculum Development for Gifted Learners," in *Planning Effective Curriculum for Gifted Learners,* J. VanTassel-Baska, ed., Denver, CO: Love.

Mecca, A. M., N. J. Smelser, and J. Vasconcellos, eds. 1989. *The Social Importance of Self-Esteem.* Los Angeles, CA: University of California Press.

Miller, J. P. and W. Seller. 1985. *Curriculum Perspectives and Practice.* New York, NY: Longman.

Nias, J. 1989. *Primary Teachers Talking.* New York, NY: Routledge.

Ornstein, A. C. and F. Hunkins. 1988. *Curriculum: Foundations, Principles, and Issues.* Englewood Cliffs, NJ: Prentice-Hall.

Parker, B. 1972. *A Mingled Yarn.* New Haven, CT: Yale University Press.

Rogers, C. 1969. *Freedom to Learn; A View of What Education Might Become.* Columbus, OH: C.E. Merrill Publishing Company.

Rosenberg, M. 1979. *Conceiving the Self.* New York, NY: Basic Books, Inc.

Slavin, R. 1990. "Point-Counter Point: Ability Grouping, Cooperative Learning and the Gifted", *Journal for the Education of the Gifted,* 14(1):3–8.

Spring, J. 1972. *Education and the Rise of the Corporate State.* Boston, MA: Beacon Press.

VanTassel-Baska, J. 1992. *Planning Effective Curriculum for Gifted Learners.* Denver, CO: Love.

Welsh, P. 1990. "Fast-Track Trap: How 'Ability Grouping' Hurts Our Schools, Kids and Families," *The Washington Post,* September 16:B1, 4.

Index

About the Authors

STEVEN X. GALLAS

STEVEN GALLAS is a school psychologist in the Williamsburg/James City County School District in Virginia. He holds a bachelor's degree from Kutztown State University and a master's from Millersville University. Gallas is a Certified School Psychologist in Virginia and Pennsylvania, specializing in family systems, and has written several articles.

GAIL HARDINGE

GAIL HARDINGE is a school psychologist in the Williamsburg/James City County School District in Virginia. She earned her bachelor's degree from Virginia Commonwealth University and master's and Ed.S. from The College of William and Mary. She is currently working on her Ed.D. in Counseling and School Psychology at The College of William and Mary. Hardinge is a Certified School Psychologist in Virginia. Her research interests include consultation and collaboration and integrating family and school issues.

HERBERT HIRSCH

HERBERT HIRSCH is currently Professor of Political Science at Virginia Commonwealth University. He holds a bachelor's degree from Concord College, a master's degree from Villanova University, and a Ph.D. from the University of Kentucky. Hirsch teaches courses in American government and the politics of violence, war, and genocide. His book publications include *Persistent Prejudice: Perspectives on Antisemitism* (1988) edited with Jack Spiro, *The Right of the People* (1980), *Learning to Be Militant* (1973) with David Perry, *Comparative Legislative Systems* (1971) with M. Donald Hancock, and *Poverty and Politicization: Political Socialization in an American Sub-Culture* (1971). He has also published numerous articles.

WILLIAM F. LOSITO

WILLIAM F. LOSITO is the Heritage Professor of Education at The College of William and Mary. He received a bachelor's degree from The University of Dayton and a Ph.D. from Indiana University. He completed postdoctoral training at the Hastings Center in the Teaching of Ethics in Higher Education and at Harvard University in Moral Education. Losito teaches courses in social and philosophical foundations of education and ethics, and has published articles on these topics.

GAIL McEACHRON-HIRSCH

GAIL McEACHRON-HIRSCH is an Assistant Professor in Teacher Education at The College of William and Mary. She received bachelor's and master's degrees from Arizona State University; a Certificate of Studies from Oxford University, Great Britain; and a Ph.D. from the University of Texas at Austin. McEachron-Hirsch teaches courses in social studies, language arts, elementary curriculum and instruction, and classroom management and has published articles on these topics.

CHARLES O. MATTHEWS

CHARLES O. MATTHEWS is currently an Associate Professor of Education in the Counseling Program at The College of William and Mary. He received a bachelor's degree from Davidson College, a master's from Harvard University, and a Ph.D from Duke University. Matthews teaches courses in advanced theories of counseling and psychotherapy, human sexuality, and group theory and techniques and has published articles on these topics.

LOUIS P. MESSIER

LOUIS P. MESSIER is an Associate Professor of Education in the Special Education Program at The College of William and Mary. He earned a bachelor's degree from Johnson College and a master's and Ed.D. from Boston University. Messier teaches courses in psychopathology and emotional disorders of children and adolescents, characteristics and psychology of mental retardation, and psychoeducational assessment and has published articles on these topics.

JOYCE VANTASSEL-BASKA

JOYCE VANTASSEL-BASKA is the Jody and Layton Smith Professor of Education in the Gifted Education Program at The College of William and Mary and also serves as Director of the Center for Gifted Education. She received a bachelor's degree, master's in education, master's in English, and Ed.D. from the University of Toledo. Her book publications include: *Effective Curriculum Planning for the Gifted* (1992), *Excellence in Educating the Gifted* (1989) with John Feldhusen and Ken Seeley, *Patterns of Influence on Gifted Learners: The Home, the Self, and the School* (1989) edited with P. Olszewski-Kubilius, and *Comprehensive Curriculum for Gifted Learners* (1988) with J. Feldhusen, K. Seeley, G. Wheatley, L. Silverman and W. Foster. She has also published numerous articles.

CHRISTINE S. WALTHER-THOMAS

CHRISTINE S. WALTHER-THOMAS is an Assistant Professor of Education in the Special Education Program at The College of William and Mary. She received bachelor's and master's degrees from the University of Utah and a Ph.D. from the University of Kansas. Walther-Thomas teaches courses in learning disabilities, teaching exceptional children with learning problems, current trends and legal issues in special education, and resource/consulting teaching and has published articles on these topics.

SANDRA BRUBAKER WARD

SANDRA BRUBAKER WARD is an Assistant Professor of Education in the School Psychology Program at The College of William and Mary. She earned a bachelor's at The College of William and Mary and a master's and Ph.D. at The Pennsylvania State University. She is a Nationally Certified School Psychologist and a Certified School Psychologist in Virginia and Pennsylvania. Ward teaches courses in school psychology, psychosocial assessment and clinical methods, and intelligence testing and has published articles on these topics.

THOMAS J. WARD

THOMAS J. WARD is an Assistant Professor of Education in the Educational Foundations Program at The College of William and Mary. He received a bachelor's degree from LaSalle College and a master's and Ph.D. from The Pennsylvania State University. Ward teaches courses in research methods and advanced statistics in education and has published articles in areas of school psychology, counseling, testing, and achievement.

KAORU YAMAMOTO

KAORU YAMAMOTO is a Professor of Education in the Graduate School of Education at the University of Colorado at Denver. He received a bachelor's degree in Industrial Chemistry from the University of Tokyo, a master's and Ph.D. from the University of Minnesota, and did postdoctoral work at the University of Minnesota, the University of Wisconsin, and the University of Cambridge, England. Yamamoto's research interests include self, stress and coping, teaching, creativity, human development in the lifespan, and human movement and communication. Selected book publications include *Beyond Words: Movements Observation and Analysis* (1988), *Children in Time and Space* (1979), *Death in the Life of Children* (1978), *Individuality: The Unique Learner* (1975), *The Child and His Image: Self-Concept in the Early Years* (1972), *Teaching: Essays and Readings* (1969), and *The College Student and His Culture: An Analysis* (1968).